Predictive Analytics and Generative AI for Data-Driven Marketing Strategies

In providing an in-depth exploration of cutting-edge technologies and how they are used to support data-driven marketing strategies and empower organizations to make the right decisions, *Predictive Analytics and Generative AI for Data-Driven Marketing Strategies* includes case studies and examples from diverse marketing domains. This book demonstrates how predictive analytics and generative AI have been successfully applied to solve marketing challenges and drive tangible results. This book showcases emerging trends in predictive analytics and generative AI for marketing and their potential impact on the future of data-driven marketing. This book is meant for professionals and scholars to gather the skills and resources to use predictive analytics and generative AI effectively for marketing strategies.

This book:

- Examines the different predictive analytics models and algorithms, such as regression analysis, decision trees, and neural networks, and demonstrates how they may be utilized to get insightful conclusions from marketing data.
- Includes generative AI techniques, such as generative adversarial networks (GANs) and variational autoencoders (VAEs), showcasing how these techniques can generate synthetic data for marketing insights and decision-making.
- Highlights the importance of data-driven marketing choices and illustrates how generative AI and predictive analytics may be quite useful in this context.
- Integrates the principles of data science with marketing concepts, offering a cohesive understanding of how predictive analytics and generative AI can power data-driven marketing decisions.
- Presents the recent advances in predictive analytics and generative AI and discusses how they can affect the area of data-driven marketing.

Artificial Intelligence, Machine Learning, Data Analytics and Automation for Business Management

Rajesh Dey, *Senior Commissioning Editor, CRC Press, Taylor & Francis Group*

The series presents a comprehensive exploration of how organizations strategically leverage technology to achieve their goals and maintain competitiveness in rapidly evolving industries. With contributions from experts across multiple disciplines, including computer science, business management, and data science, the series adopts an interdisciplinary approach, offering diverse perspectives and fostering cross-functional collaboration. In an era defined by rapid technological innovation and digital transformation, the book series on computational intelligence, data analytics, and emerging technology for business management serves as an indispensable resource for professionals, researchers, and students seeking to harness the power of technology to drive organizational growth and success.

- This series includes works on the latest advancements in computational intelligence, data analytics, and emerging technologies to offer invaluable insights into leveraging cutting-edge tools and methodologies to drive organizational success.
- This series emphasizes practical applications, featuring real-world case studies, examples, and best practices that demonstrate how these technologies can be effectively implemented to address business challenges and drive innovation.
- A multidisciplinary series draws on principles from management, engineering, economics, and other disciplines to effectively leverage technology for organizational success.
- Comprising professional insights, reference materials, and case studies, this series delves into key concepts essential for effective technology for management success.
- This series serves as an indispensable resource for scholars, practitioners, and decision-makers committed to driving innovation and sustainable growth in the digital age.

Predictive Analytics and Generative AI for Data-Driven Marketing Strategies
By Hemachandran K, Debdutta Choudhury, Raul Villamarin Rodriguez, Jorge A. Wise, and Revathi T

For more information about this series, please visit: https://www.routledge.com/Artificial-Intelligence-Machine-Learning-Data-Analytics-and-Automation/book-series/AIBM

Predictive Analytics and Generative AI for Data-Driven Marketing Strategies

Edited by
Hemachandran K, Debdutta Choudhury,
Raul Villamarin Rodriguez,
Jorge A. Wise and Revathi T

CRC Press
Taylor & Francis Group
Boca Raton London New York

CRC Press is an imprint of the
Taylor & Francis Group, an **informa** business
A CHAPMAN & HALL BOOK

Front cover image: PSboom/Shutterstock

First edition published 2025
by CRC Press
2385 NW Executive Center Drive, Suite 320, Boca Raton FL 33431

and by CRC Press
4 Park Square, Milton Park, Abingdon, Oxon, OX14 4RN

CRC Press is an imprint of Taylor & Francis Group, LLC

Library of Congress Cataloging-in-Publication Data
Names: K., Hemachandran, editor. | Choudhury, Debdutta, editor. |
Rodriguez, Raul Villamarin, editor. | Wise, Jorge A., editor. | T., Revathi, (Theerthagiri) 1989- editor.
Title: Predictive analytics and generative AI for data-driven marketing strategies / edited by Hemachandran K, Debdutta Choudhury, Raul Villamarin Rodriguez, Jorge A. Wise and Revathi T.
Description: First edition. | Boca Raton, FL : CRC Press, 2025. |
Series: Artificial intelligence, machine learning, data analytics and automation for business management | Includes bibliographical references and index.
Identifiers: LCCN 2024024620 | ISBN 9781032748917 (hardback) |
ISBN 9781032751320 (paperback) | ISBN 9781003472544 (ebook)
Subjects: LCSH: Marketing–Data processing. | Marketing–Technological innovations. |
Artificial intelligence–Marketing applications.
Classification: LCC HF5415.125 .P735 2025 |
DDC 658.800285/63–dc23/eng/20240904
LC record available at https://lccn.loc.gov/2024024620

ISBN: 978-1-032-74891-7 (hbk)
ISBN: 978-1-032-75132-0 (pbk)
ISBN: 978-1-003-47254-4 (ebk)

DOI: 10.1201/9781003472544

Typeset in Times
by codeMantra

Contents

About the Editors

Hemachandran Kannan is a professor in the Department of Artificial Intelligence & Business Analytics at the School of Business, Woxsen University, India, and holds the Zita Zoltay Paprika of Decision Sciences and Business Economics and Course5i-Chair Professor of Business Analytics and Machine Learning. He has been a passionate teacher with 15 years of teaching experience and 5 years of research experience. He is a strong educational professional with a scientific bent of mind, highly skilled in artificial intelligence (AI) and business analytics. After receiving a PhD in embedded systems, he started focusing on interdisciplinary research. He served as an effective resource person at various national and international scientific conferences and panel discussions. He also gave lectures on topics related to AI and business analytics. He was bestowed as best faculty at Woxsen University in 2021–2022 and at Ashoka Institute of Engineering & Technology in 2019–2020. He has rich working experience in natural language processing, computer vision, building video recommendation systems, building chatbots for human rights (HR) policies and education sector, automatic interview processes, and autonomous robots. He is currently working on various real-time use cases and projects in collaboration with industries such as Advert Flair, Nosh Technologies, Course5i, and Apstek Corp. He has organized many international conferences, hackathons, and ideathons. He owed four patents to his credentials. He has a life membership in estimable professional bodies. He is an open-ended, positive person who has a stupendous peer-reviewed publication record with more than 35 journals and international conference publications. As of now, he has authored three books and edited seven books in CRC Press, Taylor and Francis, and IGI Global.

Debdutta Choudhury is an academician with 18 years of corporate experience spanning manufacturing, BFSI, technology, and education domains. He has spent most of his career in sales and marketing with exposure to sales strategy, sales management, corporate strategy, integrated marketing communication, corporate finance, and general management. He teaches marketing courses and has a research interest in technology in marketing, sustainability, and pedagogical innovations. He has published several book chapters and cases and presented them in research conferences. At Woxsen, he handles various accreditations and new initiatives.

Raul Villamarin Rodriguez is the Vice President of Woxsen University and holds the Steven Pinker Professor of Cognitive Psychology and Classavo Chair Professorship in Integrative Research and Digital Learning. He is an adjunct professor at Universidad del Externado, Colombia; a member of the International Advisory Board at IBS Ranepa, Russian Federation; and a member of the IAB, University of Pécs Faculty of Business and Economics. He is also part of the PRME i5 Expert Pedagogy Group – India representative.

He holds a PhD in artificial intelligence and robotics process automation applications in human resources. His specific areas of expertise and interest are machine learning, deep learning, natural language processing, computer vision, robotic process automation, multi-agent systems, knowledge engineering, and quantum artificial intelligence. He has experience and feels comfortable using Prolog, Java, C++, Python, R/RStudio, Julia, Swift, Scala, MySQL, and Spark, among others. He is a registered expert in artificial intelligence, intelligent systems, and multi-agent systems at the European Commission, a nominee for the Forbes 30 Under 30 Europe 2020 list, and an awardee in the Europe India 40 under 40 Leaders. Alongside this, he is a member of the GRLI Deans and Directors cohort. He is a regular keynote speaker and panel moderator at various national and international conferences or summits such as Machine Learning (ML) Conference (Singapore). Additionally, he is a member of the Harvard Business Review Advisory Council, the ETS Business School Advisory Council (BSAC) in India, and the Institute for Robotics Process Automation & Artificial Intelligence.

He has co-authored two reference books: *New Age Leadership: A Critical Insight* and *Retail Store'e*. He has more than 70 publications to his credit. He is a weekly contributing writer to various magazines in the field of analytics and emerging technologies. Alongside this, he is a journal reviewer and associate editor in various publications such as Institution of Electrical & Electronics Engineers (IEEE).

Jorge A. Wise got a PhD from EGADE Business School. He stood out in professional activities from 1980 to 2000 working in national and international firms. In 1998, he joined Monterrey Tech (ITESM) as a professor of marketing and international business. In 2014, he was appointed as the Director of the Center of Excellence for Competitiveness and Entrepreneurship at CETYS University. Later, he was appointed as the dean of the brand new CETYS Graduate School of Business. In those years, he was recognized as a member of the Mexican National Research System from CONACYT (The Mexican Council for Science and Technology).

He is an international professor who works in the United States, Latin America, and Europe. His latest appointments are at CEIPA Business School, Colombia, and at IESEG School of Management, France. He is also a visiting professor at WOXSEN University, Hyderabad, India, and Pforzheim University, Germany. He is recognized for his work in marketing, international business, strategic management, and family businesses.

T. Revathi is an academician with 7 years of research experience in computer vision and 3 years of teaching in universities. She has spent most of his career in research with exposure to computer vision, applied mathematics, machine learning, and deep learning.

She teaches data analytics courses and has a research interest in technology in artificial intelligence. She has published several research papers in journals and conferences. At Woxsen, she is one of the members of AI Research Centre.

Contributors

Mir Aadil
Woxsen University
Hyderabad, India

Yashaswini Aavula
Woxen University
Hyderabad, India

Shalom Mariam Aeby
Woxsen University
Hyderabad, India

Ezendu Ariwa
Warwick University
Coventry, United Kingdom

Yellamati Aseesh
Woxsen University
Hyderabad, India

Jayasimha Avaldhar
Woxsen University
Hyderabad, India

Darahas Bolisetty
Woxsen University
Hyderabad, India

Bhogineni Sankha Chakradhar
Woxsen University
Hyderabad, India

Divyansh Chittranshi
Woxsen University
Hyderabad, India

K. Mani Teja Chowdary
Woxsen University
Hyderabad, India

Jeevan D'Mello
Zenesis Corporation
Dubai & Woxsen University
Hyderabad, India

Preethi Dharmendar
Woxsen University
Hyderabad, India

Chinna Swamy Dudekula
Engineering and Environment Department
Northumbria University
Newcastle, UK

Rohith Emandi
Woxsen University
Hyderabad, India

Viyyapu Chaitanya Ganesh
Woxsen University
Hyderabad, India

Anisha Gupta
Woxsen University
Hyderabad, India

Nikhil Gupta
Woxsen University
Hyderabad, India

Pepe Gutierrez
University of Burgos
Burgos, Spain

S. R. Hareesh
Woxsen University
Hyderabad, India

Morri Sri Harsha
Woxsen University
Hyderabad, India

Ponthala Harshavardhan
Woxsen University
Hyderabad, India

Mrudula Sai Inampudi
Woxsen University
Hyderabad, India

Rahul Kalra
Woxsen University
Hyderabad, India

Sakshi Karwa
Woxsen University
Hyderabad, India

K. V. Rajesh Kumar
School of Business
Woxsen University
Hyderabad, India

Pokala Pranay Kumar
MPS Data Science
University of Maryland
Baltimore, Maryland

Neelam Kumari
Dublin Business School
Dublin, Ireland

Tolem Kusuma
Woxsen University
Hyderabad, India

P. Mohan Sai Manikanta
Woxsen University
Hyderabad, India

Deepthi Mecharla
Woxsen University
Hyderabad, India

Pratik More
School of Business
Woxsen University
Hyderabad, India

Mosuri Muniratnam
Woxen University
Hyderabad, India

Narsimlu Naganolla
Woxsen University
Hyderabad, India

P. Santosh Sreeram Naidu
Woxsen University
Hyderabad, India

Bharathi Nakkella
Woxen University
Hyderabad, India

Bhargav Narsimgoju
Woxsen University
Hyderabad, India

K. V. Swetha Niharika
Woxsen University
Hyderabad, India

Dasoju Nikhileswar
Woxsen University
Hyderabad, India

Premsai Paidisetty
Woxen University
Hyderabad, India

Lokesh Palimkar
Woxsen University
Hyderabad, India

Adarsh Reddy Pannala
Woxsen University
Hyderabad, India

Zita Zoltay Paprika
Corvinus Business School
Budapest, Hungary

Hithakrith Parshetty
Woxsen University
Hyderabad, India

Shaik Iqbal Pasha
Woxsen University
Hyderabad, India

Anil Pise
University of the Witwatersrand
Johannesburg, South Africa

Philipp Plugmann
Interdisciplinary Periodontology and Prevention
SRH Hochschule für Gesundheit Gera
Gera, Germany

Shiva Sai Kiran Pothula
School of Business
Woxsen University
Hyderabad, India

A. Naga Sai Purushotham
Woxsen University
Hyderabad, India

Adith Raj
Woxsen University
Hyderabad, India

M. Chithik Raja
College of Computing and Information Sciences, Information Technology Department
University of Technology and Applied Sciences Salalah
Dhofar, Sultanate of Oman

V. Vedhik Mohan Rao
Woxsen University
Hyderabad, India

Ankannagiri Harika Reddy
Woxsen University
Hyderabad, India

Jalapally Raja Sai Saketh Reddy
Woxsen University
Hyderabad, India

K. V. Meghana Reddy
Woxen University
Hyderabad, India

M. Nagender Reddy
Woxsen University
Hyderabad, India

Mayreddy Indu Reddy
Woxsen University
Hyderabad, India

Ramidi Pooja Reddy
Woxsen University
Hyderabad, India

Kalal Rukmini
Woxsen University
Hyderabad, India

Bharath Sah
Woxsen University
Hyderabad, India

Bhagyam Saiteja
Woxsen University
Hyderabad, India

Suneeth Samuel. N
Woxsen University
Hyderabad, India

Nidhi Shetty
Woxsen University
Hyderabad, India

Gurram Shilpa
Woxsen University
Hyderabad, India

Surya Shivannagari
Woxsen University
Hyderabad, India

Shreya
Woxsen University
Hyderabad, India

Prudviraj Reddy Singireddy
Woxsen University
Hyderabad, India

Nelapatla Swetha
Woxsen University
Hyderabad, India

Vaishnavi Tadepally
Woxen University
Hyderabad, India

Deepak Durga Prasad Timanani
Woxsen University
Hyderabad, India

Vaishnavi Tirunagari
Woxsen University
Hyderabad, India

Suraj Tunk
Woxsen University
Hyderabad, India

Maniteja Vallepu
Woxsen University
Hyderabad, India

Mugil Vijey
Woxsen University
Hyderabad, India

Yashwant Sai. N
Woxsen University
Hyderabad, India

Preface

In the era of digital revolution, the interaction between predictive analytics and generative AI represents a paradigm shift in marketing strategies. This book, *Predictive Analytics and Generative AI for Data-Driven Marketing Strategies*, serves as a beacon for marketers, data scientists, and business leaders seeking to harness the full potential of these cutting-edge technologies.

This book commences with an exploration of the fundamental principles that reinforce predictive analytics and generative AI. We delve into how these technologies use historical data and recognized patterns to forecast future trends and create unique, actionable insights. This groundwork sets the stage for understanding their profound impact on data-driven marketing strategies.

The subsequent chapters of the book are dedicated to showcasing how predictive analytics and generative AI empower businesses to make informed decisions, personalize marketing efforts, and optimize consumer experiences. Through a blend of theoretical knowledge and practical case studies, we illustrate the transformative role of these technologies in digital marketing. We highlight their capability to analyse vast amounts of data, identify patterns, and generate specific business insights that drive successful marketing strategies.

Furthermore, this book addresses the ethical considerations and challenges that accompany the deployment of AI in marketing. We accentuate the importance of using these powerful tools responsibly, ensuring privacy, fairness, and transparency in all marketing practices.

Predictive Analytics and Generative AI for Data-Driven Marketing Strategies is more than just a book; it is a comprehensive guide designed to equip readers with the knowledge and tools needed to excel in the fast-paced world of digital marketing. By blending the technical aspects of predictive analytics and generative AI with practical marketing applications, we aim to inspire innovation and drive success in data-driven marketing endeavours.

We are thankful to all the contributors who shared their insights and experiences, making this book an invaluable resource for anyone looking to navigate the complex landscape of contemporary marketing. It is our hope that readers will find this book not only informative but also inspiring, opening new avenues for exploration and innovation in the field of data-driven marketing.

1 Introduction to Predictive Analysis and Generative AI

Pepe Gutierrez, Rahul Kalra, Bharath Sah, and Narsimlu Naganolla

1.1 PREDICTIVE ANALYSIS, FROM YESTERDAY TO TODAY

In the rapidly evolving landscape of the digital world, where data reigns supreme, the convergence of predictive analytics, LLMs-LMMs, and generative artificial intelligence (AI) stands as a beacon guiding marketers toward unprecedented insights and strategies. This chapter serves as a gateway to this transformative realm, demystifying the core concepts and principles that underpin predictive analytics and LLMs-generative AI, setting the stage for a profound exploration of their applications in data-driven marketing.

Imagine looking into a crystal ball to view potential outcomes based on past whispers rather than to see your fate. This is basically the appeal of predictive analysis, a method that predates both the technology used to perform it and its use. Though we frequently identify it with state-of-the-art algorithms and massive amounts of data, its origins are surprisingly old, dating back centuries, and it has developed with our comprehension of the world. This chapter explores the rich history of predictive analysis, showing how it developed from crude origins to the complex instruments that shape our modern world.

1.1.1 The Origin of Predictive Analysis

One of the earliest applications of predictive modelling was made by merchants at Lloyd's of London, who utilized ship trip data to estimate hazards and determine insurance rates centuries before computers. This straightforward exercise established the groundwork for comprehending how historical trends influence potential futures.

1.1.2 1950s–1960s: Statistical Analysis Reveals Hidden Correlations

After the world's wars ended, attention turned to understanding and reconstruction. Regression analysis and other statistical techniques gained popularity during this time, enabling businesses and researchers to find patterns and connections in data. For example, businesses could forecast client demand and improve inventory control by examining sales data. Despite being less advanced than their contemporary

DOI: 10.1201/9781003472544-1

equivalents, these methods represented a substantial advancement in the use of data to support well-informed decision-making.

1.1.3 1970s–1990s: Revealing Big Data's Secrets

Data gathering and analysis entered a new era with the advent of the information age. With the development of data mining tools, it became possible to uncover patterns hidden inside large databases. Thanks to developments in processing power and storage capacity, this era witnessed the development of sophisticated algorithms and models. These technologies revolutionized industries by detecting fraudulent transactions and anticipating credit risks. They also created new opportunities for utilizing the hidden narratives included in the data.

1.1.4 The Future the Unfolded Unparalleled Possibilities

Revolutions were made, and technology advanced in ways unfathomable. The "big data" boom necessitated even more advanced technologies. The field of machine learning, and deep learning in particular, transformed forecasting capacities. Personalized suggestions and healthcare outcome prediction are just two instances of how these algorithms are influencing our daily lives.

Looking Ahead: Predictive analysis is still developing as we approach a future fuelled by data. Consider applying it to create individualized learning models or forecast climate change. The options appear to be endless.

This historical look serves as a reminder that predictive analysis is a human endeavour driven by curiosity and a desire to comprehend the world around us, not merely a piece of technology. By advancing and embracing its potential while taking ethical considerations into account, we may harness its power to create a more promising future.

1.2 WHAT IS PREDICTIVE ANALYSIS?

Have you ever wondered how streaming services recommend the perfect show, or how online stores suggest items you might buy? It is not magic, but rather the power of predictive analysis, a fascinating field that unlocks insights from data to anticipate future possibilities.

However, what precisely is it? Predictive analysis, to put it simply, is the technique of projecting future possibilities utilizing past data and complex algorithms. It is like having a superpowered data detective sifting through enormous data sets in search of hints and piecing them together to create a picture of what might be in store.

1.2.1 Predictive Analytics: Navigating the Future

- The Essence of Predictive Analytics

  Predictive analytics, at its core, is a powerful tool that harnesses the wealth of historical data to predict future trends and behaviours. By leveraging statistical algorithms and machine learning techniques, marketers gain the ability to foresee market dynamics, consumer preferences, and potential risks. This chapter initiates readers into the foundational concepts, emphasizing the significance of historical data as the bedrock upon which predictive models are built.

- Techniques and Algorithms in Predictive Modelling

  To comprehend predictive analytics, it is essential to delve into the techniques and algorithms that fuel its predictive prowess. Regression analysis, decision trees, and machine learning algorithms are explored in detail, offering readers a comprehensive understanding of the diverse tools available. This knowledge empowers marketers to select the most suitable approach based on their specific objectives and data set characteristics.
- The Ethical Imperative in Predictive Analytics

  As we traverse the terrain of predictive analytics, ethical considerations come into sharp focus. This chapter underscores the importance of responsible AI usage and ethical decision-making in the realm of marketing. It prompts marketers to reflect on the potential biases embedded in historical data and the ethical implications of predictive modelling, urging a balanced and conscientious approach in leveraging data for marketing insights.

1.2.2 Consider It This Way

- **Weather Forecast**: Meteorologists can determine whether it will rain or be sunny tomorrow by looking at historical weather patterns, temperature variations, and air pressure.
- **Credit Score**: Banks use your credit score to determine whether to approve your application based on your income, spending patterns, and financial history. This helps them evaluate your likelihood of repaying a loan.
- **Online Platforms**: They use information about your browsing and purchasing habits to determine which products you are most likely to be interested in and then display relevant ads to you based on those predictions.

1.2.3 What Are the Key Ingredients of Predictive Analysis?

- **Data**: The prediction models' fuel source. The more precise and pertinent the data, the more accurate the projections will be.
- **Algorithms**: Intricate mathematical algorithms that examine data, spot trends, and draw conclusions. Consider them the secret to transforming data into meaningful insights.
- **Statistical Methods**: Employed to assess the forecasts' dependability and accuracy to make sure they are not merely educated guesses.

Even though predictive analysis has a lot of potential, it is important to approach it critically. It is critical to comprehend these models' limitations, any biases in the data, and the moral issues relating to algorithmic fairness and human privacy. Predictive analysis will continue to influence our world as long as data are more readily available and technology keeps developing. Knowing its fundamentals will enable you to ask wise questions and make better judgements for the world around you as well as for yourself in this more data-driven future.

1.2.4 Peering beyond the Horizon: Predictive Analysis's Future

Imagine a world in which financial institutions anticipate fraud in real time, cities dynamically modify traffic flow to avoid congestion, and healthcare providers are able to prevent illnesses before they arise. These are not futuristic dreams but rather hints at the revolutionary possibilities of predictive analysis, a discipline that can drastically alter our world in the years to come.

Predictive analysis has already had a significant impact on several industries, but there are still a ton of intriguing possibilities for the future.

1.2.5 Together Let Us Uncover What Lies Ahead

- **Supercharged by Data**: Predictive model evolution will be further fuelled by the massive growth of data. The amount of data that will be available will be enormous, ranging from the ubiquitous sensors in our devices to the ever-increasing volume of online interactions. This will provide deeper insights and open the door to even more precise and nuanced forecasts, especially when combined with improvements in data processing and storage capacities.
- **More Intelligent Algorithms**: Envision AI models that not only forecast but also provide a rationale, fostering comprehension and confidence. Quantum computing may also increase speed and complexity, opening up hitherto unimaginable possibilities.
- **Human Power**: Do not think that one size fits all. With personalized insights on your learning, health, and other areas, predictive analysis will become more personal and provide you the ability to make wise decisions.
- **Ethics Matter**: As this power increases, ethical questions also do. For everyone to benefit, not just a chosen few, we need to have an honest conversation and pursue responsible development.
- **Seeing the Unseen**: Consider being able to accurately foretell climate patterns or anticipate disasters before they occur. Predictive analysis has the potential to address humanity's most pressing issues and aid in navigating our complex world.
- **Robots and Humans**: Do not be afraid of the robot tyrants! In a collaborative future, machines will process data and uncover hidden patterns, while humans will provide context and ethics.

As we have uncovered the prowess of predictive analysis, let us dive deep into the world of generative AI.

1.3 TO UNDERSTAND WHAT GENERATIVE AI IS, LET US LOOK AT WHAT AI IS

1.3.1 Artificial Intelligence, a Computer's Way of Understanding

Artificial intelligence is the imitation of human intelligence that is processed by machines, especially computers. The application of AI includes expert systems, natural language processing, machine vision and speech recognition.

AI systems function by taking large amounts of labelled training data, analysing the data for correlations and patterns, and using these patterns to make future predictions about future states. In this way, if a chatbot is given the text samples, it may learn to engage in conversations with the people or an image recognition programme can learn to recognize and describe items in photographs by analysing millions of instances. New, rapidly improving generative AI techniques that can create realistic text, images, music, and other media.

Now, coming back to the topic at hand, let us understand what generative AI is.

1.4 GENERATIVE AI

Generative AI has created excitement and stunned the whole world with its potential to reshape how knowledge work can be done in business functions and industries throughout the whole economy. Around all the functions, such as customer operations, software development, sales, and marketing, it is positioned to revolutionize jobs and improve performance.

In recent years, the rapid speed of AI development and the public release of AI-powered tools like ChatGPT, Gemini, Perplexity.ai, GitHub, Copilot, and DALL-E have peaked all the widespread attention, alarm, and optimism from around the world. These tools are examples of generative AI, a class of machine learning tools that can generate new content such as text, images, music, or video—by analysing patterns in existing data.

1.4.1 Generative AI: Crafting Innovation and Personalization

- **Unveiling Generative AI**

  Transitioning seamlessly from predictive analytics, the chapter introduces readers to the realm of generative AI—a transformative force in content creation, and personalized communications. Generative AI multimodal models, LLMs-LMMs such as GPT-4, are spotlighted for their ability to create human-like text, images, and videos and innovate content with unprecedented creativity. This section provides a glimpse into the capabilities of generative AI, inviting us to envision a future where AI becomes a creative ally.
- **The Dynamics of Generative AI**

  Generative AI transcends the traditional boundaries of content creation, infusing marketing strategies and communications strategies, with unparalleled dynamism. Campaigns can be optimized with personalized content, enhancing customer engagement and driving conversion rates. The chapter elucidates the ways in which generative AI can be harnessed to craft innovative marketing initiatives, from dynamic email campaigns to personalized website content, ushering in a new era of customer-centric communication.

Generative AI and LLMs-LMMs are the fundamental elements in this decade and as such must be considered and used at this time.

- **Responsible AI Practices**

  Just as in predictive analytics, ethical considerations accompany the integration of generative AI. LLMs-LMMs into consumer strategies. The chapter emphasizes the ethical imperative of using AI responsibly and transparently. It addresses concerns related to the potential misuse of generative AI, ensuring that marketers are equipped with the knowledge to navigate the ethical complexities of personalized marketing driven by AI-generated content.

1.4.2 The Key Characteristics of Generative AI

See Figure 1.1.

- **Content Creation**

  Generative AI excels at the creative aspect as it creates entirely new content, such as text, images, videos, and music, instead of simply analysing existing data. The advanced ability of generative AI produces novel content that resembles real-world data, unlike other AI applications that focus on tasks like classification or prediction.

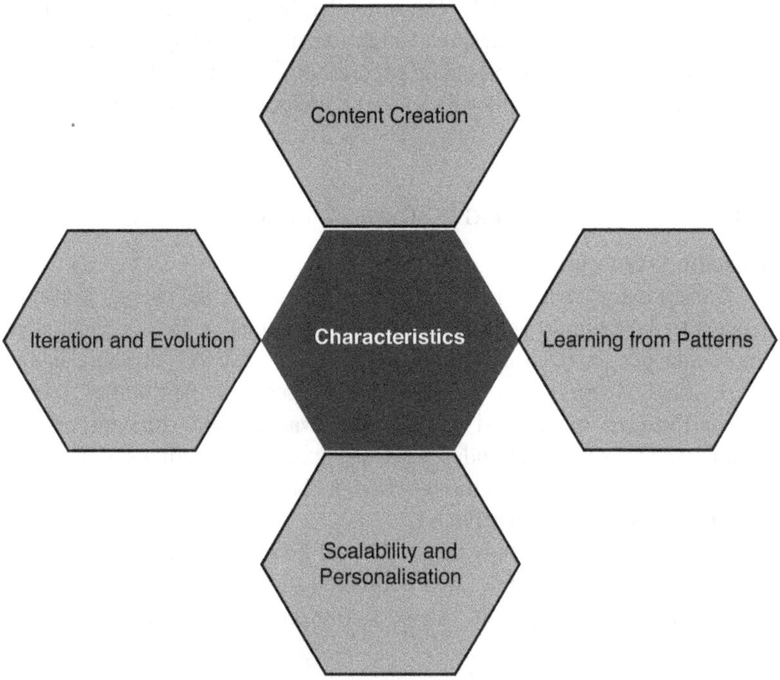

FIGURE 1.1 Characteristic of generative AI.

- **Learning from Patterns**
  To achieve learning from patterns, it analyses massive amounts of data that consist of text, images, videos, etc., to identify the underlying patterns and relationships that connect various pieces. This allows it to understand the rules of how these data are structured and what makes them realistic.
- **Scalability and Personalization**
  Once the algorithm is trained, the generative AI can create personalized content at scale. For example, it can generate unique product descriptions for individual customers tailored to their specific preferences and past purchases. This level of personalization was previously impossible due to the time and resources constraints.
- **Iteration and Evolution**
  Generative AI models are always learning and evolving every minute. They improve their capacity to generate high-quality, realistic content over time by analysing fresh data and receiving feedback. This constant development guarantees that the generated content is both relevant and effective.

1.4.3 Generative AI's Diverse Impact across Industries

Generative AI, which uses computer power to produce entirely new content, is rapidly penetrating several sectors, changing the norms of how people used to interact with information and unleashing a flood of previously unimaginable creative potential. Let us look at how this technology is changing several fields (Figure 1.2).

- **Marketing**
  From Mass Messages to Microtargeting: Consider targeted ads that speak directly to your interests, product descriptions based on your previous purchases, and even immersive AR experiences that allow you to try on clothes, glasses, etc., digitally. This is the effectiveness of generative

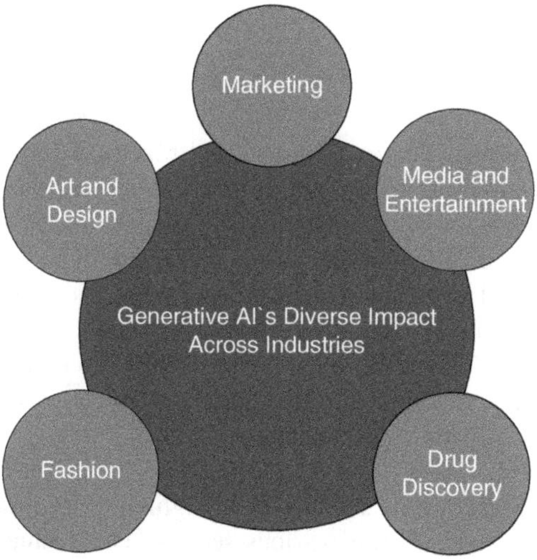

FIGURE 1.2 Generative AI's diverse impact across industries.

AI in marketing. Brands can now utilize algorithms to analyse vast customer data, crafting unique content that resonates on an individual level. Netflix's tailored thumbnail pictures, which increase click-through rates, demonstrate this trend. Generative AI envisions a future in which marketing thrives on individual understanding, forming stronger relationships, and achieving greater results.

- **Media and Entertainment**

  Beyond the Blockbuster Formula: Imagine AI composing music in any genre, quickly generating screenplays that react to audience tastes, or creating video game levels of infinite variety. Generative AI is bringing new inventiveness to media and entertainment. Artists may work with AI tools to produce distinct music genres, authors can experiment with AI-generated story concepts, and game developers can build more immersive and diverse experiences. This technology does not replace current creatives; rather, it empowers them to explore unexplored territory and push artistic boundaries.
- **Drug Discovery**

  From Trial and Error to Precision Design: Generative AI is proving to be a valuable friend in the time-consuming and costly drug development process. Consider AI models quickly creating compounds and molecules with precise properties, which might lead to advances in illness treatment. Researchers have previously used AI to create a promising chemical that fights antibiotic-resistant bacteria, demonstrating the technology's promise. Aside from new medications, generative models may tailor treatment regimens based on individual patient data, opening the path for more accurate and effective healthcare.
- **Fashion**

  From Trends to Personalized Couture: Let us just imagine that AI is developing original clothing designs based on your style choices, 3D prototypes for faster manufacturing, and even personalized fashion suggestions. Generative AI is changing the fashion business. Brands may adapt designs based on individual preferences, streamline manufacturing using AI-generated prototypes, and provide customers with tailored suggestions, resulting in a more engaging and efficient fashion experience.
- **Art and Design**

  Bridging the Gap Between Human and Machine: Imagine AI creating elaborate digital art pieces, writing compelling music based on your mood, or even developing architectural models that push the limits of creativity. Generative AI is broadening the scope of art and design. Artists may collaborate or work with AI technologies to experiment with new styles, produce individualized artwork, and work with machines to explore unexplored creative territory. This technology is not intended to replace human artists rather, it provides new tools for broadening artistic expression and opening doors to previously unthinkable opportunities.

This insight into generative AI's many uses highlights its immense potential to transform businesses and empower various sectors. This technology is guiding in a future rich with innovation, personalization, and advancement, from personalized marketing to expedited drug research, AI-powered music creation to tailored fashion designs. As generative AI evolves, the possibilities are endless, and one thing is certain, it will play a critical role in creating the future in a variety of sectors.

Generative AI is a step change in the evolution of AI. As many companies strive to adapt and implement generative AI, recognizing the technology's potential to offer value to the economy and society at large will help shape crucial decisions.

1.5 BRIDGING THE GAP: CONVERGENCE OF PREDICTIVE ANALYTICS AND GENERATIVE AI

1.5.1 The Work of Synergy

- **Improved Decision-Making**
  Businesses can make better judgements because of the combination of generative AI and predictive analytics. Businesses can create creative strategies that adapt to the changing demands and preferences of their clientele by combining generative creativity with predictive insights.
- **Real-Time Adaptation**
  By combining generative AI and predictive analytics, businesses can dynamically modify their strategies in response to new market trends and customer behaviour patterns. Businesses may stay competitive and ahead of the curve in quick-paced markets because of this agility.
- **Personalization at Scale**
  At scale, personalization is made possible by the marriage of generative AI and predictive analytics. Businesses are able to provide highly targeted campaigns and products that connect with specific consumers by analysing large amounts of data and producing creative content. This leads to increased brand loyalty and engagement.
- **Talent Development**
  To fully utilize generative AI and predictive analytics, a staff with the necessary skills is needed. Employers must fund talent development programmes to give staff members the skills they need in data science, machine learning, and creative design.
- **Cooperation and Joint Ventures**
  Working together is frequently necessary to address the difficulties and take advantage of the potential presented by the convergence of generative AI and predictive analytics. Businesses should look to collaborate with academic institutions, technology companies, and other industry peers to share best practices, gain insights, and co-invent solutions that advance society.

1.5.2 Opportunities and Difficulties

- **Ethical Concerns**
  The ethical implications of the combination of generative AI with predictive analytics include the possibility of algorithmic bias and the responsible

use of consumer data. To foster consumer trust and reduce ethical risks, businesses using AI-driven projects should place a high priority on accountability, fairness, and openness.

- **Regulatory Compliance**

  As generative AI and predictive analytics continue to evolve at a rapid rate, regulatory frameworks may find it difficult to keep up. In order to maintain individual privacy rights and comply with data protection rules, organizations need to negotiate complicated regulatory environments.

1.6 CONCLUSION: PAVING THE WAY FOR DATA-DRIVEN COMPANIES

In conclusion, the "Introduction to Predictive Analytics and Generative AI" chapter serves as a compass for marketers venturing into the realm of data-driven strategies. By laying a robust foundation in predictive analytics and introducing the creative potential of generative AI, this chapter equips readers with the essential knowledge and ethical considerations necessary for the transformative journey that lies ahead. As the narrative unfolds, marketers are beckoned towards the subsequent chapters, where real-world applications, case studies, and best practices illuminate the path to a future where data-driven companies are synonymous with innovation, personalization, and responsible AI usage.

FURTHER READINGS

Francois Chollet. 2021. *Deep Learning with Python.* Manning Publications Co.

Cognite. The Definitive Guide to Generative AI for Industry. Cognite.

Marcus du Sautoy. 2019. *The Creativity Code: Art and Innovation in the Age of AI.* The Belknap Press of Harvard University Press.

Viktor Mayer-Schönberger and Kenneth Cukier. 2017. *Big Data: A Revolution That Will Transform How We Live, Work, and Think.* John Murray.

University of Alberta. 2024. Ethical Considerations - Using Generative AI - Subject Guides. The University of Alberta.

Upwork. 2023. Generative AI vs. Predictive AI: Differences and Applications. Upwork.

2 Fundamentals of Data-Driven Marketing

Morri Sri Harsha, Yellamati Aseesh, and Anil Pise

2.1 INTRODUCTION

2.1.1 Definition

A marketing approach called "facts-pushed advertising" makes use of analytics and statistics to inform strategic picks, improve advertising and marketing, and provide a greater tailored customer enjoyment. It entails collecting, examining, and extrapolating facts from numerous assets so that it will comprehend the tendencies, behaviours, and patterns of customers. Businesses might also enhance ROI (Return on Investment) and customer engagement by using records to expand centred and efficient advertising campaigns.

2.1.2 Overview

Businesses' information of and interactions with their target audience have passed through a full-size exchange due to the transition from conventional advertising to records-driven strategies. Conventional advertising had a one-length-fits-all approach and normally relied on mass media, together with print, radio, and TV. With few tools at their disposal, entrepreneurs have been every now and then compelled to make judgements based totally extra on gut feeling rather than hard information.

The emergence of virtual generation and the growth of online systems have furnished agencies with substantial get admission to information created via patron interactions. As a result of this variation, information-pushed advertising and marketing emerged, whilst advertisers began the use of system mastering, synthetic intelligence, and statistics analytics to improve their approach. More accurate, concentrated on, tailor-made communications, and ongoing optimization based on real-time facts are made viable via this shift.

2.1.3 Relevance in the Context of Contemporary Business

Data-pushed advertising is turning into more and more essential in trendy corporate environment for a number of motives:

Precision Concentrated: Organizations might also pinpoint the particular characteristics, behaviour, and inclinations of their goal marketplace via examining information. As a result, much less money is wasted on unrelated audiences and greater correct concentrated on is made possible.

DOI: 10.1201/9781003472544-2

Personalization: Content may be created that is pertinent and tailored to each individual customer way to records-pushed advertising. Personalization improves customer delight, builds emblem loyalty, and increases conversion charges.

Efficiency and Optimization: Using actual-time information insights, entrepreneurs can continually enhance their efforts. By the use of an iterative method, marketing campaigns may be optimized for efficiency and tactics may be adjusted to reflect transferring market conditions [1].

Measurable Return on Investment: Data-pushed marketing, in assessment of conventional advertising, gives quantifiable measurements and key performance signs (KPIs). This makes it viable for businesses to evaluate the campaign's effectiveness and adjust their plans as important.

Competitive Advantage: Businesses that correctly use records-driven advertising have an advantage over their rivals due to the fact they are able to continue to be bendy, hastily adjust to converting marketplace situations, and more appropriately satisfy client expectancies.

2.2 KEY CONCEPTS IN DATA-DRIVEN MARKETING

2.2.1 Customer Segmentation

A key element of records-driven advertising and marketing is customer segmentation, that is the dividing of a target marketplace into discrete groups according to specific attributes. By focusing on quantifiable traits like age, gender, income, education, and marital status, demographic segmentation lets in corporations to personalize advertising messages for positive agencies of people. In order to create campaigns that resonate with clients on an emotional level, psychographic segmentation explores their psychological and lifestyle attributes, along with values, pursuits, and personality. Using behavioural segmentation, marketers may additionally target specific necessities by way of grouping clients in step with their behaviour, inclusive of brand loyalty and purchase habits. Through the customization of messaging, offers, and studies, personalized marketing procedures boom purchaser engagement, increase conversion costs, construct logo loyalty, and optimize advertising and marketing go back on investment. Businesses build deeper relationships with clients by means of mastering about and accommodating man or woman possibilities. This fosters greater interplay, customer loyalty, and, sooner or later, corporation fulfilment [2].

2.2.2 Data Collection and Sources

Businesses concerned in statistics-pushed advertising need to recognize the variations among first-celebration, second-birthday party, and third-celebration information. Data can also take many unique forms. Through sources like website analytics and transactional data, first-celebration statistics—received directly from customer interactions on an organization's systems—offers insightful statistics approximately the patron base. In order to sell cooperative advertising initiatives and enhance facts richness, cooperating corporations may additionally percentage first-birthday celebration records for mutual advantage, that is known as "2nd-birthday celebration facts." However, 0.33-birthday party information, that is collected and mixed from different assets, provides an organization's very own datasets by offering further info like behavioural and demographic information [3].

Privacy and ethical issues are major issues on the subject of information-pushed advertising and marketing. Maintaining moral facts-collecting approaches is important to setting up credibility and shielding brand integrity. This involves maintaining openness and getting people's explicit agreement concerning the statistics this is accrued and the way it will likely be used. Ensuring that client statistics is blanketed from potential breaches and unauthorized get entry to requires robust information security procedures. Techniques like anonymization and aggregation can help allay privateness worries by means of imparting insights while shielding private information. In addition to being required through law, adhering to data safety legal guidelines like the CCPA and GDPR suggests a commitment to moral information practices. In this case, constructing patron trust and upholding a robust emblem image require carefully navigating the records panorama.

2.2.3 Data Analytics and Insights

The direction from raw records to actionable insights is significantly aided by analytics equipment and technology, which encompass records visualization, statistical analysis, device mastering, and consumer relationship management (CRM) systems.

Tools for statistical analysis use methods like regression analysis and descriptive records to discover styles and relationships in records. Predictive analytics is made viable by means of machine getting to know algorithms, a powerful factor that uncovers styles in massive datasets to assist organizations in expecting destiny traits and offer tailor-made guidelines.

D3.Js, Tableau, and Power BI are a few examples of statistics visualization technologies which could flip complex datasets into visual representations. This improves interpretability, which allows strategic selection-making by means of making insights simpler for marketers and choice-makers to realize and explicit.

CRM systems integrate information from several assets to offer an entire image of patron interactions. Businesses are able to monitor purchaser trips, tailor messages, and enhance connections as an end result.

The main objective of data analytics is to offer sensible insights for nicely-informed choices. Setting up pertinent Key Performance Indicators (KPIs) is critical for gauging the effectiveness of marketing campaigns and ensuring that they are consistent with strategic targets. Customer group segmentation and analysis resources in customizing advertising plans to personal tastes, and ongoing campaign optimization incorporates in-the-moment adjustments depending on performance indicators and A/B checking out [4].

Machine getting to know algorithms-powered predictive analytics gives groups the capability to foresee destiny trends, purchaser conduct, and market shifts. Proactive selection-making is made viable via this foresight, which continues techniques ahead of the opposition. Essentially, the combination of these analytics tools and technology permits a statistics-pushed strategy that directs businesses towards strategic success in product creation, advertising and marketing, and popular operations.

2.3 IMPLEMENTING DATA-DRIVEN STRATEGIES

2.3.1 Building a Customer-Centric Culture

Businesses aiming to prosper in state-of-the-art aggressive environment must prioritize aligning their company with patron necessities, underscoring the need for a patron-centric lifestyle. There are several blessings to this alignment:

First of all, setting the requirements of the consumer first improves customer happiness, which in turn produces better items, services, and experiences all around. Customers who might be happy with a logo are extra inclined to apply it once more and to advocate it to others.

Secondly, by showing honest willpower to pleasurable and surpassing customer expectancies, a client-centric approach promotes more patron loyalty. Long-term success depends closely on consumer loyalty as it is from time to time much less luxurious to get repeat enterprise than to find new ones.

Thirdly, businesses that position an excessive priority on customer delight set up a favourable popularity for his or her emblem, which inspires phrase-of-mouth referrals and favourable internet critiques. This right emblem belief draws in new enterprise and maintains the preserve of modern customers.

Finally, firms with a sturdy purchaser awareness are more ready to adjust to moving marketplace situations. Through constant monitoring of purchaser feedback and records, companies are able to directly adjust their plans in reaction to converting wishes.

In order to set up a client-centric culture, agencies should prioritize education and development tasks that allow the body of workers members to make records-driven alternatives. This involves tackling vital topics like:

Data literacy is coaching a group of workers and participants on the basics of records literacy that will nicely examine and use statistics to make choices.

Technology Proficiency: Teaching analytics gear and technology, inclusive of CRM systems, statistics visualization equipment, and platforms like Google Analytics, to customers.

Customer-Centric Attitude: Developing a client-centric mindset among the team of workers members in any respect organizational levels, motivating them to comprehend the necessities of customers, empathize with them, and utilize facts to make choices that place the desires of the patron first.

Teamwork and Communication: To make sure that patron insights are shared and used throughout the organization, training packages must encompass a sturdy emphasis on powerful conversation and teamwork. This will assist to break down organizational silos.

2.3.2 Campaign Optimization

Campaign optimization techniques, which include A/B and multivariate testing, are critical due to the fact they let entrepreneurs take a look at numerous additives and perceive the fine versions for higher overall performance.

A/B checking out reveals the higher-acting model of an advertising and marketing piece by using evaluating variations (A and B) of the identical, such as an electronic mail subject line or website. By the use of this technique, marketers may additionally optimize destiny efforts primarily based on measurable reactions and make information-driven decisions.

Multivariate testing, then again, assesses numerous iterations of various components concurrently that allows you to decide how they affect overall performance as a whole. When examining elaborate interactions in a marketing campaign, such as experimenting with one-of-a-kind headlines and pictures and making contact with-to-movement combinations, this technique is quite beneficial.

The technique of using information to beautify campaigns is non-stop and incorporates a number of essential factors, including:

Performance Metrics: Determine and display key overall performance indicators (KPIs) that are pertinent to the goals of the campaign, which include engagement degrees, click-on-through prices, and conversion rates.

Iterative Analysis: Examine campaign performance statistics on an ordinary basis to identify traits and styles. This recurrent evaluation aids in figuring out which advertising factors are attractive to the goal demographic and what changes are probably required.

Segmentation Analysis: Examine how various consumer segments carry out with the purpose of understanding why responses vary. This consciousness directs the improvement of custom-designed and centred advertising and marketing for unique target market segments.

Customer Enter: Include remarks from social media, surveys, and purchaser remarks inside the analysis. Complementing quantitative statistics with qualitative insights is the comprehension of patron emotions.

Through the mixing of these methodologies into the optimization technique, marketers can also continually beautify and optimize their efforts. Effective, resonant, and adaptable advertising and marketing campaigns are guaranteed via information-pushed choice-making grounded on A/B testing, multivariate checking out, and in-depth performance metrics evaluation.

2.3.3 Real-Time Personalization

Dynamic content and recommendation engines provide real-time personalization, that is a mighty tactic to enhance purchaser reports and inspire engagement and conversion.

Customizing internet site content, email campaigns, and different advertising and marketing materials in actual time primarily based on personal information is known as dynamic content material. For example, an e-commerce internet site can also offer a personalized and relevant experience by dynamically displaying items based on a consumer's past purchases or cutting-edge browsing behaviour.

Recommendation engines are pushed by information algorithms that look at previous person behaviours, alternatives, and comparable consumer profiles to provide tips for items or information that might be of hobby to certain users. By the use of a personalized strategy, firms may additionally provide pointers which can be greater applicable to their clients, which will increase customer satisfaction and conversion rates.

A thorough hold close of each purchaser's unique route and preferences is vital to customize messaging relying on their behaviour. Important approaches for this customized technique encompass:

Behavioural Tracking: Track and compare patron behaviour throughout a variety of touchpoints, along with website visits, e-mail conversations, and social media participation, by way of using facts. The basis for creating communications which are tailored to the pursuits of the consumer is these statistics.

Campaigns That Are Induced: Set up induced campaigns that are computerized and react to precise occasions or movements from clients. One way to re-engage customers and urge a purchase is to send them a personalized email with special offers once they abandon their online shopping cart.

Segment-Specific Messaging: Tailor communications to the pastimes and behaviours of diverse consumer segments. This guarantees that messages are pertinent and resonate with every demographic, boosting advertising and marketing efforts' efficacy.

Through using recommendation engines, dynamic content, and tailor-made messaging in line with patron movements, corporations may additionally set up deeper relationships with their target audience. This custom-designed method increases engagement and conversion rates while also enhancing patron happiness.

2.4 MEASURING AND EVALUATING PERFORMANCE

2.4.1 Key Performance Indicators (KPIS)

The effectiveness of records-driven advertising and marketing depends on the definition of pertinent Key Performance Indicators (KPIs), which offer quantifiable measurements to assess overall performance and direct well-informed choice-making. The following are important KPIs and techniques for tracking and assessing facts-driven advertising achievement:

Conversion Rate: This degree shows what proportion of leads or website traffic completes a favoured hobby, such as submitting a form or completing a purchase. Tracking the conversion rate makes it easier to evaluate how well advertising and marketing campaigns are accomplishing their desires.

Client Acquisition Cost (CAC): A measure of the expenses involved in acquiring a new patron. CAC is computed by dividing total marketing costs using the range of recent clients received. In popular, lower CAC is higher for low priced consumer acquisition.

Customer Lifetime Value (CLV): CLV forecasts the net profit that a customer will offer to the enterprise in the course of their association with it. Optimizing advertising approaches for lengthy-time period fulfilment requires a knowledge of CLV.

Click-Through Rate (CTR): This degree evaluates the proportion of folks that click on an advertising or link out of all the impressions. CTR sheds light on the potency of advertising creatives and the applicability of the material.

Churn Rate: Over a certain time period, the fee at which purchasers discontinue making use of a service or product is measured. Reducing attrition is crucial to keeping robust clients.

Engagement Metrics: Information on how actively and favourably customers have interaction with advertising and marketing content can be gleaned from metrics like e-mail open costs, time spent on a website, and social media interactions.

2.4.2 Methods for Monitoring and Assessing Achievement

Employing Analytics Instruments: Use programmes like Adobe Analytics or Google Analytics to screen and examine pertinent KPIs. These tools provide information on person conduct, campaign overall performance, and website traffic.

Establish Specific Objectives: Establish quantifiable, unique targets for each advertising and marketing attempt. Defined goals serve as achievement standards and direct the selection of pertinent KPIs.

Frequent Monitoring: Make it a habit to check KPIs on a common foundation. Monitoring in real-time or nearly real-time permits for the early detection of traits and the well timed modification of campaigns while vital.

Data Quality Assurance: Consistently audit and validate records sources to assure facts dependability and correctness. Incomplete or inaccurate records would possibly result in defective evaluation and poorly knowledgeable selections.

Data Visualization: To provide KPIs a visual representation, use information visualization tools to generate dashboards and reviews. Visualization improves understanding and makes insights less complicated to speak to stakeholders.

Organizations may additionally achieve important insights into the effectiveness of their records-pushed advertising and marketing tasks and make sensible selections to maximize subsequent campaigns by way of establishing and frequently monitoring these KPIs.

2.4.3 Return on Investment (ROI)

Evaluating the economic performance of information-pushed advertising tasks calls for computing the Return on Investment (ROI). The ROI calculation is as follows:

$$\text{ROI} = (\text{Net Profit}/\text{cost of investment}) * 100$$

where

Net profit is the quantity of money made from the advertising and marketing campaign minus all the expenses incurred, which includes those for analytics software, advertising, and different related expenses.

The term "cost of funding" refers to all of the marketing campaign's out-of-pocket spending, along with those for workforce, generation, marketing, and content production and shipping.

To proficiently carry to stakeholders the significance of statistics-pushed advertising and marketing endeavours, the subsequent procedures are essential:

Evidently, Specify Your Desires: Give stakeholders context with the aid of in reality mentioning the campaign's pursuits and coordinating them with greater well-known corporate goals.

Calculate Outcomes: Provide hard information and figures to illustrate the campaign's effectiveness, highlighting vital signs along with more income, extra customers, or higher patron delight.

Benchmark against Goals: Draw attention to overachievements or provide suggestions for improvement by contrasting actual results with original targets.

Attribution Modelling: Use attribution fashions to reveal how different advertising and marketing channels and touchpoints motivated conversions, providing you with complete information on the impact of the advertising blend.

Create a Story: Craft a story that narrates the marketing campaign's adventure from start to finish, enabling stakeholders to emotionally identify with its triumphs.

Exchange Knowledge and Discoveries: Share campaign accomplishments in addition to training discovered to expose your dedication to ongoing development and to fostering trust inside the organization's statistics-pushed strategy.

Visuals are used to present complicated records graphically, using charts, graphs, and tables to help stakeholders recognize the significance of facts-pushed advertising projects.

By enforcing these tactics, businesses can also persuade stakeholders to go back on investment (ROI) in their data-pushed advertising initiatives, win over funding, and guarantee the continued fulfilment of records-pushed strategies.

2.5 CHALLENGES AND CONSIDERATIONS

2.5.1 Data Privacy and Compliance

Organizations that use information-pushed advertising ought to take legal responsibilities under consideration, in particular in relation to facts protection laws just like the General Data Protection Regulation (GDPR). Here is how organizations can comply with those requirements and navigate them:

Principles of Data Protection: Comply with the fundamental guidelines set forth in laws just like the GDPR. This involves getting express consent earlier than processing statistics, making sure that it is miles accurate, and putting strong safeguards in place to protect personal records.

Justification for Processing within the Law: Determine and file in element the prison justification for dealing with non-public statistics. A valid justification have to be in area before any personal data is accrued and used, making certain that it is used for the supposed reason.

Rights of Data Subjects: Respect the rights of statistics topics, including the capability to view, amend, and cast off private information. Create powerful processes to respond to requests from records subjects in a timely and transparent way.

Data Breach Response: To quickly identify, report, and handle any records breaches, create and position into motion a radical plan for responding to data breaches. Organizations have to frequently tell the correct authorities and impacted parties within positive deadlines as a way to comply.

Data Protection Impact Assessments (DPIAs): To determine the viable effect of statistics processing on human beings' privacy and to use mitigation measures, DPIAs must be carried out for excessive-danger processing sports.

It is critical to strike a balance between privacy issues and personalized advertising as a way to uphold regulatory compliance and purchaser self-assurance. The following are some methods to strike this balance:

Explicit Consent: Before accumulating and making use of a person's non-public information, get their specific consent. Make it apparent why records are being amassed, and provide customers the selection to consent to or item to ensure processing operations.

Anonymization and Pseudonymization: Use techniques like information anonymization and pseudonymization to protect non-public records whilst obtaining precious insights from blended statistics. This protects privacy and allows for useful evaluation.

Integrate privacy concerns into the planning and creation of goods, services, and promotional campaigns. This is called "privateness by layout." By taking a proactive stance, the risk of non-compliance is reduced due to the fact privacy is given priority from the start.

User Education: Inform users of the security precautions in place to steady their records as well as how they will be applied. In addition to fostering acceptance as true, open communication empowers humans to make knowledgeable choices about sharing their private statistics.

Organizations might also efficiently control the challenges of statistics-pushed marketing while setting up and preserving audience consider by using coordinating approaches with felony responsibilities and putting a high priority on user privacy.

2.5.2 Technology Integration

It may be difficult to embrace and combine new technologies in fact-driven advertising because of quite a few problems, including problems integrating antique structures, a lack of vital abilities, and competition to change. Organizations must prioritize interoperability, engage in the body of workers' education, use efficient alternate control strategies, and take a phased integration strategy to address these issues. Important actions include selecting exceptional generation suppliers via in-depth exams and tackling statistics switch problems with tricky techniques. Long-term fulfilment relies upon on compatibility and scalability, which incorporates choosing technology that paints nicely together, taking future enlargement into consideration, doing huge performance testing, and setting sturdy security features in the vicinity. In the long term, incorporated technologies come to be extra resilient and successful when destiny-proofing entails predicting technological enhancements and growing monitoring and preservation strategies.

2.6 CASE STUDIES AND EXAMPLES

2.6.1 Highlight Effective Data-Driven Marketing Initiatives

The e-commerce behemoth Amazon has cemented its role in the use of information-pushed advertising procedures; its personalized advice engine is one of its most fantastic functions. Amazon makes use of a plethora of personal facts to observe browsing patterns, shopping patterns, and product opinions. The advice engine, that is pushed through state-of-the-art device getting-to-know algorithms, makes predictions about objects based on personal alternatives, which enhances purchaser engagement and increases conversion charges. A custom-designed buying revel is fantastic for clients, growing their pleasure and loyalty.

Similarly, the famous song-streaming provider Spotify uses data-pushed advertising to enhance consumer experience with tailor-made playlists, as confirmed by the "Discover Weekly" campaign. In order to broaden an advanced image of every user's particular musical choices, Spotify explores their listening styles by examining genres, artists, and song selections. Collaborative filtering is utilized by the advice set of rules to evaluate humans with comparable tastes and provide new and suitable music. This method has stepped forward user retention at the website and generated top feedback from users who cost the guidelines' accuracy, strengthening the bond between customers and the platform.

2.6.2 Examine the Finest Practices and Lessons Discovered from Leaders in the Field

Both Amazon and Spotify emphasize unique techniques and provide insightful insights into the arena of records-pushed advertising. The mystery to Amazon's fulfilment is its large use of statistics, which incorporates lots of datasets containing transactional and behavioural facts. This technique offers complete information on client possibilities. The e-commerce behemoth has tested the cost of keeping up with technology changes by making an investment in gadget-mastering-powered state-of-the-art algorithms that improve the accuracy of customized hints.

Conversely, Spotify emphasizes the price of ongoing adaptation and generation. The song streaming service performs exceedingly properly because it makes use of machine learning models, which can be constantly learned from personal conduct, making sure that personalized recommendations continue to be applicable through the years. Setting consumer engagement measures, such as the amount of time spent on the website online and the wide variety of songs listened to, as a top precedence, suggests how properly customised advertising paintings to maintain and please purchasers.

Netflix, an outstanding player within the area, enhances data-driven advertising and marketing with the aid of making use of dynamic storytelling and content material personalization. Netflix gives customized content recommendations based on person behaviour analysis and offers specific reviews, such as interactive storytelling in series like "Bandersnatch." Increased viewer happiness and favourable phrase-of-mouth are the final results, highlighting the price of customized content and modern paperwork.

Additionally, Netflix highlights the cost of A/B trying out content optimization, automatically evaluating the efficacy of various capabilities and guidelines. This iterative system demonstrates Netflix's willpower to break new ground and offer revolutionary reports while enabling ongoing optimization based totally on client choices.

In end, these case studies show how industry leaders have efficiently implemented facts-driven advertising techniques, highlighting the importance of thorough data utilization, ongoing generation, funding in modern algorithms, and utilizing A/B checking out for optimization. Companies may additionally study loads from these lessons to improve their own records-pushed marketing campaigns and higher meet the converting demands in their goal market.

2.7 FUTURE TRENDS IN DATA-DRIVEN MARKETING

2.7.1 New Technological Developments and Their Effects on Marketing

Data-pushed advertising and marketing already heavily is based on synthetic intelligence (AI) and device mastering (ML), which strength recommendation engines, personalization, and predictive analytics. Currently, artificial intelligence (AI) is being used in chatbots and digital assistants to enhance consumer interactions and provide real-time assistance. The application of AI and ML in advertising is predicted to grow in the future. As predictive personalization advances, it will be able to expect real-time client preferences and demands. Customer segmentation may be advanced through ML algorithms so that it will additionally come across diffused tendencies and behaviours for greater precise and focused marketing.

As 5G generation is being deployed, it is going to provide faster and more dependable net access if you want to have a favourable effect on cellular stories and the intake of multimedia content. 5G is expected to enhance cellular stories within the destiny via enabling greater immersive and facts-wealthy content material. Furthermore, 5G will facilitate the vast use of Virtual Reality (VR) and Augmented Reality (AR) apps in advertising, providing users smooth, wonderful stories.

The Internet of Things (IoT) is currently having a power on devices like as wearables and clever domestic home equipment, which might be generating large volumes of records for individualized marketing and consumer insights. Hyper-personalization will be made possible in the future through IoT, so as to permit marketers to gather statistics in real time from linked devices to create customized offers and advertising messages. Smart tool behavioural facts will tell greater specialized advertising, marketing, and product pointers.

Users' interactions with digital fabric are already being altered by way of voice seek and smart assistants, which have an influence on search engine optimization (search engine optimization) approaches. In the future, as entrepreneurs optimize their content for voice search and conversational interfaces come to be increasingly crucial in customer interactions, conversational marketing will become more and more famous. Voice-activated commerce is likewise expected to grow in the future, converting the e-trade scene as a smart assistant boost to enable greater common voice-activated purchases and transactions. These technical tendencies spotlight how digital advertising is changing and the way businesses have to adjust to take gain of those traits to offer more attractive and customized purchaser studies.

2.7.2 Forecasts on the State of Data-Driven Marketing in the Future

Increased international statistics privateness policies will pressure entrepreneurs to prioritize moral statistics practices and benefit express consent, resulting in great changes to privateness-first marketing. In order to cope with rising issues regarding statistics privacy, marketers will refocus their efforts on acquiring and using first-birthday party facts immediately from customers. With its capability to provide customers with immersive and tasty reviews, augmented reality (AR) is set to end up being a critical factor in advertising campaigns, in particular in the retail and e-commerce industries. AR will remodel how products are visualized, allowing for immersive pre-purchase experiences and digital strive-one.

Blockchain era is anticipated to emerge as extra widely used in the privacy and protection space, in particular in the protection and authentication of patron records. Blockchain technology has the capacity to enable authenticated consumer identities, ensuring particular targeting and tailor-made experiences and mitigating the likelihood of information breaches. Metrics associated with customer experience (CX), consisting of Net Promoter Score (NPS) and customer contentment, could be given greater weight in assessing the efficacy of advertising and marketing campaigns. The creation of seamless, customized customer journeys throughout numerous touchpoints turns into the number one recognition.

The improvement of thorough purchaser profiles for more efficient personalization could be made viable by the unification of purchaser facts from various assets, a good way to make this feasible is by using unified customer facts systems (CDPs). Real-time records processing can be made less difficult by means of superior CDPs, enabling entrepreneurs to react speedily to the choices and behaviours of their customers. With an emphasis on moral advertising and marketing techniques and corporations that aid social ideals, environmental, social, and governance (ESG) marketing will grow in significance and positively impact trade.

AI-generated equipment will assist in creating dynamic and personalized content, from product descriptions to photograph additives in marketing substances. This will lead to breakthroughs in each AI-generated content material and creativity. AI will enhance creativity through supporting entrepreneurs come up with ideas and offer records-pushed insights to make content material as impactful as possible. All of these traits point to a dynamic shift in advertising techniques that prioritize patron connection and happiness above privateness worries, experiential advertising, and moral advertising and marketing.

2.8 CONCLUSION

In the end, the research into records-pushed advertising has revealed a number of essential insights that spotlight its progressive impact on current employer procedures. The communique has explored the complexities of placing records-driven methodology into practice, together with the whole lot from the transition far away from traditional strategies to the essential emphasis on patron-centricity. Important ideas like real-time personalization, moral information acquisition, and client segmentation were emphasized, underscoring their vital characteristic in developing advertising and marketing campaigns that are both centred and memorable. Considerations, together with evaluating ROI, negotiating obstacles like facts safety and technological integration, and measuring effectiveness with pertinent KPIs have grown to be important for successful deployment.

Upon contemplation of case studies touching on distinguished enterprise gamers, including Amazon, Spotify, and Netflix, it is apparent that statistics-driven procedures may be efficiently used to enhance patron engagement and happiness. Looking in advance, new technology like artificial intelligence, 5G, and the Internet of Things will have an effect on information-pushed advertising and marketing in the future and gift formerly unheard-of chances for innovation and individualized patron stories. Nevertheless, no matter these developments, long-term success relies upon on a willpower to privacy-first techniques, augmented fact integration, and user revel in measurements.

It is critical to stress the continued importance of records-driven advertising projects. Adaptability to change is important in an era characterized by way of fast technology innovation and transferring expectations from customers. Companies that use statistics-pushed insights to their benefit may match the wishes of cutting-edge customers for individualized reviews and build long-lasting relationships. Organizations are positive to be at the vanguard of innovation and originality in content material improvement, customer reviews, and ordinary campaign strategies way to the ongoing optimization and refining made viable by facts-driven strategies. Prioritizing ethical and responsible facts and practices is important to maintaining transparency in communication, regulatory compliance, and public self-assurance. To position it virtually, information-driven advertising is a strategic want that permits agencies to overcome obstacles, seize new possibilities, and build lengthy-lasting connections with their goal market.

REFERENCES

1. Grandhi, B., Patwa, N. and Saleem, K. (2021). Data-Driven Marketing for Growth and Profitability. *EuroMed Journal of Business*, 16(4), 381–398.
2. Redding, S. (2015). *The data-driven marketing manual.* NXT Books.
3. Kingsnorth, S. (2016). *Digital marketing strategy: An integrated approach to online marketing.* Kogan Page Publishers.
4. Viswanathan, V., Williams, J. R. and Bergiel, E. (2019). Data-Driven Marketing: A Practical Framework. *Journal of Direct, Data and Digital Marketing Practice.*

3 Future Trends in Predictive Analytics and Generative AI for Marketing

Suneeth Samuel. N, Yashwant Sai. N, Preethi Dharmendar, and Philipp Plugmann

3.1 INTRODUCTION

Understanding customer demands, observing market developments, and putting together attractive marketing campaigns is essential than ever before in today's rapid and constantly changing digital landscape. The traditional areas of marketing are being transformed by two innovative technologies: generative artificial intelligence (AI) and predictive analytics.

Using algorithms based on statistics and machine learning techniques, predictive analytics analyses historical information to predict future events or events. Predictive analytics provides marketers the capability to recognize patterns, forecast trends, and target advertisements with previously unattainable accuracy by using huge amounts of data. Marketers can filter through huge quantities of previous information and identify associations, associations, and trends using advanced statistical algorithms and machine learning strategies. Predictive analytics helps marketers make informed decisions by calculating customer attrition, forecasting sales and volumes, and improving their marketing efforts.

On the other side, generative AI enables machines to generate distinctive material, photographs, and even entire marketing campaigns on their own, thereby boosting AI-driven creativity to a new level through applying techniques such as machine learning and the processing of natural language, generating artificial intelligence (AI) could imitate human creativity and develop engaging advertisements on an extensive scale. This field of artificial intelligence involves educating machines to generate original content on its own, encompassing written form, images, movies, and music. Generative AI can imitate human creativity with outstanding precision using techniques such as deep learning and natural language processing, providing marketers the capacity to develop interesting personalized content on a large scale [1].

The players will look at the connection between generative AI and predictive analytics in the context of marketing in this chapter. It will also discuss these

DOI: 10.1201/9781003472544-3

technologies' current state, examine recent advances, and address future developments that have a chance to fundamentally affect how marketers communicate with their targeted market.

We will examine a wide range of topics that illustrate the groundbreaking opportunities of generative AI and predictive analytics in marketing, from advanced customization and immediate decision-making to moral dilemmas and collaborative AI. Through case studies and real-world examples, we will show the way innovative businesses are making use of these technologies to get a gain an edge over competitors and promote business growth [1].

3.2 PURPOSE OF THIS CHAPTER

The objective of this chapter is to provide advertisers an in-depth understanding of artificial intelligence (AI) generative and predictive analytics with regard to modern marketing. Our goal is to offer advertisers the understanding and understanding they need to effectively travel the evolving landscape of data-driven advertising tactics through a review of these innovative technologies [2].

1. **Training and the Foundation**: To begin with, the objective of this chapter is to educate the reader on the fundamental thoughts, methods of operation, and applications of artificial intelligence (AI) generative and predictive analytics. We give readers a solid basis for comprehending how these innovations may be utilized for revenue from marketing by offering them with clear and clear explanations of key subjects. With the implementation of AI-driven publishing and forecasting strategies, we are hoping to simplify these complex topics and allow marketers to make educated choices about their use in marketing ideas.
2. **Learning and Information**: Our further objective is to inform visitors of the latest recent advances, patterns, and business standards in artificial intelligence (AI) and statistical analysis for advertising. By an in-depth examination of previous studies, conversations with professionals in the field, and actual instances, we offer helpful insights on how leading businesses use these advances in order to enhance client relationships, optimize their advertising spend, and acquire an edge over their competitors. Companies may keep apprised of the latest developments in technology for marketing and take advantage of these emerging possibilities by keeping up on the latest developments in artificial intelligence (AI) generative and predictive analytics.
3. **Motivation and Recommendations**: Furthermore, by providing innovative applications and instances of achievement of machine learning and generative artificial intelligence in advertising, this section aims to motivate and guide users. We want to capture the curiosity of readers and encourage them to think about novel ideas for their individual advertising strategies by demonstrating creative uses and practical execution strategies. In addition, we provide practical guidance and recommendations to advertisers who desire

to effectively accept and make use of artificial intelligence (AI) and predictive analytics, thereby allowing them to easily and competently discuss the complicated world of Intelligence-driven advertising.

3.3 CURRENT LANDSCAPE

Innovation is abundant in the areas of generative AI and predictive analytics.

1. **Acceptance and Implementation Are Rising**: Predictive analytics has become widespread, helping organizations in a wide range of industries to predict customer preferences, simplify procedures, and reduce risks. Current knowledge and decision-making can be further enhanced by connection with the Internet of Things (IoT). Personalized learning, treatment research, and creative creation of content are just some of the industries wherein generative AI is finding practical uses and is no longer restricted to research labs.
2. Advancement Has Been Fueled by Advances in Technology: Methods for deep learning such as Generative Adversarial Networks (GANs) are pushing the limits of both generative and predictive abilities, and machine learning algorithms continue to evolve. Advanced and complex models have been made accessible by infrastructure enabling cloud computing and processor speed improvements.
3. It is Important to Choose between Trust and Clearness: Both generative and predictive models are currently under greater scrutiny as ethical issues about data privacy and fairness and potential biases are increasingly known. The field of "explainable AI" (XAI) is gaining in prominence. It promotes the development of transparent and interpretable models to build trust among users in their applications.
4. Talent and Publicly Accessible Assets Facilitate Partnership: There is a rising number of skilled employees who can create, set up, and supervise these technologies. Open-source projects promote collaboration, quickening up invention and liberalizing access to resources and tools.

   Predictive analytics has expanded into fresh fields such as predicting weather patterns, optimizing supply chains, and reducing risks to the environment. Uses for generative AI have been researched in targeted advertising, generating artificial intelligence (AI) models by teaching them using artificially generated information and even creating realistic simulators for many areas.

   Predictive analytics and generative AI offer tremendous opportunities for expansion in the years to come, broader usage, and an increasing impact on numerous areas of everyday life.

However, important parts of this journey are solving moral problems, ensuring that cutting-edge innovations are utilized wisely, and utilizing them to change culture for a better future.

3.4 TECHNOLOGICAL ADVANCES

Technological advances have thrown up previously unthinkable opportunities and abilities for marketers, with statistical analysis and generative artificial intelligence (AI) approaching new heights. Begin to examine some of the significant advances impacting the area of generative AI and predictive analytics in marketing [3].

3.4.1 Innovative Machine Learning Techniques

The development of powerful machine learning techniques is one of the most significant advancements in predictive analytics. Deep learning, combined methods, and neural networks are just a few of the technologies that have made it possible for marketers to derive deeper insights from complex and unstructured data sets.

Advertisers may identify minor correlations, patterns, and trends that conventional statistical techniques could have overlooked by using sophisticated algorithms. In areas like forecasting demand, churn forecasting, and segmentation of consumers, this allows more accurate predictions and smarter choices [2].

3.4.2 The Concepts of Natural Language Generation (NLG) and Natural Language Processing (NLP)

Technology like natural language generation (NLG) and natural language processing (NLP) have completely altered the way marketers produce and assess written material. With the application of NLP algorithms, advertisers can derive emotion and significance from written information, like social media, posts, customer reviews, and other sources of text [2].

On the other hand, NLG offers marketers the capacity to generate autonomous creation, which appears human. This technology is extremely useful when creating massive, specific descriptions of items, articles, and email marketing. Advertisers may supply their target audience with much more relevant and appealing material through the use of NLP and NLG [2].

3.4.3 Cloud Computing and Big Data Infrastructure

The ability to scale and availability of generative AI and predictive analytics tools has been significantly enhanced by the widespread use of cloud-based computing and big data infrastructures. Without needing to incur major capital spending, marketers can use robust computing abilities immediately with cloud-based platforms like Microsoft Azure, Google Cloud Platform (GCP), and Amazon Web Services (AWS) [1].

Due to the increasing accessibility of technology, businesses of all sizes are now able to take advantage of sophisticated analytics and AI capabilities. Small and medium-sized businesses, in particular, are able to employ generative AI and predictive analytics for marketing purposes [1].

3.4.4 Machine Learning That Is Automated (AutoML)

Systems for automated machine learning (AutoML) have altered the playing field for advertisers who want to employ predictive analytics without needing plenty of knowledge in the field of data science. Marketers may develop predictive models with minimal effort due to these platforms, which ease the steps of choosing features, building a model, and parameter modification [4].

AutoML technologies relieve managers from the computational challenges of modeling, enabling users to zero in on extracting insight from data and via predictive models in real marketing applications. This happens by making machine learning capabilities.

Future applications for marketing might become more transformative due to the rapid advancements in artificial intelligence (AI) generative and predictive analytics. As these innovations grow, the key to achieving their full potential while completely transforming the landscape of marketing will be to properly use them, providing moral issues and human understanding of the utmost importance [5].

3.5 FUTURE IMPLICATIONS

Future impacts of advances in technology in artificial intelligence (AI) and predictive analytics for marketing will be major and broad. With the growing complexity and actual time processing capacity of machine learning algorithms, businesses could be expecting an enormous shift in the way they communicate with consumers. With AI-powered systems constantly altering material, deals, and overall experiences to match each consumer's unique needs and preferences, personalization will eventually reach higher levels. In addition, advertisers will be able to predict consumer habits with unprecedented accuracy owing to the integration of generative AI with predictive analytics, allowing proactive rather than reactive approaches to marketing. Along with increasing the rate of conversion and customer happiness, this predictive agility will strengthen brand advocacy and commitment. Also, we can anticipate the development of entirely novel advertising structures and platforms as AI technologies develop, thanks to innovations such as voice-controlled assistants, online influencers, and virtual reality. Predictive analytics and generative artificial intelligence together have a chance to transform advertising, moving away from an unchanging, universal approach to a changing, tailored, engaging interaction with consumers. Given the rapid pace at which technology is developing in the future, marketers are going to require an ongoing learning and modification strategy. The sets of abilities and strategies employed by marketers have shifted in addition to predictive analytics and generative AI. Keeping current awareness of constantly changing developments, acquiring new skills and techniques, and achieving all that is possible from these advances will all require regular training and upgrading of their skills. In addition, advertisers must create a setting wherein rejection is seen as an opportunity for growth and innovation. In a more changing and uncertain marketplace, marketing may put itself at the cutting edge of creativity and create equitable growth and an edge over rivals by developing a culture of unchanged growth and adaptation.

3.6 CHALLENGES AND CONSIDERATIONS

Advertisers encounter plenty of challenges and variables that are important to their performance if they employ artificial intelligence (AI) generative and predictive analytics for their marketing. Among these difficulties is ensuring the privacy and accuracy of information. Huge amounts of information required to train predictive algorithms and allow based on artificial intelligence publishing present an obstacle for advertisers. It is essential to make sure that this information is accurate, reliable, and conforms to confidentiality regulations like the CCPA and GDPR. In addition, because customers are growing increasingly worried about their confidentiality, it is essential that we maintain openness and the ethical use of consumer data so as to gain and retain their confidence.

Advertisers have to reduce bias caused by algorithms and assure fairness in artificial intelligence decision-making procedures alongside solving data-related problems. The dependability and effectiveness of artificial intelligence (AI) and statistical analysis can be compromised by biases that have become entrenched in databases or algorithms and which consequently perpetuate prejudiced behaviors or unjust results. For researchers to efficiently detect and remove bias, solving this issue calls for additional efforts in the governance of data, and computational openness, including the inclusion of diverse the creation of model's groups. The ability to scale and incorporate artificial intelligence and predictive analytics technology within the present marketing framework is a further factor that advertisers have to keep under consideration. Delivering solutions based on AI needs seamless integration with automation platforms, customer relationship management (CRM) platforms, and other crucial technologies. Effective implementation and sustainability over time rely on ensuring compatibility and adaptability among different platforms while reducing changes to ongoing operations [6].

The legal and societal consequences of employing AI for advertising have to be addressed by advertisers. There are numerous hard moral problems concerning the proper application of artificial intelligence, its impact on society as a whole and the way it affects the buying habits of consumers. Through successfully handling these barriers and variables, advertisers can harness the revolutionary possibilities of predictive analytics and generative AI for everyone while creating trustworthiness, inspiring imagination, and driving lasting expansion in the constantly shifting world of modern marketing.

3.7 ETHICAL AND SOCIAL IMPACT

Additionally, issues about algorithmic unfairness and bias are raised by the increasing prevalence of AI in marketing. By accidentally preserving prejudices identified in the information, artificial intelligence systems trained upon previous information can deliver prejudiced outcomes or exacerbate injustices in society. Marketers must confirm test, and continually analyze algorithms in hopes of proactively conquering these prejudices. In addition, promoting diversity and inclusion in AI teams of developers may reduce biases and ensure equitable outcomes during advertising efforts [3].

The widespread adoption of artificial intelligence for advertising has implications for civilization that exceed computational bias. Machine learning (AI)-driven robotics have a chance to disrupt traditional schedules, prompting concerns regarding loss of employment or inequality in the economy. Advertisers have to be mindful of the way their based on artificial intelligence efforts will impact the community as a whole and explore methods to mitigate their adverse effects on those who are less fortunate. To ensure a more inclusive and equitable future, this could mean supporting workforce upgrading and training programs or exploring different forms of financial power.

In negotiating these ethically difficult and culturally complicated issues, marketing has a duty to uphold ethical norms, promote transparency, and have significant discussions with partners. In the age of digital media, businesses may embrace the groundbreaking capabilities of artificial intelligence (AI) with predictive analytics while encouraging creativity, fostering confidence, and creating improvements in society through implementing ethical AI principles and social accountability.

3.8 CONCLUSION

In brief, statistical analysis and generating machine learning (AI) have an opportunity to transform advertising in the years to come. These advances in technology have an enormous capacity to completely alter way business's view, communicate with, and delight consumers, as we have witnessed through this chapter [1].

We have seen ways advertisers use data-driven knowledge and Intelligence-driven imagination to drive creativity and effectiveness throughout their initiatives, from the present-day status of statistical analysis and generative artificial intelligence to the advances in technology driving their development. A compelling outlook for the next phase of advertising is offered by the potential of hyper-individualization instantaneous decision-making powered by AI imagination, which will allow companies to connect with consumers deeply and deliver them experiences that have more of an impact. Deployment of artificial intelligence (AI) and predictive analytics does not come absent challenges, nevertheless, as was typical with any breakthrough technology. Marketers face a complex landscape with ethical, technological in nature, and societal implications to handle, including safeguarding information and bias in algorithms to connectivity and scalability [7]. With meticulous, clear, and moral management in addressing those challenges, advertisers might effectively utilize artificial intelligence (AI) tools while minimizing related hazards and dangers. Looking in advance, artificial intelligence (AI) generative and predictive analytics have a bright and exciting future in advertising. In a market that has grown more rapidly, changing, and profitable, marketing can stay ahead of the game and encourage sustained expansion as well as creativity by embracing a mindset of continuous development and adaptation. Advertisers are able to establish a time wherein based on artificial intelligence marketing delivers customized, captivating and memorable occasions to consumers across the world by prioritizing moral concerns while providing benefits [1].

Before we embark on an adventure into the next phase of advertising, let us embrace the use of the groundbreaking possibilities of generative AI and predictive analytics to build an equitable and creative future where consumers and businesses grow alongside one another side.

REFERENCES

1. Hastie, T., Tibshirani, R., & Friedman, J. (2009). *The Elements of Statistical Learning: Data Mining, Inference, and Prediction.* Springer Science & Business Media.
2. Goodfellow, I., Bengio, Y., Courville, A., & Bengio, Y. (2016). *Deep Learning (Adaptive Computation and Machine Learning Series).* MIT Press.
3. Radcliffe, N. J., & Surry, P. D. (2011). *Predictive Analytics: The Future of Business Intelligence.* John Wiley & Sons.
4. Doshi-Velez, F., & Kim, B. (2017). Towards a rigorous science of interpretable machine learning. https://doi.org/10.48550/arXiv.1702.08608
5. Kohavi, R., & Provost, F. (1998). Glossary of terms. *Machine Learning*, 30(2–3), 271–274.
6. Ganie, S. M., Malik, M. B., & Arif, T. (2021). Early prediction of diabetes mellitus using various artificial intelligence techniques: a technological review. *International Journal of Business Intelligence and Systems Engineering*, 1(4), 1–22. https://www.inderscienceonline.com/doi/abs/10.1504/IJBISE.2021.122759
7. Kondapaka, P., Khanra, S., Malik, A., Kagzi, M., & Hemachandran, K. (2023). Finding a fit between CXO's experience and AI usage in CXO decision-making: evidence from knowledge-intensive professional service firms. *Journal of Service Theory and Practice*, 33(2), 280–308.

4 Analytical Prospective on Fashion Industry
Data-Driven Strategies

Shreya, Ankannagiri Harika Reddy, Vaishnavi Tirunagari, and Rajesh Kumar K V

4.1 INTRODUCTION

The fast fashion industry is one of the most powerful global fashion players, giving a new look to the trends. This shift has had a shock wave effect on how consumers interact with clothing and has also had a big ramification on the environment. The very quick construction and destruction of clothes have resulted in an unfathomable amount of waste. This adds to environmental degradation across the globe. As sustainability increasingly emerges as a key factor, it is a turning point for the fashion industry. It needs to develop and introduce some schemes that decrease the negative influence on nature but also secure its long-term growth and competitiveness in a highly volatile market.

Emphasizing the Indian market, European markets, and global consumer trends, we shall understand the challenges and opportunities in sustainability that the fashion industry faces in this introductory chapter, which builds on the Indian context. The objective of underpinning the comprehension of the barriers would be achieved through an analysis of the context of the fashion industry in India. Although awareness levels are gradually moving in the right direction, there are a few issues that still need to be addressed that call for the establishment of a reverse supply chain network to free value from waste materials. The recognition of the importance that the creation of public awareness and community participation have for promoting sustainable practices in India is where this discussion focuses.

However, by widening the angle to take a global view, we deal with the challenges related to textile recycling in Europe, therefore showing that the fashion industry stakeholders should associate together in order to solve the environmental problems caused by the rapid expansion of the sector. Research-based insights help the authorities realize the importance of combined actions to tackle the intensifying nature of environmental problems. Shifting to a supplementary focus, we look at the diverse side of analytics that connect customers and fashion retail. We convey that merchants face difficulties in predicting and accommodating shifting customer preferences; however, new analytics technologies drive the supply chain adjustments and rise of customer satisfaction to another level.

DOI: 10.1201/9781003472544-4

Moreover, we delve into the complexities of predicting sales in the fashion industry, focusing on the challenges posed by demand and diverse product offerings. We explore methods for enhancing the accuracy of sales forecasts in an evolving market. These methods involve leveraging user-generated content and search queries. Additionally, we discuss product redesign as a strategy for repurposing less popular items. While we acknowledge the challenges of achieving perfection in both aesthetics and functionality through this process, we highlight the importance of embracing solutions.

This opening chapter aims to provide readers with an understanding of sustainability issues and innovative solutions within the fashion sector by synthesizing insights from research fields. It lays the foundation for exploration in chapters enriching ongoing discussions on sustainable fashion practices and their impact on global industry stakeholders.

4.2 METHODOLOGIES

We are delving into how novel ideas and statistical techniques are revolutionizing fashion analytics in this investigation. In spite of obstacles such as exceptional occurrences like the COVID-19 pandemic, we begin by evaluating statistical methods for trend forecasting, such as averages and regression. Next, we talk about cutting-edge techniques like clickstream tracking and Google Trends integration, which have the potential to completely transform fashion's predictive analytics by providing insights into consumer behavior and industry trends. Additionally, we explore the importance of product redesign and the use of the Grouping Genetic Algorithm for upcycling in fashion. Product redesign aims to extend garment lifespan and reduce environmental impact, while Grouping Genetic Algorithm helps optimize the selection of modular components for sustainability and consumer preferences.

Turning our attention to consumer analytics, we emphasize how important it is for guiding decision-making and improving the general customer experience in fashion retail. We talk about techniques including data gathering, customer segmentation using descriptive analytics, demand forecasting, and customer lifetime value prediction using predictive analytics. Changeover Matrix In fashion retail, modeling has become a sophisticated technique to forecast shifts in client segments. By utilizing sophisticated algorithms and past data, companies may predict changes in consumer behavior, which enables targeted advertising campaigns, inventory control, and client loyalty initiatives. Future trends and developments, like integrating with emerging technologies and collaborating with data scientists by retailers, hold the potential to improve predictive analytics in the fashion sector and propel success and innovation, even in the face of hurdles.

4.2.1 STATISTICAL METHODS FOR FASHION TREND FORECASTING

The fashion industry is always changing due to a number of causes including economic situations, cultural transformations, and sociological changes. For fashion retailers to remain ahead of the competition, precisely predicting these trends is essential. Fashion trends are often predicted using statistical methods; in this investigation, we explore some of the most important statistical methods, such as regression, exponential smoothing, and averages. Moreover, we tackle the difficulties presented by extreme values, emphasizing the consequences of exceptional occurrences such as the COVID-19 pandemic.

a. **Averages**
   A key statistical metric, averages give a central tendency that symbolizes the typical value in a set of data. Averages are frequently used in fashion trend forecasting to examine past data and spot trends. Retailers can learn about the general level of demand, for example, by computing the average sales of particular products over time. But depending just on averages has its drawbacks, especially when it comes to catching the subtleties of quickly evolving fashion trends and adapting to unexpected changes in customer preferences.
b. **Moving Average and Weighted Moving Average**
   An extension of an average, a moving average is the average of a given number of data points over a moving window. This technique is especially helpful in bringing underlying trends to light by mitigating short-term variations. By giving varying weights to distinct data points, weighted moving averages give recent observations greater weight. Moving averages remove noise from random changes, which aids in the identification and prediction of emerging trends in the context of fashion trend forecasting.
c. **Exponential Smoothing**
   An advanced statistical method called exponential smoothing gives historical observations exponentially diminishing weights. Because it highlights recent data, this approach is very adaptable to changes. Exponential smoothing helps predict fashion trends by catching the latest patterns in consumer behavior. Because of its flexibility, it can be used to forecast trends with brief lifespans or abrupt changes in consumer demand. However, the efficacy of this approach depends on the assumption of a continuous, smooth trend and necessitates careful parameter tweaking.
d. **Regression for Seasonal and Minor Yearly Changes**
   One effective method for simulating the relationship between variables is regression analysis. Regression analysis can be used in fashion trend forecasting to determine how seasonal and small annual changes affect trends. For instance, a regression model taking into account variables like temperature, holidays, and fashion events may be used to forecast sales of winter clothing. Regression analysis offers insightful information, but it makes the assumption that variables have a linear connection, which may not always adequately capture the intricate dynamics of fashion trends.
e. **Limitations in Handling Extreme Values**
   Although statistical approaches are useful for identifying trends, they are not always well-suited to handle extreme numbers or outliers. An important example is how the COVID-19 epidemic upset conventional predicting methods. Unpredictable events are difficult for statistical methods based on past data to adjust to, which results in incorrect forecasts. The pandemic's

abrupt changes in consumer behavior, hiccups in the supply chain, and unpredictability in the economy serve as a stark reminder of how inadequate conventional statistical techniques are for handling extreme values.

f. **Adapting Statistical Methods to Unforeseen Events**

Statistical approaches must be adjusted to account for unanticipated events such as the COVID-19 pandemic in order to improve the robustness of fashion trend forecasting. Forecasting models can be made more resilient by including real-time data inputs, machine learning techniques, and scenario analysis. In addition to providing flexibility and adaptation to shifting trends, machine learning techniques—like deep learning and ensemble approaches—can incorporate non-linear patterns that statistical methods would overlook.

4.2.2 Innovative Methods for Predictions in Fashion Analytics

As technology progressed, fashion analytics changed as well, bringing with it new techniques to improve forecast accuracy and tactical decision-making. We investigate three state-of-the-art methods in this investigation: Clickstream tracking on non-transactional websites, product forecasts enhanced by Google Trends, and supply chain cost components taken into account in conjunction with forecast error reduction. Predictive analytics in the fashion sector is being revolutionized by these techniques, which offer a comprehensive understanding of customer behavior, market trends, and operational efficiencies.

a. **Clickstream Tracking on Non-Transactional Websites**

Clickstream tracking is keeping an eye on and evaluating how users interact with a website. This method was previously used on e-commerce platforms to comprehend the user journeys that resulted in transactions. Expanding clickstream tracking to non-transactional websites, however, provides special insights into customer preferences, hobbies, and browsing habits in the field of fashion analytics. Through the examination of clicks, page views, and time spent on different fashion-related content, businesses can identify new trends, vogue looks, and possible influencers influencing customer decisions.

Fashion blogs, social networking sites, and online magazines are examples of non-transactional websites that act as virtual catwalks for users to peruse fashion trends, styles, and commentary without having to commit to a purchase right away. These sources of clickstream data can be quite helpful in spotting trend precursors, enabling fashion firms to react ahead of time to changing customer tastes. Large volumes of clickstream data can be processed by machine learning algorithms, which can then be used to identify trends, forecast new fashions, and provide consumers with tailored recommendations.

b. **Utilizing Google Trends for Improved Product Forecasts**

Google Trends has developed into a potent instrument for forecasting consumer demand and interest in a variety of sectors, including the fashion industry. This platform compiles search data to show the trending popularity of particular search terms. Fashion firms can use Google Trends to get up-to-date information on the newest trends in accessories, colors, and designs. Through the examination of certain fashion-related keywords or phrases, firms are able to make well-informed judgments on product development, marketing tactics, and inventory control.

For example, if searches for "sustainable fashion" increase, a business may decide to put more emphasis on environmentally friendly collections. More precise estimates of customer demand are made possible by incorporating Google Trends data into forecasting algorithms, which lowers the possibility of overstock or lost opportunities. Brands can also match their digital marketing initiatives to popular subjects to increase exposure and interaction.

4.2.3 Consideration of Forecast Error Reduction and Supply Chain Cost Components

In order to optimize supply chain operations, predictive analytics in the fashion sector needs to go beyond trend forecasting. Businesses can balance satisfying demand and reducing operating costs by integrating supply chain cost components with prediction error reduction tactics. Forecasting models can be improved with the use of advanced analytics, such as predictive modeling and machine learning, which continuously learn from historical data and adjust to shifting market conditions.

Moreover, a holistic approach to decision-making is made possible by incorporating supply chain cost components, such as production, transportation, and inventory holding costs, into predictive analytics models. For example, managing inventory levels and dynamically altering production volumes based on demand estimates can dramatically lower holding costs. Supply chain data can be analyzed by machine learning algorithms to find trends that let businesses implement "just-in-time" production processes and increase overall efficiency.

4.2.4 Integration and Synergy of Innovative Methods

When these cutting-edge techniques are combined and optimized, predictive analytics' full potential in the fashion industry becomes apparent. Supply chain optimization assures economical and flexible operations, Google Trends improves product projections based on real-time search data, and clickstream tracking offers insights into changing consumer preferences. By combining these strategies, fashion businesses may develop a strong predictive analytics framework that is compatible with the industry's fast-paced and dynamic environment.

For example, clickstream data can be used by a fashion brand to spot rising interest in a specific style on non-transactional websites. The popularity of the trend among internet searches might then be confirmed using Google Trends data. By using these insights into the predictive analytics model, the manufacturing and distribution processes may be guided, reducing prediction mistakes and lowering supply chain expenses.

4.2.5 Redesign Technique in Upcycling

Upcycling is a sustainable fashion industry strategy that entails creating new, high-quality things out of discarded materials or existing products. A crucial part of this process is redesigning, which includes a variety of methods for giving old or abandoned objects new life. The importance of product redesign in the fashion business, the modularization process for creating product families and cutting costs, and the use of grouping genetic algorithms for intelligent redesign and optimization are all explored in this investigation.

a. **Significance of Redesign in the Fashion Industry**

In the fashion sector, product redesign has several uses, from resource efficiency and sustainability to adapting to shifting consumer preferences. The urge to prolong clothing's lifespan and lessen the environmental impact of rapid fashion and excessive consumption is one of the main drivers for redesign. Fashion brands may revive their items through redesign, bringing them into line with current trends and customer expectations. Additionally, the fashion industry is increasingly embracing circular economy principles, and redesign plays a key role in this transition. By upcycling existing garments or materials, brands contribute to the reduction of textile waste and promote a more sustainable and responsible production cycle. Redesign also fosters creativity and innovation, challenging designers to think beyond traditional design norms and reimagine the potential of discarded materials.

b. **Modularization Process for Product Family Creation and Cost Reduction**

The process of designing a product such that its components may be assembled and customized more easily is known as modularization. The modularization method becomes a potent tool for developing product families and cutting production costs in the context of upcycling and sustainable fashion. Fashion brands can build a variety of products using a common set of elements by creating garments with modular or replaceable parts. This method eliminates the need to create brand-new molds and patterns for every product, improving design adaptability while streamlining manufacturing procedures. This reduces production costs and the industrial process's total environmental impact.

Additionally, modularization satisfies customer desires for distinctive and customized solutions. Consumers can customize their outfit selections by mixing and matching modular components, giving them a sense of personal style. This personalization feature strengthens the bonds between the brand and the customer while also adding value to the products.

c. **Grouping Genetic Algorithm for Intelligent Redesign and Optimization**

The redesign process is enhanced by the use of sophisticated algorithms, such as the Grouping Genetic Algorithm (GGA), which adds intelligence and optimization. Inspired by natural selection and genetics, GGA is a heuristic algorithm that works well for combinatorial optimization tasks, making it appropriate for the intricate world of fashion design.

GGA can be used in the upcycling context to strategically group and arrange design elements according to predetermined goals. For instance, it can concurrently reduce waste, increase aesthetic appeal, and maximize the usage of recycled materials. The program generates a variety of optimum combinations by taking into account many design aspects, including color, texture, and pattern.

Additionally, GGA is able to adjust over time to shifting consumer trends and tastes in design. The algorithm constantly improves its suggestions in response to changing consumer preferences, making sure that upcycled goods continue to be relevant and appealing. Given how quickly trends can change in the fashion industry, adaptable intelligence is very useful.

d. Integration of Redesign Techniques

Fashion brands can integrate these strategies in a synergistic way to develop a comprehensive and effective approach to upcycling through redesign. The basis for developing a variety of product offers while using the fewest resources possible is provided by modularization. After that, the Grouping Genetic Algorithm arranges and chooses modular components in a way that maximizes both resource efficiency and visual attractiveness. A fashion brand might use modularization, for example, by creating clothing with removable collars, sleeves, or embellishments. The best combinations of these modular pieces would then be suggested by the Grouping Genetic Algorithm, which would cleverly assess consumer preferences, production limitations, and sustainability objectives. The end product is a selection of repurposed goods that follow fashion, cut waste, and provide customers with a customized experience.

4.2.6 Sustainability and Circular Economy Practices in Fashion

The fashion business faces a wide range of sustainability-related issues, from waste and overconsumption to the depletion of natural resources. Innovative solutions to these problems are desperately needed as consumer awareness of environmental issues rises. This investigation focuses on two crucial tactics to bring about a paradigm shift in the fashion industry toward sustainability and circular economy practices: modularization as a design strategy and the usage of the Grouping Genetic Algorithm (GGA) for sustainable product design.

a. Challenges in the Fashion Industry

The 'take, make, dispose' method of the fashion industry's classic linear model has had serious negative effects on the environment and society. The usage of non-renewable resources, fast fashion cycles, and excessive consumption all lead to waste, pollution, and moral dilemmas. Comprehending and addressing these obstacles is crucial for the sector to shift toward more environmentally friendly methods.

The massive carbon footprint of the textile industry, the tremendous amounts of water needed for dyeing and finishing, and the tons of unsold or abandoned clothing that need to be disposed of are some of the sustainability concerns. These problems are made worse by the need to meet the ever-evolving demands of consumers and trends, which creates a vicious cycle of wasteful manufacturing that is hard to escape.

b. Modularization as a Design Strategy for Sustainability

A viable answer to various sustainability issues facing the fashion industry is modularization, a design approach that entails building goods with interchangeable or modular components. Through resource efficiency, waste reduction, and garment longevity extension, this technique turns the linear paradigm into a more circular one.

A uniform collection of components can be transformed into a range of goods by fashion designers by dissecting a garment into modular parts like sleeves, collars, or accessories. This makes recycling, repairs, and improvements easy as well as enabling the reuse of materials. Modular components allow customers to mix and match, encouraging personalization and lowering the need for ongoing purchases.

Furthermore, by encouraging a closed-loop system, modularization is consistent with the tenets of the circular economy. When a garment's lifecycle comes to an end, its modular components can be disassembled and the individual parts recycled or used to create new goods. With this strategy, the environmental impact of textile waste is greatly reduced, and a more sustainable fashion ecology is fostered.

c. Grouping Genetic Algorithm for Sustainable Product Design

A clever and adaptable method for handling the challenges of sustainable product design in the fashion industry is the Grouping Genetic Algorithm (GGA). Natural selection and genetics serve as inspiration for GGA's exceptional problem-solving abilities in combinatorial optimization. This makes it especially well-suited for the wide range of variables found in fashion, including color, texture, and pattern. GGA may select and arrange modular components optimally in the context of sustainable design to accomplish numerous goals at once. It can, for example, save waste, make the most of repurposed or environmentally friendly materials, and guarantee aesthetic appeal. The algorithm offers a dynamic response to the dynamic environment of sustainable fashion by adjusting to shifting consumer preferences and market trends.

Fashion firms can benefit greatly from GGA's assistance in supply chain optimization by using it to guide their decisions about distribution networks, production methods, and material procurement. Through the consideration of several aspects, such as social responsibility, cost-effectiveness, and environmental impact, the algorithm helps to build a fashion supply chain that is more ethical and sustainable.

d. Integration of Modularization and GGA

The implementation of modularization and GGA together for sustainable product design demonstrates their synergy. The basis for producing a wide variety of goods with less resource consumption is provided by modularization, and GGA enhances the optimization of modular components with an intelligent layer. Fashion manufacturers can use modularization by creating clothing with interchangeable parts that take into account aspects like material recyclability, durability, and simplicity of disassembly. Subsequently, GGA is employed, examining diverse design factors and customer inclinations to suggest ideal pairings of modular elements. As a result, a variety of sustainably designed goods that satisfy customer desires, environmental objectives, and aesthetic standards are produced.

e. **Achieving a Paradigm Shift**

The apparel industry can undergo a paradigm shift toward sustainability and circular economy principles by implementing GGA in conjunction with modularization. A comprehensive strategy covering the full product lifecycle—from design and production to use and disposal—is needed to handle this change. For modular design to be widely used, it is imperative that designers, manufacturers, and consumers understand its advantages and guiding principles. Fashion manufacturers have the opportunity to set an example by integrating modularization into their design processes and informing customers about the advantages this strategy has for the environment and society.

The industry's capacity to adjust to changing conditions is further improved by incorporating GGA into sustainable design methods. Because the algorithm is flexible, it can adapt to changing customer tastes, new trends, and developments in environmentally friendly materials and technology. This adaptability is essential to preserving sustainable fashion methods' relevance and viability in a changing marketplace.

f. **Overcoming Challenges and Future Prospects**

Although modularization and GGA present encouraging alternatives, obstacles still stand in the way of the garment industry's widespread adoption of sustainable methods. The necessity for technology infrastructure, cost concerns, and change resistance are obstacles that designers, producers, legislators, and consumers must work together to overcome. However, integrating cutting-edge technology like 3D printing for on-demand manufacturing and blockchain for transparent supply chains has the potential to improve the efficacy of sustainable practices. These innovations support the circular economy's tenets and lessen the waste, energy use, and environmental impact of the fashion industry as a whole.

4.2.7 Customer Analytics Methodologies in Fashion Retail

Success in the fast-paced and ever-changing world of fashion retail depends on having a solid understanding of consumer behavior. Fashion retailers are using customer analytics, a multifaceted method of studying consumer data, as a pillar to adjust their strategies in response to changing market trends. This investigation explores the customer analytics approaches used in the fashion retail industry, looking at the steps involved in gathering data and applying descriptive and predictive analytics.

a. **Overview of Customer Analytics in Fashion Retail**

In order to obtain useful insights, customer analytics in fashion retail entails the methodical gathering, examination, and interpretation of customer data. With the help of statistical methods, machine learning, and data mining, this multidisciplinary strategy can identify patterns, preferences, and trends among a retailer's clientele. Enhancing the overall consumer experience, streamlining marketing tactics, and providing information to decision-making processes are the main objectives. Remaining competitive in a market where consumer tastes are constantly shifting requires staying on top of trends and comprehending customer behavior. Retailers are able to shift from general strategies to tailored, targeted approaches that appeal to their particular client segments because to the power of customer analytics.

b. **Data Collection from Internal and External Sources**

The gathering of varied data from internal and external sources forms the basis of customer analytics. Information created inside the retailer's environment, such as transaction logs, customer profiles, and inventory data, is referred to as internal data. Outside of the retailer's walls, external data sources can include competition analysis, social media interactions, and more general market trends.

4.2.8 Internal Data Collection

Retailers can get a better grasp of customer behavior by using transaction data, which provide insightful information about product affinity, purchase habits, and customer preferences. Retailers may enhance client retention and personalize their marketing efforts by generating extensive consumer profiles through the consolidation of demographic, purchase history, and engagement variables. Retailers may also identify popular products and successfully manage stock by keeping an eye on inventory levels and sales data. This helps them meet client demand while eliminating excess inventory and stockouts.

4.2.9 External Data Collection

Retailers may adjust their tactics in real time by gaining insights into customer sentiment, preferences, and new trends through the analysis of social media interactions. Retailers can also find whitespace possibilities and improve their strategy by studying the tactics and market positioning of their competitors. Additionally, maintaining a watch on macroeconomic data, cultural changes, and wider market trends offers a thorough grasp of the retail environment, enabling retailers to stay ahead of the curve and make wise judgments.

4.3 PRE-PROCESSING OF DATA

Pre-processing is necessary to guarantee the obtained raw data's quality, applicability, and suitability for analysis. There are multiple processes involved in this, such as integration, transformation, and cleansing.

4.3.1 Cleaning

Data cleaning is essential to guaranteeing the accuracy and dependability of a dataset. It includes operations like eliminating duplicates, fixing mistakes, and handling missing entries. By preserving data consistency and integrity, this procedure makes it possible to conduct more thorough studies and make well-informed decisions. Furthermore, outlier detection is essential for spotting and managing anomalies that could skew analyses and produce false insights. Analysts can improve the validity and reliability of their results by ensuring that their conclusions are indicative of the underlying data distribution by recognizing and managing outliers.

4.3.2 Transformation

While categorization transforms raw data into categorical variables for analytical procedures, normalization standardizes data formats and units for meaningful comparisons. In order to prepare data for reliable analyses, both are essential.

4.3.3 Integration

Integrating data from several sources to provide a full picture and enhance analysis using a range of viewpoints is known as data integration. Analysts can find hidden patterns and linkages by integrating data sources, which may not be obvious when looking at separate datasets separately. Furthermore, data aggregation is essential for summarizing information at several levels, such as time intervals or client segments.

More detailed insights are made possible by aggregating data, allowing analysts to pinpoint anomalies, trends, and patterns at various levels of specificity. When combined, data aggregation and integration improve the breadth and depth of analysis, enabling organizations to make decisions that are well-informed and grounded on a comprehensive understanding of their data.

4.3.4 Application of Descriptive Analytics

In descriptive analytics, historical data is analyzed and summarized to give a quick overview of previous trends and occurrences. This stage aids in pattern recognition, customer preference analysis, and marketing campaign performance evaluation in the context of fashion retail.

4.3.5 Customer Segmentation

Demographic segmentation gives a basic insight of the client base by grouping customers according to factors like age, gender, and geography. By focusing their marketing efforts and product offerings on particular demographic groups, firms can increase relevance and engagement through the use of segmentation strategies. Behavioral segmentation, on the other hand, focuses on examining consumer behavior, such as preferred channels, frequency of purchases, and product categories.

By comprehending the ways in which consumers engage with their brand, companies may create more specialized marketing plans that speak to the interests and requirements of certain consumers. RFM analysis also classifies clients according to the frequency, recentness, and monetary value of their contacts. This method aids companies in identifying their most valuable clients, setting marketing priorities, and tailoring customer retention plans to each client's degree of participation. When combined, these segmentation strategies help companies better understand and cater to their broad clientele, which in turn spurs expansion and profitability.

4.3.6 Market Basket Analysis

Product placement, bundling tactics, and cross-selling opportunities can all be optimized by firms by using product affinity research, which offers insights into which goods are frequently bought together. Businesses can strategically display complementary items to boost sales and improve the overall consumer experience by knowing the links between various products. Recommendation systems also use market basket analysis information to provide customers with customized recommendations.

Through targeted marketing campaigns, these systems increase engagement and boost sales by making relevant product or service recommendations based on historical purchase behavior analysis. Product affinity analysis and recommendation systems work together to give companies more insight into the preferences of their customers and enable them to customize their offers to suit specific demands, which in turn increases customer happiness and loyalty.

4.4 APPLICATION OF PREDICTIVE ANALYTICS

To predict future patterns and behaviors, predictive analytics makes use of statistical algorithms and historical data. Predictive analytics makes proactive decision-making, individualized marketing strategies, and inventory management possible in the fashion retail industry.

4.4.1 Demand Forecasting

By using historical sales data to forecast demand patterns, seasonal trend analysis helps firms plan production and inventory more effectively for varying seasons. Businesses can effectively allocate resources by anticipating changes in demand and modifying their strategy based on historical trends. Moreover, the utilization of machine learning models in demand forecasting improves accuracy by integrating many aspects, such as outside influences on consumer behavior.

By using sophisticated algorithms to evaluate large, complicated data sets and produce more accurate forecasts, these models help firms make well-informed decisions and successfully adjust to shifting market conditions. When combined, machine learning-based forecasting and seasonal trend analysis allow organizations to better fulfill customer demand and manage their operations.

4.4.2 Customer Lifetime Value (CLV) Prediction

Through churn prediction and CLV models, predictive analytics is essential to customer relationship management. CLV models make use of predictive analytics to project a customer's future value, which helps allocate funds for customer acquisition and retention initiatives. Businesses can effectively allocate resources, concentrating on obtaining and retaining high-value consumers, by comprehending the potential long-term worth of each customer.

Furthermore, churn prediction makes use of predictive analytics to pinpoint clients who are likely to leave, allowing for proactive retention initiatives like tailored marketing campaigns or loyalty plans. Businesses can reduce customer attrition and retain a devoted client base by spotting and resolving possible churn issues early on. This will ultimately boost profitability and long-term performance.

4.5 TRANSITION MATRIX MODELING FOR CUSTOMER SEGMENTATION

Success in the ever-changing world of fashion retail requires an ability to comprehend and predict consumer behavior. Conventional techniques for consumer segmentation frequently fail to capture the subtle changes over time between different categories. A clever method that not only foretells these transitions but also offers insights for enhancing consumer experiences is revealed: transition matrix modeling. This investigation explores the complexities of transition matrix modeling, how fashion retailers use it to predict consumer segment transitions, and how companies might use this technology to improve customer experiences.

4.5.1 Understanding Transition Matrix Modeling

Changeover Matrix A statistical method known as modeling is used to capture how things move or transition between various states or segments over specific time periods. Customer segments in the context of fashion retail are discrete groups that are based on demographics, preferences, or purchase patterns. The cornerstone of this modeling strategy is the transition matrix, a square matrix whose elements each represent the likelihood of shifting from one segment to another.

The rows and columns of the transition matrix are arranged to correspond to the various client segments. The possibility that customers will switch from one segment to another within a given time frame is indicated by the probabilities in the matrix. Businesses can create an early transition matrix, a useful tool for forecasting future consumer segment migrations, by evaluating historical data.

4.5.2 Prediction of Customer Segment Transitions

In order to keep ahead of trends and adjust their tactics appropriately, fashion merchants must be able to predict shifts in their client segments. Changeover matrix in order to generate a baseline matrix, modeling makes use of past consumer data, including browsing patterns, purchase histories, and interactions with marketing efforts. The customer segments and their transition probabilities are shown in this matrix as of right now.

Businesses use a variety of algorithms, such as Markov Chain models and machine learning approaches, to forecast future transitions. These algorithms calculate the likelihood that a client will switch from one segment to another by examining patterns in past data. Markov Chain models are especially well-suited to representing the dynamic and ever-changing character of consumer behavior in fashion retail due to their iterative nature.

In contrast, machine learning algorithms use sophisticated statistical methods and predictive analytics to find patterns and correlations within large datasets. These models offer a more sophisticated knowledge of segment transitions by adapting to shifting consumer preferences and market developments.

4.6 APPLICATION OF THE TRANSITION MATRIX TO OPTIMIZE CUSTOMER EXPERIENCES

When transition matrix modeling is used to improve client experiences in fashion retail, it truly has value. Businesses may adapt their marketing, product offerings, and overall strategy to match changing customer needs once they have a solid forecast of client segment migrations. The transition matrix can be used in the following practical ways:

a. **Personalized Marketing Campaigns**

   With the help of the transition matrix, fashion merchants may create marketing campaigns that are specifically targeted at particular customer categories. For example, marketing efforts can concentrate on promoting formal attire during a season when there is a significant likelihood of customers moving from the "casual wear" category to the "formal wear" section.

b. **Inventory Management**

   Inventory management and planning are aided by the ability to forecast changes in client segments. Retailers can reduce overstock or stockouts by modifying their stock levels in response to expected changes in demand. This guarantees that the appropriate items are offered to satisfy changing consumer tastes.

c. **Customer Loyalty Programs**

   Refinement of loyalty programs is possible for retailers with an understanding of segment transitions. Businesses can cultivate client loyalty and enhance the probability of recurring purchases by providing incentives or rewards that correspond with the predicted preferences of migrating segments.

d. **Enhanced Customer Service**

   Customer care teams can anticipate customer needs by having knowledge regarding segment transitions. For instance, if a pattern of customers switching between segments as a result of sizing dissatisfaction is observed, the shop can take steps to enhance sizing data and lower returns.

e. **Product Development**

A useful source of information for product development methods is the transition matrix. Retailers may lead the way in product innovation and launch products that cater to client preferences and developing trends by identifying categories with high transition probability.

4.7 CHALLENGES AND CONSIDERATIONS

Although transition matrix modeling provides insightful analysis, there are obstacles and factors to take into account when using it in fashion retail. The quality and granularity of the data used to create the first transition matrix have a significant impact on the forecast accuracy. Predictions that are erroneous might result from biased or incomplete data, which highlights the significance of data diversity and quality.

Not only that, but the fashion sector is dynamic, which makes it difficult to forecast sudden changes in consumer behavior. External variables that may not be fully reflected by historical data alone, such as fashion trends, prevailing economic situations, or world events, can have a significant impact on consumer choices. Because of this, companies need to use real-time analytics and market intelligence in addition to transition matrix modeling.

4.8 FUTURE DIRECTIONS AND INNOVATIONS

Transition Matrix Modeling is expected to undergo further advancements in the fashion retail industry given the changing landscape of customer analytics. Prediction granularity and accuracy can be improved through integration with cutting-edge technology like artificial intelligence, natural language processing, and image recognition. Sentiment analysis of social media interactions and customer reviews can offer more information about the preferences and sentiments of customers, which helps to strengthen transition matrix models.

Furthermore, working together, data scientists and fashion merchants can create frameworks and algorithms that are unique to the fashion business and address its particular problems. The approaches that retailers use to comprehend and adjust to these shifts must also develop in tandem with the ongoing evolution of client expectations.

4.9 DISCUSSION

4.9.1 Multi-Criteria Decision-Making (MCDM) Methodologies for Circular Economy (CE) Challenges

When it comes to managing the intricacies of circular economy (CE) problems, Multi-Criteria Decision-Making (MCDM) techniques are essential, particularly in sectors like fashion that struggle with environmental concerns. A level of complexity is added by integrating the Fuzzy Decision-Making Trial and Evaluation Laboratory (DEMATEL), which enables a sophisticated comprehension of the difficulties and how they relate to one another.

When using Fuzzy DEMATEL, issues are ranked systematically in relation to the fashion industry's transition to a circular economy. To account for the uncertainty present in real-world decision-making situations, fuzzy logic is used. The research attempts to untangle the complex web of issues and their effects using Fuzzy DEMATEL, providing insights that can guide strategic decision-making for sustainable practices.

The ranking of challenges is one of the methodology's main components. "Lack of traceability" is the main issue, as determined by a thorough analysis with Fuzzy DEMATEL. This problem captures the difficulties of monitoring and accounting for items and resources across the course of their lives, which is essential to the fashion industry's goal of becoming circular. The methodology offers a quantitative measure of the difficulties' influence, which enables stakeholders to prioritize their efforts depending on the extent of the impact. It goes beyond just listing the challenges.

In addition, the difficulties are divided into groups according to the causes and effects of each group. The rowi – coli values serve as markers, indicating the type of difficulties. Challenges with negative values are categorized as belonging to the effect group and are therefore more vulnerable to outside influences. Positive values, on the other hand, identify obstacles within the cause group and label them as forces that hinder industrial management's adoption of circular economy methods.

The designation of 'Lack of traceability' as the most essential concern shows its severe impact on circular economy practices in the fashion industry. This problem arises from cultural beliefs and practices that cause fashion goods to be disposed of inappropriately, making it more difficult to include them in circular processes. The challenge is further compounded by the underdeveloped reverse supply chain network in places like India, which limits the amount of waste materials available to businesses interested in adopting circular economy methods [1].

The cause-and-effect teams offer an organized framework for taking action. Problems that belong to the cause group include "Weak technical know-how," "Inefficient performance evaluation system," and "Reluctance to adopt a new business model." These are examples of systemic problems that require quick action. These difficulties obstruct the smooth adoption of circular economy principles in the fashion sector. It is imperative to tackle them in order to establish pathways toward sustainable practices and effective resource management.

On the other hand, issues in the effect group, such as "insufficient recyclable materials," "inadequate high quality," and "lack of certifications," are results impacted by a number of variables. These difficulties highlight how crucial it is to deal with the underlying causes inside the cause group in order to remove obstacles later on. It is essential to take a comprehensive, integrated approach that emphasizes cooperation and communication throughout the fashion industry's value chain.

4.9.2 Causal Linkages and Ranking of Challenges

Causal relationships and the ranking of obstacles that follows are essential elements in the strategic evaluation of problems that sectors face, especially when it comes to the fashion industry's transition to sustainable and circular practices. These linkages as a guide for stakeholders, giving them a thorough grasp of the difficulties and how they are interconnected.

The illustration of causal relationships is a useful tool for decision-makers in the complex world of sustainable practices in the fashion business. The relationships between the numerous problems are represented visually in Figure 2, which also deconstructs the web of factors that add to the complexity of implementing circular economy (CE) practices. The diagram's arrows indicate the causal relationships between the difficulties and show the direction of their influence.

Causal links help prioritize solutions by drawing attention to issues that require urgent attention. Problems do not exist in a vacuum; rather, they are part of an ecosystem, and solving one could have a ripple impact on others. 'Lack of traceability' and 'Problem in collection and separation' stand out as issues that need to be addressed immediately. These problems are related because the efficiency of the processes involved in collection and separation is directly impacted by the efficacy of traceability systems. The fact that "Lack of traceability" has been highlighted as a major obstacle highlights how deeply it affects CE practices in the apparel sector. This is a complex problem that involves both structural flaws and societal behaviors. Stakeholders can better understand the intricacy of the cause-and-effect interactions linked to "Lack of traceability" thanks to the visual representation shown in Figure 2. The problem stems from the way society views fashion waste and is made worse by the lack of a robust reverse supply chain, especially in places like India.

Similarly, 'Problem in collection and separation' shows up as a difficulty closely related to traceability. Efficient collection and careful separation procedures are essential for the successful reuse and recycling of fashion materials [2]. Gathering waste materials is not the only difficult part of the job; another is sorting through the various materials that are used in the fashion business. This difficulty highlights the requirement for reliable waste management and logistics systems that can manage the complexity of various material configurations.

A quantitative aspect is added to the significance of challenges when they are ranked according to rowi + coli values. The biggest obstacle in this situation is the "absence of certifications." Both the influencing impact (rowi) and the influencing impact (coli) are taken into account while determining this ranking. "Lack of certifications" has a pivotal position in the hierarchy of problems, reflecting its pervasive impact on the garment industry's ability to successfully adopt CE practices.

'Absence of certificates' is significant because of how it affects customer behavior and industry confidence. Consumers can be reassured of a brand's dedication to sustainability through certifications. Lack of such credentials might make consumers skeptical, which affects their decisions to buy and prevents the development of circular processes. This problem goes beyond internal business procedures, highlighting how crucial consumer confidence and outside perceptions are to the success of sustainable projects.

4.9.3 Forecasting in the Fashion Industry

The fashion industry presents a number of unique problems to forecasting, including low forecasting ability and high demand volatility. Forecasting in this sector is a complex task. Accurately forecasting future wants is complicated by the dynamic nature of consumer tastes and the quick change of fashion trends. Fashion retailers must implement advanced forecasting models in order to efficiently meet client requests and maximize inventory management [3].

The fashion industry's dynamic terrain is a major factor contributing to its forecasting issues. [4] point out that every season, almost 95% of the fashion products in a collection are replaced, highlighting the necessity of accurate and flexible forecasting techniques. Because of the industry's emphasis on rapid turnovers and the steady inflow of new designs, forecasting models that can handle significant demand volatility are required. The article presents an autoregressive forecasting model, a potent tool for calculating predicted demands and their variances, in order to address these issues. Because autoregressive models can capture patterns and trends across time, they are particularly useful for fashion forecasting. Autoregressive models are frequently employed in time-series analysis. These models use historical data, seasonality, and trend-specific information to forecast future values based on prior observations.

Fashion retailers can use the autoregressive forecasting model as a strategic tool as it provides information about predicted product demand as well as the variance related to these predictions. In a sector where demand fluctuations must be accurately predicted and where the forecasting horizon is short, this level of detail is critical. The model offers a more accurate depiction of the uncertainty involved in predicting fashion products by taking variances into account. One important topic covered in the context of forecasting is how to determine the ideal inventory levels. Numerous factors, such as selling price, demand uncertainty, and customer compromise, affect these levels. The way these elements interact highlights how difficult inventory management is in the fashion sector.

Optimal inventory levels are significantly influenced by customer compromise. Customers may choose not to make a purchase at all or, in the event of inventory shortages, they may compromise by buying substitute products if they are offered. This tendency is especially important in the fast-paced fashion sector, where customers could change their minds depending on what is available. Retailers must comprehend this factor and include it into their inventory management plans in order to reduce revenue losses and uphold consumer pleasure.

The best inventory levels are harder to determine when demand is unknown. The autoregressive forecasting model takes demand prediction variances into account to help evaluate and quantify this uncertainty. Determining the ideal inventory levels is harder the more unpredictable the situation. Retailers have to walk a tightrope between satisfying consumer demand and preventing overstock, which can result in price reductions and losses.

The profitability of inventory is significantly impacted by selling price, another significant element. Retailers may choose to keep higher inventory levels if the selling price exceeds the order cost in anticipation of possible strong demand. On the other hand, merchants may err on the side of smaller inventory levels in order to reduce risks and losses if there is a large degree of demand uncertainty or if the selling price is not appreciably higher than the order cost.

4.9.4 Customer Segmentation and Analytics in Fashion Retail

In the ever-changing and cutthroat world of fashion retail, customer segmentation and analytics are vital. Comprehending and classifying consumers according to their actions yields important information for focused advertising campaigns, customized interactions, and effective use of resources. Here, the conversation is on the use of transition matrices for predictive analysis, the segmentation of customers according to recency values, and the significance of broadening the scope of segmentation to include frequency and monetary value.

Sorting clients according to their recency values is the first step in the customer segmentation process. In this instance, "recent" means how long it has been since a customer has interacted with you or made a transaction. This segmentation method is useful since it makes it easier to distinguish between different consumer segments with different levels of involvement and buying habits. Consumers who have not engaged with the brand for a long time are probably going to behave differently and have different preferences than those who have recently interacted with it. The transition matrix is an effective tool for forecasting the number of clients in each market sector and the revenue those clients are anticipated to bring in over the course of the following 6 and 12 months. This matrix provides a forward-looking view by encapsulating the dynamics of client migration between segments. Retailers can make proactive decisions in areas like inventory management, marketing campaigns, and customer retention strategies by utilizing past data and observed transitions to predict future patterns [5].

The research becomes more comprehensive and successful when it goes beyond recency values to add criteria like frequency and monetary value in client segmentation. The frequency with which a customer purchases offers valuable information about their involvement and loyalty. Conversely, monetary value measures the amount that consumers spend and represents their share of total revenue. Retailers are able to customize strategies according to the various demands and preferences of distinct client categories by including these factors, which provide a more sophisticated picture of customer behavior.

The retail fashion industry's diversified consumer base makes it clear how important it is to develop segmentation. Customers differ greatly in their behaviors, and they are not all made equal. While some consumers might buy frequently, others would only sometimes make expensive purchases. Retailers may create individualized marketing campaigns, loyalty plans, and product recommendations that appeal to each category by taking these subtleties into account. To further foster their loyalty, high-frequency and high-value customers might be targeted with special offers, early access to new collections, or premium loyalty programs. Customers who have a history of making few purchases, on the other hand, can find that re-engagement campaigns, exclusive discounts, or tailored product recommendations spark their interest in the brand again.

Furthermore, the growth of segmentation makes it possible to analyze customer behavior over time in a more thorough manner. Retailers can detect patterns, preferences, and possible changes in consumer behavior by examining the purchase habits of various client groupings. Proactively addressing issues allows for prompt modifications to marketing plans, inventory scheduling, and general business operations.

4.9.5 Redesign Model for Product Development

This redesign model's fundamental feature is the application of a genetic and modular algorithm. Using the modular approach, an article of clothing is disassembled into discrete components, or modules, each of which represents a particular feature or function. Each module's design fitness is determined by taking into account parameters including fabric qualities, seam type, machine type, and seam length. This detailed assessment makes sure that every part is evaluated according to how it uniquely contributes to the overall functioning and design. Natural selection served as the inspiration for the genetic algorithm, a computational optimization method that improves the designing process even further. By iteratively sifting through a population of possible solutions to discover the best one, genetic algorithms simulate the process of evolution. This algorithmic method makes it possible to explore a variety of modular element combinations in the context of clothing redesign, which makes it easier to create creative and effective design solutions.

Important factors taken into account for design fitness are fabric qualities, seam type, machine type, and seam length. The type of machine used effects the overall quality and precision of the stitching, while the choice of seam affects the garment's structural integrity and appearance. The overall fit and appearance are influenced by the seam length, while fabric properties include material qualities including sustainability, durability, and texture. The redesign process makes sure that the final clothes not only satisfy practical and aesthetic standards, but also follow sustainable practices by assessing these characteristics.

A case study is used to support the redesign system's viability and provide empirical proof of its efficacy. The suggested methodology is practically validated through a case study on a rebuilt Swedish corporation. The outcomes show how much time might be saved by using a modular and genetic algorithm method instead of more labor-intensive manual procedures. The suggested modularized model provides a more effective option to the current situation, in which manual operations depend on the knowledge and abilities of designers for jobs ranging from parts extraction to reconstruction. The process is streamlined and a large amount of time is saved thanks to the modular approach, which allows for systematic redesign operations based on past redesign data.

An example of design fitness utilizing a reference product—a t-shirt, for example—showcases the advantages and practicality of the suggested model. The model shows how versatile it is for many types of clothing by taking comparable functional components from the reference product and extracting them for the target function. Additionally, the model can be expanded to extract components from different products, increasing its application in a variety of industries.

REFERENCES

1. Kannan, V. R., & Tan, K. C. (2005). Supplier selection and assessment: Their impact on business performance. *Journal of Supply Chain Management*, 41(2), 23–35.
2. Choi, T. M., & Cheng, T. C. E. (2020). Fashion retail operations: A review. *International Journal of Production Economics*, 220, 107464.
3. Farsijani, H., & Lee, L. H. (2018). Sustainable fashion supply chain: Lessons from H&M. *Sustainability*, 10(1), 1–19.
4. Beheshti-Kashi S, Lutjen M, Stoever L, Thoben KD. trendfashion-a framework for the identification of fashion trends. Informatik, In: Cunningham D, Hofstedt P, Meer K, Schmitt I. Jahrestagung der Gesellschaft für Informatik, Informatik 2015, Informatik, Energie und Umwelt. Gesells chaft für Informatik; 2015.
5. Christopher, M., & Peck, H. (2004). Building the resilient supply chain. *International Journal of Logistics Management*, 15(2), 1–14.

5 Predictive Analytics Techniques for Marketing

Deepthi Mecharla, Jayasimha Avaldhar, and Kalal Rukmini

5.1 INTRODUCTION

Predictive analytics has become an essential component for optimising strategic decisions and prioritising consumer needs within the dynamic realm of marketing. This article conducts a comprehensive analysis of predictive analytics methods that are customised for use in marketing applications. This paper examines the methodologies, applications, advantages, and also obstacles associated with predictive analytics in the field of marketing. Through the provision of all perspectives on current developments and emergent patterns, the objective of this article is to furnish marketers with the information and resources necessary to effectively utilise predictive analytics as a catalyst for expanding enterprises and improving customer satisfaction.

Moreover, this investigation tackles the intrinsic difficulties and ethical implications linked to predictive analytics in the field of marketing, including but not limited to the concerns regarding data privacy, algorithmic bias, and interpretability. Through a critical evaluation of these concerns and the formulation of potential resolutions, the objective of this paper is to cultivate a comprehensive comprehension of predictive analytics and enable marketers to traverse the intricacies of data-driven decision-making ethically and responsibly. This extensive investigation functions as a guide for marketers seeking to harness the revolutionary capabilities of predictive analytics to stimulate business expansion, cultivate customer allegiance, and attain a competitive edge in the data-centric marketplace of the present day. By adopting predictive analytics as one of the strategic necessities and capitalising on its predictive capabilities, marketers can initiate an ongoing process of innovation and prioritisation of customers, thereby driving their organisations towards long-term viability and prosperity [1].

5.2 DATA COLLECTION AND PREPARATION

The data collection and organisation of data are one of the fundamental stages in the predictive analytics procedure, upon which accurate predictive modelling is built. This chapter explores the importance of these processes and also provides an overview of the most effective methods for guaranteeing the integrity and dependability of data utilised in predictive modelling initiatives.

DOI: 10.1201/9781003472544-5

5.2.1 The Significance of Collecting Data

Predictive modelling is dependent on the accessibility of high-quality data. Therefore, identifying and gathering pertinent data sources constitutes the initial phase of the data acquisition procedure. Examples of such sources include customer databases, transaction archives, web analytics, social media platforms, and external data providers. By leveraging a wide range of data sources, marketers can acquire an all-encompassing comprehension of market trends and consumer behaviour, which empowers them to formulate more precise forecasts and well-informed decisions.

5.2.2 Preprocessing and Data Cleaning

Preprocessing and data cleaning are the essential stages within the data preparation procedure, serving the purpose of rectifying data quality concerns and laying the groundwork for subsequent analysis. This includes encoding categorical variables, standardising and transforming data, handling missing values, and removing duplicates [1].

5.3 PREDICTIVE ANALYTICS TECHNIQUES

Predictive analytics techniques have also brought about a paradigm shift in the manner in which marketers comprehend consumer behaviour, forecast market trends, and enhance marketing strategies.

Predictive analytics, encompassing both conventional statistical models and sophisticated machine learning algorithms, grants marketers the ability to derive practical insights from data and execute well-informed decisions that propel organisational triumph. This chapter provides an in-depth analysis of predictive modelling, examining a wide range of algorithms and techniques that are specifically designed to meet the distinct requirements of marketing initiatives. This extensive investigation examines the diverse predictive analytics methodologies employed in the field of marketing, including their practical implementations and benefits.

5.3.1 Regression Analysis

Regression analysis is a fundamental method of predictive analytics that is extensively employed in the field of marketing and aims to ascertain the correlation between independent and dependent variables. Regression models are also employed by marketers to forecast quantitative outcomes, including customer lifetime value, market share, and sales, by analysing a range of marketing inputs including advertising expenditure, pricing tactics, and promotional endeavours. Through the examination of past data and the identification of critical performance determinants, regression analysis empowers marketers to effectively allocate resources, evaluate the effectiveness of marketing endeavours, and predict future results with an exceptionally precise level of accuracy.

Interpretability is a fundamental advantage of regression analysis, as it furnishes valuable insights regarding the strength and direction of the association between variables.

Furthermore, regression analysis enables the testing of hypotheses, enabling marketers to evaluate the predictive model's validity and the statistical significance of predictors.

Although regression analysis is known for its adaptability, it does possess specific constraints, especially when confronted with high-dimensional data or non-linear associations. During such circumstances, more advanced methodologies, such as decision trees or machine learning algorithms, might provide more accurate prognostications [2].

5.3.2 Classification and Decision Trees

Classification and decision trees are highly effective predictive analytics methodologies employed to discern patterns in marketing data and segment customers. In decision trees, decision-making processes are visually depicted through nodes, with each node signifying a decision that is derived from input variables and culminates in either a classification or prediction. Classification and decision tree models are utilised by marketers to divide consumers into discrete segments according to psychographic attributes, demographic characteristics, or purchasing behaviour. Then, customised marketing strategies can be implemented to target these segments, resulting in increased consumer engagement and conversion rates.

A primary benefit of decision trees is their straightforwardness and interpretability, as they furnish a visually coherent and instinctive depiction of the processes involved in making decisions. Decision trees are highly suitable for managing categorical variables and predictor interactions, rendering them highly valuable in marketing scenarios that involve intricate criteria for making decisions.

Nevertheless, decision trees are susceptible to overfitting, particularly when confronted with unbalanced or chaotic data. To address this potentiality, strategies including regularisation, ensemble methods (e.g., random forests), and pruning can be implemented to enhance the capacity of decision tree models to generalise.

5.3.3 Clustering Analysis

A technique used to combine similar data elements based on shared characteristics or behaviours is clustering analysis. Clustering analysis is a marketing technique that allows practitioners to discern discrete consumer segments or market segments that possess similar attributes. Insights into the distinct requirements and preferences of various customer segments can be obtained by marketers through the aggregation of customers according to variables including geographic location, purchasing behaviour, and product preferences.

As a result, this enables the implementation of focused marketing initiatives, tailored product suggestions, and improved customer satisfaction.

Clustering analysis identifies natural patterns or groupings within data without the need for labelled examples, which is one of its benefits. Additionally, it is beneficial for exploratory data analysis and the revelation of concealed insights. Capable of managing high-dimensional and large datasets.

One limitation of clustering analysis, in addition to its benefits, is the subjective determination of the optimal number of clusters, which may hurt the quality of the clustering outcomes.

Instability regarding the selection of the distance metric or clustering algorithm. Complicated interpretation of cluster significance, particularly in high-dimensional spaces [2].

5.3.4 Time Series Analysis

The utilisation of time series analysis is critical in examining temporal data as it enables the identification of recurring patterns, trends, and seasonal variations. Time series analysis is frequently employed in the field of marketing to make informed decisions regarding demand, sales, and campaign optimisation. Through the examination of historical sales data and market trends, marketers can predict forthcoming demand, discern seasonal variations, and efficiently distribute resources to satisfy consumer demands.

Utilising exponential smoothing techniques and time series models like ARIMA (Autoregressive Integrated Moving Average), marketers can optimise inventory management, pricing strategies, and promotional activities while ensuring precise forecasts. Time series analysis has the benefit of capturing trends and temporal dynamics in data. It generates precise predictions for forthcoming time intervals by utilising past data.

Additionally, irregularly spaced or absent data points can be managed.

One limitation of time series analysis is its assumption of stationarity, which states that the statistical properties of the time series remain constant throughout its duration. Potentially challenged by long-term forecasting and predicting sudden trend shifts. Exposure to outliers or anomalies has the potential to introduce distortions into forecasts.

5.3.5 Machine Learning Algorithms

Machine learning algorithms, such as support vector machines, neural networks, and random forests, provide sophisticated predictive functionalities and are being progressively employed in marketing contexts. With the ability to decipher intricate patterns and correlations within extensive datasets, these algorithms empower marketers to extract valuable insights and generate precise predictions. Neural networks find applications in various domains, such as customer review sentiment analysis, customer attrition prediction modelling, and personalised product recommendation systems. Marketers can attain a competitive advantage through the utilisation of machine learning algorithms, which enable them to execute highly targeted marketing campaigns, enhance client experiences, and stimulate business expansion. It can capture complex patterns and relationships within data, such as nonlinearities and interactions between predictors, which is one of its primary advantages. Particularly effective concerning extensive and heterogeneous datasets. Furthermore, provides adaptability and expandability in managing a wide range of marketing applications and datasets.

Nonetheless, training with such voluminous quantities of annotated data may prove to be an expensive or time-consuming endeavour. And Insufficient interpretability, particularly about intricate models such as neural networks or ensemble methods. Particularly susceptible to overfitting when confronted with high-dimensional data or intricate model architectures.

Analytical techniques vary in their strengths and limitations; therefore, the selection of a particular technique is contingent upon the particular demands of the marketing endeavour in question. To make informed decisions in the current competitive marketplace, marketers can effectively utilise these techniques to extricate valuable insights from data by comprehending their underlying principles and trade-offs.

5.4 KEY ADVANTAGES OF PREDICTIVE ANALYTICS IN MARKETING

Predictive analytics has become a staple of modern marketing tactics, providing several benefits that also enable marketers to make data-driven choices, improve consumer experiences, and drive corporate success. In this in-depth examination, we look into the fundamental benefits of predictive analytics in marketing, demonstrating how it alters marketing tactics and produces concrete outcomes.

5.4.1 Enhanced Targeting Accuracy

One of the most significant advantages of predictive analytics in marketing is its potential to increase targeting precision. Predictive analytics allows marketers to better segment their target audience by analysing past data and also discovering patterns in consumer behaviour. This enables targeted content and offers that resonate with certain client demographics, resulting in increased engagement and conversion rates.

Predictive models may also forecast consumer behaviour, such as buy propensity, likely to churn, and preferred communication channels, allowing marketers to tailor their marketing efforts appropriately. Marketers may also improve their marketing strategies and increase their return on investment (ROI) by targeting the appropriate audience with the right message at the right time [3].

5.4.2 Personalised Customer Experiences

Predictive analytics enables marketers to provide personalised experiences by identifying individual preferences and requirements. Marketers may use predictive models to construct dynamic customer profiles that provide a full perspective of each customer's interactions, preferences, and purchase history. Within this information, marketers can send tailored content, product suggestions, and offers that are relevant to each consumer, resulting in increased engagement and loyalty.

Personalisation has become a critical distinction for firms seeking to stand out in a competitive market. According to studies, 80% of consumers prefer to conduct business with companies that provide personalised experiences. Marketers may strengthen customer connections and generate repeat business by using predictive analytics to create personalised experiences across channels such as email, websites, and mobile applications.

5.4.3 Improved Campaign Efficacy

Predictive analytics helps marketers optimise campaigns for optimal efficacy. Predictive models may discover the best channels, marketing tactics, and timing for future advertising by analysing previous campaign performance and consumer reaction data. Predictive analytics may also assist marketers in foreseeing prospective hurdles or impediments and adapting their tactics accordingly.

Predictive models, for example, can analyse consumer data to determine which groups are most likely to respond to a specific offer or campaign. Marketers may increase campaign response rates and conversion rates by tailoring messages and offers to these demographics. Predictive analytics may also help companies optimise their marketing budgets by assigning money to the most productive channels and approaches.

5.4.4 Risk Mitigation

Predictive analytics helps marketers detect and reduce risks in their marketing activities. Predictive models, for example, can predict customer turnover or detect possible fraud issues before they become a problem. By proactively addressing these risks, marketers may take preventive actions to retain consumers, protect brand reputation, and reduce financial losses. For example, a telecoms corporation may utilise predictive analytics to identify customers who are likely to churn based on their consumption and behaviour. By providing targeted retention offers or incentives, the organisation may lower turnover and keep important clients. Similarly, predictive analytics may assist marketers in identifying prospective fraudsters by analysing patterns of suspicious behaviour, allowing them to take action to avoid fraudulent acts [4].

5.4.5 Capitalising on Emerging Opportunities

Predictive analytics enables marketers to discover and capitalise on new possibilities before their competitors do. Predictive models can identify unexplored market sectors, new product opportunities, or evolving consumer preferences by analysing market trends, consumer behaviour, and competition intelligence. This early identification of possibilities provides marketers with a competitive advantage, allowing them to innovate and adapt to changing market conditions.

For example, a retail organisation may utilise predictive analytics to uncover patterns in consumer preferences and purchase behaviour. By analysing sales data and social media trends, the corporation may spot emerging trends and capitalise on them quickly by launching new goods or marketing campaigns. Similarly, predictive analytics may assist marketers in identifying untapped market segments or specialised markets that provide prospects for corporate growth.

To summarise, predictive analytics provides several benefits for marketers, ranging from greater targeting precision and personalised consumer experiences to increased campaign effectiveness and risk reduction. Marketers may use predictive analytics tools to handle specific difficulties, get actionable insights, and create meaningful business objectives. As predictive analytics evolves and becomes more accessible, its revolutionary influence on marketing will only expand, preparing organisations for success in an increasingly competitive and data-driven environment.

5.5 APPLICATIONS OF PREDICTIVE ANALYTICS IN MARKETING

The utilisation of predictive analytics in marketing has become a paradigm shift for the discipline, providing an extensive range of practical implementations in diverse marketing sectors. Predictive analytics techniques empower marketers to circumvent particular obstacles, gain valuable insights, and attain concrete business results, encompassing consumer segmentation and campaign optimisation.

This section explores the various marketing applications of predictive analytics, providing concrete illustrations and case studies that demonstrate its efficacy in fostering marketing success and attaining a competitive advantage.

5.5.1 Customer Segmentation

Customer segmentation is a fundamental component of marketing strategy as it empowers marketers to partition their intended audience into discrete clusters according to common attributes, actions, or inclinations. Sophisticated segmentation approaches are enabled by predictive analytics techniques, including machine learning algorithms and clustering analysis, which analyse massive datasets to detect patterns that might not be readily discernible using conventional segmentation methods [5].

As an illustration, a retail organisation employs predictive analytics to divide its clientele into distinct personas according to demographic characteristics, past purchases, and online conduct. The organisation increases conversion rates and engagement by customising its marketing messages and offers to each high-value segment characterised by distinct preferences and requirements.

5.5.2 Churn Prediction

Across all industries, customer attrition, or the gradual loss of customers, is a significant concern for businesses. By utilising predictive analytics, marketers can anticipate which consumers are susceptible to attrition and implement proactive strategies to retain them. Through the analysis of historical data and the identification of churn indicators, such as a decline in purchase frequency or diminished engagement, predictive models possess the capability to forecast the consumers who are most prone to churn in the future.

As an illustration, a subscription-based service provider employs predictive analytics to detect customers who exhibit initial indications of disengagement, including reduced platform usage or absence of interaction. The implementation of targeted incentives and personalised communications by the company effectively mitigates customer attrition and preserves valuable clientele.

5.5.3 Demand Forecasting

The ability to anticipate future demand for products or services and optimise inventory levels, production schedules, and supply chain operations is contingent upon demand forecasting.

Predictive analytics methodologies, including time series analysis and machine learning algorithms, empower marketers to effectively anticipate demand through the examination of past sales data, market trends, and external determinants of demand.

As an illustration, a manufacturer of consumer goods employs predictive analytics to estimate the demand for its products in various channels and regions. Through the integration of internal sales data with external factors including weather patterns and economic indicators, the organisation can produce more precise demand forecasts, minimise superfluous inventory costs, and prevent stockouts.

5.5.4 Campaign Optimisation

To maximise return on investment and accomplish marketing objectives, it is vital to optimise marketing campaigns. Predictive analytics methodologies assist marketers in enhancing a multitude of facets of their marketing campaigns, encompassing targeting, messaging, channel choice, and timing. Through the examination of historical campaign performance and consumer response data, predictive models possess the capability to discern the most efficacious campaigns and subsequently allocate resources.

For example, an e-commerce retailer optimises its email marketing campaigns using predictive analytics. Through the examination of email engagement metrics, purchase history, and perusing patterns of customers, the organisation discerns the most receptive segments and customises its email content and promotions to effectively connect with each segment.

Subsequently, increased conversion rates, click-through rates, and open rates all contribute to the retailer's revenue expansion.

5.6 ETHICAL CHALLENGES AND CONSIDERATIONS

Within the dynamic realm of predictive analytics for marketing, substantial ethical concerns and obstacles abound. In an era when marketers rely heavily on data and sophisticated analytics methods to influence business results, it becomes critical to address ethical quandaries and minimise potential threats to consumer confidentiality, equity, and openness.

This chapter delves into the ethical implications and obstacles that are linked to the utilisation of predictive analytics in the field of marketing, while also planning approaches to mitigate them.

5.6.1 Privacy Concerns

Regarding predictive analytics for marketing, safeguarding consumer privacy is among the most significant ethical concerns. As marketers amass and scrutinise extensive quantities of personal data to inform predictive models, apprehensions emerge concerning the suitable application and protection of this data. Consumers anticipate that their data will be managed responsibly through the provision of explicit consent and transparency regarding its intended utilisation. To safeguard consumer privacy rights throughout the data lifecycle, marketers are obligated to comply with data protection regulations, including the California Consumer Privacy Act (CCPA) and the General Data Protection Regulation (GDPR) [6].

5.6.2 Bias and Fairness

The potential for bias in algorithms and models is an additional ethical dilemma in predictive analytics. Prevalent or exacerbating preexisting disparities and prejudice, biased algorithms may result in the unjust treatment of specific demographic cohorts. Inadvertent discrimination against marginalised communities or reinforcement of stereotypes rooted in ethnicity, gender, or socioeconomic status are both potential consequences of biased algorithms. To promote equity and mitigate bias, marketers must conduct thorough evaluations of algorithms to ensure transparency and fairness, identify and mitigate sources of bias in data and algorithms, and establish mechanisms that hold accountable those who identify biases and provide redress.

5.6.3 Transparency and Accountability

Transparency and accountability are fundamental tenets that underpin data-driven marketing that operates ethically. Regarding the accumulation and processing of consumer data, marketers must be transparent by providing consumers with easily accessible information regarding how their data is utilised and distributed. In addition, marketers ought to bear responsibility for the decisions and actions executed by the findings of predictive analytics, guaranteeing compliance with regulatory obligations and ethical principles. Transparency cultivates confidence among stakeholders and consumers, thereby bolstering the organisation's credibility and standing.

5.6.4 Data Security and Integrity

The preservation of consumer data security and integrity is an essential ethical obligation that marketers must uphold. Consumers may suffer severe repercussions as a result of security incidents and data breaches, such as identity theft, financial deception, and loss of privacy. To prevent unauthorised access, disclosure, or modification of consumer data, marketers must implement stringent data security measures, such as encryption, access controls, and routine security audits. Through the protection of data integrity and security, marketers establish a rapport with stakeholders and customers and showcase their dedication to ethical data practices [6].

5.6.5 Responsible Use of Predictive Analytics

The ethical implementation of predictive analytics in marketing ultimately necessitates a steadfast dedication to responsible data practices that are founded upon the principles of openness, impartiality, and responsibility. During every stage of the data lifecycle—from data acquisition and processing to model development and deployment—ethical considerations must be a top priority for marketers. By cultivating an organisational culture that prioritises ethical consciousness and integrates ethical considerations into decision-making processes, marketers can effectively utilise predictive analytics to stimulate business expansion while maintaining the confidence of customers and the respect of society at large.

In conclusion, the use of predictive analytics in marketing presents inherent ethical challenges and considerations. Through the implementation of measures such as addressing privacy concerns, mitigating bias and promoting fairness, ensuring transparency and accountability, and safeguarding data security and integrity, marketers can effectively navigate ethical dilemmas and establish trust with stakeholders and consumers. In a world that is becoming increasingly data-driven, ethical data practices not only safeguard the rights and interests of consumers but also contribute to the long-term viability and prosperity of marketing endeavours.

5.7 REAL-WORLD USE CASES

Real cases underscore the wide-ranging utility and advantages of predictive analytics in various industries, including finance, healthcare, retail, and e-commerce. Through the implementation of predictive analytics, businesses can stimulate expansion, enhance consumer engagement, and cultivate innovation. The aforementioned illustrations highlight optimal methodologies and acquired knowledge, furnishing marketers seeking to adopt predictive analytics endeavours within their respective organisations with invaluable insights. With the ongoing advancement and increased availability of predictive analytics, its profound influence on both the business sector and society at large will continue to expand.

5.7.1 Retail and E-Commerce

Predictive analytics is of the utmost importance in the retail and e-commerce industries for comprehending consumer behaviour, optimising product assortments, and customising marketing communications. For instance, Amazon employs predictive analytics to provide customers with product recommendations that are informed by their purchase behaviour, browsing history, and personal preferences. Through the examination of extensive quantities of data, such as product views, interactions, and purchases, Amazon's recommendation engine produces individualised product suggestions that effectively increase conversion rates and customer contentment. In a similar vein, Stitch Fix, a fashion retailer, utilises predictive analytics to customise each customer's online purchasing experience. Through the examination of customer feedback, body measurements, preferences, and algorithms, Stitch Fix generates customised apparel assortments for every client, resulting in increased customer engagement and repeat purchases.

5.7.2 Finance

Predictive analytics facilitates the ability of organisations in the finance sector to detect fraudulent activities, evaluate credit risk, and tailor financial services to individual consumers. For example, financial institutions employ predictive analytics to identify fraudulent transactions instantaneously through the examination of suspicious behaviour patterns, including atypical purchasing habits or repeated unsuccessful login endeavours. Banks can safeguard consumer accounts and avert financial losses by alerting potentially fraudulent activity. In addition, credit card companies employ predictive analytics to evaluate credit risk and establish credit limits for prospective customers. Predictive models predict the probability of default and allocate suitable credit limits by evaluating credit history, income level, and additional variables. This serves to mitigate the risk of delinquency and enhance the overall performance of the portfolio [7].

5.7.3 Healthcare

Predictive analytics assists healthcare providers in the healthcare industry with optimising resource allocation, enhancing patient outcomes, and reducing costs. As an illustration, hospitals employ predictive analytics to estimate patient admissions and subsequently allocate resources, including personnel and accommodations. Hospitals can forecast variations in demand and enhance resource allocation, resulting in superior patient care and operational efficacy through the examination of historical data that comprises patient demographics, medical records, and seasonal patterns.

Furthermore, proactive measures are taken by healthcare organisations to avert unfavourable health outcomes by identifying patients who are at risk of developing chronic diseases through the use of predictive analytics. Predictive models can, through the examination of patient data including medical history, laboratory results, and lifestyle factors, detect individuals who are at an elevated risk of developing ailments like cardiovascular disease or diabetes. The risk can then be mitigated, and patient health outcomes can be improved through the implementation of targeted interventions, such as lifestyle counselling or medication management, by healthcare providers.

5.8 EMERGING TRENDS AND FUTURE DIRECTIONS IN PREDICTIVE ANALYTICS FOR MARKETING

Recent years have witnessed a rapid evolution of predictive analytics, propelled by technological advancements, the proliferation of data, and shifting consumer preferences. As we contemplate the forthcoming period, several significant developments and trends are positioned to mould the domain of predictive analytics for marketing. This section examines the emerging trends and future orientations that are anticipated to have an impact on predictive analytics in the field of marketing in the coming years.

5.8.1 Using AI to Drive Predictive Modelling

An area of considerable importance within the realm of predictive analytics is the incorporation of machine learning and artificial intelligence (AI) methodologies into predictive modelling.

Algorithms powered by artificial intelligence, such as deep learning neural networks, provide enhanced precision and prognostic capability in contrast to conventional statistical models.

Predictive modelling enabled by AI in marketing facilitates a more refined examination of intricate datasets, resulting in more precise forecasts and practical insights.

Predictive models enabled by AI can analyse unstructured data sources, including but not limited to social media posts, customer reviews, and images, to reveal latent patterns and insights. This facilitates marketers in attaining a more profound understanding of consumer sentiment, preferences, and behaviours, thereby empowering them to develop marketing strategies that are more precise and individualised.

5.8.2 Real-Time Analysis

The adoption of real-time predictive analytics represents an additional burgeoning development in the field of predictive analytics. Predictive models have historically depended on past data to generate forecasts regarding forthcoming outcomes. Nevertheless, as the quantity and speed of real-time data production escalate, there emerges an expanding need for predictive analytics solutions capable of real-time data stream analysis and the provision of instantaneous insights.

The utilisation of real-time predictive analytics empowers marketers to promptly address evolving market dynamics, customer actions, and competitive risks. For instance, by analysing website visitor data, real-time predictive models can identify consumers who are most likely to complete a purchase within the next few minutes. This enables marketers to dynamically tailor offers and incentives to increase conversion rates.

5.8.3 Personalisation at Scale

Personalisation has emerged as a primary objective for marketers seeking to increase consumer engagement and satisfaction. Nonetheless, scaling up personalisation efforts for marketing campaigns can prove to be a formidable task, especially given the escalating quantity and diversity of consumer data. Predictive analytics provides a resolution by empowering marketers to mass-personalise marketing communications, promotions, and suggestions on the unique preferences and actions of each consumer.

The implementation of predictive modelling techniques and machine learning algorithm advancements has enabled the analysis of massive datasets and the generation of personalised recommendations for individual customers. To illustrate, predictive models can assess demographic data, browsing history, and purchase patterns of customers to suggest products or content that are most pertinent to their interests and preferences [8].

5.8.4 Explainable AI and Ethical Data Practices

The increasing prevalence of predictive analytics in the marketing sector has sparked a heightened concern for ethical data practices and the transparency of algorithmic decision-making. The concerns of marketers regarding algorithmic bias, data privacy, and consumer confidence are growing. There is an increasing demand for explainable AI techniques that can offer insights into the decision-making and recommendation processes of predictive models to address these concerns.

Explainable artificial intelligence (AI) methods empower marketers to comprehend the elements and fluctuations that impact prognostic results, thereby enabling them to detect and alleviate possible prejudices or ethical dilemmas. Furthermore, an increasing emphasis is being placed on ethical data practices, including consent management, data governance, and data anonymisation, to guarantee the responsible and ethical execution of predictive analytics initiatives.

5.8.5 Integration with Marketing Automation Platforms

With the increasing significance of predictive analytics in shaping marketing strategies, there is a mounting requirement to incorporate predictive analytics solutions into customer relationship management (CRM) systems and marketing automation platforms. Through the direct incorporation of predictive analytics into preexisting marketing protocols, organisations can optimise operations, delegate monotonous duties to automated systems, and execute marketing campaigns that are more tailored and precise [9].

For instance, by utilising predictive models to segment customers automatically, predictive analytics solutions can initiate targeted advertising or personalised email campaigns on the preferences and behaviours of each customer. This integration facilitates the dissemination of marketing messages that are more pertinent and timely, thereby increasing conversion rates and engagement [10].

In summary, advancements in artificial intelligence and machine learning, real-time analytics, scalable personalisation, ethical data practices, and integration with marketing automation platforms will significantly influence the trajectory of predictive analytics in marketing.

Through the adoption of these nascent patterns and advancements, marketers can exploit predictive analytics to acquire a more profound understanding of customer conduct, enhance marketing tactics, and stimulate enterprise expansion within a progressively competitive and data-centric environment.

5.9 CONCLUSION

In conclusion, predictive analytics has become an influential and revolutionary concept in the realm of marketing, providing an exceptional understanding of consumer conduct, market patterns, and corporate results. Throughout this paper, we have examined how predictive analytics techniques empower marketers to forecast forthcoming trends, enhance marketing strategies, and stimulate business expansion in an ever-changing and data-centric environment. Technological advancements and the emergence of big data have facilitated the extensive implementation of predictive analytics within the marketing domain. In the current era, marketers are equipped with a variety of potent tools and techniques—from rudimentary statistical models to advanced machine learning algorithms—that empower them to derive practical insights from extensive and intricate datasets.

An essential benefit of predictive analytics lies in its capacity to improve the precision of targeting and tailor consumer experiences to individual preferences. Through the examination of past data and the detection of recurring trends in consumer conduct, predictive models empower marketers to more precisely divide their target audience and provide customised messages and promotions that align with the unique inclinations and requirements of each individual. By adopting a personalised approach, marketing not only increases customer engagement and loyalty but also optimises overall effectiveness and return on investment.

In addition, predictive analytics empowers marketers to maximise the effectiveness of their marketing campaigns. Through the examination of historical campaign performance and customer response data, predictive models possess the capability to discern the optimal timing, channels, and messaging strategies for forthcoming campaigns. The implementation of a data-driven strategy for optimising campaigns results in increased response rates, decreased costs per acquisition, and enhanced marketing efficiency as a whole.

Nevertheless, despite its manifold advantages, predictive analytics also poses several obstacles that necessitate marketers' skills to fully harness its capabilities. Marketers may face numerous obstacles during the implementation of predictive analytics initiatives, including doubts regarding data quality, algorithmic bias, interpretability, privacy, and organisational preparedness. To tackle these obstacles, organisations must make a collective endeavour to allocate resources towards data quality management procedures, reduce bias in predictive models, give precedence to transparency and explainability, comply with stringent privacy regulations, and cultivate an organisational culture that embraces data-driven decision-making. Anticipating the future, the potential of predictive analytics in the field of marketing is tremendous. Novel developments, including predictive modelling enabled by artificial intelligence, real-time analytics, scalable personalisation, explainable AI, and integration with marketing automation platforms, are positioned to fundamentally transform the domain of predictive analytics and stimulate advancements in marketing methodologies [11].

Through the adoption of these nascent patterns and advancements, marketers can exploit predictive analytics to acquire a more profound understanding of customer conduct, enhance marketing tactics, and stimulate enterprise expansion within a progressively competitive and data-centric environment. The increasing development and maturity of predictive analytics will further solidify its position as a crucial strategic necessity for contemporary marketers, enabling them to effectively position their organisations for triumph in a dynamic marketplace. In summary, predictive analytics transcends its role as a marketing instrument and acts as a driver of innovation, expansion, and achievement in the era of digitalisation. By leveraging the capabilities of predictive analytics to generate practical insights and inform strategic decision-making, organisations will enhance their preparedness to succeed in a progressively intricate and competitive commercial landscape.

REFERENCES

1. Elkan, C. (2013). *Predictive analytics and data mining* (Vol. 600). San Diego: University of California.
2. Kumar, V., & Garg, M. L. (2018). Predictive analytics: A review of trends and techniques. *International Journal of Computer Applications, 182*(1), 31–37.

3. Nyce, C., & Cpcu, A. (2007). Predictive analytics white paper. *American Institute for CPCU. Insurance Institute of America*, 9–10.
4. Korn, S. (2011). The opportunity for predictive analytics in finance. *HPC Wir*; Nigrini, M. J. (2020). *Forensic analytics: Methods and techniques for forensic accounting investigations.* Hoboken, NJ: John Wiley &Sons.
5. Schiff, M. (2012). BI experts: Why predictive analytics will continue to grow. *The Data Warehouse Institute.*
6. Reichheld, F. F., & Schefter, P. (2000). The economics of E-loyalty. *Harvard Business School Working Knowledge, 10.*
7. Dhar, V. (2011). Prediction in financial markets: the case for small disjuncts. *ACM Transactions on Intelligent Systems and Technology (TIST), 2*(3), 1–22.
8. Osheroff, J. A., Teich, J. M., Middleton, B., Steen, E. B., Wright, A., & Detmer, D. E. (2007). Aroadmap for national action on clinical decision support. *Journal of the American Medical Informatics Association, 14*(2), 141–145.
9. Ganie, S. M., Malik, M. B. and Arif, T. (2022). Machine learning techniques for big data analytics in healthcare: Current scenario and future prospects. In Choudhury, T., Katal, A., Um, J. S., Rana, A., Al-Akaidi, M. (eds) *Telemedicine: The computer transformation of healthcare.* Cham: Springer International Publishing, 103–123. https://link.springer.com/chapter/10.1007/978-3-030-99457-0_6
10. Kamiński, B., Jakubczyk, M., & Szufel, P. (2018). A framework for sensitivity analysis of decision trees. *Central European Journal of Operations Research, 26*, 135–159.
11. Armstrong, J. S. (2012). Illusions in regression analysis. *International Journal of Forecasting, 28*(3), 689–694.

6 Customer Targeting and Segmentation

Hithakrith Parshetty, Lokesh Palimkar, and Rohith Emandi

6.1 INTRODUCTION

In the dynamic and competitive landscape of modern business, understanding customers has become paramount for success. Customer targeting and segmentation are pivotal strategies that enable businesses to effectively identify, reach, and engage with their target audience. In today's digital age, where consumers are inundated with choices and information, personalized marketing has emerged as a cornerstone for building meaningful relationships and driving business growth.

Customer targeting and segmentation involve dividing a heterogeneous market into distinct groups of consumers with similar characteristics, behaviors, and needs. By segmenting their audience, businesses can tailor their marketing efforts to specific segments, delivering messages and offers that resonate with each group's preferences and interests.

The importance of personalized marketing cannot be overstated in today's competitive landscape. With the rise of digital technologies and the proliferation of data, consumers have come to expect personalized experiences from the brands they interact with. Generic, one-size-fits-all marketing approaches no longer suffice in capturing consumer attention and loyalty. Instead, consumers seek relevance, authenticity, and value from the brands they engage with.

Personalized marketing allows businesses to meet these evolving consumer expectations by delivering targeted messages, offers, and experiences that are tailored to individual preferences and behaviors. By leveraging data analytics and customer insights, businesses can gain a deeper understanding of their audience, enabling them to anticipate needs, solve problems, and provide solutions that resonate on a personal level.

Moreover, personalized marketing has been shown to drive tangible business outcomes. Research indicates that personalized campaigns yield higher engagement rates, conversion rates, and return on investment compared to generic marketing efforts. By delivering relevant and timely messages to the right audience segments, businesses can increase customer satisfaction, loyalty, and lifetime value.

Furthermore, personalized marketing fosters stronger connections between brands and consumers. By demonstrating an understanding of individual preferences and needs, businesses can build trust, credibility, and loyalty with their audience. This, in turn, leads to increased brand advocacy, word-of-mouth referrals, and positive brand sentiment, driving long-term growth and sustainability.

 DOI: 10.1201/9781003472544-6

In conclusion, customer targeting and segmentation are essential strategies for modern businesses seeking to thrive in a competitive marketplace. By embracing personalized marketing, businesses can unlock new opportunities for growth, differentiation, and success. By understanding the importance of personalized marketing and adopting a customer-centric approach, businesses can build stronger relationships with their audience, drive business outcomes, and ultimately achieve sustainable growth in today's ever-evolving landscape.

6.2 FOUNDATIONS OF CUSTOMER TARGETING AND SEGMENTATION

Customer targeting and segmentation serve as foundational pillars in marketing, enabling businesses to effectively identify, understand, and engage with their target audience. This section delves into the definition and significance of customer targeting and segmentation, traces the historical evolution and development of segmentation strategies, and explores the theoretical frameworks that underpin segmentation in marketing.

6.2.1 Definition and Significance

Customer targeting and segmentation involve dividing a heterogeneous market into distinct groups of consumers based on shared characteristics, behaviors, and needs. This process allows businesses to tailor their marketing efforts to specific segments, delivering messages, products, and services that resonate with each group's preferences and interests. By targeting and segmenting their audience, businesses can maximize the relevance and effectiveness of their marketing initiatives, ultimately driving engagement, conversion, and loyalty.

The significance of customer targeting and segmentation lies in its ability to enhance marketing efficiency and effectiveness. Rather than adopting a one-size-fits-all approach, segmentation enables businesses to identify and prioritize high-value segments, allocating resources and efforts where they are most likely to yield favorable outcomes. Moreover, segmentation facilitates the development of targeted marketing strategies that resonate with the unique needs and preferences of different consumer groups, leading to increased engagement, satisfaction, and retention.

6.2.2 Historical Evolution and Development

The practice of segmentation has a rich history that dates back to the early days of marketing. While the concept of market segmentation can be traced to the pioneering work of scholars such as Wendell Smith in the 1950s, segmentation strategies have evolved significantly over time in response to changing consumer behaviors, market dynamics, and technological advancements.

Initially, segmentation strategies focused primarily on demographic variables such as age, gender, income, and geography. However, as marketers sought to gain deeper insights into consumer motivations and psychographics, segmentation approaches expanded to include factors such as lifestyle, values, attitudes, and purchase behavior.

This shift toward psychographic segmentation marked a significant milestone in the development of segmentation strategies, enabling businesses to target consumers based on shared interests, preferences, and aspirations.

In recent years, advancements in data analytics, technology, and artificial intelligence have further revolutionized segmentation practices. With the proliferation of digital channels and the abundance of data available to marketers, segmentation has become more sophisticated and granular, allowing for the identification of micro-segments and individualized targeting at scale. This evolution has empowered businesses to deliver hyper-personalized experiences to their audience, driving engagement and loyalty in an increasingly competitive landscape.

6.2.3 Theoretical Frameworks

Several theoretical frameworks underpin segmentation in marketing, providing conceptual foundations for understanding consumer behavior and market dynamics. One such framework is the psychographic segmentation model, which draws on theories of personality, motivation, and lifestyle to segment consumers based on their attitudes, values, and interests. According to this model, consumers can be grouped into distinct psychographic segments characterized by shared psychological traits and behavioral tendencies.

Another theoretical framework commonly used in segmentation is the benefits sought segmentation model, which posits that consumers seek products and services that offer specific benefits or solutions to their needs. By identifying the primary benefits sought by different consumer segments, marketers can tailor their offerings and messaging to resonate with each group's desired outcomes and aspirations.

Additionally, the usage-based segmentation model categorizes consumers based on their usage patterns, behaviors, and preferences related to a particular product or service. This approach recognizes that consumers may exhibit varying levels of engagement, loyalty, and usage frequency, necessitating differentiated marketing strategies to address their needs and motivations effectively.

In summary, the foundations of customer targeting and segmentation are rooted in the principles of understanding consumer diversity, preferences, and behaviors. By leveraging segmentation strategies informed by historical insights and theoretical frameworks, businesses can effectively identify, reach, and engage with their target audience, driving sustainable growth and competitive advantage in today's dynamic marketplace.

6.3 METHODS OF SEGMENTATION

Segmentation is a crucial process in marketing that involves dividing a heterogeneous market into distinct groups of consumers with similar characteristics, behaviors, and needs. By segmenting the market, businesses can tailor their marketing efforts to specific segments, delivering messages and offers that resonate with each group's preferences and interests. This section delves into various methods of segmentation, including demographic, psychographic, behavioral, geographic, and technological advancements in segmentation techniques.

6.3.1 Demographic Segmentation

Demographic segmentation is a fundamental method used in customer segmentation and targeting, involving the categorization of consumers based on identifiable characteristics such as age, gender, income, education level, occupation, marital status, and household size. This approach recognizes that individuals within a market exhibit diverse demographic profiles, and by understanding these differences, businesses can tailor their marketing strategies to better meet the needs and preferences of specific demographic segments.

Age is one of the most common demographic variables used in segmentation. Different age groups may have distinct preferences, behaviors, and purchasing power. For example, younger consumers (such as millennials and Gen Z) may be more tech-savvy and receptive to digital marketing channels, while older consumers (such as baby boomers) may prefer traditional media and value relationships with established brands.

Gender is another important demographic variable that can influence consumer behavior and preferences. Products and marketing messages may be tailored to appeal to specific gender segments based on their unique interests and needs. For instance, cosmetic companies often target women with skincare and makeup products, while automotive brands may focus more on male consumers in their advertising campaigns.

Income level is a key determinant of purchasing power and spending behavior. Consumers with higher incomes may be willing to pay premium prices for luxury products and services, while those with lower incomes may prioritize affordability and value. Understanding income segmentation enables businesses to develop pricing strategies and product offerings that align with the financial capabilities of different consumer segments.

Education level and occupation can also provide insights into consumer lifestyles, values, and aspirations. Highly educated professionals may seek products and services that reflect their intellectual interests and career aspirations, while blue-collar workers may prioritize practicality and utility in their purchasing decisions.

Marital status and household size are additional demographic variables that influence consumer behavior. Married couples with children, for example, may have different consumption patterns and priorities compared to single individuals or empty nesters. Businesses can customize their marketing messages and offerings to resonate with the unique needs and dynamics of different household compositions.

Overall, demographic segmentation allows businesses to identify and target specific consumer segments based on their shared demographic characteristics. By tailoring marketing strategies to resonate with the preferences and needs of these segments, businesses can enhance relevance and engagement and, ultimately, drive success in the marketplace. However, it is important to recognize that individuals within a demographic segment are not homogenous and may exhibit variations in preferences and behaviors, necessitating ongoing refinement and adaptation of segmentation strategies based on evolving consumer dynamics.

6.3.2 Psychographic Segmentation

Psychographic segmentation is a methodology used in customer segmentation and targeting that focuses on analyzing consumer lifestyles, values, beliefs, attitudes, personality traits, and interests. Unlike demographic segmentation, which categorizes consumers based on observable characteristics like age or income, psychographic segmentation delves into the psychological and emotional aspects of consumer behavior. By understanding the psychographic profiles of their target audience, businesses can create more nuanced and targeted marketing strategies that resonate with consumers on a deeper level.

Psychographic segmentation enables businesses to identify different consumer segments based on their shared psychographic characteristics, allowing for more personalized and tailored marketing approaches. Here are some key aspects of psychographic segmentation:

Lifestyle Analysis

Lifestyle segmentation involves categorizing consumers based on their activities, interests, and opinions (AIO). This includes factors such as hobbies, recreational activities, social behaviors, and cultural preferences.

For example, a fitness apparel brand may target consumers who lead an active and health-conscious lifestyle, emphasizing the importance of fitness and wellness in their marketing messages.

Values and Beliefs

Psychographic segmentation also considers consumers' values, beliefs, and ideals. This involves understanding the underlying principles and convictions that guide consumers' decision-making processes.

For instance, a sustainable fashion brand may appeal to environmentally conscious consumers who prioritize ethical and eco-friendly practices in their purchasing decisions.

Personality Traits

Personality-based segmentation identifies consumer segments based on their personality characteristics, such as introversion vs. extroversion, openness to new experiences, conscientiousness, and emotional stability.

Certain products and brands may resonate more strongly with consumers who exhibit specific personality traits. For example, adventurous and thrill-seeking individuals may be more inclined to purchase outdoor adventure gear and travel experiences.

Attitudes and Opinions

Psychographic segmentation considers consumers' attitudes and opinions toward various products, brands, and social issues. This involves understanding consumers' perceptions, preferences, and biases.

Businesses can tailor their marketing messages to align with consumers' attitudes and opinions, addressing their concerns and motivations more effectively.

Psychographic segmentation allows businesses to create more targeted and personalized marketing strategies that resonate with consumers on an emotional and psychological level. By understanding consumers' lifestyles, values, beliefs, attitudes, and personality traits, businesses can develop messaging, branding, and product offerings that appeal to the unique needs and preferences of different psychographic segments. This approach enhances consumer engagement, loyalty, and satisfaction, ultimately driving business success in the marketplace.

6.3.3 Behavioral Segmentation

Behavioral segmentation is a strategic approach used in marketing to categorize consumers based on their behaviors, actions, and patterns of interaction with products, services, and brands. Unlike demographic or psychographic segmentation, which focuses on inherent traits or beliefs, behavioral segmentation divides consumers based on their observable actions and responses to marketing stimuli. This method allows businesses to tailor their marketing efforts more precisely to meet the specific needs and preferences of distinct consumer segments. Here are key aspects of behavioral segmentation:

Purchasing Behavior

This involves segmenting consumers based on their purchasing habits, including frequency of purchases, average transaction value, product usage, and loyalty.

For example, a retailer may identify segments such as frequent buyers, occasional shoppers, first-time purchasers, or lapsed customers, each requiring different marketing strategies [1].

Usage Patterns

Segmentation by usage patterns focuses on how consumers utilize products or services. This includes frequency of usage, usage occasions, and product/service usage lifecycle.

For instance, a software company may segment its customers based on how frequently they use the software, whether they use all features or only specific ones, and how long they have been using the product.

Brand Loyalty

Behavioral segmentation also considers consumers' loyalty to brands. This involves categorizing consumers based on their level of brand loyalty, repeat purchases, brand-switching behavior, and advocacy.

Businesses may target loyal customers with rewards programs or exclusive offers to encourage repeat purchases and foster brand advocacy.

Purchase Journey

Understanding the consumer's purchase journey is essential for effective behavioral segmentation. This includes identifying different stages of the buying process, such as awareness, consideration, purchase, and post-purchase evaluation.

By mapping out the purchase journey, businesses can target consumers with relevant messages and incentives at each stage to guide them toward conversion.

Benefits Sought

Behavioral segmentation based on benefits sought involves identifying consumer segments based on the specific benefits they seek from products or services.

For example, a food manufacturer may segment consumers based on their preference for convenience, health, taste, or affordability, tailoring product offerings and marketing messages accordingly.

6.3.4 Occasion-Based Segmentation

This involves segmenting consumers based on specific occasions or events when they are most likely to make a purchase.

For instance, a beverage company may target consumers with different messaging and promotions for everyday consumption, special occasions, or seasonal events.

Behavioral segmentation allows businesses to understand how consumers interact with their products, services, and brands, enabling more targeted and effective marketing strategies. By segmenting consumers based on their behaviors, businesses can deliver personalized messages, offers, and experiences that resonate with the specific needs and preferences of each segment. This approach enhances customer engagement, satisfaction, and loyalty, ultimately driving business growth and success in the marketplace.

6.3.5 Geographic Segmentation

Geographic segmentation is a marketing strategy that involves dividing a market into distinct segments based on geographic factors such as location, climate, culture, population density, and socio-economic characteristics. By segmenting consumers geographically, businesses can tailor their marketing efforts to specific regions or locations, taking into account the unique needs, preferences, and behaviors of each segment. Here are key aspects of geographic segmentation:

Location-Based Segmentation

Geographic segmentation involves dividing consumers based on their physical location, such as country, region, state, city, or neighborhood.

Businesses may target consumers in different geographic areas with customized marketing messages, offers, and promotions that are relevant to their local context.

Climate and Environmental Factors

Climate and environmental factors play a significant role in consumer behavior and preferences. Businesses may segment consumers based on their climate zone, weather patterns, and environmental conditions.

For example, a clothing retailer may offer different product lines and promotions based on seasonal weather changes, catering to the specific needs of consumers in different regions.

Cultural and Socioeconomic Factors

Geographic segmentation takes into account cultural differences and socio-economic characteristics that influence consumer behavior. This includes factors such as language, customs, traditions, and income levels.

Businesses may adapt their marketing strategies to align with the cultural norms and values of specific geographic segments, ensuring messages and offerings resonate with local consumers.

Population Density and Urbanization

Population density and urbanization rates can impact consumer preferences, purchasing power, and lifestyle choices. Businesses may segment consumers based on urban, suburban, or rural areas.

Urban consumers may have different preferences for convenience, accessibility, and product offerings compared to rural consumers. Businesses can tailor their marketing strategies accordingly.

Localization Strategies

Geographic segmentation often involves localization strategies aimed at customizing products, services, and marketing communications to specific geographic markets [2].

Localization strategies may include adapting product features, packaging, pricing, distribution channels, and promotional campaigns to meet the unique needs of different geographic segments.

Regional Preferences and Trends

Geographic segmentation allows businesses to identify regional preferences and trends that may influence consumer behavior. This includes preferences for certain products, cuisines, fashion styles, or entertainment options.

By understanding regional preferences and trends, businesses can develop targeted marketing campaigns that resonate with local consumers, driving engagement and sales in specific geographic markets.

Geographic segmentation enables businesses to effectively target and engage with consumers in different geographic areas, maximizing relevance and impact. By tailoring marketing strategies to specific geographic segments, businesses can address the unique needs, preferences, and behaviors of local consumers, ultimately driving business growth and success in diverse markets.

Technological Advancements in Segmentation

Technological advancements have revolutionized segmentation techniques in marketing, enabling more sophisticated and dynamic approaches to customer targeting. By leveraging cutting-edge technologies such as data analytics, machine learning, and artificial intelligence (AI), businesses can gain deeper insights into consumer behavior and preferences, allowing for more precise and personalized segmentation strategies. Here are some key technological advancements in segmentation:

6.4 DATA ANALYTICS

Data analytics tools enable businesses to analyze large volumes of customer data to uncover meaningful patterns and trends. By leveraging data from various sources such as customer transactions, interactions, and demographics, businesses can gain insights into consumer behavior and preferences.

Advanced analytics techniques, including descriptive, predictive, and prescriptive analytics, allow businesses to segment customers based on their past behaviors, predict future actions, and prescribe optimal marketing strategies.

Machine Learning

Machine learning algorithms can automatically segment customers based on complex criteria and patterns. These algorithms can analyze vast amounts of data to identify hidden relationships and segment customers into homogeneous groups.

Supervised and unsupervised machine learning techniques, such as clustering algorithms (e.g., k-means clustering) and classification algorithms (e.g., decision trees, random forests), enable businesses to segment customers based on both known and unknown factors.

Artificial Intelligence (AI)

AI-powered segmentation techniques leverage advanced algorithms and neural networks to segment customers in real-time and adapt marketing strategies dynamically. AI algorithms can analyze customer interactions and feedback across various channels to identify segmentation opportunities.

Natural language processing (NLP) and sentiment analysis techniques enable businesses to analyze customer sentiment and categorize customers based on their attitudes and emotions, allowing for more targeted messaging and engagement.

Real-Time Segmentation

Real-time segmentation techniques enable businesses to segment customers dynamically based on their current behavior and preferences. By continuously monitoring customer interactions across multiple touchpoints, businesses can adjust marketing messages and offer in real-time to maximize relevance and impact.

Real-time segmentation techniques often rely on stream processing and event-driven architectures, allowing businesses to respond quickly to changes in customer behavior and market conditions.

Dynamic Targeting Approaches

Dynamic targeting approaches use algorithms to personalize marketing messages and offers for individual customers based on their unique characteristics and behaviors. By combining segmentation with personalization techniques, businesses can deliver highly relevant and engaging experiences to customers.

Dynamic targeting approaches may include recommendation engines, personalized content delivery systems, and adaptive marketing campaigns that tailor messaging and offer in real-time based on customer preferences and interactions.

Overall, technological advancements in segmentation have transformed the way businesses identify and target customers. By leveraging data analytics, machine learning, and artificial intelligence, businesses can segment customers more effectively, personalize marketing strategies, and drive better business outcomes. As technology continues to evolve, segmentation techniques will become increasingly sophisticated, enabling businesses to stay ahead in an ever-changing marketplace.

6.5 BENEFITS OF CUSTOMER TARGETING AND SEGMENTATION

Customer targeting and segmentation offer numerous benefits to businesses seeking to enhance their marketing strategies and drive success in the marketplace. By dividing a heterogeneous market into distinct groups of consumers with similar characteristics and needs, businesses can tailor their marketing efforts more effectively, leading to increased engagement, satisfaction, and loyalty. Here are some key benefits of customer targeting and segmentation:

6.5.1 Enhanced Relevance and Personalization

By segmenting customers based on shared characteristics, businesses can create more relevant and personalized marketing messages, offers, and experiences. Personalized marketing resonates with consumers on a deeper level, increasing their engagement and likelihood of conversion.

6.5.2 Improved Marketing Efficiency and Effectiveness

Customer targeting and segmentation allow businesses to allocate resources more efficiently by focusing their marketing efforts on the most valuable and receptive segments. By identifying high-potential customer segments, businesses can optimize their marketing campaigns and maximize return on investment.

6.5.3 Increased Customer Satisfaction and Loyalty

Tailoring products, services, and communications to the specific needs and preferences of different customer segments enhances customer satisfaction and loyalty. When customers feel understood and valued, they are more likely to develop strong emotional connections with the brand and become loyal advocates.

6.5.4 Better Understanding of Customer Needs and Behaviors

Customer targeting and segmentation provide businesses with valuable insights into consumer needs, behaviors, and preferences. By analyzing data from different segments, businesses can identify emerging trends, anticipate future demand, and adapt their offerings to meet evolving customer expectations.

6.5.5 Competitive Advantage and Market Leadership

Effective customer targeting and segmentation enable businesses to differentiate themselves from competitors by offering unique value propositions tailored to specific segments. By addressing niche markets and fulfilling unmet needs, businesses can establish themselves as market leaders and gain a competitive edge.

6.5.6 Optimized Product Development and Innovation

By understanding the preferences and pain points of different customer segments, businesses can develop products and services that better meet customer needs. Customer feedback and insights gathered through segmentation can inform product development decisions and drive innovation.

6.5.7 Increased Revenue and Profitability

Targeting high-value customer segments and delivering personalized offerings can lead to increased sales, higher conversion rates, and greater customer lifetime value. By focusing on the most profitable segments, businesses can drive revenue growth and improve overall profitability.

In conclusion, customer targeting and segmentation offer a wide range of benefits for businesses across industries. By understanding and catering to the unique needs and preferences of different customer segments, businesses can enhance relevance, efficiency, and effectiveness in their marketing efforts, ultimately driving customer satisfaction, loyalty, and profitability.

6.6 CHALLENGES IN CUSTOMER TARGETING AND SEGMENTATION

While customer targeting and segmentation offer numerous benefits, businesses also face several challenges in implementing these strategies effectively. Overcoming these challenges is essential to maximizing the impact of segmentation efforts and achieving desired business outcomes. Here are some key challenges in customer targeting and segmentation:

Data Quality and Availability

One of the primary challenges in segmentation is ensuring the quality and availability of data. Businesses rely on data to identify and understand different customer segments, but data sources may be incomplete, inaccurate, or outdated. Poor data quality can lead to flawed segmentation and ineffective marketing strategies.

Complexity of Segmentation Models

Segmentation models can be complex, requiring businesses to analyze multiple variables and factors simultaneously. Developing and implementing segmentation models may require advanced statistical techniques, expertise in data analysis, and specialized software tools. Complexity can hinder segmentation efforts and pose challenges for businesses with limited resources or expertise [3].

Integration Across Marketing Channels

Customer targeting and segmentation often involve targeting customers across multiple marketing channels, including digital, social media, email, and offline channels. Ensuring consistent messaging and coordination across these channels can be challenging, particularly as consumer interactions become increasingly fragmented and omnichannel marketing strategies become more prevalent.

Dynamic Nature of Consumer Preferences

Consumer preferences and behaviors are constantly evolving, making it challenging for businesses to maintain relevance and accuracy in their segmentation efforts. Segmentation models must be flexible and adaptable to changes in consumer preferences, market dynamics, and external factors. Businesses need to continuously monitor and update segmentation strategies to remain effective over time.

6.7 FUTURE TRENDS AND CONSIDERATIONS IN CUSTOMER TARGETING AND SEGMENTATION

As technology continues to evolve and consumer behavior undergoes rapid changes, the landscape of customer targeting and segmentation is also expected to evolve. Understanding future trends and considerations is essential for businesses to stay ahead of the curve and adapt their segmentation strategies to meet evolving customer needs and market dynamics. Here are some key future trends and considerations in customer targeting and segmentation:

Predictive Analytics and AI

The adoption of predictive analytics and artificial intelligence (AI) is expected to increase, allowing businesses to anticipate future trends, identify emerging customer segments, and personalize marketing strategies in real time. AI-powered algorithms will enable more accurate predictions and dynamic segmentation approaches, enhancing targeting effectiveness and efficiency.

Hyper-Personalization

Hyper-personalization involves delivering highly customized and individualized experiences to customers based on their unique preferences, behaviors, and context. Future segmentation strategies will focus on hyper-personalization, leveraging data from various sources to tailor marketing messages, offers, and experiences at an individual level.

Contextual Segmentation

Contextual segmentation considers the situational context in which customers interact with brands, products, and services. Future segmentation strategies will incorporate contextual factors such as location, time, device, and behavior to deliver more relevant and timely marketing communications that resonate with customers in specific contexts.

Ethical and Transparent Data Practices

With growing concerns about data privacy and ethical data usage, businesses will need to prioritize transparency, consent, and data protection in their segmentation efforts. Future segmentation strategies will focus on ethical data practices, ensuring that customer data is collected, used, and shared responsibly and transparently.

Integration of Online and Offline Data

As consumer interactions become increasingly omnichannel, businesses will need to integrate online and offline data sources to create a unified view of the customer. Future segmentation strategies will leverage data integration technologies to capture and analyze customer interactions across multiple touchpoints, enabling seamless targeting and personalization across channels.

Dynamic and Adaptive Segmentation Models

Segmentation models will become more dynamic and adaptive, continuously evolving based on real-time data and insights. Future segmentation strategies will employ machine learning algorithms and AI-driven analytics to automatically adjust segmentation criteria and targeting strategies in response to changing customer behavior and market conditions.

Emphasis on Customer Experience

Future segmentation strategies will prioritize enhancing the overall customer experience, focusing not only on targeting and acquisition but also on retention, loyalty, and advocacy. Businesses will adopt customer-centric segmentation approaches that prioritize long-term relationships and customer lifetime value over short-term transactions.

In conclusion, future trends in customer targeting and segmentation will be characterized by the adoption of advanced technologies, increased personalization, ethical data practices, omnichannel integration, and a focus on delivering exceptional customer experiences. By embracing these trends and considerations, businesses can stay ahead of the curve and drive sustainable growth and success in an increasingly competitive marketplace.

6.8 CONCLUSION

Customer targeting and segmentation play a pivotal role in modern marketing strategies, enabling businesses to effectively identify, understand, and engage with diverse consumer segments. Through this research paper, we have explored the foundations, methods, benefits, challenges, and future trends of customer targeting and segmentation.

We have seen how demographic, psychographic, behavioral, and geographic segmentation techniques allow businesses to divide their target market into distinct segments based on various criteria such as demographics, lifestyles, behaviors, and locations. These segmentation methods enable businesses to deliver more relevant, personalized, and impactful marketing messages and offerings to their target audience, ultimately driving customer satisfaction, loyalty, and business success.

Despite the numerous benefits of customer targeting and segmentation, businesses face challenges such as data quality, integration, privacy concerns, and resource constraints. However, by addressing these challenges and embracing emerging trends such as advanced data analytics, hyper-personalization, and sustainability-driven segmentation, businesses can unlock new opportunities for growth and innovation.

In conclusion, customer targeting and segmentation are essential strategies for businesses seeking to thrive in a competitive marketplace. By understanding the diverse needs and preferences of their customers and tailoring their marketing efforts accordingly, businesses can build stronger relationships, drive engagement, and achieve sustainable growth in the long term.

REFERENCES

1. Ganie, S. M., et al. (2023). An ensemble learning approach for diabetes prediction using boosting techniques. *Frontiers in Genetics*, *14*, 1252159.
2. Akhila, G., Hemachandran, K., & Jaramillo, J. R. (2021). Indian premier league using different aspects of machine learning algorithms. *Journal of Cognitive Human-Computer Interaction*, *1*(1), 1–7.
3. Malik, M. B., et al. (2023). "Performance Evaluation and Comparative Analysis of Machine Learning Techniques to Predict the Chronic Kidney Disease." *International Conference on Artificial Intelligence on Textile and Apparel*. Singapore: Springer Nature Singapore.

7 Personalized Marketing and Recommendation Systems

K. Mani Teja Chowdary, Maniteja Vallepu, A. Naga Sai Purushotham, and Neelam Kumari

7.1 INTRODUCTION

The digital world is overflowing with data, saturating us with advertisements, entertainment, and goods competing for our attention. One-size-fits-all, traditional marketing finds it difficult to cut through the clutter, which results in "ad fatigue" and disgruntled customers. This is where suggestion and customized marketing systems come in handy, adjusting experiences and messaging to each person's unique requirements, interests, and behaviours to take a more powerful and convincing tack. Imagine entering a shop where the salesperson is familiar with your favourite brands, recalls previous purchases, and makes genuine recommendations for products you might adore. Online, personalized marketing replicates this experience by providing relevant material on the appropriate platform at the appropriate moment.

The days of generic advertising interfering with your internet experience are long gone. You may view goods based on your hobbies, deals catered to your requirements, and material linked to your interests when you enable customization. Consider a travel enthusiast who prefers to get special bargains for their ideal place rather than being inundated with generic vacation packages. Relevance stands out among the crowd, drawing interest and encouraging participation. You will feel appreciated and respected when businesses speak to your interests and are aware of your preferences. As a result, a stronger bond is created that increases loyalty and trust. Consider getting emails highlighting previous purchases or birthday wishes with customized suggestions—small actions that have a significant impact. Compare looking through a plethora of possibilities in search of the ideal product to viewing a well-chosen assortment that is tailored just for you. Personalized suggestions steer consumers toward relevant goods they are more likely to buy, greatly reducing selection fatigue. For instance, Netflix's exceptional consumer engagement and retention rates are partly attributed to their tailored suggestions.

Recommendation systems, which are complex algorithms that evaluate massive quantities of user data, are the engine driving this magic of customization. These systems create a digital profile of each user based on many factors such as demographics, social media activity, past purchases, and website interactions. They provide recommendations for goods, entertainment, or services you are likely to appreciate before

 DOI: 10.1201/9781003472544-7

you ever know it. They do this by seeing trends and correlations. Although revenue growth is a desirable result, tailored marketing has other advantages for companies as well: showing that you comprehend your clients builds trust and establishes your brand as client-focused. You may improve your products and marketing tactics by learning more about consumers' tastes and expectations and examining how they engage with tailored experiences. Bid farewell to pointless advertisements and suggestions! Personalized experiences guarantee that you find goods and information that catch your attention. Picture a shopping experience that is customized to your tastes, saving you time and energy while you look for what you need. Are you feeling overtaken by options? Personalized suggestions confidently point you in the direction of the perfect goods, eliminating the uncertainty from your shopping experience.

7.2 METHODOLOGIES

There are three primary categories of recommendation systems, each with benefits and a unique methodology:

1. **Collaborative Filtering**: Visualize people as lines connecting dots on a map according to shared preferences. This is the fundamental idea of collaborative filtering, which generates suggestions by examining user behaviour. There are two varieties available: Given two users who made comparable purchases, the system may suggest to one of them things that the other liked but has not yet found. Although this method captures intricate user interactions, it has "cold start" problems since new users do not have a history of purchases. Visualize the objects as fellow shelf neighbours. If you purchase one item, the algorithm may suggest its neighbouring items based on the purchases made by other users. Although this approach is simpler to use and effective for novice users, it ignores the intricate relationships among users.
2. **Content-based Filtering**: This method concentrates on the attributes of the objects themselves rather than on user behaviour. Consider it as creating a profile of your preferences based on previous purchases. The algorithm may suggest action-packed movies with high ratings and action tags if you like a fast-moving action movie. While this is simple to set up and effective for novice users, it misses important information provided by user interactions.
3. **Hybrid Methodologies:** Hybrid systems incorporate several approaches, realizing their limits. Consider recommending movies using both item-based and user-based techniques. This may get around each one's shortcomings and provide suggestions that are more reliable and accurate. These systems may be more difficult to build and manage, however. In what way, then, do these systems convert data into recommendations? There are many strategies used, each having advantages and disadvantages of its own: In a multidimensional space, users and objects are points linked by lines that depict their interactions [1].

This space is compressed using matrix factorization, which makes hidden linkages and patterns visible. Although this method is quite effective at capturing intricate user-item interactions, it may be computationally costly and need big datasets. Recall the example of the user map [1]. These algorithms identify individuals who have your interests (your neighbours) and suggest products they enjoy that you have not yet looked at. Although it has problems with cold starts and does not record all user-item connections, this is clear-cut and easy to understand. These potent algorithms are modelled like the human brain and can extract intricate correlations from large volumes of data. They can handle many data kinds and capture complicated user-item interactions, but they are often opaque, complex, and need a large amount of processing power.

7.3 SELECTING THE APPROPRIATE INSTRUMENT

Several criteria determine which suggestion method is most appropriate for you. Do you own a large collection of item properties and user interactions? If not, less complex techniques could be more appropriate. How often do you come across brand-new products or users? This is a problem for collaborative filtering; content-based approaches may perform better. Do you have to know the rationale behind any recommendations? Neighbourhood-based techniques are more transparent, but deep learning techniques may be opaque. How many things and users must you manage? Deep learning and matrix factorization are capable of handling large-scale systems, but they need greater resources. Although these fundamental ideas serve as a basis, the field of recommendation systems is always changing. These are a few noteworthy trends:

By combining dynamic user preferences and real-time context, sophisticated algorithms are elevating personalization to new heights. For a smooth user experience, recommendations now span many touchpoints and are not limited to a single platform. AI is blending the boundaries between marketing and one-on-one interactions by tailoring whole experiences, from communication preferences to product offers [2].

Changing Relationships with Information and Morality. The way that clients interact with agencies has been profoundly altered by the virtual surroundings. Customers now need individualized reviews which might be tailored to their very own necessities and pursuits; they are no longer happy with prevalent messaging and one-length-fits-all strategies. Personalized advertising and marketing are becoming increasingly popular because of this developing need, which enables organizations to construct stronger relationships, boost client engagement, and in the end spur improvement.

7.4 FINDINGS

At the heart of personalization lies data. Website/app behaviour (clicks, searches, and purchases), email interactions, social media activity, demographics, and purchase history—these diverse data points paint a vibrant picture of individual preferences and behaviours. However, harnessing this power responsibly requires careful consideration of ethical considerations. Transparency: informing users about data collection and usage is paramount. User consent: obtaining explicit permission to leverage data builds trust [2]. Data security: robust measures safeguard personal information against breaches. Avoiding bias: algorithms must be designed to prevent unfair discrimination based on protected characteristics.

The ability to personalize seamlessly across various marketing channels unlocks immense potential. Imagine landing pages dynamically adjusting based on previous searches, product recommendations appearing as if they read your mind, and navigation paths customized to your browsing history. This level of dynamic engagement fosters a sense of discovery and encourages exploration. Forget generic blasts. Segmented email lists cater to specific interests, while dynamic subject lines pique curiosity. Personalized product offers based on purchase history entice further exploration and triggered emails based on specific actions (e.g., the abandoned cart) nudge customers towards completion.

Targeted ads ensure relevance in the bustling social media sphere. Algorithms curate content suggestions based on past interactions, while personalized messaging in direct messages creates a one-on-one feel. Take personalization to the next level with recommendations based on real-time behaviour and context. Imagine receiving location-specific offers while travelling or product suggestions based on the time of day. This hyper-personalized approach fosters an immediate and impactful connection. They provide a specially customized listening experience by considering social connections, listening history, and preferred genres. Amazon uses data to anticipate consumer requirements and increase conversions. Examples of this include customized product recommendations, dynamic search results, and "frequently bought together" suggestions. Users may easily browse the extensive content collection and find new favourites with the aid of movie and programme suggestions based on watching history, ratings, and genre interests.

Personalization will not be limited to static suggestions in the future. Entire experiences are customized to each person's tastes. The product offers change according to user browsing habits, communication techniques change to suit different personality types, and loyalty plans are customized for every user. This degree of experience customization strengthens bonds on an emotional level and takes relationships with customers to new heights.

Customization is a strategic need, not merely a fad. In the constantly changing digital world, organizations may create enduring consumer connections, encourage brand loyalty, and achieve sustainable development by ethically using data, implementing customization across all touchpoints, and adopting ethical standards. Recall that customization is a process that is driven by data, regulated by ethics, and ultimately intended to forge sincere relationships with every client. It is not a panacea. Customized Advertising: Exceeding Clicks and Conversions—Getting Around the Ethical Maze and Revealing Upcoming Patterns

The practice of customizing experiences and messages for each user, known as personalized marketing, has completely changed the online market. Its influence extends far beyond a rise in clicks and conversions; it also shapes brand perceptions, customer relationships, and the fundamentals of marketing. However managing this revolutionary potential is not without its difficulties and moral dilemmas, which call for careful thought. Future trends indicate even more customization, but they also need prudent expansion. These are exciting times.

Increased clicks and conversions are quantifiable successes, but tailored marketing has a deeper effect. Imagine entering a shop where every element, including the product displays and suggestions, speaks to your tastes. This smooth experience on the internet equals sincere curiosity piqued by targeted content, which results in more in-depth social media conversations, longer website visits, and greater email open rates.

Product recommendations and offers that are tailored to the requirements of the person encourage purchases, sign-ups, and other desirable activities. Loyalty, repeated business, and enhanced brand support are all bolstered by a sense of worth and understanding. Although these advantages may be measured with concrete performance measures, customization has more power than just data. Customers experience a feeling of belonging, trust is developed, and good emotional relationships are fostered. Imagine getting a social media ad that is exactly in line with your interests right now or a birthday email that offers you a tailored discount on your favourite product. These customized interactions create a strong impression that improves consumer relations and brand attachment.

The revolutionary potential of personalization is entwined with an intricate ethical web. Three crucial issues need our attention when we integrate consumer data into marketing: algorithmic bias, data privacy, and customization fatigue. Ignoring these moral issues runs the danger of destroying the very trust that we work so hard to establish.

Nowadays, personal information is like money. Customers want transparency and control over its usage as they become more conscious of its worth. This calls for moving away from "take-it-or-leave-it" permission forms and toward a sincere conversation. Opt-in choices have to be unambiguous, succinct, and easily available. Complex legalese buried in countless pages undermines confidence, while fine-grained control gives customers the freedom to decide what customization and data they want to contribute.

In addition to permission, safe handling and storage are critical. Strong security protocols protect confidential information from intrusions, and appropriate deletion procedures make sure that out-of-date or unnecessary material is removed from circulation. Recall that maintaining data privacy is essential to upholding consumer rights, fostering trust, and satisfying legal requirements.

Despite their seeming impartiality, algorithms can reflect the biases present in the training set of data. Consider a recommendation system that unintentionally reinforces past housing discrimination by prioritizing loan approvals for people living in certain zip codes. If such biases are allowed to run rampant, they may produce unfair and discriminating results that outweigh the advantages of customization for whole populations.

To mitigate algorithmic prejudice, proactive steps must be taken. It is critical to use a variety of data sets that accurately represent the demographics of your target market. Potential problems may be found and fixed with the use of human supervision, fairness measurements, and regular audits of algorithms for prejudice [3]. Recall that algorithms are instruments, not miracles. We can guarantee genuinely equitable and inclusive customization for everyone by accepting their limits and actively reducing prejudice.

7.5 CHALLENGES

Overly aggressive customization might backfire, much like a persistent salesman who keeps approaching you with uninvited offers. Imagine feeling as if you are being monitored and controlled by constantly getting alerts about items you have never thought about [4]. This "personalization fatigue" damages credibility and may even turn off clients.

Finding a balance between respect and relevancy is crucial. Pay attention to customization that improves the consumer experience rather than compromises their privacy. Use data to understand each person's requirements and preferences so that you may provide ideas that are authentic rather than overwhelming.

Context and frequency are important. Constant pop-ups are annoying, but targeted email offers based on surfing history are pertinent [3]. Give unsubscribe alternatives that are transparent and respect the user's decision to opt-out. Recall that customization is a luxury, not a necessity. The secret to its long-term success is building and maintaining trust by decency.

The ethical terrain of customization requires ongoing attention to detail and a dedication to morality. Three values that should never be compromised are transparency, justice, and respect for user privacy. Through proactive resolution of these issues, we may use the potential of customization to establish significant bonds, provide authentic benefits, and establish enduring partnerships.

It is not only morally required but also practically necessary for businesses to address these issues. Customers are becoming leery of intrusive methods, and biased algorithms or the unethical use of data may swiftly undermine confidence.

7.6 FUTURE SCOPE OF THE RESEARCH

Though recommendation and personalized marketing technologies are still developing, the following intriguing prospects lie ahead: More advanced algorithms will anticipate your requirements before you do, providing even deeper insights and suggestions. A cohesive and consistent consumer experience will be produced via seamless customization across all touchpoints, including websites, apps, social media, and physical shops. Picture-fully customized experiences, down to the product selection and communication methods.

Based on your previous purchases, your preferred bookshop may put up a reading list for you and suggest authors you would like. The information universe is enormous, and it may be difficult to navigate on your own. Personalized filters that suggest products we may enjoy based on our prior behaviour, tastes, and the collective knowledge of others are what recommendation systems are for. How do these magic boxes operate, though? Let's examine the many kinds of recommendation systems, their methods, and the compromises that exist between them.

Notwithstanding the difficulties, customized marketing has a bright future ahead of it. Emerging patterns suggest that more in-depth consumer insights will be uncovered by sophisticated AI algorithms, allowing for hyper-personalized experiences catered to specific requirements and preferences. Personalized experiences will go beyond specific channels to provide a unified and coherent user experience across websites, applications, social media, and physical retail locations.

Personalization will go beyond making product suggestions and include customization of whole experiences, ranging from product offers to communication methods. Imagine getting bespoke physical shop layouts, loyalty programmes that match your interests, or even content curation that is specifically chosen only for you. More ROI, stronger brand loyalty, and more consumer happiness are all promised by these trends. However, ethical use and responsible growth are crucial. As customization develops, transparency, diversity, and user permission will be essential tenets.

While personalized marketing has great promise, there are drawbacks as well. It is our responsibility as marketers to use this influence sensibly, giving algorithmic fairness, data protection, and ethical behaviour priority. This implies informed consent, giving people control over their data, and being transparent about the gathering and use of their data. To guarantee equitable and inclusive customization, actively audit algorithms for biases and put mitigation techniques into place. Give users the right to opt out, prioritize safe data storage, and reduce data collecting. We can create a future where the advantages of customization are fully realized by addressing it responsibly and ethically. In this new era of marketing, we can develop trust with consumers, drive sustainable growth, and promote meaningful relationships.

7.7 CONCLUSION

Personalized marketing is becoming the cornerstone of effective consumer interaction rather than just a trendy term. The challenge is now "how" to personalize in an efficient, moral, and sustainable way rather than "if" to do so. The complex world of recommendation systems, the data that underpins customization, and its effects on various marketing channels have all been covered in this chapter. However, the tale is not over yet.

Personalized marketing has several advantages that go far beyond memorable phrases. Research indicates that customized suggestions may raise conversion rates by as much as 70%, and customized email marketing achieves click-through rates that are six times greater than those of generic campaigns. Real-world business benefits include increased revenue, a greater customer lifetime value, and stronger brand loyalty. In turn, customers gain from a more engaging and relevant experience, which saves them time and effort when trying to discover what they need.

Personalization has great power, but it also carries great responsibility. Using enormous volumes of user data gives rise to questions regarding possible biases, transparency, and privacy. It is imperative for us as marketers to give ethical practices like user permission, data security, and algorithm explainability a priority. Building trust via openness in data gathering and use promotes positive customer relationships. Furthermore, reducing algorithmic bias guarantees inclusive and equitable experiences for everyone, irrespective of preferences or demographics.

Exciting potentialities abound for individualized marketing in the future. With its capability to create dynamic content in real-time, make predictive hints, and section clients extra exactly, artificial intelligence (AI) can alternate the game. Imagine residing in a world wherein your move-to retailer is aware of exactly what you need earlier than you say it, imparting pointers for the best outfit based totally on your earlier purchases, the climate, or even your emotional country.

The future lies in creating a smooth, customized experience across all touchpoints rather than focusing just on one-on-one encounters. Imagine entering a shop where a selection of things that are relevant to you has already been chosen based on your past internet browsing activity. Or imagine being able to seamlessly connect the online and offline worlds by having tailored offers appear on your phone as you walk by a real business.

Personalization will go beyond just suggesting products. Brands will tailor their marketing strategies, loyalty plans, and even their product lines. Imagine getting birthday wishes based on your own tastes or loyalty points based on your shopping habits. Real connection and appreciation will be fostered when the distinction between commercial and personal interactions becomes hazier.

Although technology facilitates customization, its effectiveness depends on comprehending the human factor. Though they are strong instruments, algorithms cannot take the place of true consumer knowledge, empathy, and inventiveness. Striking a balance is essential, using technology to augment rather than replace human talents. Instead of being intrusive or exploitative, personalized encounters should seem human, pertinent, and kind.

Although it is no longer a panacea, personalization is a precious tool in a marketer's toolbox. We can comprehend the total ability of the generation to offer memorable patron reports and enduring connections with the aid of emphasizing ethical behaviour, the use of it responsibly, and preserving a human touch. As we navigate this thrilling destiny, permit's preserve in thoughts that customization is a method to an end: building real relationships with our consumers and supplying significant value.

REFERENCES

1. Recommender Systems: Behind the Scenes of Machine Learning-Based Personalization. (2021, July 27). AltexSoft. https://www.altexsoft.com/blog/recommender-system-personalization/
2. Huang, F. (2021, November 16). Personalized Marketing Recommendation System of New Media Short Video Based on Deep Neural Network Data Fusion. *Journal of Sensors*. https://doi.org/10.1155/2021/3638071
3. 5 Best Practices for Effective Personalized Product Recommendations. (n.d.). Mailchimp. https://mailchimp.com/marketing-glossary/personalized-product-recommendations/
4. Hemachandran, K., Tayal, S., Kumar, G. S., Boddu, V., Mudigonda, S., & Emudapuram, M. (2020). A technical paper review on vehicle tracking system. In *Proceeding of the International Conference on Computer Networks, Big Data and IoT (ICCBI-2019)* (pp. 698–703). Springer International Publishing.

8 Pricing Optimisation Using Predictive Analytics

K. V. Swetha Niharika, S. R. Hareesh, and Ezendu Ariwa

8.1 INTRODUCTION

Pricing optimisation is a critical factor in determining market competitiveness, maximising profitability, and fostering sustainable development in the ever-evolving realm of commerce. Conventional methods of pricing, although proficient in their own regard, frequently fall short in the clarity and flexibility required in the swiftly changing business environment of the twenty-first century. Nevertheless, the emergence of predictive analytics has provided organisations with a robust set of tools that enable them to gain a more profound understanding of consumer behaviour, market trends, and competitive dynamics. This chapter delves into the complex relationship between pricing optimisation and predictive analytics, providing a thorough guide for capitalising on data-driven approaches to succeed in a progressively competitive market (Lindsey et al., 2014).

8.2 A COMPREHEND OF PREDICTIVE ANALYTICS

Predictive analytics is an interdisciplinary field that emerges from the convergence of data mining, machine learning, and statistical analysis techniques. This methodology embodies a proactive stance towards data analysis, with the dual objective of comprehending past patterns and predicting forthcoming developments and trends. Predictive analytics is fundamentally predicated on the methodical scrutiny of historical data patterns in order to discern correlations, trends, and associations that may provide insights for subsequent decision-making endeavours. By utilising sophisticated algorithms and computational models, predictive analytics empowers organisations to derive practical insights from extensive datasets that would otherwise be concealed or disregarded.

Predictive analytics is fundamentally concerned with enabling organisations to proactively anticipate and make necessary preparations for forthcoming events and developments. Through the utilisation of patterns in historical data, predictive analytics offers significant insight into prospective risks and opportunities. Predictive analytics provides a strategic edge to organisations by facilitating informed decision-making grounded in data-driven insights, as opposed

DOI: 10.1201/9781003472544-8

to relying on intuition or imputed judgements, regarding customer churn, sales trends, and emergent market trends.

Predictive analytics is distinguished by its adaptability and feasibility in a wide range of sectors and domains. Organisations spanning a wide array of industries, including finance, healthcare, retail, and manufacturing, can effectively utilise predictive analytics to optimise resource allocation, enhance strategic decision-making processes, and drive operational efficiency. Through the utilisation of sophisticated statistical methods and machine learning algorithms, predictive analytics empowers organisations to acquire a more profound comprehension of intricate data environments, reveal latent patterns, and extract practical insights that generate value for the business.

Furthermore, predictive analytics functions as a potent instrument for alleviating the harm and unpredictability that are intrinsic in the contemporary, ever-changing business landscape. By analysing trends and patterns in historical data, organisations can identify potential risk factors and implement preventative measures to lessen their impact. Predictive analytics empowers organisations to proactively resolve potential issues, such as credit risk assessment, supply chain optimisation, and fraudulent activity identification, in order to prevent the escalation of substantial liabilities or disruptions.

In addition, predictive analytics is crucial for recognising and leveraging nascent prospects in markets that are undergoing rapid change. Through the examination of market trends, consumer behaviour, and competitor strategies, businesses are able to discern unexplored market segments, forecast changes in consumer preferences, and proactively modify their operational approaches to exploit nascent prospects. Predictive analytics enables organisations to penetrate new markets, enhance customer engagement initiatives, and promote new products with the foresight and insights necessary to maintain a competitive edge in the dynamic business environment of the twenty-first century.

In summary, predictive analytics serves as a potent instrument to extract practical insights, minimise potential hazards, and exploit nascent prospects in the data-centric society of the twenty-first century. By leveraging the capabilities of sophisticated algorithms and computational models, organisations can acquire more profound understandings of their data, facilitate more informed decision-making, and foster innovation and sustainable growth. With the growing adoption of data-driven decision making and digital transformation by organisations, predictive analytics will inevitably assume a more significant role in determining the trajectory of business operations in various sectors and industries (Deprez, Antonio and Boute, 2020).

8.3 THE IMPORTANCE OF PREDICTIVE ANALYTICS IN THE OPTIMISATION OF PRICING

Pricing optimisation is an essential element of corporate strategy, with the objective of maximising profits, market share, and revenue while managing intricate internal and external variables. Pricing optimisation, at its essence, entails the calculated establishment of prices for products or services with the intention of attaining intended business goals. Amidst this ever-changing environment, predictive analytics arises as a potent instrument, enabling enterprises to formulate well-informed pricing determinations through the utilisation of past data, customer perceptions, and market fluctuations (Bekiroglu et al., 2018).

Pricing optimisation is significantly influenced by predictive analytics, which formulates effective pricing strategies by utilising historical sales data, customer demographics, competitor pricing strategies, and market trends. Through the examination of extensive datasets, predictive analytics algorithms reveal associations, patterns, and trends that have an impact on the purchasing behaviour and price sensitivity of consumers. Predictive analytics utilises sophisticated statistical methods and machine learning algorithms to discern critical determinants of demand and price elasticity. This empowers businesses to establish ideal price levels that effectively reconcile the generation of revenue and the contentment of customers.

An important benefit of utilising predictive analytics for pricing optimisation is its capability to interpret and analyse intricate datasets in order to reveal practical and implementable insights. Predictive analytics algorithms can discern patterns and trends in consumer behaviour through the analysis of historical sales data. This empowers organisations to comprehend the ways in which alterations in pricing influence customer demand and subsequent purchasing choices. This understanding enables businesses to dynamically adapt their pricing strategies in order to take advantage of favourable market conditions and minimise potential hazards.

In addition, predictive analytics empowers organisations to forecast shifts in market dynamics and competitor conduct, thereby facilitating a competitive advantage. Organisations can discern emergent pricing trends and adapt their pricing strategies accordingly by monitoring market trends and competitor pricing strategies. By adopting this proactive stance, organisations can effectively maintain their competitive edge in a swiftly changing market, thereby optimising their capacity to acquire market share and stimulate revenue expansion.

Within the realm of pricing optimisation, predictive analytics analyses past data and forecasts future outcomes through the utilisation of numerous statistical models and algorithms. Regression analysis, which investigates the relationship between pricing variables and sales performance in order to determine the optimal price point for maximising revenue or profit margins, is a frequently employed method. In addition, support vector machines, neural networks, and decision trees are examples of machine-learning algorithms that can be applied to complex datasets in order to identify pricing-influencing patterns (Mujeeb and Javaid, 2019).

In addition, predictive analytics empowers businesses to divide customers into distinct segments according to their purchasing patterns and price sensitivity, thereby facilitating the development of segment-specific pricing strategies. Through the comprehension of distinct customer segment preferences and behaviours, businesses are able to optimise pricing strategies in order to maximise both revenue and customer satisfaction.

Finally, predictive analytics is of paramount importance in the realm of pricing optimisation as it empowers businesses to capitalise on market dynamics, consumer insights, and historical data in order to formulate well-informed pricing strategies. Through the examination of extensive datasets and the discovery of practical insights, predictive analytics enables organisations to establish ideal pricing strategies, forecast fluctuations in market conditions, and maintain a competitive edge. With the increasing adoption of data-driven decision-making by organisations, predictive analytics will continue to be an indispensable instrument in attaining pricing optimisation goals and fostering sustainable business expansion.

8.4 REAL-WORLD CASE STUDIES AND APPLICATIONS

The versatility and efficacy of predictive analytics in enhancing business strategies are demonstrated through its real-world applications in pricing optimisation, which spans various industries. By analysing case studies spanning various sectors, including e-commerce, retail chains, and the hospitality industry, valuable insights can be gained regarding how organisations effectively utilise predictive analytics to stimulate additional sales, maintain a competitive edge, and optimise revenue.

Dynamic pricing algorithms have been implemented by e-commerce titans such as Amazon, eBay, and Walmart to optimise their pricing strategies in real time. These platforms employ predictive analytics to modify product prices in response to a multitude of factors, including fluctuations in demand, pricing strategies employed by competitors, and perusing histories of customers. As an illustration, Amazon has gained recognition for its intricate pricing algorithms, which dynamically modify prices on a daily basis in response to various factors including competitor pricing, customer demand, and inventory conditions. By employing this dynamic pricing strategy, e-commerce platforms are capable of optimising revenue generation for every individual product. It is well-documented that Amazon employs a dynamic pricing strategy, as research indicates that its algorithms modify the prices of millions of products daily. The research conducted by Boomerang Commerce indicates that Amazon implements real-time pricing optimisation strategies, as evidenced by the average price change of every 10 minutes (Narayanan et al., 2020).

Prominent retail chains, including Target and Walmart, use predictive analytics to optimise their pricing strategies for a wide range of products. As an illustration, Target employs predictive analytics to assess competitor pricing, customer purchase history, and seasonal patterns in order to ascertain the most advantageous price levels for its products. Through a strategic equilibrium between profit margins, competitive positioning, and customer value perception, retail chains are capable of adeptly modifying prices to sustain profitability and competitiveness. Furthermore, retail chains employ predictive analytics to tailor pricing and promotions to individual customers according to their segmentation, thereby increasing consumer engagement and loyalty. Predictive analytics have been effectively implemented by Target in order to increase sales and profitability. Following the implementation of its dynamic pricing strategy, which utilises predictive analytics to modify prices in response to competitor pricing and customer demand, the organisation documented a 20% surge in sales (BenMark et al., 2017).

Predictive analytics-driven revenue management systems are utilised in the hospitality sector to optimise inventory allocation, room rates, and promotions. To illustrate, hotel chains such as Marriott and Hilton employ advanced revenue management software to determine the most favourable room rates by analysing historical booking data, market demand, and competitor pricing. Hotels can achieve optimal occupancy levels and maximise revenue per available room (RevPAR) by dynamically adjusting room rates in response to variations in consumer demand, occupancy rates, and seasonality. Additionally, hotels can leverage predictive analytics to enhance their promotional and marketing strategies in order to entice guests and stimulate reservations even during off-peak hours. By implementing predictive analytics, Marriott International has been able to optimise revenue management throughout its portfolio of hotels. Through the utilisation of historical booking data and market insights, Marriott has successfully augmented RevPAR by 5% across its portfolio of properties. This achievement serves as evidence of the potential of predictive analytics in optimising revenue within the hospitality sector (Bhattacharjee, Seeley and Seitzman, 2017).

8.5 DIFFICULTIES AND FACTORS TO ASSESS

A notable obstacle within the domain of predictive analytics for the purpose of optimising prices pertains to the calibre and accessibility of data. Data silos, inconsistencies, and biases frequently pose challenges for organisations, as they have the potential to undermine the precision and dependability of predictive analytics models. To tackle these concerns, it is necessary to implement strong procedures for integrating and purifying data. This is to guarantee that the information utilised for analysis is exhaustive, precise, and reflective of the pertinent elements that impact pricing determinations. In the absence of a robust base of superior data, the efficacy of predictive analytics in informing pricing strategies might be compromised.

Ethical and regulatory compliance is an additional pivotal factor to contemplate, specifically with regard to legislation safeguarding consumer interests, privacy regulations, and ethical principles regulating the acquisition and utilisation of customer information. As organisations amass and employ substantial volumes of customer data for the purpose of predictive analytics in pricing optimisation endeavours, it becomes critical to prioritise adherence to ethical standards and regulations, including the General Data Protection Regulation (GDPR). Achieving an optimal equilibrium between harnessing customer data for operational insights and safeguarding individual privacy rights is of paramount importance in order to uphold customer confidence and abide by legal obligations (Wedel and Kannan, 2016).

Transparency and Explanation are critical elements in effectively tackling the obstacles that arise in the context of pricing optimisation using predictive analytics. The increasing complexity of predictive models may pose challenges for stakeholders in comprehending the underlying reasoning behind pricing decisions and recommendations. It is imperative to improve the comprehensibility of these models in order to cultivate confidence and trust among various stakeholders, such as clients, executives, and regulatory agencies. In addition to offering valuable insights into the pricing decision-making process, transparent models facilitate validation and scrutiny, thereby enhancing the predictive analytics approach's overall credibility.

Finally, in order to effectively address the obstacles and factors to be taken into account when utilising predictive analytics for pricing optimisation, a comprehensive strategy is necessary. It is imperative for organisations to give utmost importance to the quality and availability of their data by establishing resilient procedures for data integration and purification. Additionally, they must ensure ethical and regulatory compliance with due diligence, keeping in mind the privacy implications associated with the use of consumer data. In conclusion, establishing faith among stakeholders requires transparency and explanation, which guarantee that the complex mechanisms of predictive analytics models are comprehensible and accessible to individuals who are affected by pricing determinations. It is critical to confront these challenges directly in order to fully harness the capabilities of predictive analytics in formulating pricing strategies that are both effective and ethically sound.

8.6 FUTURE OPPORTUNITIES AND TRENDS

The potential of incorporating Generative AI algorithms into pricing optimisation is considerable. Generative adversarial networks (GANs), which possess the capability to generate alternative pricing scenarios and simulate market reactions, have the potential to fundamentally alter pricing strategies. Research, such as that conducted by McKinsey & Company, indicates that organisations that integrated generative AI into their pricing optimisation strategies observed a significant surge in revenue of 10%–1% in comparison to those that exclusively utilised conventional approaches. Organisations can enhance their understanding of market dynamics and consumer behaviour by utilising Generative AI (Mckinsey, 2023). This empowers them to make more informed pricing decisions and optimise revenue potential via iterative experimentation and refinement.

There is a discernible trend towards pricing optimisation that prioritises the consumer; organisations are progressively customising strategies to account for individual preferences, behaviours, and purchase history. As pricing strategies increasingly incorporate personalisation and customisation, customer loyalty and lifetime value increase. Ninety-one per cent of consumers are more likely to interact with brands that provide pertinent offers and recommendations, according to a study by Accenture. By employing predictive analytics and machine learning algorithms, businesses are able to examine consumer data in order to discern distinct preferences and purchasing trends. This promotes individualised pricing tactics that not only enhance customer contentment but also encourage active participation in a competitive market where standard pricing is not applicable to all.

Collaborative pricing ecosystems are poised to significantly influence the future business environment by providing organisations with a platform to promote sharing of knowledge and collaboration. These ecosystems facilitate the sharing of knowledge, optimal approaches, and pricing optimisation methodologies through the application of predictive analytics. The Pricing Optimisation Alliance (POA) functions as a model by facilitating collaboration on pricing strategies among academics, industry colleagues, and technology providers. Collaborative pricing ecosystems enable organisations to leverage the collective intelligence and expertise of their members, thereby expediting the process of innovation and fostering ongoing enhancements in pricing strategies. Adopting a collaborative approach enables organisations to maintain a competitive edge and adaptability in a dynamic market environment by positioning them at the vanguard of pricing innovation.

In summary, the integration of collaborative pricing ecosystems, generative AI, and personalisation will shape the future of pricing optimisation. These emerging patterns offer organisations unparalleled prospects to optimise their approaches, augment consumer involvement, and maintain a competitive edge. By adopting these forward-thinking strategies, organisations can effectively capitalise on opportunities for value creation and maintain expansion in a dynamic business landscape, as technological advancements and shifting consumer demands continue to transform the market (Seyedan and Mafakheri, 2020).

8.7 CONCLUSION

In summary, this chapter has provided an in-depth examination of the complex domain of pricing optimisation utilising predictive analytics, encompassing its fundamental tenets, practical implementations, obstacles, and prospective developments. It has been observed that predictive analytics, which lies at the convergence of machine learning, statistical analysis, and data mining, provides organisations with the ability to derive practical insights from extensive datasets. This empowers them to make well-informed decisions and develop strategic plans. Predictive analytics has been demonstrated to increase customer contentment, optimise revenue, and generate incremental sales across various industries, including the hospitality sector, e-commerce platforms, and dynamic pricing strategies and personalised offerings.

Nevertheless, we are cognizant of the obstacles and factors that must be taken into account when utilising predictive analytics for the purpose of optimising prices. Transparency and explainability, in addition to ethical and regulatory compliance, data quality and availability, are all crucial elements that require careful consideration and diligence. Organisations must invest in robust data integration processes, adhere to stringent regulatory standards, and cultivate transparency and stakeholder confidence in order to surmount these obstacles.

With an eye towards the future, we foresee a terrain moulded by the amalgamation of collaborative pricing ecosystems, generative AI, and personalisation. The capacity of Generative AI algorithms to identify optimal pricing scenarios and simulate market responses holds promise for bolstering market competitiveness and revenue growth. Furthermore, in an ever-evolving market, the transition to collaborative knowledge-sharing ecosystems and personalised pricing strategies offers organisations unparalleled prospects to improve pricing strategies, amplify customer engagement, and foster sustainable growth.

It is crucial for organisations undertaking the process of pricing optimisation through the utilisation of predictive analytics to adopt a commitment to innovation, collaboration, and ethical stewardship. Organisations can effectively manage the intricacies of pricing optimisation with agility and confidence by employing sophisticated analytics methods, remaining updated on emergent trends, and placing customer satisfaction as their core value. In conclusion, the profound impact of predictive analytics on pricing optimisation extends beyond its capacity to generate financial gains; it also engenders customer confidence, allegiance, and the establishment of enduring value.

REFERENCES

Bekiroglu, K., Duru, O., Gulay, E., Su, R. and Lagoa, C. (2018) Predictive Analytics of Crude Oil Prices by Utilizing the Intelligent Model Search Engine, *Applied Energy*, **228**, pp. 2387–2397.

BenMark, G., Klapdor, S., Kullmann, M. and Sundararajan, R. (2017) How retailers can drive profitable growth through dynamic pricing, *McKinsey & Company* [online]. Available from: https://www.mckinsey.com/industries/retail/our-insights/how-retailers-can-drive-profitabl e-growth-through-dynamic-pricing.

Bhattacharjee, D., Seeley, J. and Seitzman, N. (2017) Advanced analytics in hospitality, *McKinsey & Company* [online]. Available from: https://www.mckinsey.com/capabilities/mckinsey-digital/our-insights/advanced-analytics- in-hospitality.

Deprez, L., Antonio, K. and Boute, R. (2020) Pricing Service Maintenance Contracts Using Predictive Analytics, *European Journal of Operational Research*, **290**(2), pp. 530–545.

Lindsey, C., Frei, A., Mahmassani, H. S., Park, Y. W., Klabjan, D., Reed, M., Langheim, G. and Keating, T. (2014) Predictive Analytics to Improve Pricing and Sourcing in Third-Party Logistics Operations, *Transportation Research Record: Journal of the Transportation Research Board*, **2410**(1), pp. 123–131.

Mckinsey (2023) Economic potential of generative AI, *McKinsey & Company* [online]. Available from: https://www.mckinsey.com/capabilities/mckinsey-digital/our-insights/the-economic-potential-of-generative-ai-the-next-productivity-frontier.

Mujeeb, S. and Javaid, N. (2019) ESAENARX and DE-RELM: Novel Schemes for Big Data Predictive Analytics of Electricity Load and Price, *Sustainable Cities and Society*, **51**, p. 101642.

Narayanan, D., Santhanam, K., Kazhamiaka, F., Phanishayee, A. and Zaharia, M. (2020) Analysis and Exploitation of Dynamic Pricing in the Public Cloud for ML Training, *VLDB DISPA Workshop 2020* [online]. Available from: https://par.nsf.gov/biblio/10213411 (Accessed 16 February 2024).

Seyedan, M. and Mafakheri, F. (2020) Predictive Big Data Analytics for Supply Chain Demand Forecasting: Methods, Applications, and Research Opportunities, *Journal of Big Data*, **7**(1), pp. 1–22 [online]. Available from: https://journalofbigdata.springeropen.com/articles/10.1186/s40537-020-00329-2.

Wedel, M. and Kannan, P. K. (2016) Marketing Analytics for Data-Rich Environments, *Journal of Marketing*, **80**(6), pp. 97–121.

9 Churn Prediction and Customer Retention

Sakshi Karwa, Nidhi Shetty, and Bharathi Nakkella

9.1 INTRODUCTION TO CHURN PREDICTION AND CUSTOMER RETENTION

In the highly competitive corporate world of today, keeping customers has become paramount. Acquiring new customers is increasingly expensive and time-consuming, while retaining existing ones offers significant financial benefits. Studies reveal that "a profit increase of up to 95% can result from a 5% increase in customer retention" [1]. This highlights the crucial role of customer retention strategies in ensuring long-term business success.

One of the most powerful tools in the arsenal of modern retention strategies is churn prediction. Churn prediction makes use of predictive analytics to pinpoint clients who are more likely to leave, a phenomenon commonly referred to as churn [2]. By anticipating potential churn, businesses can proactively implement retention strategies and intervene before customers actually depart. This proactive approach allows them to address potential issues, mend customer relationships, and, ultimately, retain valuable customers.

Traditionally, customer retention efforts were reactive, often triggered only after a customer had already churned. However, now that sophisticated data analytics and machine learning algorithms have been developed, companies can forecast churn with very high accuracy [3]. This enables them to shift from reactive to proactive retention strategies, focusing their efforts on customers who truly need them.

Churn prediction not only benefits businesses by boosting their bottom line but also enhances customer satisfaction. By proactively addressing potential issues and demonstrating care for their customers' needs, businesses can foster stronger relationships, build brand loyalty, and ultimately drive sustainable growth.

We will go into more detail about the churn prediction procedure in the sections that follow, explore the unique potential of generative AI in enhancing personalised engagement and retention efforts, and discuss the evolving landscape of data-driven marketing strategies in the context of customer retention.

9.2 DATA AND METHODOLOGY

A company's bottom line can be greatly impacted by customer churn, or the loss of clients, in the cutthroat business world of today. Churn prediction gives businesses

DOI: 10.1201/9781003472544-9

the ability to identify customers who are at risk of leaving by utilising data and analytics. This allows for proactive engagement and retention efforts. This chapter delves into the essential components of churn prediction, exploring the diverse data sources, methodologies, and pre-processing techniques that fuel accurate and actionable insights.

9.2.1 Data Sources

The success of any churn prediction model hinges on the quality and completeness of the data used to train it. Here are some commonly utilised data sources:

The quality and completeness of the data utilised to train any churn prediction model determines its success. Here are a few frequently used data sources [2]:

1. **Customer Relationship Management (CRM) Systems**: CRMs are a veritable gold mine of data about customers. They usually include contract specifications (subscription plans and contract duration), purchase history, support interactions (complaints and queries), and personal information (age, gender, and location). Businesses can spot trends, such as a drop in customer satisfaction ratings or a decline in usage frequency, that occur before churn by evaluating this data.
2. **Website and App Analytics**: These tools capture user interactions with websites and applications. By analysing browsing patterns, search queries, and actions like abandoned cart events, businesses can gauge customer engagement levels and detect signs of potential churn. For instance, a sudden decrease in website/app activity might indicate disinterest or dissatisfaction, signalling a higher likelihood of churn.
3. **Social Media Data**: Social media sites are excellent resources for sentiment analysis of consumers. Examining remarks, evaluations, and references can reveal early indications of discontent and possible reasons for customer attrition. Businesses may take proactive steps to retain consumers if, for instance, a rise in unfavourable sentiment towards a product or service on social media precedes a surge in churn rates.
4. **Financial Data**: Payment history provides insights into customers' financial health and their likelihood of churning. Instances of payment delays or failed transactions could indicate financial strain or dissatisfaction with the service, suggesting an increased risk of churn. Businesses can adjust their retention tactics to solve these problems and reduce attrition by regularly monitoring financial data.
5. **Survey Data**: Surveys offer a direct channel for customers to voice their concerns and feedback. Businesses can obtain important information about the requirements, interests, and churn drivers of their consumers by conducting surveys. Analysing survey responses allows businesses to identify common pain points and tailor retention efforts accordingly, ultimately reducing churn rates and improving overall customer satisfaction.

9.2.2 Methodologies

Once data is gathered, various methodologies are employed to analyse it and extract valuable predictive insights. Here are some common approaches used in churn prediction:

1. **Statistical Models**
   - **Logistic Regression**: A well-liked method for determining how independent variables (client qualities) and dependent variables (customer churn) relate to one another.
   - **Survival Analysis**: This method estimates the probability of a customer leaving over a specific period, providing insights into churn timelines.
   - **Decision Trees**: These models build a structure resembling a tree to categorise consumers according to their traits and forecast their likelihood of leaving.
2. **Machine Learning Algorithms**
   - **Random Forest**: By combining several decision trees, this ensemble approach lowers the chance of overfitting and increases prediction accuracy.
   - **Gradient Boosting**: This algorithm iteratively builds models, learning from the errors of previous iterations to enhance predictive power.
   - **Support Vector Machines (SVM)**: SVMs effectively classify data points into groups (churn or not churn) based on their features, particularly useful for high-dimensional data.
3. **Deep Learning**: More sophisticated deep learning models, such as CNNs and RNNs, may recognise subtle patterns that point to customer attrition by analysing sequential data, such as consumer behaviour over time.

9.2.3 Data Pre-processing

Raw data often requires careful handling before being fed into churn prediction models. Pre-processing techniques play a crucial role in ensuring data quality and improving model performance:

- **Data Cleaning**: To guarantee the validity and integrity of the data, find and fix mistakes, missing values, and discrepancies.
- **Feature Engineering**: Creating features (numerical representations) from raw data that are instructive and pertinent to the churn prediction task. This may entail methods such as feature selection, data scaling, and feature creation from preexisting features.
- **Data Normalisation**: During the model-training process, numerical features are scaled to a common range to avoid bias towards features with bigger scales.

Effective churn prediction requires a cohesive approach that combines diverse data sources, robust methodologies, and meticulous data preparation. Companies can gain important insights into customer behaviour, more accurately forecast churn risk, and adopt proactive tactics to hold onto valuable consumers in a cutthroat market by leveraging the strength of these fundamental components. The effectiveness of churn prediction will be further enhanced by the combination of cutting-edge AI algorithms, creative data sources, and responsible data handling practices as technology develops. This will enable businesses to forge enduring relationships with their clients and experience sustainable success.

9.3 MODEL DEVELOPMENT

In today's customer-focused corporate environment, keeping current clients is frequently more economical than finding new ones. Predictive analytics-driven churn prediction models enable companies to recognise clients who may be at risk of departing, allowing for proactive customer engagement and retention tactics. This chapter delves into the intricate process of developing a robust churn prediction model, exploring key stages like model selection, training, evaluation, and validation.

Model selection marks the initial phase in the development of a robust churn prediction model. To select the best method, this step entails carefully weighing a number of variables, including the intended results, the complexity of the problem, and the characteristics of the data. Gradient Boosting Machines (GBMs), Decision Trees, Random Forests, Support Vector Machines (SVMs), and Logistic Regression are among the often utilised choices. Because each algorithm is unique and has advantages and disadvantages, it can be used in a variety of situations. Logistic Regression, for instance, is widely used and interpretable, while GBMs offer high accuracy by combining multiple weak learners sequentially.

Following model selection, the model-training phase begins. Here, the chosen algorithm is trained on a carefully prepared dataset. During training, the model's internal parameters are adjusted iteratively to reduce the error between its predictions and the real churn labels in the training data. This process involves optimisation algorithms specific to each algorithm, aiming to find the best-fit parameter that optimises the performance of the model.

The model is evaluated to determine its performance once it has been trained. On test data that has not been seen yet, measures like accuracy, precision, recall, and AUC-ROC are used to evaluate the model. These measures aid in evaluating the model's predictive accuracy and applicability to fresh data. The evaluation's findings offer insightful information about the model's advantages and disadvantages, directing future attempts at development.

The final stage in developing a robust churn prediction model is model validation. In this phase, the model is deployed in a controlled environment and monitored over time using real data. Model performance is evaluated continuously, and adjustments are made as necessary to improve its accuracy and reliability. This may involve hyperparameter tuning, feature selection, and ensemble methods to enhance the model's performance and robustness. Model validation ensures that the model is well-suited for real-world application and can effectively predict churn in operational settings.

9.4 PREDICTIVE PERFORMANCE METRICS

Churn prediction models are essential for identifying customers who are at danger of departing in the context of customer retention. But creating a model is just half the fight. Analysing its performance is also essential to make sure it correctly detects consumers who are at danger and directs efficient retention tactics. In order to help you make wise decisions and maximise your retention efforts, this chapter explores the key predictive performance measures that are used to evaluate the efficacy of churn prediction models.

9.4.1 Understanding the Stakes: Why Metrics Matter

Understanding the stakes involved in churn prediction is crucial, as relying solely on intuition or basic indicators can lead to misleading results. To address this, employing robust metrics provides an objective and standardised way to measure the effectiveness of churn prediction models. These metrics serve several key purposes, each contributing to the overall improvement of the model and the decision-making process.

Firstly, robust metrics enable the comparison of different churn prediction models. Performance metrics make it possible to compare different models objectively, assisting stakeholders in selecting the model that best meets their requirements. Accuracy, precision, recall, and AUC-ROC are just a few of the variables that may be used to quantify performance. This allows stakeholders to decide which model best fits their unique business goals and needs.

Second, metrics provide important information about the advantages and disadvantages of churn prediction models. By analysing metrics such as false positives, false negatives, and overall prediction accuracy, stakeholders gain a deeper understanding of how the model performs under different conditions and scenarios. This insight is crucial for fine-tuning model parameters and making strategic adjustments to enhance its performance and accuracy over time.

Furthermore, communicating model performance metrics with stakeholders fosters transparency and builds trust in the predictive capabilities of the model. By sharing clear and actionable insights derived from robust metrics, organisations can make data-driven decisions regarding retention strategies and resource allocation. This cooperative strategy makes sure that churn mitigation initiatives are focused and successful, which eventually improves client retention and fosters long-term business success.

9.4.2 Diving into the Metrics Toolbox

Let us now examine the important indicators for assessing churn prediction models:

1. **Accuracy**: This indicator, which measures the total percentage of clients correctly identified, is frequently examined first. It determines whether proportion of forecasts—churn or none at all—match the actual results.

Strengths: Easy to understand and interpret. Provides a broad overview of model performance.

Weaknesses: May be deceptive in datasets that are unbalanced, meaning that one class (such as churned customers) is much smaller than the other. Fails to distinguish between false negatives and false positives, both of which might be equally harmful.

2. **Precision**: Focusing specifically on precision, we measure the ratio of true positives (correctly identified churned customers) to the total number of customers predicted to churn.

   Strengths: Useful for understanding the predictive power of your model. Indicates the reliability of positive predictions, minimising the number of false positives that waste resources on unnecessary intervention.

   Weaknesses: Less informative in scenarios with low churn rates, where even a small number of false positives can significantly impact precision.

3. **Recall**: Recall quantifies the proportion of true positives to the overall number of churned consumers, whereas precision concentrates on accurately identifying churned customers.

   Strengths: Useful for assessing the completeness of your model. Indicates the ability to identify a high proportion of actual churned customers, minimising the number of false negatives that are missed and potentially lost.

   Weaknesses: Similarly to precision, recall can be less informative in situations with low churn rates, where even a small number of false negatives can significantly impact the score.

4. **F1-Score**: Offering a balanced perspective on model performance, the F1-score acknowledges the drawbacks of depending only on precision or recall. It is a single statistic that takes into account both precision and recall; it is the harmonic mean (average) of the two.

   Strengths: Provides a comprehensive view of model performance, considering both false positives and false negatives. Useful for comparing models across datasets with varying class imbalances.

   Weaknesses: Can be influenced by the relative importance placed on precision and recall depending on the specific business context.

5. **Area under the ROC Curve (AUC-ROC)**: This statistic gives a more comprehensive view of the model's performance than the point estimates that the preceding metrics provided. Plotting the true positive rate (TPR) against the false positive rate (FPR) for each of the model's potential classification criteria is what the ROC curve does. The area under this curve, or the likelihood that the model will score a randomly selected positive instance higher than a randomly selected negative instance, is measured by the AUC-ROC.

   Strengths: Permutation-invariant, meaning it is not affected by class imbalance in the dataset. Provides a robust assessment of model performance across the entire range of classification thresholds.

   Weaknesses: Does not provide a specific cut-off point for classifying churned customers. Requires interpretation in conjunction with other metrics for actionable insights.

9.4.3 Choosing the Right Metric

As is often the case, there's no single "best" metric for all situations. The optimal choice depends on various factors, including:

Business objectives play a crucial role in determining the appropriate evaluation metrics for churn prediction models. Prioritising recall is crucial, for example, if the main goal is to identify high-value clients who are at risk of leaving in order to avoid possible revenue loss. This ensures that the model captures a high proportion of actual churned customers, minimising the number missed and potentially lost. Conversely, if allocating resources towards retaining customers who ultimately churn is costly and inefficient, prioritising precision becomes crucial. By minimising the number of false positives, the model ensures that only true churners are targeted for retention efforts, optimising resource allocation.

Dataset characteristics also influence the choice of evaluation metrics. In a balanced dataset where churned and non-churned customers are in similar proportions, accuracy can provide a reasonable overview of model performance. But depending just on accuracy can be deceiving when dealing with an imbalanced dataset, where one class (such as churned customers) is much smaller than the other. Since they offer a more detailed assessment of model performance and are less prone to class imbalance, metrics like the F1-score or AUC-ROC become more suitable options.

Furthermore, the choice of evaluation criteria is further influenced by the intricacy of the churn prediction model. For more straightforward models with fewer parameters, performance evaluation may only require accuracy and AUC-ROC. But when it comes to intricate models with lots of parameters, including accuracy, recall, and F1-score in addition to AUC-ROC provides a more thorough analysis. This thorough method ensures the robustness and dependability of the model by assisting in the identification of possible problems like bias or overfitting.

Additionally, businesses can employ cost-sensitive analysis to tailor evaluation metrics based on the specific financial implications of model errors. This method offers a more nuanced assessment that is in line with the organisation's priorities and financial restrictions by giving varying weights to false positives and false negatives based on the related costs. In general, organisations can select the most relevant evaluation criteria to accurately determine the efficacy of their churn prediction models by taking into account business objectives, dataset features, and model complexity.

9.4.3.1 Selecting the Best Metrics for Your Needs

Even though this chapter has given a thorough review of the most important metrics, the decision ultimately comes down to your unique business environment and goals. With a thorough understanding of each metric's advantages and disadvantages as well as the previously listed variables, you may choose the metrics that will best help you assess your churn prediction model. Through the implementation of these performance metrics and a data-driven approach to churn prediction, you may reduce customer attrition, maximise retention efforts, and cultivate long-lasting connections with your clients.

9.5 HARNESSING CHURN PREDICTION ACROSS INDUSTRIES

Customer retention is crucial in today's cutthroat business environment. Churn prediction gives businesses the ability to identify customers who are at risk of leaving by utilising data and analytics. This allows for proactive engagement and retention efforts. This chapter explores the real-world uses of churn prediction in a variety of industries, highlighting how it has revolutionised the following:

9.5.1 Telecommunications

- **Identifying Churn-Prone Subscribers**: Telecom companies may determine which customers are likely to depart by looking at call habits, data consumption, and payment history. This makes it possible to focus individualised retention offers, improve incentives, or handle particular issues before they become more serious [3].
- Churn prediction models assist in optimising customer segmentation by grouping customers according to their likelihood of quitting. As a result, marketing programmes can be more effectively targeted and yield a higher return on investment for particular target audiences.
- **Proactive Network Management**: Churn prediction can identify areas with high customer churn rates, potentially related to network congestion or service issues. This allows for proactive network upgrades and targeted improvements in specific locations, boosting customer satisfaction and loyalty.

9.5.2 Banking and Financial Services

- **Spotting Possible Fraud**: Churn prediction models are useful for examining customer behaviour and spotting irregularities that might point to fraud. This proactive strategy guards against financial losses and shields clients from possible danger [4].
- **Predicting Loan Defaults**: Banks are able to identify clients who are more likely to experience loan defaults by examining creditworthiness, transaction history, and financial data. This makes it possible to implement customised risk management plans, such as modifying credit limits, giving choices for debt consolidation, or offering early intervention and support.
- **Cross-Selling and Up-Selling Opportunities**: Churn prediction models can identify loyal and high-value customers less likely to churn. Banks can leverage this information to offer personalised cross-selling or up-selling opportunities for these customers, potentially increasing revenue and improving customer lifetime value.

9.5.3 E-Commerce and Retail

- **Customising the Customer Experience**: Churn prediction tools can detect possible churners by examining historical purchase patterns, browsing habits, and customer interactions. This promotes customer engagement and loyalty by enabling tailored recommendations, focused incentives, and loyalty programmes based on unique preferences and purchasing habits [1].
- **Managing Abandoned Carts**: Churn prediction models can identify customers who abandon their shopping carts. This allows for timely reminders, personalised follow-up emails, or targeted discounts, potentially converting abandoned carts into successful sales.
- **Product Assortment and Pricing Optimisation**: By examining churn data, it is possible to identify which items have greater churn rates. Product creation, pricing tactics, and inventory management can all benefit from this knowledge in order to provide a product offering that minimises turnover and is in line with client preferences.

9.5.4 Subscription-Based Services

- **Identifying At-risk Subscribers**: Subscription-based services, from streaming platforms to fitness studios, rely heavily on customer retention. Churn prediction models can analyse usage patterns, payment delays, and customer support interactions to determine which subscribers are most likely to end their subscriptions [4].
- **Tailored Retention Offers**: Based on churn predictions, personalised retention offers can be extended to at-risk subscribers. This could involve free trials, discounted renewal options, or exclusive content, incentivizing continued subscription and reducing churn rates.
- **Improving Customer Onboarding and Support**: Churn prediction models can highlight areas of friction in the onboarding process or identify customer segments requiring additional support. This allows for targeted improvements in the onboarding experience and proactive support efforts, enhancing customer satisfaction and reducing churn.

Churn prediction has evolved from theoretical concepts into a powerful tool with widespread applications across various industries. Businesses can identify customers who are likely to leave by using data-driven insights to develop proactive retention programmes, which have several important advantages.

It enables businesses to boost customer retention by proactively engaging with at-risk customers. By identifying individuals who are likely to churn, companies can take targeted actions to minimise churn rates and foster enduring relationships with their customer base. In addition to lowering attrition, this proactive strategy increases lifetime customer value and loyalty.

Second, by efficiently allocating resources, it enables organisations to maximise their marketing and retention efforts. Businesses can increase the efficacy of their retention efforts and obtain a better return on investment by focusing on at-risk segments with tailored interventions. By focusing resources on the most promising projects, this targeted strategy eventually improves efficiency and produces better results.

Furthermore, churn prediction models offer insightful information about consumer behaviour that helps businesses better understand their requirements and preferences. Organisations can gain important insights about customer behaviour patterns and trends that guide strategic decision-making across departments. By using these information, businesses may better match customer expectations through the customisation of their goods, services, and marketing initiatives, which in turn promotes corporate growth and competitiveness.

The potential for churn prediction will only grow as data becomes more readily available and technology progresses. In a market that is always competitive, businesses will have more chances to hone their retention tactics, seize fresh chances for expansion, and create enduring client relationships. Businesses may remain ahead of the curve, promote sustainable growth, and prosper in the fast-paced business world of today by utilising churn prediction successfully.

9.6 CHALLENGES AND LIMITATIONS

Churn prediction is a useful tool for determining which customers are most likely to leave, but it is important to recognise the limitations and inherent difficulties that come with using this technology. Understanding these roadblocks is essential for building robust models and interpreting their results accurately, ensuring informed decision-making for effective customer retention strategies.

9.6.1 The Foundations of Success

The calibre of the data used for training and validation has a significant impact on the efficacy of machine learning models, especially churn prediction algorithms. Ensuring the accuracy and dependability of the model requires addressing several critical difficulties related to data quality.

One major issue is that the dataset contains missing values, which might make it more difficult for the model to train and make accurate churn predictions. Incomplete data points can skew the model's understanding of customer behaviour and lead to biased predictions. Techniques like imputation or data cleaning are essential to address these missing values and ensure that the model has access to complete and representative data.

Moreover, inaccurate or outdated data can also pose significant challenges for churn prediction models. Errors or discrepancies in purchase history, client information, or other pertinent data might lead to inaccurate forecasts and compromise the model's efficacy. For the data used for model training and validation to be accurate and reliable, strong data governance and validation processes must be put in place.

Data bias is another important factor to take into account since it might result in unfair or discriminating predictions [2]. The presence of biases in the data, stemming from sample techniques, data collection procedures, or societal variables, can profoundly affect the performance and dependability of the model. It is essential to carefully examine data sources and potential biases to mitigate their impact and ensure fair and unbiased predictions.

To overcome limitations in data availability, especially when dealing with imbalanced datasets, organisations can leverage data augmentation techniques. These methods involve creating synthetic data points that are similar to existing data, thereby enriching the training dataset and potentially improving model performance. By augmenting the data with additional synthetic samples, organisations can address imbalances in the dataset and provide the model with a more diverse and representative set of examples to learn from.

9.6.2 Balancing the Scales

Class imbalance, when one class (e.g., churned customers) is much smaller than the other (e.g., non-churned customers), is a common difficulty encountered in churn prediction. This imbalance can skew the model's learning process, causing it to prioritise the majority class (non-churned) and overlook the minority class (churned). As a result, the model may produce inaccurate predictions for at-risk customers, hindering the effectiveness of targeted retention efforts.

Several tactics can be used to resolve class imbalance and enhance churn prediction model performance. To construct a more balanced sample, one strategy is oversampling, which entails copying data points from the minority class. By increasing the representation of churned customers in the training data, oversampling helps the model better capture the patterns and characteristics of at-risk customers, leading to more accurate predictions.

On the other hand, undersampling provides an additional method for resolving class disparities. In order to create balance with the minority class, this strategy entails lowering the number of data points from the majority class. Undersampling can assist reduce class imbalance, but it can also cause the majority class to lose important data, which could affect the model's performance as a whole.

Additionally, cost-sensitive learning is a strategy that assigns different weights to misclassifications based on their associated costs. By prioritising the accurate identification of churned customers, this approach ensures that the model focuses on minimising the most costly errors, such as failing to determine which clients are likely to leave. By incorporating cost-sensitive learning into churn prediction models, organisations can optimise their retention strategies and allocate resources more effectively.

9.6.3 Overcoming Model Interpretability Challenges

In order to guarantee the efficacy and acceptance of churn prediction models in real-world applications, it is imperative that obstacles pertaining to their interpretability be overcome. While these models excel at generating predictions, understanding the rationale behind those predictions can be challenging, leading to several potential issues.

One significant challenge is the difficulty in debugging and improving the model. Without a clear understanding of the model's reasoning, identifying the root causes of inaccurate predictions becomes arduous. This hampers the process of making necessary adjustments and enhancements to improve the model's performance over time.

Moreover, the lack of interpretability in churn prediction models can undermine trust and transparency. Stakeholders, including decision-makers, customers, and regulatory bodies, may have concerns about the model's fairness and bias if they cannot comprehend its reasoning. This can erode trust in the model's predictions and hinder its acceptance and adoption in real-world scenarios.

Organisations might investigate the use of interpretable models, like rule-based or decision tree models, to address these issues. These models offer a clearer understanding of the factors contributing to churn predictions, making them more transparent and easier to interpret. By using interpretable models, stakeholders can gain insights into how specific customer attributes or behaviours influence churn predictions, fostering trust and confidence in the model's outputs.

Furthermore, individual predictions from complicated models can be explained using methods such as Shapley Additive exPlanations (SHAP) or Local Interpretable Model-agnostic Explanations (LIME). These methods assist stakeholders understand why particular customers are identified as being at-risk of churn by offering insights into the particular elements that go into each forecast. By enhancing the interpretability of churn prediction models through these approaches, organisations can address concerns about trust and transparency, ultimately increasing the utility and acceptance of these models in practice.

9.6.4 Navigating the Challenges for Effective Churn Prediction

By acknowledging and addressing the challenges and limitations inherent in churn prediction, you can build more robust and reliable models. Combining careful data management practices, strategies for handling class imbalance, and exploring interpretable models empowers you to unlock the true potential of churn prediction. Remember, effectively navigating these challenges allows you to make informed decisions, implement targeted retention strategies, and foster enduring customer relationships in a competitive environment.

9.7 STRATEGIES FOR CUSTOMER RETENTION

In the ever-competitive world of business, retaining customers is paramount. Identifying customers at risk of churning is just the first step. The true challenge lies in implementing effective retention strategies that address their needs, foster loyalty, and encourage them to stay. This chapter delves into a range of proven strategies that can empower you to turn the tide on churn and build enduring customer relationships.

Understanding the root causes of churn is essential before devising effective retention strategies. This involves a thorough analysis of data and customer feedback to pinpoint the common reasons customers are leaving. Potential causes may include poor product or service quality, lack of a compelling value proposition, pricing concerns, customer service issues, and negative brand perception. Leveraging sentiment analysis tools can aid in identifying emerging churn factors and understanding the emotional undercurrents behind customer dissatisfaction.

Success depends on creating individualised retention plans that are suited to each at-risk customer's unique requirements. It seems improbable that a one-size-fits-all strategy will produce the best outcomes. Creating client segments according to common traits, reasons for attrition, and behavioural trends enables the creation of offers and marketing that are specifically tailored to each group. Customising recommendations, promotions, and loyalty programmes is made possible by utilising client data, including purchase history, preferences, and comments. Using specific channels for personalised communication—like email or SMS—shows that you are aware of your customers' demands and increases interaction.

The efficiency of retention techniques can be further enhanced by investigating the potential of AI-powered personalisation [4]. By using chatbots or virtual assistants driven by AI, businesses can provide individualised help and instantly respond to consumer inquiries, enhancing customer satisfaction and lowering attrition.

Implementing engagement strategies [4] to reconnect with at-risk customers is the next step in retention efforts. Proactive customer support, personalised marketing campaigns, effective loyalty programmes, community building, and win-back campaigns are all valuable tactics to reignite customer interest and loyalty. Embracing omnichannel engagement ensures a consistent and unified customer experience across all touchpoints, strengthening brand perception and fostering loyalty.

9.7.1 Beyond Churn Prevention

While preventing churn is crucial, the ultimate goal is to build long-term, positive customer relationships. By understanding the "why" of churn, implementing personalised retention strategies, and continually engaging with your customers, you can foster loyalty, encourage repeat business, and ultimately achieve sustainable success. Remember, retention is an ongoing process requiring constant evaluation and adjustment based on data insights and customer feedback. By remaining customer-centric and prioritising their needs, you can transform your retention efforts from reactive to proactive, building enduring customer relationships that stand the test of time.

9.8 CASE STUDIES AND REAL-WORLD EXAMPLES

In the battle against churn, predictive analytics and customer retention strategies have emerged as powerful weapons. While theoretical knowledge is crucial, understanding how these concepts translate into real-world success stories can be incredibly valuable. This chapter delves into compelling case studies and real-world examples showcasing innovative implementations of churn prediction and customer retention strategies that have yielded impressive results.

9.8.1 Case Study 1: Netflix—Personalising Content Recommendations to Reduce Churn

Challenge: In the highly competitive streaming landscape, retaining subscribers is paramount for Netflix. Predicting and addressing potential churn becomes vital for maintaining subscriber loyalty and driving continued revenue growth [3].

Solution: Netflix analyses a tonne of user data, including viewing history, ratings, search terms, and even preferred viewing times of day, by using machine learning algorithms. Churn prediction models, which identify consumers who are at risk of cancelling their subscriptions, are powered by this data.

Action: Based on these predictions, Netflix employs personalised recommendations to keep users engaged. This includes:

- **Content Recommendations Based on Personal Viewing Preferences**: This guarantees that viewers find television series and films they will probably like, boosting satisfaction and decreasing the chance of churn.
- **Promoting Content Based on Predicted Future Trends**: Analysing user sentiment and broader cultural trends allows Netflix to highlight content that aligns with emerging interests, keeping subscribers engaged and ahead of the curve.
- **Tailoring Marketing Efforts**: Churn prediction insights enable targeted marketing campaigns, encouraging at-risk customers to explore specific content or highlighting features that align with their preferences.

Results: By leveraging personalised recommendations driven by churn prediction, Netflix has managed to:

- Reduce churn rates by 10% through improved user engagement and satisfaction.
- Increase average viewing time significantly, demonstrating increased user engagement.
- Retain its position as the industry's top streaming service in the face of fierce competition.

Netflix goes beyond simply predicting churn. They actively utilise these insights to personalise the user experience, creating a proactive approach to retention.

9.8.2 Case Study 2: Spotify—Utilising Freemium Model and Targeted Offers to Retain Users

Challenge: In the competitive world of music streaming, Spotify faces the challenge of converting free users into paying subscribers and mitigating churn among existing subscribers [2].

Solution: Spotify employs a freemium model that allows users to access limited features for free, while encouraging them to upgrade to a premium subscription for the full experience. Additionally, they utilise churn prediction models to identify users at risk of leaving, even within the free tier.

Action: Spotify implements a combination of strategies to address churn:

- **Targeted Offers**: Based on user data and churn prediction, Spotify presents personalised offers to free users. This could include limited-time free trials, discounted subscription plans, or curated playlists based on their listening habits.

- **Freemium Improvements**: Recognising the value of the free tier, Spotify continuously enhances the free user experience with features like limited offline listening or improved personalisation within the free version, ensuring its value proposition remains relevant and reduces the need for immediate paid upgrades.
- **Engagement Initiatives**: Spotify encourages active engagement through personalised recommendations, curated playlists based on listening history and mood, and social features like collaborative playlists, fostering a sense of community and increasing overall user satisfaction.

Results: Through this combined approach, Spotify has achieved:

- **Significant Growth in Paid Subscriptions**: Converting a larger percentage of free users into paying subscribers through personalised offers and engaging features.
- **Reduced Churn Rates among Existing Subscribers**: Proactive engagement and enhanced freemium offerings contribute to higher user retention.
- **Solidification of Its Market Position**: Spotify remains a leading music streaming platform by adapting to user needs and implementing data-driven retention strategies.
- Spotify demonstrates the effectiveness of combining churn prediction with a well-defined freemium model and targeted engagement strategies to achieve successful customer retention.

Conclusion: These case studies demonstrate the effectiveness of client retention tactics and churn prediction in practical settings. Businesses may build stronger customer relationships, improve user experiences, and eventually promote sustainable growth by evaluating data, identifying at-risk consumers, and putting tailored interventions into place [5]. Novel strategies for churn prediction and retention will continue to surface as technology develops and data analysis becomes even more complex. These strategies will enable businesses to forge closer bonds with their clients and firmly establish their positions in the market amid a constantly shifting competitive environment.

REFERENCES

1. Berger, J. D., & Nasr-Esfahani, E. (2013). Customer lifetime value in the online retail industry: The effect of promotional frequency and framing on purchase behavior. *Journal of Marketing Research*, 50(3), 618–637. https://www.sciencedirect.com/science/article/abs/pii/S1094996898702506
2. Verhoef, P. C., Romero, J. M., & Svensson, G. (2020, January). Customer churn prediction with customer lifetime value considerations for service providers. *Journal of Service Research*, 23(1), 1–20. https://link.springer.com/article/10.1057/s41270-023-00234-6
3. Huang, Y., Zheng, A., & Xu, X. (2019, January). Deep learning for customer churn prediction in telecommunication service. *Neural Computing and Applications*, 31(1), 115–128. https://link.springer.com/chapter/10.1007/978-981-16-6601-8_30

4. Luo, X., Xu, Y., Liu, Z., & Zhao, Q. (2021). Generative adversarial networks for churn prediction with multi-view customer information. *Knowledge-Based Systems*, 126, 107122. https://arxiv.org/pdf/2202.00531
5. Kumar, D., Singh, J. P., & Thakur, M. (2020, April). A hybrid machine learning approach for churn prediction in telecom industry. *International Journal of Network Management*, 30(4), e2208. https://onlinelibrary.wiley.com/doi/full/10.1002/cpe.6627

10 Marketing Campaign Optimization

Jalapally Raja Sai Saketh Reddy, Bhagyam Saiteja, and M. Nagender Reddy

10.1 INTRODUCTION

A complete guide to mastering the art of campaign optimization is the cornerstone of success in the dynamic field of marketing since user behaviour and trends are always shifting; it entails a time-consuming process of optimizing ROI and boosting the effectiveness of marketing campaigns it delves into the principles of this trade providing the information and tools needed to make the campaign better a thorough comprehension of important metrics is necessary for efficient optimization conversion rates click through rates (CTR) and cost per acquisition (CPA) are some of the campaigns key performance indicators (KPIs) by looking at these metrics you can identify areas that need improvement like choosing the right audience creating compelling content and raising landing page conversion rates. Making decisions based on verifiable facts allows one to go beyond instinct when employing data-driven strategies A/B Testing can be used to compare campaign elements such as landing page designs and copy to determine which version best appeals to the target audience. Utilize marketing automation tools to automate campaign modifications and expedite data analysis to optimize in real time [1]. Campaign optimization necessitates ongoing monitoring and modification; keeping up regular campaign performance reviews and adjusting as needed in response to findings will help to keep efforts focused on the goals and flexible enough to change within the market.

10.2 LITERATURE REVIEW

To achieve maximum effectiveness, marketing campaigns must be continuously assessed and improved due to the dynamic landscape in which they operate; several studies look at various aspects of optimizing marketing campaigns, giving practitioners useful knowledge; a central idea emphasizes how important it is to base decisions on facts according to research it is a good idea to use marketing analytical tools and A/B testing to identify elements that resonate with target audiences. As per reference [2], the data-centric approach can aid in the continuous improvement of the campaign message targeting strategies and creative assets, thereby leading to an increase in engagement and conversion rates. Studies also look at the benefits of personalization and omnichannel marketing; the effectiveness of marketing campaigns has been shown to be significantly increased by personalized experiences and messaging;

 DOI: 10.1201/9781003472544-10

moreover, synchronizing marketing campaigns across various channels such as social media and mobile email enhances brand consistency and maximizes visibility.

10.2.1 Setting the Foundation for Campaign Optimization

- **Defining Objective's and KPIs**: Defining objectives and KPIs clearly is the first step in building a solid foundation for campaign optimization. Here is a synopsis of this crucial action.
- **Defining the Campaign's Objectives**: What objectives does the campaign have? Is increasing revenue-generating leads driving more traffic to the website, or building brand awareness the aim? If campaign goals are well defined optimization efforts will be directed and focused.
- **Finding Permanent KPIs to Measure**: After the goals have been set, indicate the KPIs that will be used to monitor the outcome; among these metrics are social media engagement, lead generation rate, conversion rate, cost per acquisition (CPA) and website traffic select KPIs that align with the campaign objectives to gain accurate insights into the performance.
- **Coordinating Goals with the Overarching Business Plan**: Verify that the campaign objectives line up with your overall business plan. This ensures that marketing campaigns are coordinated and helps the company grow.
- **Campaign Objective**: Increase brand awareness in anticipation of a new product launch; brand mentions, website traffic, social media reach, and post engagement rate are examples of pertinent KPIs.

10.2.2 Understanding the Audience

Understanding the target audience is crucial before putting data-driven decision-making into practice in this section, we will discuss the importance of audience comprehension.

- **Developing thorough Buyer Personas**: Make detailed buyer personas or profiles of the ideal customer base including their demographics, hobbies, issues and online behaviour. By thoroughly understanding the target audience, it is able to effectively tailor the messaging and campaign elements to resonate with them.
- **Researching the Market**: Conduct market research to find out more about audience preferences, industry trends, and competition trends. This may involve the use of surveys, focus groups, and competitor analysis. By keeping an eye on the wider market context, you can strategically position the campaign and effectively meet the needs of the audience utilizing feedback from clients to learn you should never undervalue the power of customer feedback; keep a close eye on customer service inquiries, reviews, and comments on social media to gather valuable information about their expectations and experiences can make improvements to the campaign's messaging and strategy based on this feedback which will help it better reach the target audience.

10.3 DATA-DRIVEN DECISION-MAKING

In today's data-driven marketing environment, utilizing analytics power is essential to campaign optimization success. The essential elements of data-driven decision-making are examined in the sections that follow,

10.3.1 Harnessing the Power of Analytics

- **Choosing the Best Analytics Tools**: Ensure that the tools meet the campaign's demands and goals. Google Analytics, social media analytics platforms, and marketing automation platforms are popular options.
- **Analysing Data to Obtain Practical Insights**: Instead of just collecting data, develop your ability to interpret it effectively [3]. Search for partners, trends, and correlations to obtain wife information that will aid in making better optimization decisions. Aim for insights about audience demographics, campaign performance indicators, engagement metrics, and customer behaviour patterns.
- **Monitoring in Real Time to Make Quick Adjustments**: Continually utilize real-time analytics to monitor the campaign's efficacy. This makes it possible to identify areas for improvement and make adjustments quickly, ensuring that the campaign remains relevant and effective in a changing market.

10.3.2 A/B Testing Strategies

One powerful tool for making data-driven marketing decisions is A/B testing. The effective use of A/B testing is explained in the following section.

- **Creating Efficient A/B Tests**: Ensure that the hypothesis you want to test is well-defined. Compare different ad copy headlines or landing page layouts, for instance. Select a statistically significant sample size and ensure that the testing process is fair in order to obtain reliable results [4]. Making choices based on analysis of the results; Examine the results to determine which version performed better after the test. Utilize the information to refine the campaign's elements and move forward with the best option.
- **Continuous Improvement Through Iterative Testing**: Perform multiple A/B tests. Test the campaign's features frequently to identify areas that still need improvement. Use this iterative approach to optimize the campaign gradually for long-term success.

10.4 CHANNEL-SPECIFIC OPTIMIZATION

In order to maximize the campaigns, you must modify your approach for every distinct channel. The primary optimization strategies for three popular marketing channels are outlined below.

10.4.1 Social Media Campaigns

- **Creating Interesting Content**: Provide visually appealing and educational content that appeals the target audience on all platforms. Use a variety of content formats, including images, videos, infographics, and live streams, to cater to a wide range of tastes.

To encourage social interaction, start debates, organize contests, and ask questions. Using sponsored advertising to its full potential make use of the paid advertising options available on social media platforms to grow your audience and meet specific campaign goals.

Advertisements should be targeted according to the interests, demographics, and online activity of the intended audience. Regularly monitoring relevant social media metrics is advised. These metrics include things like click-through rates, impressions, reach, and engagement. Analyse these data to identify the audience's preferred content types and the areas in which the social media strategy needs to be reinforced.

10.4.2 Email Marketing

- **Email List Segmentation for Targeted Campaigns**: Sort the list into categories based on demographics, interests, buying habits and other relevant data. This makes it possible to send each recipient more interesting and pertinent targeted emails, which raise open and click-through rates.
- **Enhancing Content and Subject Lines**: Make your email subject lines compelling enough to entice the recipient to open them. Keep the email content brief, informative, and visually appealing by including obvious calls to action.
- **Lowering Attrition and Raising Open Rates**: To reduce email list churn, employ strategies like providing insightful content, providing unsubscribe links, and sending emails at the right intervals. Adapt the email's timing to the audience's actions to increase open rates.

10.4.3 Search Engine Optimization (SEO)

- **Researching and Optimizing Keywords**: By performing in-depth keyword research, you can find relevant keywords that people are using to find the target market. To maximize the website's content, strategically and naturally include these keywords on each page.
- **Increasing the SEO-Friendliness of Website's Structure**: Make sure the structure is clear and easy to follow. This entails optimizing header tags, internal linking, page titles, and meta descriptions in order to improve website crawlability and user experience.
- **Keeping Up with Search Engine Algorithms**: Since search engine algorithms are constantly evolving, it is critical to stay current with suggested practices and emerging trends in SEO. By doing this, it can be guaranteed that the website will follow search engine guidelines and remain visible in search results.

10.5 BUDGET MANAGEMENT

Careful budget management is necessary for optimized campaigns. The following section delves into strategies for allocation and optimizing the marketing budget.

10.5.1 Allocating Budget Effectively

- **Setting Budget Priorities**: Prioritize the marketing goals and objectives in order to effectively manage the budget. Consider factors like ROI potential, audience reach, and brand awareness requirements when distributing resources across different channels.
- **Return on Investment (ROI) Calculation**: Track and measure the return on investment of the marketing campaigns in order to assess their profitability. This helps determine which campaigns yield the highest return on investment and where the amount of funding should be adjusted.
- **Changing Budgets in Response to Performance**: Pay special attention to how effective the campaigns are and adjust the budget accordingly based on the results. Funds from unsuccessful campaigns should be transferred to those with a higher return on investment.

10.5.2 Cost-Per-Click (CPC) Optimization

For pay-per-click (PPC) advertising campaigns, cost-per-click (CPC) optimization is crucial to maximizing budget efficiency. Here is how you approach it,

- **Strategies for Managing Bids**: To control the amount you are willing to pay for each click, use tactical bidding strategies. Utilize tools such as automated and manual bid adjustments based on audience and device targeting, among other factors.
- **Enhancing the Quality of Advertisements**: Use attention-grabbing ad copy, relevant imagery, and proper landing page placement to increase the effectiveness of your advertisements. Higher-quality advertisements usually have lower cost-per-click (CPC) because they are more efficient and relevant.
- **Pacing and Adjustments of the Budget**: Throughout the campaign, monitor the spending amount and pace to ensure that the strategy is being followed. Make any necessary modifications to the daily or overall budget to ensure that it stays within the financial constraints.

10.6 PERFORMANCE TRACKING AND REPORTING

10.6.1 Building Comprehensive Reports

In-depth reporting is required to evaluate the effectiveness of campaigns and provide stakeholders with insights. This part outlines crucial elements for writing effective reports.

- **Determining and Disclosing Important Metrics**: Select the metrics that are most relevant to the goals and objective of the campaign. Include KPIs like website traffics, engagement rates, conversion rates, cost per acquisition (CPA), and return on investment (ROI).
- **Making Dashboards That Are Visually Appealing**: Use data visualization tools to create visually appealing and easily understood dashboards. It is possible to swiftly spot trends and communicate complex information by using tables, graphs, and charts.
- **Results Dissemination to Stakeholders**: Consider the audience's needs when writing reports. Outline the results in detail, highlighting both the areas that require improvement and the good work that has been done. In a clear and practical manner, provide recommendations and next steps.

10.6.2 Iterative Improvement

Campaign optimization is an ongoing process. This section emphasizes the value of continuous learning and adaptation.

- **Creating a Feedback Loop to Enable Ongoing Development**: Create a feedback loop to gather data from various sources. This can include customer feedback, campaign performance data, and A/B test results. Utilize these insights from these experiences to future campaigns going forward.
- **Including the Knowledge Gained in Upcoming Campaigns**: Analyse the campaign's effective and ineffective elements. Apply the insights from these experiences to future campaigns to ensure continued progress towards marketing goals.
- **Maintaining Flexibility in a Changing Marketing Environment**: The marketing industry is always evolving. Prepare to adjust the plan in response to changes in consumer behaviour, market trends, and technological advancements can ensure that the campaigns continue to be successful and relevant over time by remaining flexible and open to new ideas.

10.7 CONCLUSION

Campaign optimization is an ongoing process that calls for a blend of flexibility, data-driven insights, and strategic planning. It is a continuous accomplishment. Through the application of the comprehensive framework offered, marketers can design campaigns that perform above and beyond initial projections, yielding dependable, superior outcomes and expediting long- term viability in a dynamic marketing environment.

KEY POINTS

- **Lay the Groundwork**: Clarify the objectives and key performance indicators (KPIs) of the campaign, understand the target market through buyer personas and market research, and obtain insightful information from customer feedback.

- **Adopt a Data-Driven Decision-Making Approach**: Utilize analytics software, test ideas with A/B testing, and monitor and adjust your campaigns based on data-driven insights.
- **Optimize for Channels**: To make the approach distinct for every channel, including social media, email marketing, and SEO, create engaging content, employ targeted tactics, and stay current with industry developments and algorithm modifications.
- **Effectively Manage Budget**: Assign resources strategically based on priorities, calculate ROI to assess campaign success, and adjust budgets based on outcomes.
- **Monitor and Report on Performance**: Prepare comprehensive reports with key metrics and graphics, then communicate the results to stakeholders in an efficient manner.
- **Adopt Iterative Improvement**: Establish a feedback loop for continuous learning, incorporate what you have learned into future campaigns, and maintain your flexibility in the face of changing market conditions.

By adhering to these guiding principles and fostering a culture of continuous learning and improvement, marketers can equip themselves with the tools and techniques necessary to navigate the ever-changing marketing landscape and realize the full potential of their campaigns.

REFERENCES

1. Heinzelbecker, K. (2023). Account-Based Marketing with CRM and Marketing Automation. In *Marketing and Sales Automation: Basics, Implementation, and Applications* (pp. 189–212). Cham: Springer International Publishing.
2. Singh, J., Park, Y., & Kim, Y. (2019). A/B testing: A review of current practices and future directions. *International Journal of Information Management*, *49*(5), 158–173.
3. Akhila, G., Hemachandran, K., & Jaramillo, J. R. (2021). Indian premier league using different aspects of machine learning algorithms. *Journal of Cognitive Human-Computer Interaction*, *1*(1), 1–7.
4. Osuanah, C. C. (2024). *Foreign Direct Investment and Economic Growth in Nigeria: A Quantitative Correlational Study* (Doctoral dissertation, University of Phoenix).

11 Customer Retention Using Machine Learning Techniques in Human Resource Industry

A Systematic Literature

Gurram Shilpa, Ramidi Pooja Reddy, and Mir Aadil

11.1 INTRODUCTION

In recent years, HR companies have experienced a paradigm shift in strategy toward customer retention, owing to the ML techniques enhancements. Meritorious retention is regarded as a vital component of sustainable and increasing business operations in the competitive HR services market [1]. Conventional systems frequently fail to live up to the complex demands and high standards being evinced by contemporary customers in the digital age. Thus, there is an upsurge in the interest in using ML to strengthen workforce stiffening and customer retention strategies in HR. The goal of this systematic literature review is to unveil the utility of ML algorithms and approaches to support HR companies in their efforts to retain clients. It will integrate all the recent methods and techniques and their implementation. So, it will tamper with the current methods to offer a complete experience of the future practices, challenges, and directions in this domain.

HR sector performs the biggest role in human resources management, specialists' engagement and staff training for companies across the industries. The escalating need for well-qualified professionals and the growing complexity of employment regulations pose a huge threat to the HR industry to generate correct as well as timely information in an effective way to satisfy their customers (Figure 11.1). That is so important since the sustenance of long-term customer relationships has been one of the success factors of HR companies in retaining their competitiveness and business growth. Nevertheless, the old standards for client retention, which are established on standard operating methods and subjective decision-making, have failed to respond to the quest by customers for other transformations and alternatives.

Retention of customers is a vital aspect for a number of companies, even human resources. If a company loses its customers, it can lead to a decline in revenue and, to a larger extent, quality concerns, which can affect its long-term sustainability.

DOI: 10.1201/9781003472544-11

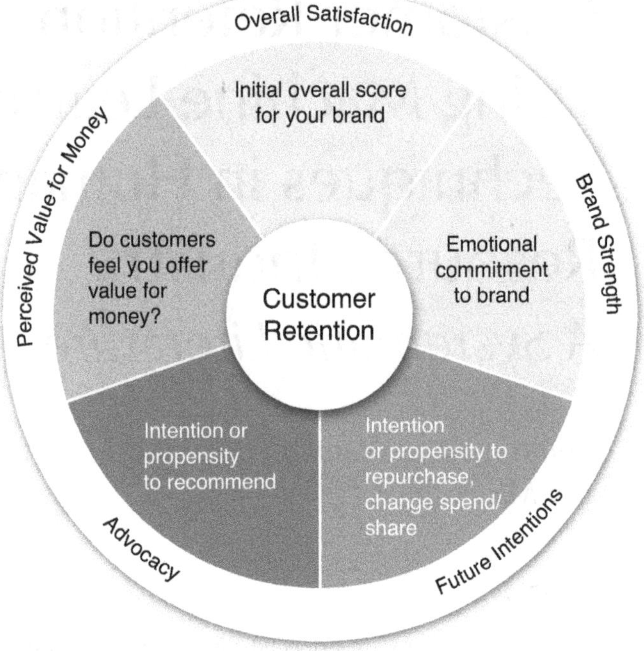

FIGURE 11.1 Churn prediction in subscription services.

These imply that the firms offering HR services become more interested in the issues pertaining to the retention of their clients [2]. One of the options that is coming up more often is customizing machine learning and then predicting churn rate and creating retention programs.

Machine learning is a process of using statistical models and algorithms to data for learning patterns so that the machines can predict accurately without being explicitly programmed [3]. In the situation of customer retention, machine learning can help identify customers by means of their behavior (patterns of usage, engagement rate, complaints, etc.) who are (probable either to terminate or to default on their contract). Several machine learning algorithms can be used in scaling customers according to the likelihood of churning.

Human Resource firms can easily understand the human resource management system more precisely due to the fact that predictive analytics can be integrated with machine learning. How people choose the companies to work for and remain with maybe they are unsatisfied, the salaries are more among other reasons, can help to determine customer retention models which fit the HR sector. Therefore, a company can plot particularized programs and messages to the ones marked as "high risk of churn" by a machine learning algorithm to lower the churn.

In addition, the machine learning techniques allow for customer retention strategies that are more flexible, adjustable, and customizable. Eclectic data fed, the network models can be re-trained to fit the changed customer mentality and taste. Human resource companies can, in this way, test the retention strategies optimally.

The machine learning has witnessed remarkable progress in recent years due to an increase in computing power, novel algorithms, and plenty of data [4]. For example, LSTM, a recurrent neural network adapted for sequential prediction, can be used to model sequential customer transactions and interactions. Using the info about customer engagement metrics in time perspective, LSTM networks can identify the churn risk that might be missed from looking at the data in total.

RecruitCo and Onboardly enterprises are those that have already adopted deep learning to ensure customer retention. To this end, they build up dedicated data science teams and use neural networks, which are tailor-made using their customers' data, to rediscover actionable insights that may also point to the forewarning of churn risk factors.

The potential of deep learning techniques to absorb vast amounts of diverse, complex information and spot the most subtle predictive signals offers the human resources industry retention of customers hope. Committing to these advanced machine-learning applications can increase customer loyalty and enhance business profitability.

11.2 LITERATURE REVIEW

Customer retention is a very key issue for businesses in various industries, including human resources. Losing customers means losing income, and for this reason, we focus on customer retention. Machine learning methods provide many new opportunities for the enhancement of customer retention through the use of data and algorithms to gain insights into customer behaviors and preferences. This literature review will look into the many recent studies about using machine learning to improve customer retention in the human resource industry.

An important emphasis of research is on machine learning that can predict customer churn, that is, the customer loss. Through knowledge of which customers are the most vulnerable to churning, businesses can choose a more focused direction to aim retention efforts. [5] designed a learning machine predicting employee turnover in Human Resource services firms. Researchers found neural networks had a big lead over logistic regression, reaching more than 80% accuracy identifying employees with a high probability of quitting. Such means implies that the HR can act before the attrition is done.

Customer lifetime value (CLV) modeling is the second most popular application of machine learning for retention. CLV forecasts the lifetime value of each customer. Machine learning enables CLV forecasting by discovering the main factors that drive value. [6] used boosted decision trees to develop a CLV model for an HR consulting firm's clients. The machine learning model combined client, contract, and economic data to measure the predicted CLV, which led to resource allocation to the retention area.

Personalizing service through tailored offerings is an important retention strategy that machine learning enables. HR services firms can leverage data mining techniques to segment customers based on characteristics and purchase history. K-means clustering and decision trees are popular for customer segmentation, as seen in [7]. Machine learning then helps predict which offerings each segment will respond to best.

Given that quality data there can be a problem of model interpretability. Many of these advanced machine learning techniques actually act as black boxes, so it is difficult to interpret or understand why some of the predictions or segmentations appear. Absence of this transparency hinders the emergence of meaningful loyalty approaches. Methods like LIME and Shapley values are being explored to improve interpretability of client churn models [8].

Ethical application of machine learning is also important for the models bring in more crucial predictions on people's lives. Biased data or algorithms can result in unfair retention practices; for instance, it may be the reason why someone was not provided with the service. [9] suggest policies for assessing ethical risks in machine learning applications for HR, for example, machine learning should be modeled from biased and trustworthy data. Transparency, auditability, and human oversight among others help to ensure ethics is implemented in AI.

The bulk of retention-focused machine learning research in HR has mainly depended upon supervised learning methods like decision trees, logistic regression, and neural networks. Nevertheless, these are the newer approaches such as reinforcement learning. Reinforcement learning is the process by which AI agents continually improve how they acquire rewards. [10] created a reinforcement learning chatbot that trains retention tactics, such as personalized discounts or customer care.

Traditionally, HR service firms evaluate many clients; however, machine learning may particularly be helpful with an additional internal aspect – retention. This approach is based on the analysis of employee engagement, performance, and survey data for the prediction of flight risk in an early stage (Figure 11.2). Thus, burnouts can be mitigated, and rewards can be given due to the development of any nuisance that could put the productivity of the firm at risk. Highly accurate churn prediction models by [11] for employers' neural networks reached over 85%.

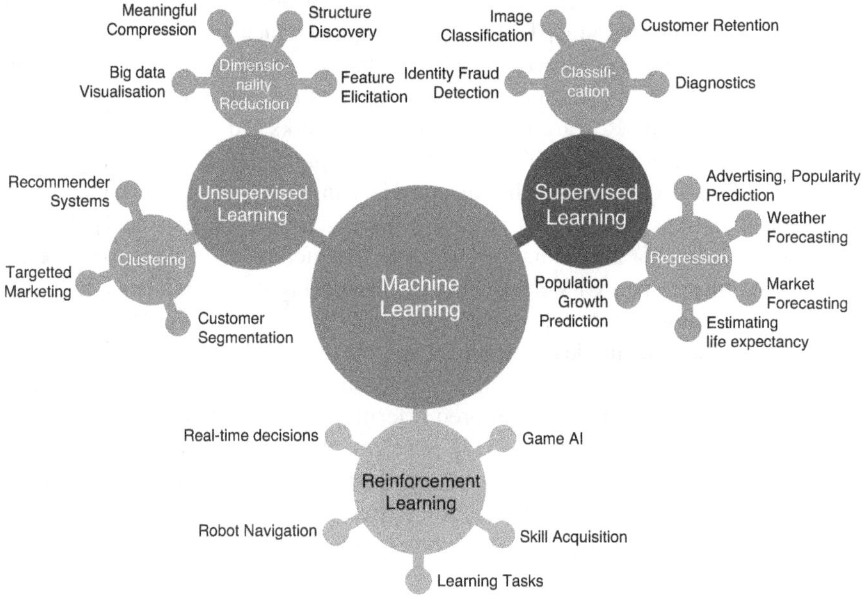

FIGURE 11.2 Customer churn prediction using Machine Learning.

Customer retention is mostly induced by external economic aspects, especially in HR. The only reason is that hiring is related to the business cycle. Techniques such as Bayesian networks can be utilized in predictive models for churn by integrating macroeconomic data. Using machine learning methods together with econometric analysis, [12] constructed a model under which the weight of economic indicators is determined by its predictive power. This boosted accuracy.

The use of ML for HR customer retention is taking its place together with new supportive technologies. Such channels like digital involvement participate in the process of collecting richer behavioral data. Cloud computing also allows complicated machine learning models to be scaled rapidly to process big datasets. But, the use of legacy IT systems can hamper the implementation of state-of-the-art technology. [13] assert IT modernization as the cornerstone of advanced analytics.

Machine learning models can be developed within individual HR firms as well as other independent bodies. However, third-party solutions are gaining popularity. SaaS churn prediction solutions like Client Savvy promise straightforward tools for the identification of at-risk clients across client segments. As the solutions develop, they provide practical machine learning capability in an affordable and easy manner without the need for significant in-house investment. Still, plug-ins are taking away customization.

The majority of papers study how early-stage machine learning applications are used for employee retention in HR, providing proof of context. Yet the full implementation and organizational use cases are rare examples to study in real life. The application of hybrid techniques looks promising, like using the combination of machine learning and statistical methods of business with what Kim et al. have studied. Future studies will measure the effectiveness in real-time applications over time.

11.3 OBSERVATIONS/SUGGESTIONS BASED ON THE EXISTING WORK

The current literature covers a full spectrum of machine-learning techniques that could be employed to predict and build customer loyalty in the HR industry. The most studied techniques are logistics regression, random forests, and neural networks. Most studies depend on HR data like employee demographics, performance metrics, and engagement survey results for machine learning to spot turnover risk. There is evidence that ML models outperform the traditional statistical methods in churn prediction in the HR sector (Table 11.1).

11.3.1 Model Evaluation Metrics

Measurements such as AUC-ROC, precision, recall, and F1-score are often used for evaluation. These metrics are used to analyze binary high versus low turnover risk classification. Alongside cost-based learning and lift charts, there is also a recommendation to count the business effect of such metrics. Interpretability techniques are adopted in order to ensure faithfulness in model predictions. The exploration on evaluation frameworks that are customized for human resource (HR) use cases is a necessity.

TABLE 11.1
Summary of Major Customer Retention Techniques using Machine Learning

Paper Title/Year of Publication	Objectives	Methodology	Results	Problem Identification
Improving Customer Loyalty in HR Services through Personalized Recommendations (2023)	To develop a recommendation system using collaborative filtering to provide personalized product suggestions and assets and its impact on customer loyalty	A matrix factorization algorithm was implemented to generate recommendations based on transaction history data.	Customer receiving personalized recommendations had a higher repurchase rate compared to the control group. The technique was able to apprehend key favorites.	Absence of tailored and applicable offers is a key driver of churn analysis in HR services.
A Hybrid Approach for Predicting Customer Churn in HR Software Services (2022)	To develop a churn prediction model that combines machine learning with statistical methods to improve accuracy over individual approaches	Blending Logistic regression with a random forest model.	The hybrid approach achieved better ROC AU (0.89) over individual modes (0.82–0.85), indicating superior overall predictive performance.	Machine learning methods alone may not fully capture complex churn patterns.
Employee Retention Prediction in Corporate Organizations Using Machine Learning Methods (2021)	To identify the reasons for employee turnover, predict employee training needs, determine effective scrutiny methods for retention, and develop a predictive model for employee retention.	The use of a survey to collect primary data and the application of ML algorithms to increase the precision of research outcomes.	The study indicated that instructing numbers is transpired as the top forecaster of employee retention.	Confronts linked to employee retention in current corporate administrations, emphasizing the vital role of workforce management and the need for strategic efforts from management to retain talent and prevent competitors from attracting skilled employees nurtured by the company.

(Continued)

TABLE 11.1 (*Continued*)
Summary of Major Customer Retention Techniques using Machine Learning

Paper Title/Year of Publication	Objectives	Methodology	Results	Problem Identification
(IERS) Intelligent Employee Retention System for Attrition Rate Analysis and Churn Prediction: An Collective Machine Learning and Multi-criteria Decision-Making Approach (2021)	Using the employee records dataset from a mid-sized Fast-Moving Consumer Goods (FMCG) company, this study aims to assess the predictive power of Deep Learning for employee churn prediction over ensemble machine learning approaches such as Random Forest and Gradient Boosting on real-time employee data and investigate the factors impacting employee attrition rate.	A method that uses ensemble or collective machine learning and multi-criteria decision-making to find out what causes employees to leave and then gives HR managers specific advice on how to keep both happy and unhappy workers around.	Deep Neural Networks outperform Random Forest and Gradient Boosting Algorithms as churn predictors, according to the actual findings of the machine learning models. For HR managers, the study offers important insights that can help with staff retention and improved incentives.	Huge attrition rates or employee turnovers Customized retention strategies are necessary
Study and Prediction Analysis of Employee Turnover Using Machine Learning Approaches (2021)	To examine and forecast employee revenue using ML approaches. Specifically, the research aimed to understand the factors influencing employee turnover and subsequently develop predictive models to forecast the likelihood of turnover for new employees.	The methodology involved the utilization of ML approaches to study and forecast employee turnover. Various classification methods were used to estimate and parallelly measure the likelihood of revenue of every fresh employee.	With an accuracy of 90.20%, Random Forest was the top-performing performance algorithm, while Naïve Bayes had the worst performance algorithm with an accuracy of 80.20%. According to the findings, employee characteristics including job position, overtime, and workload considerably impact turnover.	Hr Analytics has recognized employee revenue as a significant market challenge. In the expectation of reaping benefits, administrations often invest heavily in hiring and developing personnel. When an employee leaves, the company has to pay for the missed opportunities.

(*Continued*)

TABLE 11.1 (*Continued*)
Summary of Major Customer Retention Techniques using Machine Learning

Paper Title/Year of Publication	Objectives	Methodology	Results	Problem Identification
Predictive Model for Employee Attrition in the Indian IT Industry: A Study of Three IT Companies	The aim of the paper is to introduce a predictive model for employee erosion in the Indian IT industry by utilizing supervised machine learning algorithms. The study aims to predict employee attrition based on various features and provide insights into the factors influencing attrition rate in the IT industry.	Paper utilizes archival employee data from HR databases of three IT companies in India. A total of 1,650 employees' demographics and job-related information were collected, including age, gender, job level, and more. As part of the preprocessing steps, we reduced the dataset to 1470 observations, checked for missing values, and removed outliers. Python libraries such as NumPy and Matplotlib were used for feature selection and analysis.	The study reports an accuracy of 85% for the predictive model based on SVM model. Additionally, the results indicate that the model accomplishes better in forecasting which employees will leave the firm compared to forecasting who will not leave the firm.	To address the systemic issue of high employee turnover in the Indian IT industry and its influence on administrative performance and productivity. By developing a predictive model for employee attrition, the study seeks to provide organizations with insights to tackle the issue and improve retention, leading to improved performance and productivity in the IT sector.

(*Continued*)

TABLE 11.1 (*Continued*)
Summary of Major Customer Retention Techniques using Machine Learning

Paper Title/Year of Publication	Objectives	Methodology	Results	Problem Identification
Predicting Customer Retention of an App-Based Business Using Supervised Machine Learning (2019)	To build a model that accurately predicts which customers are likely to stay with the platform. A key challenge was overcoming imbalanced data, where there are many more non-churned customers than those who leave. By employing a quantitative and data-driven approach, the researchers developed a supervised machine learning model specifically designed to handle this data imbalance. They compared the performance of different sampling methods with both individual and combined (ensemble) machine learning models.	On building a ML model to accurately predict customer retention in an e-learning business. They tackled the problem of imbalanced data (unequal numbers of retained and churned customers) using a quantitative and data-driven approach.	That Random Sampling yielded the best accuracy in recognizing the retention class.	The challenge of effectively identifying retainable consumers from the total consumer data of an e-learning industry, especially in the context of imbalanced data, and aimed to address this issue using supervised machine learning models.

(Continued)

TABLE 11.1 (*Continued*)
Summary of Major Customer Retention Techniques using Machine Learning

Paper Title/Year of Publication	Objectives	Methodology	Results	Problem Identification
Employee Attrition Prediction in Industry Using Machine Learning Techniques, International Journal of Advance Research in Engineering and Technology	To predict employee attrition in the industry using machine learning techniques and to advance categorization precision and True Positive Rate while dropping fault rates.	Feature selection structure based on ML Classifier and analysis of different feature selection techniques	Random Forest Classifier and Decision Tree Classifier are used for grading and regression in predicting employee attrition. The Decision Tree algorithm creates a training model based on previous data sets to anticipate employee attrition decisions. Evaluation of various functional approaches regarding employee attrition classification is made using chi-square feature selection.	The need to precisely forecast employee erosion in the industry using machine learning methods. The importance by improving classification accuracy and reducing error rates in employee attrition prediction.
A Deep Learning-Based Customer Sentiment Analysis Model to Enhance Customer Retention and Loyalty in the Payment Industry (2020)	The objective of the paper is to address the challenge faced by SaMS-PSP in recalling their consumers due to more consumer churn. The key goal is to utilize sentiment analysis to modify those products and services to mix with preferences of customers, thereby enhancing customer retention and trustworthiness within SaMS-PSP.	The model demonstrates superior performance compared to conventional ML techniques. In order to reduce customer attrition within SaMS-PSP, the methodology leverages consumers' feelings using sentimental analysis to tailor services and goods to their preferences.	The deep learning-based customer sentimental analysis model shows greater performance over conventional ML methods, highlighting its capability to handle some of the big data applications like customer sentimental analysis successfully.	Improved customer retention and loyalty within SaMS – PSP can be achieved by providing cost-effective, timely, and value-added quality service. One strategy to proactively adjust products and services to customers' preferences and tastes—and, by satisfying their demands, reduce customer attrition—is to use sentiment analysis.

(*Continued*)

TABLE 11.1 (*Continued*)
Summary of Major Customer Retention Techniques using Machine Learning

Paper Title/Year of Publication	Objectives	Methodology	Results	Problem Identification
Machine Learning for Predicting Employee Attrition (2021)	HR and management to help improve employee retention	Engagement metrics like satisfaction surveys, training time Past attrition/retention Explore correlations between features and attrition using statistical analysis Train classification models to evaluate, select and optimize the best performing model Identify the most influential attrition factors based on the model feature importance Deploy model to make real-time predictions and drive retention programs	Low job satisfaction, no recent promotions, young age, areas for advancement	Current employee turnover is costly and higher than competitors

11.3.2 Algorithm Selection and Tuning

Trivial algorithms like logistic regression beat the complicated masquerading ensemble and neural network models to some extent; the latter, however, can be slightly improved. Hyperparameter adjustment is a vital task in treating overfitting and improving predictive accuracy. Algorithms like XG Boost and neural networks (particularly 'pertained' embeddings) exhibited great successes in fields similar to ours. An in-depth study of new HR-oriented algorithms with designs and other issues involved must be considered.

11.3.3 Deployment Challenges

There are only a couple of cases of large-scale implementations. Such problems as integrating them into production workflows, detecting a model drift, and scaling the infrastructure should be tackled. HR departments lack the knowledge of deployment best practices. Collaboration between data scientists and HR on developing real world platforms will be a good idea (Figure 11.3).

11.3.4 Ethics and Governance

The risks of job surveillance, biased predictions, and improper use of employee data exist. Standards for responsible ML in HR must be developed including

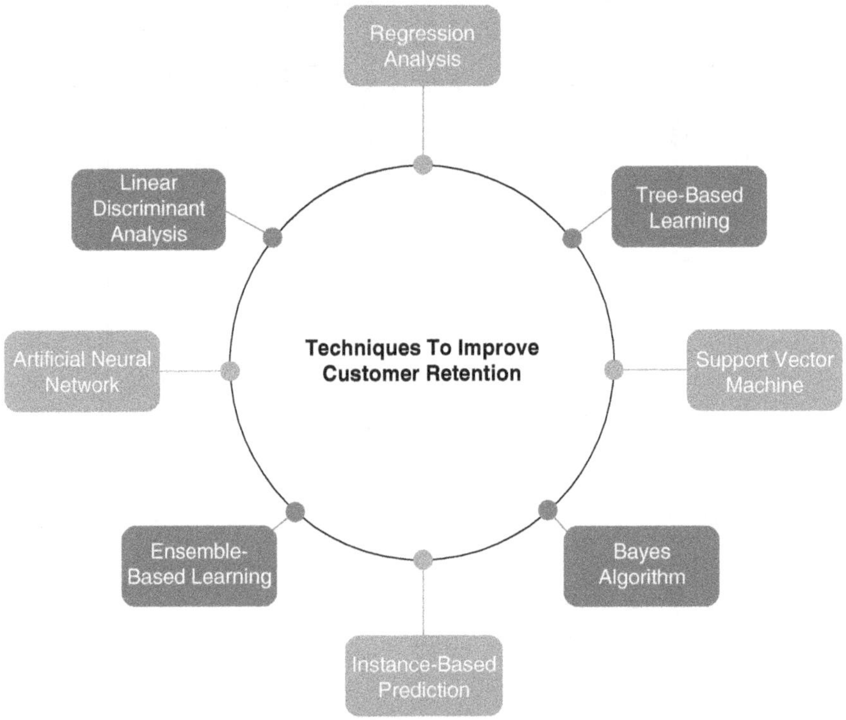

FIGURE 11.3 Building comprehensible customer churn prediction models.

transparency, auditing for fairness, and employee consent mechanisms. More investigation of ethical dilemmas is needed.

11.3.5 Targeted Retention Intervention

The bulk of work is done on prediction but less on response. Others recommend cash incentives and manager interventions for employees with high risks. Post-turnover, we propose to use knowledge-sharing platforms and alumni networks to maintain relationships. We need more innovation to provide positive, ethical retaining strategies that are driven by ML.

11.3.6 Board Talent Management Application

One HR use case is retention; the methods could also be used more broadly for skills mapping, training recommendations, team composition, and other areas. From a comprehensive perspective, talent management practices do not consider ML as integrated. Systems design and thinking grounded in employee lifecycles are permissible.

11.4 CONCLUSION

Ultimately, the literature I have investigated showed that machine learning techniques are extremely effective at increasing customer retention for human resources companies. As a matter of fact, masses of studies point to the fact that the utilization of machine learning in HR processes, such as recruiting, onboarding, training, and performance management, leads to a great increment in retention rates. The predictive functionalities of algorithms give human resource department an opportunity to know underlying factors that lead to employee mood, satisfaction, and churn rate. It facilitates accurate and timely interventions tailored to the needs of every employee for effective and sustained loyalty to the organization.

An important insight here is that machine learning techniques are able to discover relations in data that human analysts might miss. This allows the use of more focused and efficient retention strategies. To illustrate, natural language processing can interpret employee feedback and exit interviews to derive the underlying reasons for personnel turnover. Predictive modeling can subsequently identify such employees, and HR can step in with more specific incentives or career development opportunities. Such specialty retention is far more effective than wide general schemes.

On the contrary, textbooks discuss a few problems of machine learning as a learning-holding mechanism. An algorithm heavily relies on the accuracy and neutrality of the data sets in its training, and these sets must be comprehensive. While they act as support for the human brain, they cannot entirely replace the human mind and intuition. It is the most powerful application of ML in HR, which consists of algorithmic pattern recognition coupled with human conditions based on different types of industrial culture and organizational psychology. The average retention is higher overall for the human-machine combinations primarily.

Machine learning will greatly be integrated into human resources retention policies now and in the future. Along with the tearing high competition for the best class of talent, every time, organizations need advanced analytics capabilities to retain the foremost ones. ML was demonstrated to be a major saving factor for adopters in HR, with a few billion dollars in savings from the reduction of turnover. Laggard companies will naturally exit. They will not be a part of that race.

However, algorithms are important not only in HR decision-making but also in people's careers. Transparency and accountability will be essential features of ML automated retention systems. The HR teams should make certain that the defined corporate retention goals are aligned with employee's well-being. Besides, they should also look for unnoticed biases that might have dangerous or illegal implications on employee conduct.

Therefore, the literature review shows that with the help of machine learning, customer retention will increase within HR companies, but policymakers should still consider ethical use factors. This research presents an even picture of ML's achievements in retention as areas where improvement can still be done. For the HR executives who are designing retention strategies, the path ahead is to carefully integrate machine learning with the human component.

This review looked at many studies from the last 10 years that showed how machine learning can be used for HR retention such as natural language processing of employee feedback, flight risk prediction, and machine learning-powered individual career development and incentives. Altogether, the research provides strong proof that machine learning will be the key focus in the future of retention.

Finally, machine learning is an essential tool for HR organizations to keep the best talents and key human capital amid a competitive, data-driven business environment. Companies that strategically use ML for retention will gain a competitive advantage in the long run through higher workforce quality, productivity, and loyalty. However, tapping into its potential fully needs to handle data bias, ethical risks, and hybrid human-machine cooperation as well. Machine learning can take retention strategies to the next level with responsible implementation.

11.5 FUTURE SCOPE

11.5.1 Making Use of ML in the Unveiling of Deeper Retention Levels

One huge interesting prospect for future development is using machine learning in addition to mere prediction in many areas. ML used to predict employees most likely to leave could also be applied to gain insight into reasons for employees' withdrawal and the most effective retention strategy. For example, natural language processing could survey the exit interviews and conduct surveys to obtain similar dominant themes. Reinforcement learning algorithms could be used to test diverse retention resorts and identify which one yields the best results in the long term. It would allow HR to shift from reactive retention to proactive and personalized retention programs.

11.5.2 Employing Advanced Techniques Like Deep Learning and Transfer Learning

Besides, one can use more sophisticated ML techniques such as deep learning to find more divergent patterns that the human mind may not even explore. As one of the examples, neural networks can analyze employee communication data and detect expressions of dissatisfaction or disengagement at a very early stage. This could be happening even earlier than the employees think of leaving. They can discover which training programs, opportunities for professional growth, perks, etc., are most valued by different staff demographics. This would enable HR to handle each person uniquely and create rewards and retention plans that are specific to them. Transfer learning could potentially apply success achieved for retention patterns in one industry into practice for other ones, thereby reducing time to market for these strategies.

11.5.3 Including More Heterogeneous, Unarranged Data for an Entire Picture

Moreover, the other domain for success is finding extra inputs to the ML models. Currently, most initiatives are centered around demographics, compensation, performance rating, and other structured HR data. Aligning such data in the future can be used for the models to incorporate unstructured resources like employee engagement surveys, co-worker email/chat logs, or wearable device data. This way, we would not get just the "surface" feeling but rather a much more holistic view of their sentiment. Studios might as well analyze advertising job postings and level of employees' satisfaction on Glassdoor to increase the accuracy of the predictions. Interactive, on-time data is able to yield AI agents that function like online coaches that help employees and solve issues before they become problems.

11.5.4 Enhancing Diverse Interpretability and Casual Inference

Along with the growth of retention models, there is also space for further developments in the model interpretability and causal inference. Some black-box neural nets have a lack of transparency of the reasons why an employee is deemed high risk. For example, techniques such as SHAP values could be employed to explain the model predictions, build trust, and find areas for improvement. Causal AI could not just establish who is likely to resign but the most effective levers to maintain loyalty, such as compensation, career development, and management algorithms. That would make AI more action-oriented. Intensive testing and controlled experiments are required to substantiate these causal relations.

REFERENCES

1. Gupta, S., Hanssens, D., Hardie, B., Kahn, W., Kumar, V., Lin, N., & Sriram, S. (2006). Modeling customer lifetime value. *Journal of Service Research*, 9(2), 139–155.
2. Neslin, S. A., Gupta, S., Kamakura, W., Lu, J., & Mason, C. H. (2006). Defection detection: Measuring and understanding the predictive accuracy of customer churn models. *Journal of Marketing Research*, 43(2), 204–211.
3. Khan, S. A., Liang, Y., & Shahzad, S. (2015). Predicting customer churn in telecom industry using data mining techniques. *International Journal of Database Theory and Application*, 8(1), 47–58.
4. Verbeke, W., Dejaeger, K., Martens, D., Hur, J., & Baesens, B. (2012). New insights into churn prediction in the telecommunication sector: A profit driven data mining approach. *European Journal of Operational Research*, 218(1), 211–229.

5. Rahman, H. M. Mahfuzur & Raju, Valliappan. (2020). Employee Turnover Intention through Human Resource Management Practices: A Review of Literature. *International Research Journal of Multidisciplinary Scope.* 1. 21–26. 10.47857/irjms.2020.v01si02.035.
6. M. Óskarsdóttir, C. Bravo, W. Verbeke, C. Sarraute, B. Baesens and J. Vanthienen, "A comparative study of social network classifiers for predicting churn in the telecommunication industry," *2016 IEEE/ACM International Conference on Advances in Social Networks Analysis and Mining (ASONAM)*, San Francisco, CA, USA, 2016, pp. 1151–1158, doi: 10.1109/ASONAM.2016.7752384
7. Yue Li, Xiaoquan Chu, Dong Tian, Jianying Feng, Weisong Mu, Customer segmentation using K-means clustering and the adaptive particle swarm optimization algorithm, Applied Soft Computing, Volume 113, Part B, 2021, 107924, ISSN 1568-4946
8. Wang, Xing & Nguyen, Khang & Nguyen, Binh. (2020). Churn Prediction using Ensemble Learning. 56–60. 10.1145/3380688.3380710
9. Simbeck, K. (2019). HR analytics and ethics. *IBM Journal of Research and Development*, 63(4/5), 9–1.
10. Liang, K. H., Shi, W., Oh, Y., Zhang, J., & Yu, Z. (2021). Discovering Chatbot's Self-Disclosure's Impact on User Trust, Affinity, and Recommendation Effectiveness. *arXiv preprint arXiv:2106.01666.*
11. Park, W., & Ahn, H. (2022). Not all churn customers are the same: investigating the effect of customer churn heterogeneity on customer value in the financial sector. *Sustainability*, 14(19), 12328.
12. Xu, N., Li, Y., Lin, J., Yu, L., & Liang, H. N. (2022, October). User retention of mobile augmented reality for cultural heritage learning. In *2022 IEEE International Symposium on Mixed and Augmented Reality Adjunct (ISMAR-Adjunct)* (pp. 447–452). IEEE.
13. Schmidt, I., Morris, W., Thomas, A., & Manning, L. (2022). Smart systems: the role of advanced technologies in improving business quality, performance and supply chain integration. *Standards*, 2(3), 276–293.

12 A Persona-Based Approach for Churn Prediction and Retention Strategies Driven by Predictive Analytics and Generative AI

Pratik More and Shiva Sai Kiran Pothula

12.1 INTRODUCTION

The business models of most organizations have undergone a pronounced transition in the past decade, leading to a disconnect from ownership and remarkable growth in Subscription Business Models (SBMs). This transition is fuelled by the proliferation of digital access to products and services [1]. Not only are established companies like newspapers and magazines transitioning to operate on subscription models, but airlines and even car companies are switching to subscription business models. Not to mention the already existing telecom companies and emerging streaming companies like Netflix, Spotify and HBO Max.

SBMs are expected to increase customer loyalty, insights, customization of products and services, scalability and innovation [1]. However, they also face challenges, notably in terms of customer satisfaction and efforts related to customer retention. Customer churn, also referred to as customer attrition, is the propensity of customers to stop doing business with a particular company [2]. In business terms, churn is an amalgamation of two words—change and turn. It signifies the discontinuation of the contract or cancelling their subscription to the services offered or just quitting the service.

In general, there types of churns can be observed. In the first type, active churn, the customer decides to quit his contract and to switch to another provider due to several reasons. These reasons include dissatisfaction with the quality of service, high costs, lack of rewards for customer loyalty, poor customer support, lack of specific information about service disruption and forecasted resolution time, no resolution, privacy concerns, and more. In active churn, the customer finds value in the competitor's offerings and intends to switch to the competitor. In the second type, passive churn, the company stops its operations, and the customer has no choice but

DOI: 10.1201/9781003472544-12

to switch to another provider. The third type, incidental/rotational churn, is when the customer does not intend to switch to a competitor but wants to opt out of the contract for circumstantial reasons that prevent the customer from further necessitating the service, for example, financial incapacity leading to deferred payment; or movement to another geographical location where the company is not present, or the service is unavailable. Depending on the churn type, the business impact and the necessary actions to minimize churn vary.

Hence, customer churn actively indicates how well a company is performing in terms of selling its goods or services to the customer[3]. Every time a customer churns, it represents a significant loss in investment utilized to acquire that customer. A company's ability to have a high client retention rate is essential to its existence and revenue generation. Consequently, all subscription businesses strive to prevent and reduce the negative effects of customer churn. Hence, the importance of understanding how and when a customer is likely to churn is paramount. Predicting churn has become a fact of life for any company in the modern business landscape [4].

This prediction is achieved through utilization of several predictive analytics including but not limited to decision tree, random forest, clustering, regression, classification and principal component analysis [5]. Predictive Analytics can be applied to forecast sales, demand, customer churn, and new customer acquisition for a company. Additionally, predictive analytics helps predict the likelihood of customer engagement, the propensity to unsubscribe/convert, and recommendations of products, services, and advertisements to customers based on their past behaviours [6].

In general, these analytical methods came with their own challenges. The first challenge is computational in nature. As they were operating on historical data and subscription industries like telecom have collected a huge amount of data on each customer, it was a tedious and time-consuming task to analyse and predict customer churn. The second challenge is temporal in nature. As churn prediction is time-consuming, the insights derived from predictive analytics are useless, as the consumer might have already churned. There is a need for these prediction models to work on real-time basis, utilizing real-time data and historical data to accurately predict the churn in advance to take any action. With the rise of big data analytics and advancements in machine learning, traditional predictive analytics can map churn behaviour in real time.

Predicting churn is only half the problem. The second half of the problem is customer retention. Predicting churn has no value if the business is not able to utilize that information and retain the customer. Businesses usually make several efforts to retain customers, and these include engaging with customers, educating the customer, offering incentives, resolving complaints, offering long-term commitments and improving their overall service and customer experience. The overall agenda of these efforts is to make personalized recommendations to the customer to retain them. These efforts also cost substantial time and money for the business to implement. Although machine learning algorithms are perfect for extracting knowledge from historical and real-time data to predict churn, they fall apart when we use these algorithms to sense, reason, act and adapt like a business manager who is attempting to retain the customer. However, in the last few years, the technological world has been able to assemble a set of technologies into a system to enable and perform the same.

Artificial Intelligence (AI) has brought upon us the next generation of technological advancements that can simulate human intelligence to solve a particular set of problems. A game-changing advancement with ever-growing possibilities. In the context of the topic at hand, AI has the potential to build upon predictive analytics by enhancing efforts towards customer retention. AI is already playing a vital role in engaging with customer and improving overall customer service and experience. However, when it comes to devising tailor-made incentives and offers, and personalized recommendations to the target customer, the broad nature of Artificial Intelligence (AI) still falls short. In this case, a specific and purpose-driven AI mechanism called Generative Artificial intelligence (GenAI) comes into play.

The utility of the GenAI lies in its ability to create content autonomously. It analyses large databases, finds patterns, and produces content that is consistent with human-generated data. GenAI creates text, graphics, and other types of content by utilizing Deep Learning (a subset of ML and AI), all while keeping an artistic quality that can compete with human creation. In an effort to reduce churn, GenAI can create content that is specially catered to the customer's needs, previous behaviour, and preferences. Generative AI can also ensure that the client has a completely customized experience. It makes this decision based on their prior interactions with your company and the real-time customer behaviour towards the company. It is therefore improbable that two distinct customers will have a similar experience, even though both customers will be satisfied.

Given this context, it is also possible to generate Realistic Customer Personas (RCPs) based on historical and (large data sets including demographics, behaviours, past interactions, purchase/subscription behaviour, and even social media interactions) and identify patterns and predict churn with the real-time data. Real-time data enables proactive monitoring of any new patterns. The speed at which a business can understand these patterns increases the likelihood of avoiding needless churn. The RCPs can help businesses to understand customer needs and wants, develop insights to evaluate how, when and where the business needs to engage with their customers, identify emerging trends and churn behaviours, understand the customer's motives and values, influence service development and refine the marketing strategy.

Realistic Customer Personas (RCPs) are a blend of predictive analytics, machine learning algorithms and artificial intelligence. They represent the most accurate reflection of the customer based on the data they generate, which is then utilized to predict their churn. Then, GenAI can be further utilized to improve customer retention efforts by providing personalized recommendations, incentives, offers, and experiences. This chapter delves into the conceptual understanding of how these RCPs can be formulated and developed. Further, the challenges involved in RCPs are also discussed.

The rest of the chapter is structured as three sections. The first section presents a brief review of the research landscape concerning customer churn and evaluates the importance of several predictive analytical tools. Furthermore, the section also discusses the advantages of machine learning algorithms in predicting churn. The second section proposes a novel conceptual framework integrating predictive analytics, machine learning algorithms and Generative Artificial Intelligence (GenAI) to develop Realistic Customer Personas (RCPs) that can predict customer churn and provide insights into customer retention. The third section discusses the advantages, limitations and challenges of the conceptual framework.

12.2 CHURN PREDICTION AND ITS IMPORTANCE

Customer Churn is a common problem across several industries such as telecom, gaming, banking, e-commerce, streaming platforms, SaaS, insurance, retail, healthcare, hospitality, logistics, automotive, and education. Despite the industry, businesses encounter customer churn for various reasons such as high competition, varying customer preferences, lack of customer support, or low-quality product or service offerings. As academicians and marketers across the world have identified customer churn as a universal concern, they have highlighted the importance of implementing effective churn prediction strategies to address this problem. Customer churn across industries has several interconnected factors and challenges businesses face to retain customers. Some of the key reasons why customer churn is prevalent in various sectors include high competition in oligopolistic markets, constantly evolving customer expectations, quality of products and services, lack of personalization, customer service issues, pricing and value proposition, change in life circumstances, subscription-based business models, lack of data-driven insights, global connectivity, focus on customer acquisition, lack of technological advancement, and inadequate churn prevention strategies.

Apart from examining the factors that influence customer churn, marketers and academicians around the world have also highlighted the importance of predicting churn in coherence with machine learning and artificial intelligence and have underlined a glossary of reasons. The first reason, Revenue Protection, is the primary motive for predicting and preventing customer churn. Identification of customers who are at risk of churn allows companies to implement targeted retention strategies to prevent them from switching. By retaining existing customers, businesses can safeguard their revenue streams and minimize the negative impact of lost sales. In subscription-based models that have monthly, quarterly, or annual plans, customers need to be identified as having the propensity to switch and prevent the loss of revenues. Also, loyal customers tend to spend more, purchase add-on products and services, and promote the company among peers.

The second reason, Cost Savings, is a key to increasing the bottom line for any business. According to research and industry, retaining a customer can require less investment than acquiring a new customer. Hence, predicting the customers have the possibility to churn and preventing them from leaving will substantially reduce the company's cost. Companies can allocate resources to retain the customers who are at risk of leaving and avoid the excess expenses of acquiring new customers to replace the lost customers.

The third reason, Enhanced Customer Experience, is a crucial aspect for all businesses to retain their healthy pipeline. Analysing the various patterns in the concerns and issues raised by the customer provides valuable insights into customer behaviour and preferences that may help companies improve their products and services to meet the expectations of the customers. Predicting and addressing customer churn helps resolve the issues and concerns before they escalate and create an awful experience for customers. By being proactive, companies can showcase their dedication to customer satisfaction, leading to increased levels of trust and loyalty among their customers.

The fourth reason, Data-driven Retention, is a great way to minimize risk and get higher returns. Churn prediction relies on data analytics and machine learning algorithms to identify trends and patterns and to predict the future behaviour of the customers. Leveraging data-driven insights enables businesses to make informed decisions and develop targeted retention strategies. Data-driven churn prediction provides valuable insights into the company's customers' behaviour and preferences which the companies can fine-tune to improve their customer retention strategies. They can design personalized engagements, periodical offers, loyalty programmes, and customer support initiatives to enhance the overall customer experience and build stronger lasting relationships.

The fifth reason, Real-time Intervention, is an AI-powered churn prediction that involves continuous monitoring of how customers interact with a business. When signs of potential churn appear, like reduced activity or increased complaints, the system alerts the team. Businesses then step in right away, offering personalized solutions or incentives to keep customers from leaving. This quick action increases the chance of keeping customers happy and loyal. By addressing issues early on, businesses can build stronger customer relationships and boost their long-term success. Churn prediction models can be constantly improved and updated based on the newly generated data. As the churn prediction model becomes more accurate over time, businesses can stay ahead of evolving customer behaviour and churn trends, adapting their strategies accordingly.

The sixth reason, Competitive Advantage, is essential in a highly competitive market where customers can easily switch between providers. Leveraging user data to accurately predict and reduce churn can help companies gain a significant advantage in competitive markets. By fostering strong relationships and offering exceptional service, these companies become leaders in their industries, earning trust and loyalty from customers and stakeholders alike. Ultimately, reducing churn not only boosts revenue but also solidifies the company's reputation as a customer-centric brand that delivers value and cares about its customers' experiences.

The seventh reason, Personalized Engagement, means tailoring responses and offers to fit each customer's unique preferences and history. By understanding customer needs, businesses can send personalized messages, offer discounts on preferred products, or provide proactive support to prevent churn. This personalized approach makes customers feel valued and understood, increasing the likelihood of them staying loyal to the business. Ultimately, it enhances the overall customer experience, strengthens loyalty, and fosters long-term relationships. Through personalized engagement, businesses demonstrate their commitment to customer satisfaction and differentiate themselves in competitive markets, driving growth and profitability. Given these understandings about customer churn prediction, machine learning algorithms and artificial intelligence systems, it is imperative to examine how the dynamics between these aspects are explored in the research landscape. In the following section, a novel "keyword analysis" is conducted to examine the same.

12.3 A BRIEF REVIEW OF THE RESEARCH LANDSCAPE

Subscription Business Models (SBMs) date back to the early sixteenth century when newspapers and book publishers charged a fee for providing their products/services on a periodic basis. However, businesses started perceiving customer churn as a serious threat as market competition drastically increased due to industrialization post-1950s, and the earliest research related to customer churn can only be observed in the 1980s, see Figure 12.1. This graph is reflective of the number of publications per year on the Scopus database (keywords = "customer churn," number of results = "2110").

The data suggests that research interest in customer churn has rapidly grown since 2015. Thanks to advancements and breakthroughs in big data analytics, cloud computing and machine learning algorithms. These developments have allowed us to derive insights from large data sets that were not humanly possible earlier. To derive more insights from the literature, we can look at the keyword analysis of all the 2,110 documents available on Scopus. A total of 12,436 keywords were analysed, of which 135 unique keywords were identified. Looking at the top 30 keywords, see Table 12.1.

The above table demonstrates that most research concentrates on customer churn and prediction simultaneously with sales as their focus variable in the telecom industry. Other than the telecom industry, customer churn and prediction are also topics of interest in the e-commerce industry. Irrespective of the industry, the table above also demonstrates the use of various analytical tools to predict churn. These tools, in the descending order of preference, include forecasting, machine learning, decision trees, data mining, classification, logistic regression, support vector machines, random forests, neural networks, learning algorithms, artificial intelligence, deep learning, big data, regression analysis and feature selection. Other tools like XGBoost are also observed in the literature; however, it is a relatively new idea and has only recently

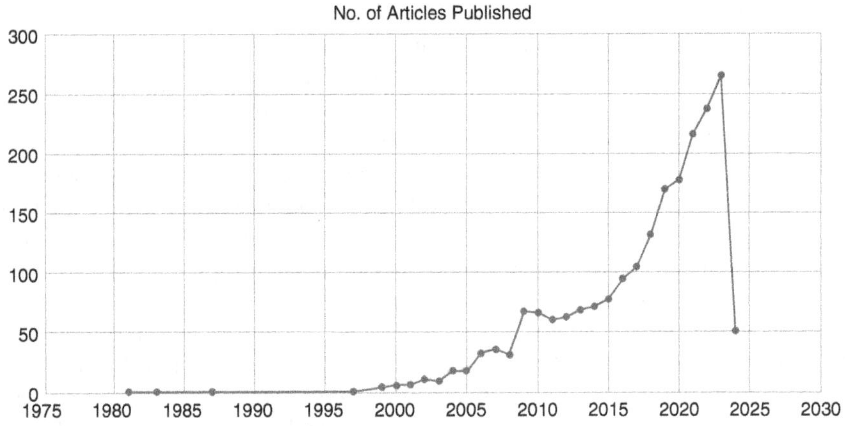

FIGURE 12.1 Number of publications per year, keywords = "customer churn," number of results (n) = "2,110", database = "Scopus."

TABLE 12.1
Distribution of Keyworks for 2,110 Documents on Scopus

Keyword	Count	Frequency Distribution (%)
Customer churn prediction	1,296	10.42
Sales	999	8.03
Customer churn	904	7.26
Telecom industry	687	5.52
Forecasting	643	5.17
Machine learning	498	4.00
Decision trees	413	3.32
Data mining	403	3.24
Customer satisfaction	260	2.09
Classification	244	1.96
E-commerce	211	1.69
Logistic regression	203	1.63
Support vector machines	201	1.61
Customer retention	198	1.59
Random forests	185	1.48
Learning systems	180	1.44
Customer relationship management	163	1.31
Public relations	147	1.18
Neural networks	127	1.02
Competition	116	0.93
Predictive analytics	114	0.91
Learning algorithms	106	0.85
Artificial intelligence	98	0.78
Deep learning	96	0.77
Big data	85	0.68
Mathematical modelling	85	0.67
Decision making	80	0.64
Regression analysis	79	0.63
Marketing	71	0.57
Feature selection	68	0.54
Others	3,392	27.27

started gaining traction. One startling insight is that most research only focuses on customer churn prediction. Hardly any research is present on customer retention. Hence, the following discussion only focuses on customer churn and prediction.

To gain a better understanding, it is necessary to examine how these prediction methods (including machine learning and artificial intelligence) have evolved over time in the backdrop of customer churn and customer prediction. This can be done by developing a temporal graph of how important prediction methods have gained traction over the last 24 years, see Figure 12.2.

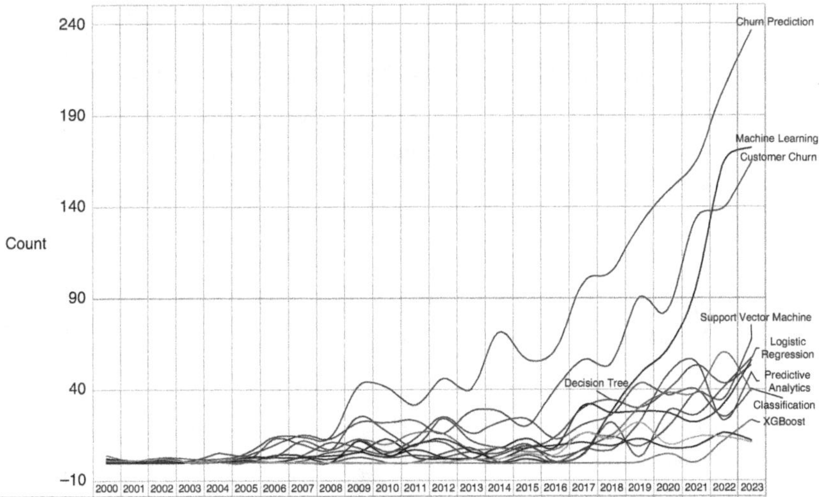

	2000	2001	2002	2003	2004	2005	2006	2007	2008	2009	2010	2011	2012	2013	2014	2015	2016	2017	2018	2019	2020	2021	2022	2023
Artificial Intelligence	0	1	1	0	0	2	0	1	6	6	3	4	3	6	2	8	9	11	9	13	8	9	16	12
Churn Prediction	2	1	3	2	2	5	14	14	14	42	41	31	46	40	71	56	61	98	104	129	148	164	204	236
Classification	0	0	3	0	0	3	3	12	7	13	6	13	25	16	22	24	13	21	26	43	37	40	25	40
Clustering	0	0	0	0	0	0	4	4	0	12	4	7	3	2	2	5	4	16	13	22	10	14	14	11
Customer Churn	1	1	2	1	5	4	10	15	13	22	22	23	16	28	28	20	40	56	54	90	83	133	139	164
Decision Tree	4	0	2	0	0	0	13	10	7	25	17	9	24	12	8	8	14	30	34	30	39	53	43	53
Logistic Regression	2	0	2	0	1	2	0	3	2	6	5	10	13	7	8	13	8	31	27	28	27	22	32	56
Machine Learning	0	0	1	0	1	0	0	0	0	0	0	0	0	2	0	4	0	5	28	48	62	95	164	172
Neural Network	2	1	0	0	0	3	3	3	4	6	13	3	2	2	8	6	7	16	15	30	38	38	60	39
Predictive Analytics	0	0	0	0	0	0	0	0	0	12	10	16	16	6	5	10	0	7	7	22	48	55	23	49
Random Forest	0	0	0	0	0	1	0	0	0	3	0	0	5	8	0	2	0	4	22	3	28	26	41	57
Support Vector Machine	0	0	0	0	0	2	0	4	11	8	3	10	11	2	4	9	3	7	14	9	19	38	35	67
XGBoost	0	0	0	0	0	0	0	0	0	0	0	0	0	0	0	0	0	0	0	0	5	0	12	23

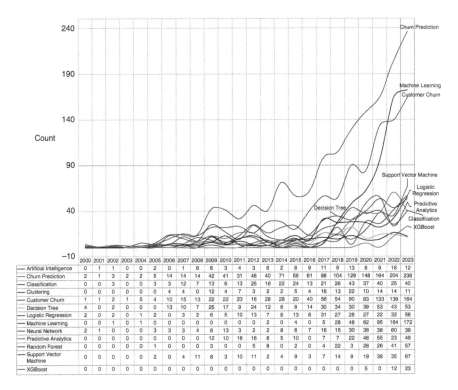

FIGURE 12.2 Graph representing the temporal evolution of customer churn and churn prediction methods.

There are several understandings that can be derived from Figure 12.2. First, there is an evolutionary relationship between the keywords "customer churn" and "customer churn prediction," indicating that most research has looked into customer churn and prediction simultaneously. The remaining lines in the graph indicate predictive methods that were used to predict churn. Second, the use of artificial intelligence and neural networks in understanding customer churn is not new, the earliest research in this domain dates to the year 2000, although the research is just conceptual in nature. Further, the earliest known analytical method used in churn prediction was "decision trees," followed by "logistic regression." Third, most empirical studies utilizing different analytical tools only began around 2005, after which a spike in empirical studies is observed. One can notice this spice for "customer churn prediction" between the years 2007 and 2008.

Fourth, this rise in interest and the increasing size of historical data that needs to be analysed has directly influenced the evolution of "predictive analytics" around 2009, which further influenced the evolution of "machine learning" around the year 2013. However, "machine learning" only took off as an area of interest only around the year 2016. This machine learning revolution is similar to the artificial intelligence revolution that is being experienced after the COVID-19 pandemic. The research involving applications of machine learning algorithms for customer churn and prediction grew rapidly until late 2021 and started to plateau from the beginning of 2022. Mainly because of the AI revolution and the increasing interest in the application of AI in this area. Fifth, analytical methods like classification, clustering, random forests, support vector machines, regression and neural networks have seen steady growth, as they are core components of machine learning algorithms and artificial intelligence systems. XGBoost is a new tool in this list, but it is observed to be growing rapidly.

The employed keyword analysis enables us to gain a preliminary understanding of the research landscape, its thriving research areas, and the prominent predictive analytical methods employed in those studies. Based on the above observations and a critical look at the current literature, a few research gaps can be identified:

1. Most research only focuses on predicting churn, and research on retaining customers is neglected.
2. Machine learning algorithms are the prominent methods for predicting churn, since artificial intelligence is a novel and broad concept. Appropriate applications of AI are yet to be examined.
3. There is no appropriate academic research on how Generative Artificial Intelligence (GenAI) can be utilized for customer retention.
4. There is no existing research concerning the application of predictive analytics and artificial intelligence to develop Realistic Costumer Personas (RCPs).

12.4 CONCEPTUAL FRAMEWORK: REALISTIC CUSTOMER PERSONAS (RCPS)

This section discusses a conceptual framework for developing Realistic Customer Personas (RCPs). This conceptual framework attempts to address the gaps found in the literature. The conceptual framework is proposed as a process with seven steps, see Figure 12.3.

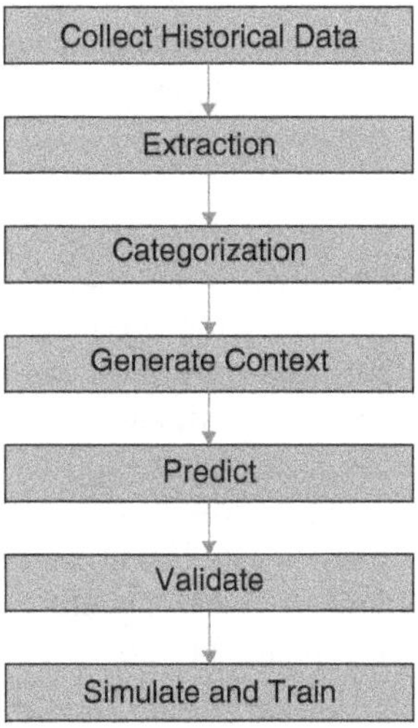

FIGURE 12.3 Proposed conceptual framework for Realistic Customer Personas (RCPs).

The first step is, "Collecting Historical Data," which most companies are already collecting from their users. This data also included the data generated by the customer through engagement with the business. The second step, "Extraction," involves extracting feature sets or characteristics from the data. There are several extraction methods already developed with varying performance levels. For instance, A method called Maximum Margin Discriminant Analysis (MMDA) was presented, which extracts features using the margin concept. It frequently performs better than conventional techniques like Kernel Fisher Discriminant Analysis (KFD) and Kernel Principal Component Analysis (KPCA) [7]. For reference, a review of numerous studies from 2005 to 2020 was performed by Jain et al. (2021) [8]. It incorporates a range of techniques suggested by earlier studies as well as the methods employed in those studies.

The third step, "Categorization," in which the extracted feature sets are classified into groups to maximize homogeneity within groups and heterogeneity between groups [9]. The analytical tools involved in this step could include random forests, classification and clustering. The groups identified using any of these methods will become the foundation for the RCPs. The fourth step, "Generate Context," is to generate extra information using GenAI. This information provides extra context, impute missing information and contextual information. The fifth step, "predict," involves bifurcating the data as per the identified heterogeneous groups and predicting the "propensity to churn" for each group. The propensity to churn is a continuous variable with a range of 0 to 1. 0 indicates no propensity to churn, 1 indicates full propensity to churn. The sixth step, "Validate," involves validation of the analytical model against alternative existing data sets. A review of validation methods for machine learning algorithms is discussed by Burzykowski et al. [10]. The seventh step, "Simulate and Train," GenAI can be used to create alternative datasets with similar characteristics to simulate various scenarios for the customer and develop training sets for machine learning algorithms. Utilizing these seven steps, a robust analytical model, that is, Realistic Customer Personas (RCPs), based on predictive analytics and GenAI is developed. Further, based on these personas and their relative "propensity to churn," GenAI can be used to generate content, customer experiences, recommendations, and incentives and deliver customer satisfaction in order to maximize customer retention.

12.5 CHALLENGES

A conceptual framework is conceptual in nature for a reason. To implement this framework theoretically or empirically a few sets of challenges need to be addressed first. This section provides a brief overview of these challenges. Because RCPs use integrated applications of predictive analytics and Generative AI (GenAI), the challenges we face with AI platforms broadly apply to RCPS also. The first challenge is "data quality." GenAI needs a lot of up-to-date data in order to be accurate. Its generated information may not be trustworthy if it lacks the necessary data. Up-to-date data is an immediate challenge for any GenAI platform, as most of them operate on old data sets. For instance, until September 2023, ChatGPT is only trained using data as early as November 2021 [11]. As of now, GenAI platforms need to be trained periodically on the latest datasets to be accurate.

This limitation directly leads to the next challenge, "real-time cost." GenAI platforms rely on huge computational capital. If the platform has to predict churn on a real-time basis, the computational cost in terms of energy, computing resources and data are very high. At some point, cost–benefit analysis will come into play. Another aspect of this challenge is "complexity." Because AI models and algorithms are complicated, learning them can be challenging. The next challenge is "context." AI responds to the prompts it has been fed by a user and can sometimes struggle to interpret them unless the prompt is precise and accurate. For instance, a study found that the majority of users found it difficult to relate the prompts to the GenAI's answers, and they frequently adopted the GenAI's recommendations word for word, even when they were incorrect. Directly leading to the incorporation of broad, inaccurate prompts and preconceived user "biases". Hence, unintentionally biased information may be presented by GenAI platforms, which could provide unfair or inaccurate results. Another major concern with RCPs will be "Consistency and Control." Because of the ways in which GenAI platforms are designed, it inevitable that the platform will provide different recommendations towards customer retention for the same RCPs. This challenge creates validation issues and hinder development of marketing and customer retention strategies.

12.6 CONCLUSION

This chapter is conceptualized on the basis of integration predictive analytics and GenAI technologies to develop Realistic Customer Personas (RCPs). First, a theoretical understanding of predictive analytics and artificial intelligence in their relationship with customer churn and prediction is discussed. A novel "keyword analysis" for literature review is performed in order to understand churn and its predictions and identify various methods used to do the same. Then, a conceptual framework is proposed with the following salient features:

- A framework that incorporates predictive analytics and artificial intelligence simultaneously
- A framework that predicts customer churn and develops customer retention strategies simultaneously.

With these salient features, the proposed conceptual framework addresses all the identified gaps in the literature. However, a plethora of challenges are needed to be addressed before the implementation of the framework, theoretically or empirically. These challenges were briefly discussed. In conclusion, it is clearly evident that artificial intelligence and GenAI platforms are revolutionizing all industries and businesses in many ways. The generative capacity of these platforms with appropriate use cases and predictive analytics can be transformed into automated business strategies. This chapter is an example of the same, at least on the levels of conceptualization and fundamentals. A lot of vision is required to derive business application of GenAI in combination with predictive analytics. We hope, this is a good enough conceptualization to start that journey.

REFERENCES

1. Y. Sharma and R. Sijariya, "Uncovering the trends and developments in subscription business models through bibliometric analysis," *Journal of Service Theory and Practice*, 2023, doi: 10.1108/JSTP-02-2023-0054.
2. S. Hurff, "Understanding Subscription Churn and Why It Matters to Your Business." Accessed: Mar. 8, 2024. [Online]. Available: https://churnkey.co/blog/understanding-subscription-churn-and-why-it-matters-to-your-business/
3. A. E. R. Sukow and R. Grant, "Forecasting and the Role of Churn in Software-as-a-Service Business Models," *iBusiness*, vol. 5, no. 1, pp. 49–57, 2013, doi: 10.4236/ib.2013.51A006.
4. E. Raafi, M. Lubis, and R. Andreswari, "Service Design through Subscription Scheme Business Model in Foodritious Start-up," in *2020 International Conference on Advancement in Data Science, E-Learning and Information Systems (ICADEIS)*, IEEE, Oct. 2020, pp. 1–6. doi: 10.1109/ICADEIS49811.2020.9277059.
5. Harvard Business School, "What Is Predictive Analytics? 5 Examples | HBS Online." Accessed: Mar. 11, 2024. [Online]. Available: https://online.hbs.edu/blog/post/predictive-analytics
6. D. Faggella, "Predictive Analytics for Marketing – What's Possible and How It Works | Emerj Artificial Intelligence Research." Accessed: Mar. 11, 2024. [Online]. Available: https://emerj.com/ai-sector-overviews/predictive-analytics-for-marketing-whats-possible-and-how-it-works/
7. I. W. Tsang, A. Kocsor, and J. T. Kwok, "Efficient Kernel Feature Extraction for Massive Data Sets," in *Proceedings of the 12th ACM SIGKDD International Conference on Knowledge Discovery and Data Mining*, New York, ACM, Aug. 2006, pp. 724–729. doi: 10.1145/1150402.1150494.
8. S. S. K. Pothula, "A Study of Factors Influencing Need for, Mode of, Sustainability of New Urban Movility," Indian Institute of Science, Bengaluru, 2023.
9. T. Burzykowski, M. Geubbelmans, A.-J. Rousseau, and D. Valkenborg, "Validation of Machine Learning Algorithms," *American Journal of Orthodontics and Dentofacial Orthopedics*, vol. 164, no. 2, pp. 295–297, Aug. 2023, doi: 10.1016/j.ajodo.2023.05.007.
10. A. Radford and Z. Kleinman, "ChatGPT Can Now Access Up to Date Information - BBC News." Accessed: Mar. 11, 2024. [Online]. Available: https://www.bbc.com/news/technology-66940771

13 Sentiment Analysis and Social Media Marketing

Mrudula Sai Inampudi, Mayreddy Indu Reddy, Viyyapu Chaitanya Ganesh, and Zita Zoltay Paprika

13.1 INTRODUCTION

The development of social media platforms has drastically changed the marketing environment in the current modern digital age. Social media such as Facebook, Instagram, and Twitter have marked themselves to be critical conduits for businesses in order to engage with their target audience to create brand identity and build valuable relationships with their consumers. The growth of these online platforms has helped customers with unparalleled access to information, goods and services by helping them shape their views, attitudes, and purchase habits (Smith, 2019).

In this technological revolution, sentiment analysis has become a key tool for firms that are trying to work through the complicated environment of social media marketing. This subset of Natural Language Processing (NLP) enables organisations to collect, examine and interpret the sentiment from the social media data. The sentiment analysis uses of complex algorithms and machine learning models that allows marketers to acquire comprehensive knowledge about the customer sentiment, opinions and emotions represented across numerous platforms of the social media (Pang & Lee, 2008).

Sentiment analysis, often known as opinion mining, plays an effective role in extracting and categorising views, attitudes, and emotions from the textual data. Through the integration of sentiment analysis and social media marketing, it gives marketers a deeper knowledge of customer attitudes (e.g., customer preferences, etc.) about their offerings by analysing the user data, which includes remarks, reviews, comments, posts, and feedback. Finally, determining the language expressed (positive, negative, or neutral mood) for a better understanding of how the customers perceive their brand and offerings.

By understanding the significance of sentiment analysis in social media marketing, organisations can discover new ways to get insights about the audience, personalise their messaging, and ensure the company drives through success in the competitive digital market.

Various ways to do sentiment analysis is through the Lexicon-based Approach; the use of lexicons of sentiment-bearing words indicates how it is viewed (positive, negative, or neutral) and categorises text by computing its overall sentiment score based on the sentiment ratings of the individual words. The other ways are "Machine learning models" and "Deep Learning Techniques."

DOI: 10.1201/9781003472544-13

13.2 APPLICATIONS OF SENTIMENT ANALYSIS IN SOCIAL MEDIA MARKETING

The Sentiment Analysis is an important instrument that helps marketers in different aspects of social media marketing, allowing them to come up with practical insights from user-generated content and refine their marketing approaches.

Below are some important uses of sentiment analysis in social media marketing:

Campaign Monitoring: With enormous money invested to create and execute social media initiatives. For example, When a cosmetics company launches a new marketing campaign promoting its latest skincare line on a social media platform like Instagram, with the help of sentiment analysis, the marketing team can observe favourable sentiments through customer's excitement and unfavourable sentiments through customer's concerns with the price and swiftly modify their message approach.

Brand Reputation Management: It is important for organisations to prioritise maintaining a positive brand reputation. For example, when a fast-food chain faces a viral social media backlash after a customer shares a video of a disappointing meal experience on a social media platform like Twitter. Then, the sentiment analysis tools will alert the brand's social media team about the negative sentiment surrounding the incident. By addressing the concerns transparently and taking proactive steps to rectify the situation, the brand can successfully minimise its reputational damage.

Product Feedback Analysis: Customers frequently share their ideas, experiences and product evaluations on social media channels, making it an invaluable source of information. Sentiment analysis can help analyse a large volume of feedback and acquire insights. Taking the example of a newly released smart phone, users can express their excitement about the phone design and camera features through comments on social media and some may showcase their dissatisfaction about the battery life of the phone, citing the major drawback. The tech company can consider these comments and work to optimise the product's performance and drive through continuous improvement.

13.3 SENTIMENT ANALYSIS TECHNIQUES AND TOOLS

Sentiment analysis, also known as opinion mining, is the process of determining the sentiment or emotion expressed in a piece of text. It involves analysing text data (such as reviews, social media posts, or customer feedback) to understand the underlying emotions and attitudes. Every method offers unique benefits and proficiencies for researching emotion in various settings. Here, we look at three noteworthy methods and tools for sentiment analysis:

13.3.1 Lexicon-Based Analysis

Lexicon-primarily based sentiment analysis is based on predefined dictionaries or lexicons containing words and phrases associated with fantastic, bad, or impartial sentiment. Each word or phrase inside the lexicon is assigned a sentiment score, indicating its polarity.

When reading text information, lexicon-based approaches calculate the overall sentiment rating through aggregating the sentiment ratings of individual phrases or phrases present in the textual content. By evaluating the overall sentiment score to a predefined threshold, the text may be classified as expressing superb, bad, or impartial sentiment.

Lexicon-based total evaluation is specifically beneficial in eventualities wherein area-unique know-how is to be had, allowing for tailored sentiment evaluation in specialised domain names including finance, healthcare, or era. However, lexicon-primarily based strategies may also warfare with nuances in language, context-based sentiment, and the need for non-stop updates to the lexicon to house evolving language utilisation.

13.3.2 Machine Learning Models

Machine-gaining knowledge of techniques offers a records-pushed method to sentiment analysis, in which algorithms learn how to classify sentiment mechanically from labelled education records. Supervised mastering algorithms, including help vector machines (SVM), logistic regression, and naive Bayes classifiers, are usually used for sentiment evaluation duties.

In supervised gaining, knowledge of the set of rules is skilled on a dataset in which each piece of text is labelled with its corresponding sentiment class (e.g., tremendous, poor, and impartial). The set of rules learns to discover styles and relationships within the text facts which are indicative of sentiment, permitting it to classify unseen text as it should be. Scalability and flexibility are features of machine learning models which enable the integration of various data representations and capacities to enhance performance. These fashions can generalise well to unseen data, making them suitable for sentiment analysis obligations across distinct domain names and languages.

13.3.3 Deep Learning Methods

Deep gaining knowledge of strategies has revolutionised sentiment analysis by enabling models to capture complex styles and semantics in textual content information routinely. Gaining knowledge of architectures, including recurrent neural networks (RNNs), convolutional neural networks (CNNs), and transformers, has proven impactful effects in sentiment evaluation duties. CNNs are particularly good at identifying important sentence patterns and structures by removing hierarchical aspects from textual content statistics. Transformers are highly effective for sentiment analysis tasks because they take advantage of self-interest processes to capture contextual statistics and long-range dependencies. Deep mastering strategies offer ultra-modern performance in sentiment analysis, especially in scenarios in which the statistics are large-scale and complex. These models can automatically study representations of text facts without the need for hand-made functions, which is mainly for greater sturdy and accurate sentiment evaluation consequences.

In precis, sentiment evaluation strategies and tools embody a range of procedures, all presenting specific strengths and abilities for studying sentiment in text statistics. Through effective implementation of these tactics, advertising firms can gain significant insights into customer sentiment, inform strategic decision-making, and enhance their advertising campaigns in an increasingly data-driven landscape.

13.4 SENTIMENT ANALYSIS IN SOCIAL MEDIA LISTENING

Social media listening has become an essential practice for businesses looking to identify and understand the views, opinions, and discussions of their customers on social media platforms. Organisations can learn important information about consumer attitude, emerging trends, and marketing tactics by analysing these discussions. Sentiment analysis plays a critical role in social media listening by enabling organisations to classify and measure the sentiment conveyed in online discussions. Here, along with real-world examples, we learn how businesses might use sentiment analysis in social media listening:

Brand Monitoring and Reputation Management: Businesses use sentiment evaluation to monitor mentions of their brand on social media structures and gauge usual sentiment toward their products or services. Organisations can identify changes in consumer views and proactively address any bad sentiment by tracking sentiment traits over time.

Example: An international purchaser electronics enterprise monitors social media conversations about its modern-day telephone release. With the help of sentiment analysis, the company observed an increase in poor sentiment related to battery overall performance problems. Using this insight, the organisation speedy releases a software program update to deal with the difficulty, mitigating terrible sentiment and retaining its logo recognition.

Product Feedback and Improvement: Sentiment evaluation helps organisations to analyse customer feedback and evaluations on social media to understand sentiment closer to precise products or capabilities (Rodriguez, Hemachandran, & Sairam, 2023). By categorising remarks as high quality, poor, or neutral, agencies can discover areas for product development and prioritise function enhancements primarily based on purchaser sentiment.

Example: A main cosmetics emblem video display units social media conversations about its new skincare line. Through sentiment analysis, the logo identifies overwhelmingly tremendous sentiment toward a brand-new moisturiser but discovers bad sentiment concerning the packaging layout. In reaction, the brand changed the packaging based on consumer feedback which led to an increase in the sales of the company.

Competitive Analysis: Sentiment analysis permits organisations to compare sentiment in the direction of their emblem with that of competition, providing insights into aggressive strengths and weaknesses. Through the process of comparing sentiment towards competitors, businesses can identify opportunities for differentiation and manage environments in which competitors may have an advantage over them.

Example: A hospitality chain makes use of sentiment analysis to examine client sentiment in the direction of its lodge homes with sentiment closer to competition' houses. With this analysis, the chain identifies areas in which competitors succeed, such as customer support, and employs strategies to enhance its personal offerings and maintain competitive inside the marketplace.

Campaign Monitoring and Optimisation: Businesses leverage sentiment analysis to screen the sentiment surrounding their advertising and marketing campaigns on social media structures. Agencies can assess the efficacy of campaigns, learn about audience responses, and make necessary adjustments to maximise campaign success by real-time sentiment analysis.

Example: A clothing retailer launches a new advertising campaign on social media to sell its spring series. The store uses sentiment analysis to monitor customer feedback on the campaign and finds that most of the comments are positive and compliment the event's modern style.

Encouraged via this fantastic sentiment, the store allocates additional budget to increase the campaign duration, ensuing in increased brand cognizance and sales.

In precis, sentiment analysis plays an essential position in social media listening via enabling corporations to screen, examine, and reply to patron sentiment on social media structures. Groups can obtain valuable insights into consumer views, identify areas for improvement, and extend data-driven initiatives to enhance logo recognition and drive business growth by effectively utilising sentiment evaluation.

13.5 CHALLENGES AND LIMITATIONS OF SENTIMENT ANALYSIS

Despite its utility in extracting valuable insights from textual facts, sentiment analysis is not always without its demanding situations and limitations. Here, we discuss some of the important thing challenges and boundaries related to sentiment analysis:

Contextual Understanding: One of the number one demanding situations confronted through sentiment analysis algorithms is the problem in understanding context and sarcasm in text facts. Language is inherently complicated, and terms or phrases may also additionally bring one in every of a type meanings relying on the context wherein they are used. Sarcasm, irony, or diffused nuances in language can regularly be misinterpreted by means of sentiment evaluation algorithms, fundamental to inaccuracies in sentiment type.

Example: A tweet that announces "Great, every other Monday!" may be interpreted as effective sentiment through a sentiment evaluation algorithm due to the presence of the phrase "amazing," despite the underlying terrible sentiment conveyed by the phrase "any other Monday."

Language Nuances: Sentiment analysis fashions may also come upon demanding situations when reading textual content statistics in specific languages or dialects. Languages vary extensively in phrases of syntax, grammar, and cultural context, making it difficult to increase one-length-fits-all sentiment analysis fashions. Furthermore, dialects and regional variations inside languages can similarly complicate sentiment evaluation tasks, requiring specialised techniques for accurate evaluation.

Furthermore, geographical differences and dialects within languages can also make sentiment evaluation jobs more difficult and necessitate the use of specialist approaches for correct evaluation.

Example: Sentiment evaluation fashions skilled in English textual content records may additionally warfare to appropriately classify sentiment in text written in languages with different grammatical structures or linguistic conventions, inclusive of Chinese or Arabic.

Data Bias: Bias in sentiment analysis models can arise from several resources, alongside imbalanced datasets, cultural biases, or sampling biases. Imbalanced datasets, where one sentiment class is overrepresented compared to others, can result in biased version predictions and faulty sentiment types. Additionally, cultural biases inherent in schooling information can impact the generalizability of sentiment analysis fashions across numerous populations.

Example: A sentiment analysis version skilled on social media records predominantly from English-speakme users may showcase biases closer to English-speakme cultural norms and expressions, leading to inaccuracies while applied to textual content facts from different cultural contexts.

Even if sentiment analysis provides invaluable insights into the attitudes and feelings of customers, it is critical to recognise and resolve the method's drawbacks and difficulties. Organisations can increase the accuracy and dependability of sentiment evaluation results, which will subsequently improve their marketing and selection-making tactics, by being aware of these issues and implementing the necessary mitigation techniques.

13.6 CASE STUDIES AND PRACTICAL EXAMPLES

13.6.1 The Social Listening Strategy of Coca-Cola

Global beverage giant Coca-Cola uses sentiment analysis to keep an eye on discussions about its products on social networking sites. Coca-Cola may adjust its advertising strategies and product offers by gaining important insights about consumer views and preferences through sentiment analysis of trends.

- For instance, when a new beverage taste is introduced, Coca-Cola keeps an eye on social media discussions to see how people are responding at first. The corporation uses sentiment research to determine that consumers have a very favourable opinion of the new flavour, complimenting both its flavours and package. Coca-Cola increased its marketing expenditure to promote the newly introduced flavour in response to the positive feedback it received, which boosted sales and customer engagement (Kim, 2014).

13.6.2 Airbnb

It uses sentiment analysis to examine user comments and ratings that are submitted on its website. Airbnb is a well-known marketplace on the internet for travel and accommodations. With the help of this, Airbnb is now able to understand the areas for growth and also provide the required insights into satisfaction levels of the clients by classifying their comments as good, negative, or neutral.

As an illustration, Airbnb analyses feedback from consumers using sentiment analysis to find reoccurring themes and opinions on how clean the unit is. The organisation found a pattern of unfavourable attitudes regarding sanitary issues in some of its listings as a result of this investigation being carried out. As a result of this, Airbnb started making its rules strict when it comes to customer cleanliness and also started a campaign to raise awareness regarding hygiene, which further increases user happiness and platform trust.

13.6.3 Starbucks Advertising Campaigns Monitoring

The global network of coffee shops keeps an eye on customer perception of its promotional activities on social media by employing sentiment analysis. Starbucks closely looks at the audience sentiment in real-time to understand the success of their campaigns, catch the audience responses, and make necessary changes to improve the marketing campaign's effectiveness.

For example, it starts an annual marketing strategy to promote its holiday-themed goods and drinks. Starbucks uses sentiment analysis to track and also understand the discussions about their ads on the internet and found out that their customers have different opinions. While certain consumers are excited and looking forward to the holiday goods, others are worried about availability and cost. As a result, Starbucks makes changes in its advertising language to meet its consumer demands and launches temporary promotions to boost sales and engagement over the holiday—Christmas season.

13.6.4 Nike's Comparative Analysis

Nike, a multinational athletic apparel and footwear corporation, uses sentiment analysis to compare its brand sentiment against rivals and do competitive analysis. Nike determines chances for uniqueness and regions with superiority by comparing customer attitudes toward the company's products with those of its rivals.

Nike, for instance, compares customer opinion toward their athletic shoes with attitude toward rival businesses using sentiment analysis. After carrying out this investigation, Nike found out that when it comes to quality and also innovation, the customers have a positive opinion of Nike's products. With the help of this knowledge, Nike makes sure to use these positive reviews in its marketing campaigns as it becomes an advantage for the brand. By tacking all this, it became the industry leader for sports footwear.

These real-life examples show us how various companies in different sectors made use of sentiment analysis in order to understand the customers, make tactical decisions and produce good positive results for the business in the continuously changing social media marketing. Businesses can find areas for growth, increase client engagement, and subsequently achieve their marketing goals more successfully by utilising sentiment research.

13.7 FUTURE TRENDS AND INNOVATIONS

The industry is aiming at gaining more growth and also innovation as all the companies are continuously leveraging the research on sentiments of the customers in social media marketing. The upcoming developments in the sentiment analysis region are being shaped by various new trends and also innovations, which the marketers in the present are trying to use in order to improve their marketing tactics and also understand how the customers feel. Below are the upcoming changes and also patterns that are significant in sentiment analysis:

Emotions Recognition

Organisations can now recognise distinct emotions represented in text data and expand above basic categorisation of sentiment thanks to emotion detection, which is a big leap in sentiment analysis.

Businesses can get a better understanding of their customer's views and reactions on their products and also make changes in their marketing and advertising strategies by identifying the customer emotions such as happiness, sadness, rage and amusement.

For example, a retail business makes the use of sentiment analysis and emotional recognition to understand the reactions of its customers to the business's most recent marketing and advertising campaign. With the help of the given analysis of the most common emotions gathered by customer feedback, the business makes changes in its messaging and come up with campaigns that get connected with the target audience more successfully.

Multilingual Sentiment Analysis

The need for multilingual sentiment analysis is only going to increase as firms expand into more diversified international markets (Zhang et al., 2016). With the help of using multilingual sentiment analysis, the businesses can assess the sentiments of audiences that giving the brand a deeper grasp of the sentiments of their customers in different marketplaces.

For instance, to track consumer sentiment throughout its global client base, an international technology corporation uses multilingual sentiment analysis. When the brands have more precise insights into the regional variations of customer preferences, needs and opinions through the sentiment analysis of the various languages, they can easily customise their promotional strategies and efforts of product adaptation to meet their target audience.

Cross-Platform Collaboration Sentiment Research

In order for organisations to obtain a comprehensive understanding of customer sentiment, they must conduct cross-platform sentiment research, as consumers interact across a variety of social media sites and internet channels. This gives a deeper understanding of the sentiments of the customers across all the channels by data integration of various sources like blogs, social networking platforms, review sites and forums.

For instance, to track consumer opinions across social media, discussion boards, and product review sites, an e-commerce store uses multi-platform sentiment analysis. This shop can improve the experience of the customer by gaining a deeper knowledge on the overall sentiment of the brand, understanding the developing trends and finally responding to the feedback of the customers quickly by combining the sentiment data from a variety of channels.

Integration with Generative AI and Predictive Analytics
Improving marketing tactics and consumer experiences could be achieved by combining sentiment analysis with these two fields of study. The brands can use the findings of sentiment analysis that are generated with the help of forecasting and AI driven data development to know the customer demands on their preferences, marketing campaigns customisation and finally provide engaging and relevant content to their customers.

For instance, to forecast client satisfaction and pinpoint possible areas for enhancement of service, a hospitality organisation combines sentiment analysis with predictive analytics. The brand forecasts the sentiments of the customers and then come up with methods that can improve the guests experience there which finally leads to customer loyalty and satisfaction. This is done by properly understanding and analysing the sentiment patterns and feedbacks of the customers.

The future phase of the sentiment analysis in the social media marketing is defined by multilingual analysis, corporation with predictive analytics and generative AI, recognition of emotions and cross-platform integration. In this more connected and fast moving data-driven world, the brands can come up with more happening marketing strategies, develop a more comprehensive understanding into customers feelings and eventually provide great significant experiences to the customers with the help of technology.

13.8 CONCLUSION

To conclude, for almost all the organisations sentiment analysis has become an important tool which provides them information that is very insightful from social media and then apply those changes to their marketing campaigns and plans. By looking into the sentiments of the customers displayed on the social media platforms, the businesses understand the views of consumers, habits and interests on a better note. We have looked at the many uses, methods, difficulties, and potential developments of sentiment analysis in social media marketing in this chapter.

The marketing efforts of businesses can be improved by using sentiment analysis as it gives a multitude of chances which eventually develops a strong connection with the target markets, starting from brand sentiment tracking to analysing the feedback and improving marketing campaigns. Businesses that successfully use sentiment analysis can:

Customise Messaging: With the use of sentiment analysis, organisations can create material and communication that reaches and also talk to their target market, this helps in boosting marketing campaigns' efficacy and encouraging the audience's interaction on social media.

Tracking of the Brand Image: Organisations may proactively handle their brand reputation by keeping an eye on sentiment patterns of their customers. The companies can then try to address bad sentiment and leverage positive sentiment to improve the brand perception and commitment.

Promoting Customer Engagement: Sentiment analysis helps in assisting the companies in finding relevant ways to interact with their target audience or market, there after replying to their client comments, and eventually create deep relationships on social media.

Organisations need to be up to date with new trends and technology in the ever-evolving digital landscape in order to maintain competitive in the ever-evolving field of sentiment analysis. The advancements in the technology give a fascinating opportunities to the companies to understand the target audiences attitudes and lead to more successful campaigns.

The sentiment analysis helps organisations to completely make use of the data of their social media that offers awareness on how to improve the interaction of customers, strategic decision making and finally lead to the success of the company in a world that is so much into data. In this digital era, the organisations need to adopt to sentiment analysis as a major part of their promotion so that the organisations can stay ahead of their competitors.

REFERENCES

Kim, Y. (2014). Convolutional neural networks for sentence classification. *Proceedings of the 2014 Conference on Empirical Methods in Natural Language Processing (EMNLP)*. 2014. Doha, Qatar.

Pang, B., & Lee, L. (2008). Opinion mining and sentiment analysis. *Foundations and Trends® in Information Retrieval*, *2*(1–2), 1–135. https://doi.org/10.1561/1500000011

Rodriguez, R. V., Hemachandran, K., & Sairam, P. S. (2023). *Coded Leadership: Developing Scalable Management in an AI-Induced Quantum World*. CRC Press.

Smith, J. (2019). The impact of social media on consumer behavior. *Journal of Marketing Research*, *24*(3), 56–78.

Zhang, Z., et al. (2016). Cross-platform sentiment analysis of social media data. *IEEE Transactions on Knowledge and Data Engineering*, *28*(4), 1043–1056.

14 Generative AI Techniques for Marketing

Divyansh Chittranshi and Pokala Pranay Kumar

14.1 OVERVIEW OF GENERATIVE AI

Generative AI is a fascinating field that involves systems capable of creating other systems. It is a relatively new area within AI that encompasses generative design, a method where computers generate various design solutions based on specific inputs and constraints. In this process, humans play a crucial role by providing the program with the desired outcomes initially. The program then explores different possibilities, adjusting inputs and calculating outcomes through a series of "What If?" scenarios. Unlike traditional testing or simulation methods, generative AI does not rely on predefined inputs or measurements, allowing for a wide range of interpretations and outcomes. However, by guiding the process with theoretical conditions and manageable inputs, generative AI ensures that all results are systematically refined and improvable. This approach incorporates intelligent tools and produces unique outputs, providing designers with genuine alternatives to explore and refine further.

14.2 IMPORTANCE OF GENERATIVE AI IN MARKETING

Generative AI has become increasingly prevalent in marketing, thanks to ongoing technological advancements and innovation. Its primary significance lies in personalizing messages and enabling marketers to effectively target a wide audience. Through generative AI, analyzing consumer data and identifying patterns has become much simpler, allowing marketers to segment potential customers based on various factors such as behavior, demographics, and geography. Real-time content optimization is another crucial aspect facilitated by generative AI, ensuring that the right message reaches the right customer at the right time. Unlike in the past, where content had to be scheduled in advance, generative AI automates content optimization and delivery, enhancing both conversion rates and consumer satisfaction. Additionally, with the growing importance of social media and e-commerce platforms, the demand for appealing and interactive content has surged. Generative AI supports marketers in creating unique and engaging content through innovative design and intelligent systems. In fact, generative design was ranked eighth in the top 10 strategic technology trends for 2019, highlighting its pivotal role in digital transformation due to its customization and innovation capabilities in production. By leveraging consumer data and analytics, marketers can enhance the visual identity of their advertisements to cater to diverse consumer preferences. With continued implementation, generative AI is poised to revolutionize marketing in the future.

DOI: 10.1201/9781003472544-14

14.3 OBJECTIVES OF THE WORK

The primary aim of this project is to assess the effectiveness of generative AI methods in marketing compared to traditional techniques. This will involve conducting a thorough review of existing literature and juxtaposing the findings with insights from industry professionals to ascertain the feasibility of integrating generative AI into modern marketing practices. Another key objective is to outline and elucidate various generative AI models and methodologies applicable to marketing. By offering a comprehensive inventory and taxonomy of these models, along with their practical marketing applications and potential outputs, this project aims to serve as a valuable reference guide for leveraging generative models in marketing endeavors. Achieving this objective entails delving deep into academic literature to understand the technical intricacies of different generative models and categorizing methodologies suitable for marketing applications. Furthermore, the project aims to devise a novel, model-based marketing strategy emphasizing scalability and content diversity. By harnessing the power of generative models to develop a data-driven approach, the project endeavors to enhance the quality and speed of marketing delivery compared to conventional methods. It is anticipated that the fluidity of generative models in autonomously generating new content based on specified parameters will enable scalability and expedited delivery. This model will be integrated into a broader software-based system with the aim of automating and optimizing the entire marketing and content management process. Such a system could be deployed in centralized marketing management setups akin to marketing agencies or in decentralized environments, encompassing a network of marketing experts within larger organizations, as proposed by Professor John Yen et al.

14.4 APPLICATIONS OF GENERATIVE AI IN MARKETING

How can generative AI be used to create personalized content for marketing campaigns?

Generative simulated intelligence innovation can possibly change advertising endeavors by making individualized content that reverberates with the main interest group. Generative man-made intelligence can produce profoundly customized showcasing messages that are applicable to individual inclinations, interests, and needs. This procedure can support commitment and further develop the client experience, bringing about expanded change rates and better advertising return for money invested [1]. The proficiency-driven methodology of generative computer-based intelligence saves time for key preparation and developing purchaser connections, permitting advertisers to effortlessly make differentiated and excellent substance [2]. Generative man-made intelligence might computerize showcasing content creation by surveying convoluted information, for example, media plans and content, and afterward making new and one-of-a-kind proposals in light of examples and realities it has learned [1]. Continuous survey and improvement can assist generative artificial intelligence with making more customized content for promoting endeavors [1]. Generative simulated intelligence might track down designs for designated showcasing endeavors and convey customized ideas in view of client inclinations and authentic way of behaving [1]. This innovation rearranges and works for the enormous scope age of customized and designated content, permitting organizations to contact their target group all the more proficiently [1]. Generative AI has had a huge impact on the marketing business, with tailored suggestions, targeted advertising, and interactive experiences becoming more prominent in campaigns [1]. Brands may maintain their competitiveness in the marketing business by remaining current on the latest breakthroughs in generative AI [1].

What are the potential applications of generative AI in improving customer engagement and targeting?

Generative AI has various potential marketing uses, including increased customer interaction and targeting. One significant feature of generative AI is its capacity to find previously unknown patterns and trends in consumer journeys [1]. This allows marketing teams to examine customer behavior and preferences and produce individualized marketing materials that appeal to their target audience [1]. Generative AI can increase marketing creativity and efficacy by automating content development, design, and strategy [1]. Furthermore, by democratizing data, generative AI solutions enable marketing teams to swiftly understand and apply data to make informed decisions without the requirement for data scientists or IT experts [2]. Generative simulated intelligence can make customized and compelling advertising materials that resound with the interest group via preparing and calibrating the model utilizing gathered information, for example, client associations, market patterns, and authentic showcasing efforts [1]. This can help advertising groups focus on the fitting crowd, upgrading content, and customizing client encounters, eventually improving buyer commitment and focusing on promoting [1].

In what ways can generative AI be utilized for market research and trend analysis in marketing?

Generative man-made intelligence has made new channels for showcasing examination and pattern investigation. One of the most well-known uses of generative artificial intelligence in promoting is content creation, picture or video creation, and website streamlining (Search engine optimization) [3]. At the point when appropriately developed, generative artificial intelligence can productively figure out market and client information, bringing about better-designated advertising endeavors [4]. What is more, advertisers can utilize generative artificial intelligence to concentrate on contest conduct, survey customer feelings, and test new item thoughts. The quick production of bits of knowledge provided by generative computer-based intelligence takes into consideration speedier independent direction and improved results [5]. One more significant use of generative computer-based intelligence in advertising is the robotization of showcasing activities and site design improvement. Generative simulated intelligence, specifically, might be utilized to produce manufactured message information labeled with different perspectives, like positive, nonpartisan, or negative, which helps feeling examination [6,7]. Generative computer-based intelligence can likewise rapidly assess huge volumes of information, helping to promote in better figuring out client inclinations, interests, and ways of behaving [1]. Nonetheless, it is imperative to feature that involving generative man-made intelligence innovation for showcasing yields that clients straightforwardly cooperate with could bring about purchaser reactance [8]. At last, promoting and deals associations might utilize generative simulated intelligence arrangements like ChatGPT, Jasper, Einstein GPT,

Rapidely, Manychat, and Flick. These innovations can assist advertisers with getting the upper hand by permitting them to more readily comprehend market patterns, client conduct, and inclinations [9].

The application of generative AI technology in marketing has the potential to transform how marketing strategies are developed and implemented. The capacity to create tailored content that reflects individual tastes, interests, and demands may boost engagement and client loyalty. The availability of numerous generative AI technologies, such as ChatGPT, Jasper, Einstein GPT, Rapidely, Manychat, and Flick, can enable marketers to better understand market trends and consumer behaviors and make educated decisions. Generative AI may automate marketing content development, resulting in more efficient and successful campaigns suited to specific consumers. Customer behavior and preference analysis may aid in the identification of patterns for targeted marketing efforts as well as the provision of tailored recommendations based on user preferences and previous activity.

Yet, one should be aware that there may be some limits and biases of the generative AI technology, which could include, for example, reinforcing the existing biases and suggesting new ones. While this technology develops and new features appear, it should be checked and adjusted continuously [10]. Moreover, further study is needed to uncover the actual use of generative AI in marketing such as how the technology can be used to boost retargeting and customer engagement. Overall, applying generative AI in marketing opens up a whole new exciting dedicated to the use of tailored ads that engage the target consumers.

14.5 BENEFITS AND CHALLENGES OF IMPLEMENTING GENERATIVE AI IN MARKETING STRATEGIES

Integrating generative AI into marketing strategies presents numerous advantages, such as enriching personalization and tailoring content to specific target audiences, fostering customer engagement through interactive chatbots and virtual assistants, and streamlining the analysis of extensive marketing data. Nonetheless, there are various challenges associated with leveraging generative AI in marketing endeavors. These include ethical considerations regarding data privacy and the imperative of utilizing high-quality training data to ensure the accuracy and dependability of outcomes [8]. Additionally, the intricate nature of implementing generative AI systems and the necessity for ongoing maintenance and updates present additional obstacles for businesses seeking to integrate this technology into their marketing initiatives. In essence, while generative AI holds great promise for enhancing marketing strategies, organizations must carefully weigh the potential benefits against the challenges before fully embracing these technologies in their operations.

14.6 ETHICAL CONSIDERATIONS IN USING GENERATIVE AI FOR MARKETING PURPOSES

Ethical considerations in using generative AI for marketing purposes are paramount in the digital age. While the technology has the potential to revolutionize personalized marketing strategies, there are concerns surrounding consumer privacy, consent, and transparency. The use of AI-generated content raises questions about the authenticity and ownership of the material produced, blurring the lines between what is real and artificially created. Marketers must also consider the impact of targeted advertising on vulnerable populations and the potential for algorithmic bias to perpetuate stereotypes or discrimination. Maintaining ethical standards when implementing generative AI in marketing campaigns requires careful deliberation and adherence to principles of fairness, accountability, and respect for individual rights.

14.7 FUTURE IMPLICATIONS AND TRENDS OF GENERATIVE AI IN MARKETING

Generative AI in marketing holds tremendous promise for reshaping the future of advertising and consumer engagement. As this technology evolves, it is poised to transform how businesses connect with their target audiences, delivering more personalized and captivating content than ever before. By harnessing deep learning algorithms, generative AI can sift through vast datasets to gain insights into consumer preferences and behaviors, enabling marketers to fine-tune their campaigns with unparalleled precision. Furthermore, the capacity of generative AI to craft lifelike text, images, and videos paves the way for innovative storytelling and creativity in marketing strategies. With ongoing advancements in this field, we can anticipate a shift toward immersive and interactive customer experiences that blend the physical and digital realms seamlessly. As organizations embrace generative AI tools, they will be better positioned to anticipate trends, respond to evolving consumer needs, and maintain a competitive edge in today's fast-paced marketplace.

14.8 CONCLUSION

In summary, generative AI techniques stand poised to revolutionize the marketing landscape, offering fresh solutions to longstanding challenges. From crafting personalized content to harnessing predictive analytics, these tools empower companies to better connect with their target audiences. Despite facing hurdles like ethical dilemmas and data privacy issues, the advantages of integrating generative AI into marketing strategies are undeniable. As technology progresses, it is vital for businesses to adopt these innovative techniques to remain competitive in today's digital-centric environment. With thoughtful strategies and effective implementation, generative AI has the potential to redefine marketing practices and fuel success for organizations of every size.

REFERENCES

1. Generative AI and the Future of Marketing. (n.d.). Retrieved February 24, 2024, from https://www.marketingevolution.com/knowledge-center/generative-ai-and-the-future-of-marketing
2. Top 10 Transformative Use Cases of Generative AI in .... (n.d.). Retrieved February 24, 2024, from https://www.linkedin.com/pulse/top-generative-ai-use-cases-2024-rami-huu-nguyen-e4xwe/
3. 7+ Use-Cases of Generative AI in Marketing. (n.d.). Retrieved February 24, 2024, from www.delve.ai/blog/generative-ai-marketing

4. 6 Ways to Use Generative AI for Your Marketing. (n.d.). Retrieved February 24, 2024, from martech.org/6-ways-to-use-generative-ai-for-your-marketing/
5. How Generative AI Can Boost Consumer Marketing. (n.d.). Retrieved February 24, 2024, from https://www.mckinsey.com/capabilities/growth-marketing-and-sales/our-insights/how-generative-ai-can-boost-consumer-marketing
6. Generative AI in Marketing: 5 Use Cases. (n.d.). Retrieved February 24, 2024, from https://www.forbes.com/councils/forbescommunicationscouncil/2023/04/03/generative-ai-in-marketing-5-use-cases/
7. Generative AI in Marketing: Benefits & 7 Use Cases in 2024. (n.d.). Retrieved February 24, 2024, from research.aimultiple.com/generative-ai-in-marketing/
8. A Practical Guide for Marketers Who Want to Use GenAI. (n.d.). Retrieved February 24, 2024, from https://hbr.org/2023/12/a-practical-guide-for-marketers-who-want-to-use-genai
9. 6 Generative AI Tools to Consider for Marketing and Sales. (n.d.). Retrieved February 24, 2024, from https://www.techtarget.com/searchcustomerexperience/tip/Generative-AI-tools-to-consider-for-marketing-and-sales
10. Hemachandran, K., Tayal, S., George, P. M., Singla, P., & Kose, U. (Eds.). (2022). *Bayesian reasoning and Gaussian processes for machine learning applications.* CRC Press.

15 Privacy and Ethical Considerations in Data-Driven Marketing

Mosuri Muniratnam, K. V. Meghana Reddy, and Yashaswini Aavula

15.1 INTRODUCTION

In the current data-driven marketing, the use of data-driven techniques has increasingly emerged as an effective method for assessing buyer behaviour, improving performance adequacy, and driving business success. Over time, the rapid spread of data-driven advertising systems creates major security concerns and moral consequences. This section analyses the evidence-based environment of data-driven advertising, highlighting its importance and the urgent need for robust safeguards and moral structures in this ever-evolving climate.

15.1.1 Background of Data-Diven Marketing

Data-driven promoting utilize expansive client data, usually accumulated across various automated stages, to immediate and further create exhibiting endeavours. This approach relies upon present-day assessment, automated thinking, and artificial intelligence strategies to create imperative pieces of data and architect publicizing tries to individual clients. The amazing extension in the number of cutting-edge stages, electronic amusement and online business has in a general sense added to the improvement of data-driven displaying, outfitting publicists with remarkable opportunities to get client encounters. The ascent and improvement of data-driven advancing can be followed back to the rising spread of digitalization in client participations. Right when people interact with online stages, they create an electronic record that publicists can take a gander at to get pieces of data into their tendencies, approaches to acting and purchasing penchants. Using a data-driven approach engages the execution of zeroed in on and modified advancing endeavours, dealing with the part of resources and extending the overall suitability of exhibiting tries.

15.1.2 Importance of Privacy and Ethics

Data-driven showcasing offers promising possibilities, however it additionally raises significant worries with respect to protection and morals. In the given circumstance, the meaning of protection cannot be misrepresented. The collection of broad datasets

DOI: 10.1201/9781003472544-15

by organizations, which much of the time incorporate delicate individual data, leads to a remarkable trepidation over the potential for data breaks and unlawful use. There is a developing acknowledgement among purchasers with respect to the meaning of individual data, prompting an uplifted craving for transparency and control comparable to its assortment, stockpiling, and usage. Data-driven showcasing includes moral contemplations that go past data security, enveloping the proper and impartial utilization of purchaser data. Advertisers are confronted with the test of finding some kind of harmony between giving custom fitted encounters and maintaining the standards of individual security. The need for moral standards that focus on client government assistance is featured by the opportunities for data abuse, including designated control and separation. Moreover, the moral part of data-driven advertising envelops the assessment of authorization and transparency. The moral idea of acquiring informed assent from people before the assortment and usage of their data is of vital significance. Conveying data rehearses in a straightforward way cultivates certainty and empowers shoppers to pursue very much educated choices in regards to their protection.

15.2 FUNDAMENTALS OF DATA PRIVACY

15.2.1 Definition and Scope of Data Privacy

Data protection, inside the domain of data-driven showcasing, relates to shielding people's independence in dealing with their own data that is accumulated, used, and held by associations for promoting targets. Data security is an assortment of ideas and practices that ensure people's privilege to be educated about the data being accumulated, its expected reason, and the capacity to direct its utilization and spread.

Data privacy in this context involves various crucial aspects:

Data collection encompasses the primary method of representing the precise categorizations of personal data that are gathered for marketing purposes, encompassing, but not limited to, names, email addresses, driving records, and purchase records. Data storage refers to the secure storage of collected data, which involves implementing measures to mitigate the risks of unauthorized access, unintentional loss, or misuse. The utilization of data encompasses the explicit representation of the intended application of the collected data for marketing endeavours, encompassing customization, targeted advertising, and customer segmentation. The topic of data sharing pertains to the potential exposure of personal data to external entities, necessitating the establishment of transparent information regarding the recipients of the data and the acquisition of explicit consent from individuals. The concept of individual control pertains to granting individuals the capacity to access their own data, demand its rectification or removal, and exercise their entitlement to decline involvement in data gathering or marketing endeavours that they consider unfavourable. An in-depth understanding of the concept and extent of data protection is crucial for upholding ethical standards in data-driven marketing strategies. By adhering to these principles, advertisers can establish trust with consumers, ensure responsible use of data, and effectively provide the appropriate environment. In a world dominated by data, this promotes a sustainable and ethical approach to marketing.

15.2.2 Legal Frameworks and Regulations

The importance of data protection has been recognized by states and regulatory agencies, leading to the development of legitimate policies and regulations. Adherence to these guidelines is crucial for organizations engaging in data-driven advertising. Within the European Affiliation, the General Data Protection Regulation (GDPR) has established stringent criteria for the handling of personal data, mandating explicit agreement from individuals and affording them the option to be disregarded. Data protection concerns in the US are also addressed by various state regulations, such as the California Consumer Privacy Act (CCPA). Customers are given the option to understand the specific personal data being collected and the current usage, as well as the option to decline the collection of their data. Comprehending and abiding by these authentic frameworks is not just a legal imperative but also a significant ethical principle in data-driven marketing.

15.2.3 Key Concepts in Privacy Protection

The rising reliance on data-driven promoting techniques requires an extensive cognizance of essential standards in shielding privacy. This section will investigate these critical points, underscoring their significance in safeguarding individual protection while working with moral showcasing procedures.

1. **Transparency and Assent**: This idea focuses on the spread of data to people with respect to the social event, use, and dispersal of their own data. Straightforward and effectively justifiable protection strategies that unequivocally address these ways of behaving are critical. Moreover, the demonstration of securing express agree before the assortment or usage of delicate data effectively develops trust and empower people to pursue very much educated choices in regards to their own data.
2. **Data Minimization and Anonymization**: The demonstration of social affairs exclusively the data that is fundamental for specific advertising targets, effectively limits the amount of data held and lessens the probability of its inappropriate usage. Likewise, the act of anonymizing data through the expulsion of and by recognizable data effectively upgrades individual protection and moderates the potential for openness in case of safety breaks.
3. **Data Security**: Carrying serious areas of strength for our conventions is fundamental to shield individual data from unapproved access, openness, alteration, or obliteration. Guaranteeing data uprightness and forestalling breaks require the execution of encryption instruments, access runs, and regular security reviews.
4. **Individual Freedoms and Control**: people must claim independence over their own data. This envelops the qualification to get, right, or erase individual data, as well as the privilege to protest its utilization for specific goals. The execution of frameworks that empower people to practice their privileges shows a guarantee of maintaining their security and developing a feeling of certainty.

5. **Responsibility and Consistence**: It is the obligation of organizations to guarantee consistence with data insurance rules and moral standards. Staying informed on relevant guidelines like the Overall Data Security Guideline (GDPR) and California Customer Protection Act (CCPA) ensures adherence to legitimate necessities and exhibits a commitment to faithful treatment of data.
6. **Moral Use**: The arrangement of data social affair and usage with moral qualities is pivotal. It is fitting for advertisers to avoid participating in strategies that might be seen as meddling, manipulative, or segregating. The use of data for legitimate promoting reasons, while at the same time keeping moral standards and protecting individual security, is of most extreme significance.

By integrating these key standards into their functional methodologies, endeavours may successfully arrange the complexities of data-driven showcasing in a capable way. The foundation of trust with shoppers and the advancement of reasonable and moral showcasing strategies in the computerized period can be worked with by putting accentuation on transparency, data minimization, security, and individual control.

15.2.4 Comparative Analysis of Global Privacy Laws

In the time of data-driven showcasing, the ability to accumulate and examine purchaser data offers huge open doors as well as critical obstructions. In a period of developing worldwide interconnectivity, it is essential for people to focus on the assurance of individual data security. This requires a careful understanding of the legitimate system in different geological regions. In this section, an assessment and juxtaposition of key worldwide security regulations will be led, with specific accentuation on the Overall Data Assurance Guideline (GDPR), the California Buyer Protection Act (CCPA), and other significant principles. The goal is to highlight the shared characteristics and differentiations between these regulations inside the structure of data-driven promotion. A striking qualification can be seen in the degree of these guidelines. The GDPR, established by the European Association in 2018, is material to all elements that handle the individual data of people living in the EU, regardless of the association's geological area. This broad extension lays out a thorough norm for protecting data on an overall scale. Conversely, the California Shopper Protection Act (CCPA), which was carried out in California in 2018, only relates to endeavours that assemble the individual data of California residents outperforming foreordained levels. One eminent qualification relates to the privileges presented to people. Both the Overall Data Insurance Guideline (GDPR) and the California Buyer Security Act (CCPA) give people the privilege to get to, right, and delete their own data. By the by, the GDPR gives further qualifications, for example, the consent to move data and the valuable chance to bring up criticisms against computerized independent direction. The consideration of these strengthening privileges awards people improved power over private data inside the European Association. Despite the fact that there are varieties, there are additionally a few likenesses. In both the GDPR and CCPA, there is a necessity for transparency in the methods of data securing. Organizations are committed to furnish people with data in regards to the idea of the data accumulated, the goal of the assortment, and the beneficiaries of the data.

Moreover, the two prerequisites require that organizations take on reasonable safety efforts to shield individual data against unapproved access, divulgence, adjustment, or destruction. In option to these key regulation, there are extra significant regulations that are impacting the data security environment. Brazil's Overall Assurance Regulation (LGPD), established in 2020, shows specific likenesses to the GDPR, in particular in its accentuation on individual freedoms and the obligation of data regulators. The Individual Data Security Regulation (PIPL) of China, which was carried out in 2021, puts a critical accentuation on the protection of data and forces impediments on the transmission of data across public boundaries. Data-driven showcasing drives deal with a huge issue in successfully exploring the multifaceted idea of these fluctuated restrictions. Businesses that work on an overall scale should comply with a different scope of regulations, which expects them to assess the singular guidelines in every ward cautiously. This habitually involves creating a multi-layered consistent methodology and changing arrangements as per the geological area of the data subject. Given the continuous advancement of the worldwide legitimate scene, keeping up with progressing endeavours to accomplish administrative harmonization is basic. This is important to give a reasonable methodology that advances development while at the same time safeguarding individual protection in an interconnected world.

15.3 ETHICAL FRAMEWORKS IN DATA-DRIVEN MARKETING (FIGURE 15.1)

Moral contemplations in promoting rehearses are pivotal, especially in the domain of data-driven advertising where the potential for abuse of buyer data is huge. Advertisers should explore the sensitive harmony between utilizing data for designated crusades and regarding individual security freedoms. One key moral thought

FIGURE 15.1 Ethical considerations in AI marketing strategies.

is the straightforward and capable utilization of customer data. Advertisers ought to be candid about their data assortment techniques, purposes, and beneficiaries. Also, they ought to guarantee that data use lines up with shoppers' assumptions and regards their independence (Figure 15.1).

Another moral thought is the rule of reasonableness. Separation in light of variables like race, orientation, or financial status ought to be kept away from in data-driven advertising. Predispositions in calculations and dynamic cycles can sustain disparities and dissolve trust. Advertisers need to effectively distinguish and amend any inclinations inside their data and calculations to maintain reasonableness and advance moral-promoting rehearses.

Moreover, the moral treatment of client data includes getting educated assent. People ought to have the potential chance to comprehend how their data will be utilized and give express agreement to its assortment and handling. Advertisers should likewise think about the standards of data minimization, gathering just the data vital for the expected reason. This training regards security as well as decreases the potential for data breaks and abuse.

15.3.1 Ethical Decision-Making Models

In the realm of information-driven advertising, ethical considerations hold significant importance. Organizations exert immense influence by collecting, analysing, and utilizing consumer data. In order to ensure conscientious and ethical actions, it is imperative to prioritize the comprehension and implementation of moral navigation systems. This study examines three distinct ethical frameworks: utilitarianism, deontology, and morality, highlighting their advantages and disadvantages in the context of data-driven marketing.

1. **Utilitarianism**: It emphasizes the maximization of overall happiness and the minimization of harm. In the context of information-driven advertising, it may suggest that the moral choice is the one that benefits the majority, regardless of whether it involves giving up a specific protection or autonomy. Using targeted advertising to promote public health initiatives should have been considered morally justified due to its anticipated societal benefits.

   However, utilitarianism can be criticized for its failure to consider individual rights and its failure to account for the possibility of unforeseen consequences. Moreover, this also gives rise to concerns over the definition of "joy" and the methods of measurement, potentially leading to biased practices.
2. **Deontology**: It emphasizes the importance of adhering to moral principles and abiding by predetermined laws, regardless of the outcomes. In the context of information-driven marketing, deontological ethics would argue that prioritizing individual rights, such as security and autonomy, is essential, irrespective of its impact on the market's profitability. For example, a deontological perspective may support strict restrictions on data collection and targeted advertising, even if it reduces advertising reach.

   However, deontology can be criticized for its extreme rigidity and failure to adequately account for contextual factors. In specific scenarios, it may be deemed necessary to deviate from established regulations in order to achieve a more significant objective. Furthermore, the task of defining universally accepted moral principles might prove challenging within a diverse and evolving global context.

3. **Virtue Ethics**: This paradigm emphasizes the cultivation of exemplary personal attributes, such as reliability, integrity, and compassion. It encourages individuals to make decisions based on the actions that a prudent person would take when faced with similar circumstances. In the realm of information-driven marketing, an ethical approach would involve the questioning of whether a judicious advertiser would endorse this instruction. This could lead to a greater emphasis on transparency in data collection, prioritizing customer protection, and avoiding misleading marketing tactics. It heavily relies on individual judgement and comprehension, potentially leading to variations in dynamics among different individuals and organizations.
4. **Rights-Based Approach**: It emphasizes fundamental common liberties, such as the right to security, freedom of expression, and non-separation. When it comes to information-driven marketing, it is necessary to ensure that advertising campaigns adhere to these fundamental rights. For example, it would promote the acquisition of explicit consent for data collection and the utilization of data in a manner that avoids oppressing individuals or communities.

   The efficacy of the privileges-based approach can be assessed by the complexity of delineating and modifying different liberties. Furthermore, there is a prevailing argument that not all liberties are universally recognized, and the interpretation and implementation of certain rights may be influenced by social, legal, and cultural contexts.

15.3.2 Industry Code of Conduct

Numerous ventures have laid out sets of principles to direct moral conduct in promoting rehearses. These codes frequently address standards of transparency, decency, and responsibility. For example, the American Showcasing Affiliation (AMA) and the Information and Promoting Affiliation (DMA) give moral rules to advertisers.

Sticking to industry sets of rules assists advertisers with lining up with all-inclusive moral principles. These codes normally incorporate arrangements connected with buyer assent, honest publicizing, and dependable information use. Advertisers ought to find out more about and coordinate these codes into their techniques to guarantee moral way of behaving in the undeniably information-driven scene.

15.3.3 Dangers and Difficulties

While information-driven showcasing offers various advantages, it accompanies intrinsic dangers and difficulties that require cautious thought from a moral outlook. One critical gamble is the potential for protection breaks. Wrong treatment of individual data can prompt information spills, fraud, and disintegration of buyer trust. Advertisers should execute strong safety efforts to defend shopper information and moderate these dangers.

One more test is the moral ramifications of designated promoting. While customized promoting can upgrade client experience, it can likewise raise worries about control and interruption. Advertisers should work out some kind of harmony among personalization and regarding individual protection, keeping away from rehearses that might be seen as obtrusive or manipulative.

The advancing scene of innovation and information examination presents the test of remaining in front of moral contemplations. Advertisers need to consistently evaluate and refresh their moral structures to line up with innovative headways and changing purchaser assumptions.

15.4 RISK AND CHALLENGES

15.4.1 Potential Privacy Risks in Data-Driven Marketing

Information-driven advertising, although providing numerous advantages, is accompanied by possible risks that require careful assessment. One significant risk involves the unauthorized access or breach of sensitive consumer data. Organizations' vast amounts of data become attractive targets for malicious actors seeking to exploit or trade personal information. Inadequate safety measures can lead to the occurrence of information breaches, resulting in significant consequences for both individuals and entities involved.

Another security concern arises from the extensive profiling and monitoring of client behaviour. The continuous monitoring of online activities, in conjunction with advanced research, has the potential to generate specific profiles that may exceed the level of privacy desired by users. The heightened level of surveillance has the potential to undermine the sense of safety and autonomy, thereby leading to unintended consequences and growing uncertainty.

The lack of transparency in information practices poses an additional risk. The absence of transparency in communicating with customers regarding the acquisition, management, and application of personal data can lead to a decline in confidence. The significance of transparency in risk management rests in its capacity to motivate individuals to make educated choices about their personal information and guarantee that companies are held responsible for their activities.

15.4.2 Challenges in Maintaining Ethical Standards (Figure 15.2)

Adhering to ethical principles in e-commerce is an ongoing challenge, influenced by several factors. One important aspect to consider is the rapid pace of technological advancements, which often surpasses the progress of ethical frameworks. Advertisers may have challenges in adapting their strategies to emerging technologies while ensuring continuous ethical considerations.

The complexity of information processes inside biological systems poses an additional challenge. As data is collected from various sources and orchestrated for the purpose of inquiry, ethical dilemmas may arise around the ownership of information, consent, and the possibility of unforeseen consequences. The examination of these complexities necessitates a proactive approach to addressing ethical guidance and a commitment to ongoing evaluation and enhancement (Figure 15.2).

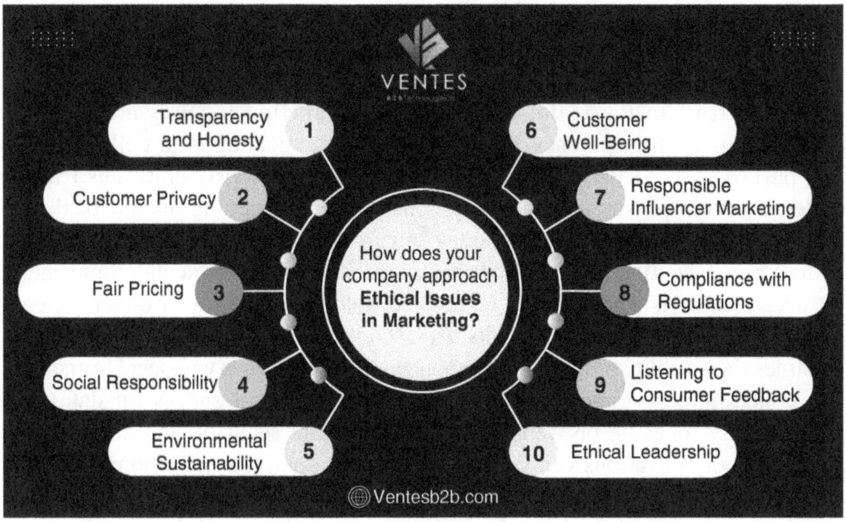

FIGURE 15.2 Approach to ethical issues in marketing.

Moreover, the challenge of achieving promotional objectives, such as increasing commitment or conversion rates, can occasionally lead to ethical dilemmas. Advertisers may be tempted to prioritize short-term gains over long-term ethical considerations, playing a risk to both brand reputation and customer trust.

15.4.3 Impact of Consumer Trust

In the period of big data, data-driven marketing has turned into the foundation of many organizations' success. By utilizing customer data to customize encounters and target campaigns, organizations can accomplish noteworthy outcomes. However, the effectiveness of this approach relies on a critical variable which is customer trust. This essay explores the significant effect of customer trust on data-driven marketing, examining its advantages, potential pitfalls, and techniques for building trust in the digital landscape.

One of the main advantages of buyer trust lies in its capacity to open the maximum capacity of data-driven marketing. At the point when customers trust a brand's data rehearses, they are bound to share their data promptly, giving significant experiences that fuel more viable personalization. This transparency permits organizations to tailor their informing, item suggestions, and offers to individual preferences, prompting expanded commitment and conversion rates.

Besides, customer trust encourages brand loyalty and positive brand perception. At the point when purchasers feel their data is secured, respected, and utilized ethically, they develop a sense of dedication and loyalty towards the brand. This positive affiliation converts into rehash business, positive word-of-mouth, and a readiness to draw in with future marketing campaigns.

However, the lack of consumer trust can have devastating consequences for data-driven marketing efforts. At the point when consumers have worries about data privacy or see unethical data practices, they become more resistant to sharing data and drawing in with customized promoting. This can prompt separation, lower change rates, and, surprisingly, negative brand opinion, eventually compromising marketing effectiveness.

Building trust in the realm of data-driven marketing requires a multifaceted approach. Firstly, transparency is principal. Communicating data collection practices, purposes, and safety efforts transparently and obviously cultivates trust and enables buyers to pursue informed decisions. Moreover, getting unequivocal assent prior to gathering any delicate data shows regard for individual security privileges.

Moreover, executing powerful data safety measures is fundamental. Solid encryption, access controls, and standard reviews console buyers that their data is defended against unapproved access and breaks. At last, complying to significant data security guidelines shows obligation to ethical practices and consistence with legal frameworks.

In conclusion, customer trust serves as the bedrock of successful data-driven marketing. By focusing on transparency, assent, data security, and administrative consistence, organizations can construct trust and open the maximum capacity of data-driven promotion. This trust, in return, fosters brand loyalty and positive brand perception and, ultimately, drives business success in the age of data.

15.4.4 Technological Advancements and Privacy Risks

Data-driven marketing has been revolutionized by the rapid growth of technologies like artificial intelligence (AI) and the Internet of Things (IoT), offering remarkable prospects for customized experiences and focused marketing. Nevertheless, these technological improvements also bring out new and complex security issues that require meticulous deliberation. One significant risk is associated with the increased quantity and level of detail in data collection. Computer-based intelligence algorithms, powered by vast amounts of data, have the capability to generate detailed profiles of individual behaviour and preferences. This extends beyond the realm of internet connectivity, as Internet of Things (IoT) devices such as smart home appliances and wearables gather sensitive data regarding our physical environment and even health information. The vast collection of information gives rise to concerns over surveillance, as individuals feel constantly monitored and require control over their data.

Moreover, the increased application of artificial intelligence in data analysis raises issues regarding algorithmic bias. The predispositions that arise from the information utilized in the development of artificial intelligence models have the potential to incite oppressive actions in the pursuit of promoting endeavours. For example, unbalanced computations may unfairly concentrate on particular socioeconomic factors or disregard individuals based on their perceived characteristics. This has the potential to cause harm to individuals at any given moment and erode confidence in the advertising strategies employed.

Another significant and urgent concern pertains to the possibility of exerting control and provocation. Simulated intelligence has the capability to tailor promotional messages and deliver them in ways that use cognitive biases or influence consumer purchasing decisions. This phenomenon gives rise to ethical concerns about the preservation of freedom and consumer autonomy, as individuals may inadvertently be swayed towards choices that do not align with their optimal interests.

Mitigating these hazards necessitates the implementation of a proactive approach. Directness, from the beginning, is essential. Buyers require transparent and concise information regarding the collection, utilization, and investigation of their data, especially using artificial intelligence calculations. Moreover, the effective management of information is of utmost importance. Organizations should implement protocols that restrict data collection, ensure data security, and empower individuals with control over their data. Finally, it is imperative to incorporate ethical considerations into the design and enhancement of artificial intelligence employed in promotional endeavours. Algorithmic bias should be thoroughly tested and mitigated, and clear explanations should be provided for AI-driven decisions.

Considering all factors, whereas revolutionary advancements provide significant benefits for data-driven marketing, they also introduce novel and intricate security obstacles. By prioritizing transparency, effective information management, and ethical artificial intelligence enhancement, advertisers can consistently navigate this emerging landscape, fostering consumer trust and ensuring ethical marketing practices in the future.

15.5 PRIVACY-ENHANCING TECHNOLOGIES (FIGURE 15.3)

15.5.1 Overview of Privacy-Enhancing Technologies

Privacy-enhancing technologies (PETs) imply an extent of instruments and strategies expected to shield individuals' insurance while, at this point, thinking about the collection and treatment of data. These advancements intend to restrict the perils related to data-driven promoting practices via completing instruments like data encryption, pseudonymization, and anonymization.

15.5.2 Role of Encryption and Anonymization

Encryption assumes a fundamental part in data-driven displaying by ensuring that delicate data stays secure during transmission and limit. By scrambling data, publicists can prevent unapproved access and defend individuals' security honours. Anonymization, of course, incorporates disposing of really conspicuous

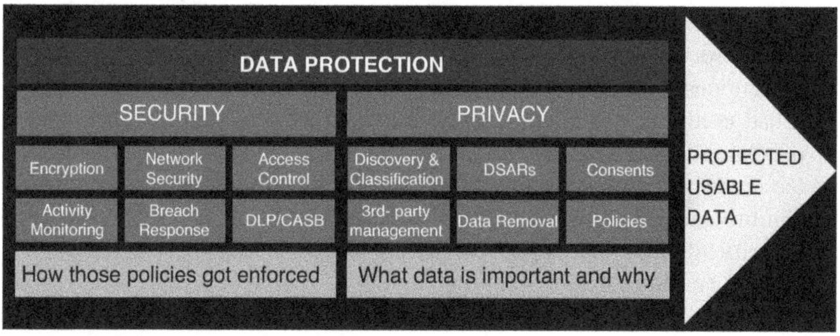

FIGURE 15.3 Data protection.

data from datasets, thinking about examination and centring without subverting individuals' assurance (Figure 15.3).

15.5.3 Emerging Advances for Security

Technology advancement continues to drive improvement in the field of safety redesigning progressions. From differential assurance to homomorphic encryption, new procedures are being made to address the creating troubles of data security in advancing practices. These emerging advances offer promising responses for changing the necessity for data-driven encounters with individuals' security concerns.

15.5.4 Challenges and Limitations of Implementing PETs

There are various impediments and limitations that organizations should defeat while carrying out security improving advancements, or PETs. The trouble of integrating PETs into current frameworks and methodology is a significant deterrent that might require a huge speculation of time and data. Moreover, it very well may be trying to find some kind of harmony among ease of use and security on the grounds that severe protection guidelines may adversely influence the client experience. Significantly more noteworthy intricacy emerges from the need to keep up with consistency when changing administrative principles. A hesitance to execute new innovation or changing well established strategies may likewise come from partners, like interior groups and outer accomplices. At last, regardless of whether PETs seem like promising answers for further developing protection, organizations should cautiously design, contribute, and stay committed to beat these impediments.

15.6 CASE STUDIES

15.6.1 Notable Examples of Privacy Breaches

1. Marriott International Data Breach

   2018 saw the discovery of a data theft impacting as many as 500 million customers of Marriott Global's Starwood Lodgings division. Delicate data, including addresses, names, and Visa numbers, were compromised during the long-term breach that occurred before it was detected. The significance of data security and the need for organizations to take necessary steps for prevention to keep away from breaches were featured by this event. Since it had compromised client data (Figure 15.4), it was liable to fines under the Overall Data Security Guideline (GDPR). With decrease the impacts of the break and comply to GDPR guidelines, the organization worked with administrative bodies, set up superior safety efforts, and gave character security administrations and remuneration to the affected gatherings.

2. Yahoo Data Breaches

   Yahoo had a few data violations somewhere in the range of 2013 and 2016, uncovering the confidential data of billions of clients. The organization experienced extreme monetary and brand hurt because of these

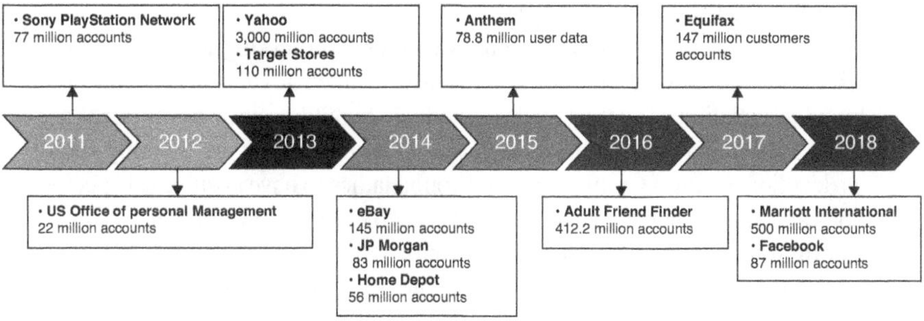

FIGURE 15.4 Marriott International Data Breach timeline of events.

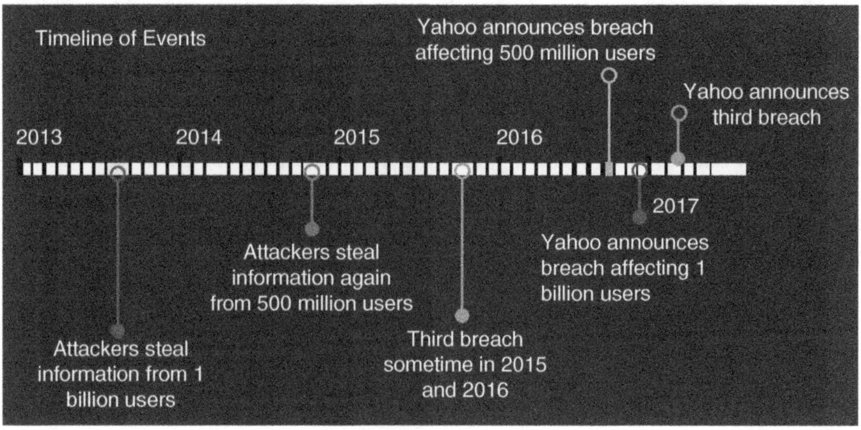

FIGURE 15.5 Yahoo Data Breach timeline of events.

violations, which were among the greatest ever. In light of the data infractions, the company went under administrative examination under data protection regulations, like the GDPR and the California Buyer Security Act (CCPA). Determined to stick to lawful norms and recapture client trust, the organization really tried to fortify its security conventions, immediately uncovered any infractions, and joined forces with administrative bodies to investigate and determine the issues (Figure 15.5).

15.6.2 Success Stories in Ethical Data-Driven Marketing

1. The Transparency Initiative of Patagonia

   Patagonia, a company that has the fame of being Renowned for its commitment to environmental and social responsibility, is an outdoor clothing maker. Patagonia started the "Footprint Chronicles" project in 2017, which gives clients bare essential data about the natural and social impact of its things. By embracing transparency and drawing in buyers to make informed choices, Patagonia has manufactured a steadfast client base and isolated itself in trouble-pressed market.

2. Real Beauty Campaign by Dove

   One of the most striking instances of moral promoting to date is Dove's "Real Beauty" crusade. Dove has successfully taken advantage of a more profound association of feeling with individuals by addressing conventional aesthetic norms and supporting variety. The organization has additionally shown its devotion to empowering ladies and young ladies to have positive self-perceptions and fearlessness by supporting projects like the Bird Confidence Venture.

3. Community-Centric Approach of Airbnb

   Being a trailblazer in the sharing economy, Airbnb has changed individual's travel and track down new protests. Airbnb has promoted a dependable and clear culture that has facilitated worries about security and insurance. Occurrences of these components consolidate character check, client analysis, and host informative classes. Trustworthiness, assortment, and validity are key pieces of Airbnb's social class-driven method.

15.7 BEST PRACTICES

In the age of data-driven marketing, striking a balance between achieving business goals and upholding ethical principles is paramount. This chapter outlines several key principles for responsible data marketing, emphasizing the importance of data minimization, transparency, security, compliance, and ethical usage.

- Regulatory bodies expect an essential part in maintaining guidelines and rules associated with data security and moral displaying practices. In light of safety breaks and tricky exhibiting practices, these associations regularly take fast action to look at, rebuff, and put resistance down. This is a layout of the manner in which regulatory bodies have addressed such episodes (Figure 15.6).
- **Data Break Admonitions**: Various managerial frameworks, similar to the General Data Security Rule (GDPR) in Europe and the Medical Care Versatility and Obligation Act (HIPAA) in the US, anticipate that affiliations should quickly tell affected individuals and authoritative specialists in the event of a data break. Failure to concur with these advance notice essentials can achieve basic disciplines.
- **Fines and Disciplines**: Regulatory bodies have the situation to compel fines and disciplines on affiliations seen as dismissing data security guidelines or partaking in unscrupulous publicizing practices. These fines can move in reality depending upon the nature and level of the encroachment, as well as the affiliation's consistency history.
- **Consent and Transparency Essentials**: Rules, for instance, the GDPR, stress the meaning of gaining unequivocal consent from individuals preceding social occasions or taking care of their own data. Managerial bodies could examine affiliations' consent parts and transparency practices to ensure consistency with these necessities.
- **Assessments and Surveys**: Regulatory bodies, as often as possible, direct assessments and audits to assess affiliations' consistency with data security guidelines and rules. These assessments may be set off by complaints from individuals, reports of data breaks, or proactive noticing.

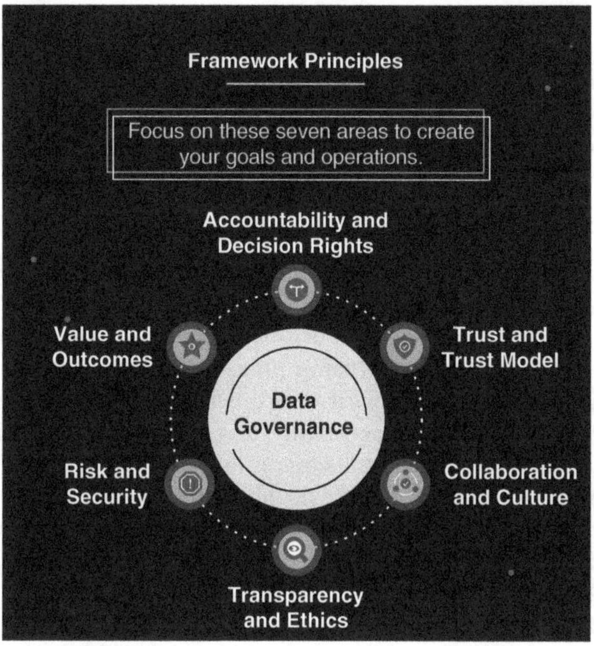

FIGURE 15.6 Framework principles in data governance.

- **Authoritative Heading and Approval Exercises**: Managerial bodies reliably disperse bearing reports and admonitions to help relationship with sorting out their responsibilities under data security guidelines and rules. In examples of obstruction, these workplaces could give cautions, medicinal action plans, or formal necessity exercises to drive relationship to address encroachment and hinder future episodes.

15.8 FUTURE TRENDS

15.8.1 Evolving Privacy Regulations

Protection guidelines undergo constant updates in order to be informed about the rapid advancements in data-driven technologies. Countries and regulatory bodies worldwide are actively enhancing and expanding privacy regulations in order to address the increasing threats. The General Data Protection Regulation (GDPR) implemented by the European Union serves as a notable example, as it has established a comprehensive standard for safeguarding data. The General Data Protection Regulation (GDPR) places significant emphasis on customer permission, data transparency, and the right to be forgotten, thereby shaping privacy policies worldwide. In addition, it is worth noting that certain nations, such as Brazil (Lei Geral de Protecao de Dados or LGPD) and California (California Purchaser Security Act or CCPA), have implemented or enhanced protection regulations, hence influencing the administrative framework. The increasing concerns over security have led to a growing inclination towards implementing more rigorous and comprehensive requirements. Anticipated security solutions will prioritize algorithmic accountability, data portability, and enhanced individual rights regarding confidential information. In the ever-changing administrative landscape, advertising and organizations must remain adaptable and adhere to regulatory requirements in order to navigate the unpredictable landscape of policies.

15.8.2 Technological Advances and Ethical Implications

The emergence of technological advancements, particularly in the areas of predictive analysis and artificial intelligence, offers a range of anticipated advantages and ethical dilemmas in the realm of data-driven marketing. The utilization of sophisticated computations, automated dynamic processes, and the potential for unintentional biases give rise to ethical concerns. In order to achieve a harmonious balance between progress and ethical responsibility, it is essential to engage in continuous evaluation and implement proactive measures to address these obstacles (Floridi et al., 2018; Mittelstadt et al., 2016). The evident significance of ethical considerations in the enhancement of innovation and organization is growing. The ethical use of computerized reasoning, often known as artificial intelligence, involves regulating inherent biases in calculations, promoting openness in dynamic systems, and fostering inclusion within model training datasets. Emerging technologies such as unified learning and homomorphic encryption are being developed to enhance the security of client data in the context of contemporary research (Yang et al., 2019; Shokri et al., 2017). Effective collaboration in conversations around ethical advancements in artificial intelligence and technology is essential for partners involved in data-driven marketing. A proactive approach entails adhering to ethical principles in artificial intelligence, fostering collaborative efforts across many fields, and consistently guiding the field towards achieving a balance between progress and reliable practices.

15.8.3 The Future Landscape of Data-Driven Marketing

The integration of artificial intelligence technology, personalized experiences, and advanced analysis is expected to play a significant role in shaping the future of data-driven marketing. The significance of ethical considerations in determining advertising strategies will become increasingly substantial as consumer expectations continue to evolve. This section examines the possible methods and modifications in the data-driven advertising environment, taking into account the evolving relationship between consumer expectations for innovation and ethical obligations (Smith, 2020). The integration of augmented reality (AR), virtual reality (VR), and the Internet of Things (IoT) platforms will provide innovative perspectives to the field of data-driven marketing. Advertisers must skilfully manage the ethical considerations surrounding the collection and utilization of data from organized devices and real-life experiences. Moreover, the advancement of voice search and conversational artificial intelligence is expected to significantly alter the manner in which advertisers engage with consumers, necessitating ethical considerations in the social event and management of voice data. As data-driven marketing progresses, it is crucial to establish a balance between development and capable work, ensuring the security of customer data and the preservation of confidence. Organizations that adopt ethical considerations not only effectively manage operational conditions but also cultivate long-lasting customer relationships founded on principles of transparency and respect for privacy.

15.8.4 Privacy and Ethics in the Age of Big Data and AI

The arrival of the digital age has brought about a time of unprecedented gathering and obtaining of data. "Large data" encompasses the vast quantities of data produced via our everyday actions, allowing artificial intelligence (AI) to gather information, make forecasts, and potentially impact human behaviour. The aforementioned breakthroughs present undeniable benefits in various domains including as healthcare, banking, and marketing. However, they also give rise to noteworthy apprehensions pertaining to security and ethics. In the current context, it is crucial to achieve a cohesive balance between the influence of data and the inherent rights to privacy. An important concern pertains to the substantial volume and quantifiable characteristics of the compiled data. An individual's life can be comprehensively analysed by examining their programme preferences, online entertainment connections, location tracking, and purchasing history. The collected data can be utilized for precise marketing, profiling, and potentially quantifying the influence on dynamic cycles. Furthermore, the problem is further intensified by the lack of openness in the methods employed for data collection, resulting in individuals being unaware of the extent to which their data is collected and utilized. The dissemination of biases using artificial intelligence algorithms can lead to the implementation of prejudiced tactics, particularly in domains such as marketing and business applications. Moreover, the potential for exerting control through personalized alerts and tailored notifications gives rise to concerns regarding unrestricted navigation and human coordination. The informed decision-making capacity of consumers is being undermined. The task of addressing these challenges is not solely the responsibility of legislative and administrative bodies, but also falls upon business and technology developers. Ensuring data privacy, consent, and control necessitates the implementation of robust security protocols. It is imperative that individuals are afforded the opportunity to access personal data, comprehend its use, and exercise their right to refuse objectionable data collection methods. On the other hand, it is imperative for organizations to prioritize effective data management, which encompasses safeguarding data security and upholding ethical standards within their promotion strategies. The importance of mechanical improvements in addressing security concerns is crucial. Anonymization and differential security strategies have the potential to provide valuable insights while simultaneously safeguarding individuals' identities. Furthermore, it is crucial to enhance the progress of ethical frameworks for artificial intelligence (AI) that prioritize principles of morality, openness, and responsibility. In the realm of massive data and simulated intelligence, effectively addressing the ethical intricacies necessitates the implementation of a comprehensive and multifaceted framework. The value of collaboration among government agencies, entrepreneurs, technologists, and individuals is of utmost importance. By giving priority to data security, promoting transparency, and implementing reliable artificial intelligence practices, it is possible to effectively harness the potential of these technologies for beneficial purposes, while also protecting the fundamental right to privacy in our technologically advanced society.

15.9 CONCLUSION

After conducting a comprehensive evaluation of the fundamental security and ethical concerns addressed in this section, several significant patterns emerge. In the current era of data-driven marketing, the primary concern is ensuring the highest level of significance in protecting customer security. The global recognition of the necessity for robust security measures is exemplified by regulatory frameworks such as GDPR, LGPD, and CCPA. The moral dimensions are inherent in every phase of data-driven advertising, encompassing both the generation of calculations and the implementation of personalized campaigns. Continuous investigation is necessary to address the presence of biases in calculations, the dependable utilization of artificial intelligence, and the efficient management of customer data. The task of reconciling social progress with ethical principles is a complex endeavour, necessitating organizations to prioritize the equitable and transparent utilization of information. The effective and ethical utilization of predictive analysis and AI in marketing necessitates the enhancement of ethical standards and industry norms in conjunction with advancements in technology. In light of the dynamic atmosphere and the uncertain interplay between security, ethics, and innovation, it is crucial to promote appropriate data practices. Companies involved in data-driven marketing must adopt a proactive stance towards ethical considerations. Organizations should allocate resources towards the education of their staff on the robust legal environment and the cultivation of ethical standards in the field of data-driven marketing. Place a significant emphasis on transparency in the collection and management of data, ensuring that explicit consent is obtained from users prior to utilizing their data for marketing purposes. Maintain ethical standards for artificial intelligence, ensuring that computations are conducted and utilized with considerations of worth, responsibility, and openness. In order to foster ethical values for data-driven marketing, active participation in organized industry collaborations is essential. This entails the promotion of consumer autonomy and collective responsibility. The objective is to enhance client engagement by implementing data regulation. Please provide other details. Incorporating these criteria can contribute to the establishment of a sustainable and ethical future for data-driven marketing within associations. Therefore, individuals can effectively navigate the influential political environment and establish credibility with their clients, fostering trustworthy relationships based on ethical data management principles.

REFERENCES

Floridi L, et al. AI4People—An ethical framework for a good AI society: Opportunities, risks, principles, and recommendations. *Minds Mach.* 2018;28(4):689–707.

Mittelstadt BD, et al. The ethics of algorithms: Mapping the debate. *Big Data Soc.* 2016;3(2):1–21.

Shokri, S., Mahmoudvand, S., Taherkhani, R., & Farshadpour, F. Modulation of the immune response by Middle East respiratory syndrome coronavirus. *J cell phys*, 2019;234(3): 2143–2151.

Smith J. Navigating the GDPR: The implications for data-driven marketing. *J Mark Technol.* 2020;4(2):87–95.

Yang, Y., Zhang, Q., Gao, W., Fan, C., Shu, Q., & Yun, H. (2022). Design on face recognition system with privacy preservation based on homomorphic encryption. *Wireless personal communications*, 123(4), 3737–3754.

16 Price Prediction and Optimization in Predictive Analytics and Generative AI for Data-Driven Marketing Strategies

Premsai Paidisetty, Darahas Bolisetty, and Bhargav Narsimgoju

16.1 INTRODUCTION

Any business strategy with the objective at maximizing profitability while sustaining a competitive edge in the market has to involve pricing optimization. It involves employing a systematic strategy to determine the ideal pricing for a product or service taking consideration of a range of factors such as consumer behaviour, production costs, market demand, and competition. A company's revenue and market share can be significantly affected by effective pricing strategies. We will look at the key elements of pricing optimization in this introduction, including different strategies, the importance of decisions based on data, and the implementation of generative AI and predictive analytics.

16.1.1 Overview of Pricing Strategies

Pricing strategies are methods that companies use to determine how much to charge for their goods or services. Typical price techniques include the following:

- **Cost-Plus Pricing**: Determining the selling price by reducing the production cost by a markup. Price setting based on the prices of rivals in the market is known as competitive pricing.
- **Value-Based Pricing**: The choice regarding price is chosen according to the customer's perception of the importance of the good or service.
- **Dynamic Pricing**: Changing prices instantly in response to financial conditions such as rivals, consumer demand, and other aspects.

DOI: 10.1201/9781003472544-16

- **Penetration Pricing**: Establishing minimal beginning costs in order to rapidly gain share of the market.
- **Price Skimming**: Pricing things highly in the beginning and then progressively reducing them over time.

Profitable pricing minimization requires an awareness of these tactics and the selection of the best one for a specific good or trade niche.

16.1.2 Importance of Data-Driven Pricing Decisions

Making data-driven price selections entails figuring out the best way to price through data analysis and insights. This approach allows businesses to:

- Recognize the choices and payment readiness of your customers [1].
- Examine the competition environment and market dynamics [1].
- Determine financial advantages and possible risks.
- Make price tactics more effective for various product categories and client groups [1].

In current cutthroat marketplace, if organizations had possession of enormous quantities of information that may be utilized to obtain an edge over others, data-driven pricing decisions are essential.

16.1.3 Role of Predictive Analytics and Generative AI in Pricing Optimization

The optimization of pricing is greatly aided by generative AI and predictive analytics through:

- Estimating pricing efficiency and demand forecasting [1].
- Determining the best pricing tactics to increase sales and profits [1].
- Price judgements and modifications that are automated and depend upon current information [1].
- Producing insights on the interests and habits of customers [1].
- Pricing models that are optimized for various trade conditions and situations [1].
- By utilizing AI and advanced analytics, firms may better adjust their pricing plans to the ever-changing trends in the market [1].

16.2 DATA COLLECTION AND PREPARATION FOR PRICING ANALYSIS

16.2.1 Gathering Relevant Data Sources

- **Transactional Data**: Trades data with date stamps, amounts offered, and past price included.
- **Product Data**: Characteristics like the attributes, specs, and classifications of a product.

- **Market Data**: Market data from rivals, standards in the sector, and economic trends [1].
- **Customer Data**: Population statistics, buying behaviours, devotion to clients, and comments.
- **External Data**: Cyclical nature, meteorological information, electronic media attitude, and financial variables.

16.2.2 Data Cleansing and Pre-processing

- **Handling Missing Values**: Utilize methods like mean, median, or forecasting to impute values that are missing.
- **Outlier Detection**: Exceptions that potentially distort the research or modelling outcomes should be identified and dealt with [1].
- **Data Formatting**: Regulate or equalize mathematical properties to guarantee level integrity.
- **Encoding Categorical Variables**: Use methods as one-hot encoding or label encoding to translate variables with categories through arithmetic formats [1].
- **Feature Scaling**: To avoid bigger size characteristics taking centre stage, scale mathematical characteristics to a comparable frequency [1].

16.2.3 Feature Selection and Engineering for Pricing Analysis

- **Univariate Feature Selection**: To find parameters of substantial predictive ability, consider attributes via empirical methods such as ANOVA or chi-square [1].
- **Feature Importance**: To determine the significance of an attribute for cost prediction, utilize ensemble approaches or decision trees as algorithms.
- **Dimensionality Reduction**: Utilize methods such as principal component analysis (PCA) or product mining to decrease the dataset's density while maintaining pertinent data.
- **Time-Series Features**: For identifying variations across time, use spatial elements like as trends, cyclical nature, and deferred data.
- **Domain-Specific Features**: Provide elements like price flexibility or instability that are unique to the pricing area.

16.3 PREDICTIVE MODELLING TECHNIQUES

Algorithms and methodologies known as predictive modelling approaches have been used in the analysis of past data to forecast future results. Prediction modelling aids in the forecasting of consumer demand, ideal prices, and client behaviour in the environment of pricing analysis and management [2].

16.3.1 Regression Analysis for Price Elasticity Estimation

- To determine price elasticity, or the degree that consumer consumption is sensitive to market fluctuations, regression analysis—more specifically, linear regression—is frequently employed [2].

- Cost is the factor that is independent at this scenario, while amount sold, or income was the factor that is dependent. A regression model is then constructed [2].
- The predicted cost flexibility is represented by the statistic of the pricing parameter in the regression equation [2].
- To take into consideration nonlinear relations among cost and need, advanced approaches like log-linear regression or log-log regression may be utilized [2].
- Regression methods that analyse info over a number of units or divisions, including the regression of panel data, variable factor regression analysis, or ordinary least squares (OLS) regression, can all be used to evaluate elasticity [2].

16.3.2 Machine Learning Algorithms for Demand Forecasting

Demand prediction is the process of projecting anticipated consumer demand for a good or service using past performance information along with other pertinent variables [4].

Machine learning algorithms offer a wide range of techniques for demand forecasting, including:

- **Time-Series Forecasting**: Prediction on the basis of past time-series data can be done using methods such as ARIMA, SARIMA (Seasonal ARIMA), or Prophet [4].
- **Regression-Based Forecasting**: Regression methods including retail slope regression, lasso model, and linear modelling are able to include other factors that predict including pricing, promotions, and seasons [4].
- **Ensemble Methods**: To increase forecasting accuracy, methods including XGBoost, Random Forest, and Gradient Boosting Machines (GBM) merge several ineffective learners [4].

Demand forecasting relies heavily on feature engineering, which selects and transforms pertinent predictions including past sales data, marketing campaigns, economic indicators, and outside demand-influencing elements.

16.3.3 Econometric Models for Pricing Optimization

Econometric models are used to study pricing approaches and optimize price using statistical tools with the theory of economics [2].

Techniques commonly used in econometric modelling for pricing optimization include:

- **Structural Equation Modelling (SEM)**: The complex connections among hidden variables (like price sensitivity and brand loyalty) and observable variables (like pricing and market share) can be estimated using structural equation modelling (SEM) [2].

- **Discrete-Choice Models**: Models like multilayer logarithm as well as multinomial logarithm are utilized to look at consumer preferences for branding as well as rival items that vary in terms of pricing and feature sets [2].
- **Price Response Models**: These models take into account variables as flexibility, cross-price impacts, along with substitution impacts while estimating the influence of price changes on demand [2].

In order to establish parameters and justify assumptions regarding consumer behaviour as well as market structure, econometric models frequently use data from surveys of consumers, market research, and experiments. Because they provide information for price elasticity, demand forecasting, and the impact of pricing decisions on consumer behaviour and marketplace results, each of these predictive modelling tools is essential to pricing research and optimization. The precise goals, data qualities, and analytical needs of the pricing optimization work all influence the technique selection [2].

16.4 UNDERSTANDING PRICE ELASTICITY

16.4.1 Concept of Price Elasticity and Its Significance

- The quantity demander's reactivity to market fluctuations is measured by price elasticity. It calculates how much the amount needed will change by percentage for every 1% change in price [2].
- The formula for price elasticity of demand (PED) is: PED = (% Change in Quantity Demanded)/(% Change in Price) [2].
- Businesses can better understand clients' pricing sensitivity by utilizing price elasticity. A price increase will cause a proportionately higher reduction in the volume searched for if demand is elastic (PED > 1), and the opposite will be true if price decreases. Quantities requested is less affected by price fluctuations if demand is inelastic (PED < 1) [2].
- **Significance**: Cost-effectiveness judgements, product placement, revenue maximization, as well as market segmentation all depend on pricing elasticity. Companies can use it to learn how pricing adjustments would affect revenue and demand [2].

16.4.2 Estimating Price Elasticity Using Predictive Analytics

Price elasticity is capable of being determined employing predictive analytics methods like fiscal models, machine learning algorithms, and regression analysis [3].

- **Regression Analysis**: To determine the cost elasticity coefficients, correlate volume required upon price along with other pertinent variables (such as income and competitor prices) [3].
- **Machine Learning Algorithms**: When trying to estimate demand, train models on past prices, volumes sold, and other characteristics. Price elasticity is subsequently inferred using the models [3].

- **Econometrics Models**: When estimating price elasticity, one might use statistical methods like as discrete-choice models or log-linear regression to account for a variety of demand-affecting variables [3].

Predictive analytics may calculate price elasticity by evaluating past sales data and adding appropriate factors to offer a glimpse of how price changes impact desire.

16.4.3 Interpreting and Leveraging Price Elasticity Insights for Pricing Decisions

- **Interpreting Price Elasticity**: The greater reactivity of customer demand to financial fluctuations is indicated by a higher absolute value of price elasticity. While inelastic demand indicates that raising prices would boost revenue, elastic demand indicates cutting prices could improve total revenue [2].
- **Leveraging Insights for Pricing Decisions**: Businesses can use price elasticity estimates to optimize pricing strategies. For example:
  - **Setting Optimal Prices**: Taking the price elasticity of demand into account, modify price to optimize revenue or profit [2].
  - **Dynamic Pricing**: Use dynamic pricing techniques that utilize estimations of the elasticity of prices and demand that are current [2].
  - **Product Differentiation**: Depending on how sensitive to price each market segment is that adjust prices accordingly [2].
  - **Promotional Strategies**: To successfully boost consumer demand, establish promotions or discounts based on understanding of price elasticity [2].

Businesses can improve their earnings and profitability as meeting consumer demands by knowing and utilizing price elasticity information to support pricing choices.

16.5 OPTIMIZATION ALGORITHMS FOR PRICING

When developing a pricing plan, optimization strategies are essential because they help companies find the best prices to meet their goals along with limits and maximizing revenue or profit [3].

16.5.1 Overview of Optimization Techniques

- By taking into account specific goals and limitations, methods of optimization seek to identify the optimal solution from a range of workable solutions for a particular issue [3].
- According to particular boundaries, optimization might entail either maximizing or decreasing a function that is objective, such as profit, expenses, and value [3].
- Here are lots of different optimization techniques and algorithms that can be used, such as integer programming, dynamic programming, linear and nonlinear programming, and metaheuristic techniques like virtual annealing and genetic algorithms [3].

16.5.2 Linear and Nonlinear Optimization Models

- **Linear Optimization**: Considering situations involving straight goals with linear constraints, linear programming (LP), represents a popular optimization method. In order to either maximize or reduce the target function, it entails determining the most appropriate values for the decision variables [3].
- **Nonlinear Optimization**: Optimization challenges using nonlinear conditions called a desired product constitute the domain of nonlinear programming, or NLP. In these situations, the best solutions are found using nonlinear optimization methods including genetic algorithms, gradient descent, and Newton's method [3].

16.5.3 Constraint Optimization for Pricing Strategy Formulation

When developing a pricing strategy, firms must take into account an array of constraints, including those related to manufacturing capacity, resource limits, legal requirements, & market dynamics. This is the place how constraint optimization gets to action [4].

- **Linear Programming for Pricing**: Choices regarding prices that are tied to limitations like manufacturing expenses, consumer demand, along with pricing rules can be made using linear programming [4].
- **Nonlinear Programming for Pricing**: Selling techniques which involve nonlinear connections among factors, like price elasticity with nonlinear function of costs are optimized using nonlinear methods [4].
- **Integer Programming for Pricing**: In order to deal with separate variables for decision-making, integer programming expands upon linear programming. As a consequence, this may be utilized for price selections with integer amounts, including price per unit and discounted quantities [4].

16.6 IMPLEMENTATION STRATEGIES

Pricing concepts and findings are translated through workable plans and procedures inside an organization as part of optimizing pricing adoption methods [2]. Here are some strategies

16.6.1 Integrating Predictive Models into Pricing Decision-Making Processes

- Gain an in-depth knowledge of the price strategies while corporation goals as the models of prediction are intended to facilitate [2].
- Discover suitable reports, assure that all the information is available, and check its accuracy before using material for validation and training prediction models [2].
- Participate on behalf of cross-functional teams to implement predictive models with the operations including costing procedures that are currently within place [2].

- In order to assist pricing specialists, understand and make efficient use of all the facts produced by predictive models, empower them with training and support [2].
- Predictive models should be regularly assessed and improved in accordance with comments and outcome indicators to boost overall validity and precision over the years [2].

16.6.2 Deploying Pricing Optimization Algorithms in Real-World Scenarios

- Based on the distinctive goals, limitations, and attributes of the company's atmosphere, select the most successful cost optimization algorithms [3].
- When implementing pricing optimization strategies with practical settings, they should be developed and validated employing past information along with simulated methodologies [3].
- To make sure the consistency, dependability, and effectiveness of price optimization strategies for real-world settings, establish rigorous evaluation and verification procedures [3].
- For the purpose to execute the necessary modifications, track and evaluate how optimization of prices methods influence important performance indicators like income, earnings, & client satisfaction [4].
- Repeat step including refine valuing algorithmic optimization constantly at response to suggestions from actual customers & evolving market circumstances [4].

16.6.3 Addressing Implementation Challenges and Considerations

- Take steps to address issues regarding the overall accuracy in the information, which include prejudices, deviations, and value gaps, as these might have an effect on the way pricing optimization methods and models for prediction function.
- By using forecasting techniques and optimization techniques, taking into thought moral and governmental issues such as customer confidentiality, equality, openness, and market methods.
- Through embrace partners at the start of the procedure, outlining the advantages with predictive pricing methods, & clearing up any confusion and issues, you may manage organizational change and opposition.
- Consistently invest money and assets towards training employees, technological solutions, statistical facilities, & continuous assistance and upkeep of predictive pricing capabilities.

16.7 VALIDATION AND TESTING

When developing and putting into practice pricing optimization & forecasting models, evaluation and verification constitute crucial processes [2]. The aforementioned processes guarantee the simulation's accuracy, dependability, and efficacy in practical situations.

16.7.1 Validating Predictive Models Using Historical Data

- Optimization of pricing uses machine learning algorithms that are trained and validated using previous information [4].
- Methods like outlier validation, time-series validation, and cross-validation are frequently used to evaluate the performance of a model on unidentified information [4].
- Forecasting model precision is frequently measured using parameters like Mean Absolute Error (MAE), Mean Squared Error (MSE), or Root Mean Squared Error (RMSE) [4].

16.7.2 A/B Testing and Experimentation for Pricing Strategies

- Clients have been randomly assigned to various price structures with treatments in A/B testing in order to evaluate their reaction and assess the effect on important KPIs [4].
- Corporations are able to evaluate various pricing ideas in safe conditions through exploration, which aids in determining their most successful methods [4].
- Designing and analysing costs studies is able to be accomplished through methods like binomial experiments and randomized controlled trials (RCTs) [4].

16.7.3 Measuring and Evaluating the Effectiveness of Pricing Optimization Efforts

- The success for pricing optimization initiatives can be measured by key performance indicators (KPIs) like earnings, profitability, acquiring clients, preservation, & value over time [4].
- The beneficial effect for optimizing pricing tactics in company outcomes is measured through the use on comparative evaluation, before and following research, with analysis of trends [4].
- Other information on the efficacy of pricing approaches originates from comparisons with rivals, market studies, and subjective input from consumers [2].

Organizations can guarantee the efficacy along with dependability associated with their price optimization and forecasting activities through setting strict verification and evaluation protocols in place. This will boost productivity and decision-making processes.

16.8 FUTURE TRENDS AND OPPORTUNITIES

Future developments along with possibilities with optimization of prices and forecasting have been determined by shifting consumer habits, company surroundings, and technological breakthroughs [5].

16.8.1 Emerging Technologies and Trends in Pricing Optimization

- **Blockchain Technology**: Blockchain facilitates secured and accessible deals, opening the door to creative pricing methods including price fluctuations that utilize immediate information through smart contract execution [5].
- **Internet of Things (IOT)**: IoT devices can offer useful product utilization information, which makes demand-based pricing structures and customized pricing arrangements that consider the unique behaviours of individual customers possible [5].
- **Edge Computing**: Real-time processing and evaluation of information to the boundary of the network is made possible by edge computing, which speeds up the process of making decisions regarding flexible rates as well as individualized services [4].
- **Augmented Reality (AR) and Virtual Reality (VR)**: Digital exhibitions and collaborative priced scenarios are two examples of comprehensive pricing techniques that are potentially facilitated by AR and VR technology, that can also improve the customer experience [4].

16.8.2 Potential Applications of Generative AI in Pricing Strategies

There are several intriguing possibilities for generative artificial intelligence in pricing techniques, especially with regard to GANs (generational adversarial networks) along with additional generative algorithms [3].

- **Price Optimization and Scenario Generation**: Artificially generated information is often produced using generative artificial intelligence (AI) models, including Generative Adversarial Networks (GANs), to train pricing algorithms & simulate price situations [4].
- **Personalized Pricing and Recommendation Systems**: According to past performance, current market conditions, and unique consumer preferences, generative artificial intelligence (AI) systems can produce tailored price predictions [4].
- **Dynamic Pricing and Market Simulation**: As a way to enhance pricing techniques within real-time with forecast the outcome of price adjustments for revenue and profitability, generative artificial intelligence (AI) models can mimic market conditions along with customer relationships [4].

16.8.3 Opportunities for Further Research and Innovation in Predictive Pricing Analytics

Forecasting price analysis has many opportunities for study along with innovation, tiggered by the increasing amount of knowledge available, developments in the fields of AI and machine learning, as well as changing corporate environments [4].

- **Interpretable Machine Learning**: Create comprehensible machine learning methods that describe intricate correlations throughout pricing factors & the buying habits that deliver concrete insights regarding pricing selections [3].

- **Bayesian Methods for Uncertainty Quantification**: Examine Bayesian methods with the pricing model measurement of uncertainty with the objective to incorporate data from experts within pricing techniques and enable effective decision-making over ambiguity [6].
- **Multi-Agent Reinforcement Learning**: Examine how to maximize pricing techniques for rapidly changing and competitive marketplaces by modelling price-driven fluctuations using reinforcement learning with multiple agents' methodologies [1].
- **Fairness and Bias in Pricing Algorithms**: Develop reasonable pricing structures that reduce prejudiced results and guarantee that different customer segments are treated equally in an attempt to deal with worries regarding unfairness and prejudice with buying methods.

Corporations can discover novel opportunities to boosting choices regarding pricing, improving client loyalty, and fostering profitable development with comparable and rapidly changing markets through investigating these novel technologies, utilizing artificial intelligence (AI) through pricing techniques, and improving studies on forecasting cost analytical thinking.

16.9 CONCLUSION

In the end, adjusting prices is essential to maximize profits and preserving market dominance. Key components of optimal pricing will be emphasized in the above outline, including numerous pricing techniques, and the significance of data-driven decisions, with the function of generative artificial intelligence and predictive analytics.

16.9.1 Summary of Key Takeaways

- Pricing based on value, price plus cost, adaptive pricing, as well as additional pricing techniques provides various methods for figuring out the most favourable costs in goods and services.
- Obtaining appropriate information sources, cleaning and preparing the information, and employing statistical modelling strategies to determine prices are all part of data-driven pricing decisions.
- Through predicting consumer demand, evaluating the elasticity of prices, and optimizing price selections according to real-time data and knowledge, predictive analytics and generative AI help with price optimization.

16.9.2 Importance of Data-Driven Pricing Optimization in Marketing Strategies

- Organizations may study trends in the market, comprehend what customers want, and improve pricing techniques to increase sales and profitability by using data-driven pricing decisions.
- Businesses may obtain an unfair advantage regarding price enhancement, adjust to changing circumstances in the market, and offer clients with individualized price experience through the use of data analytics and cutting-edge technologies.

16.9.3 Future Outlook for Predictive Analytics and Generative AI in Pricing Decisions

- Blockchain, Internet of Things, edge computing, and AR/VR are examples of modern technologies that open up new possibilities for customized pricing plans and pricing optimization.
- Technologies like price improvement, scenario creation, customized prices, including variations with methods of pricing show the potential of generative AI, which includes GANs.
- Predictive price analytics presents chances to conduct additional study with innovation in the areas of comprehensible machine learning, multi-agent reinforcement learning, Bayesian approaches for quantifying unpredictability, and tackling unfairness and prejudice in cost methods.

REFERENCES

[1] Verma, S., & Sharma, R. R. K. (2018). Role of Big Data Analytics in Pricing Optimization. *International Journal of Management, Technology, and Social Sciences (IJMTS)*, 3(1), 1–8.

[2] Levy, D., & Smets, F. (2010). Price setting and price adjustment in some European Union countries: Introduction to the special issue. *Managerial and Decision Economics*, 31(2–3), 63–66.

[3] Kohavi, R., et al. (2009). Online Experimentation at Microsoft. *Proceedings of the 15th ACM SIGKDD International Conference on Knowledge Discovery and Data Mining.* Paris, France.

[4] Jain, A., et al. (2019). A Survey of Deep Generative Models for Learned Priors. *IEEE Transactions on Pattern Analysis and Machine Intelligence*, 41(12), 2941–2958.

[5] Tapscott, D., & Tapscott, A. (2016). *Blockchain Revolution: How the Technology behind Bitcoin Is Changing Money, Business, and the World.* New York, NY: Penguin.

[6] Ganie, S. M., & Pramanik, P. K. D. (2024). A Comparative Analysis of Boosting Algorithms for Chronic Liver Disease Prediction. *Healthcare Analytics*, 100313.

17 Synthetic Data Generation for Marketing Insights

Bhogineni Sankha Chakradhar,
Mugil Vijey, and Suraj Tunk

17.1 DEFINITION AND OVERVIEW

Synthetic statistics is made of units of numbers which might be made to seem like real-international statistics but do not include any personal information that might be used to discover a person. Real records frequently have private information in it, but faux statistics is made nameless so they can be shared and analyzed without worrying about privateness. Statistical modeling, fast processing, and algorithms for system mastering are some of the techniques used to make this fake information.

17.2 IMPORTANCE IN MARKETING RESEARCH

In advertising and marketing research, getting access to proper facts is very essential for figuring out how human beings act, what they like, and how the market is changing. But a few problems include getting actual customer facts, like privacy legal guidelines like GDPR and CCPA. Synthetic records are a solution because they offer specialists real information units to study at the same time as nevertheless protecting human privacy. Marketing specialists can study a lot about how people behave and what they like through the usage of fake records. This technique would not invade people's privacy or wreck any guidelines.

17.3 COMPARISON WITH REAL DATA

Real statistics are the truest statistics there are, but they also pose large dangers to safety and privacy. Real information frequently has in my opinion identifiable facts, or PII, in it, which means that it may be stolen or misused. Synthetic information, then again, gets rid of these problems by using creating nameless record sets that also have the statistical homes of real data violating privateness. Even though faux statistics may not replicate how humans act in the actual international, it is still a useful device for research and evaluation.

DOI: 10.1201/9781003472544-17

17.4 FOUNDATIONAL CONCEPTS

To use faux facts correctly in advertising studies, you want to recognize the basic thoughts at the back of it. Some critical thoughts are:

Data Privacy and Security: In marketing studies, protective human beings' privateness may be very crucial. This hassle can be solved via synthetic facts, which create sets of nameless data that protect privateness at the same time as nonetheless being beneficial for evaluation. Synthetic records lower the threat of breaches of privacy and legal noncompliance by way of disposing of statistics that can be used to discover someone.

Data Generation Techniques: Random sampling, statistics processing, and generative opposed networks (GANs) are a number of techniques used to make fake data. There are pros and cons to every approach that depend upon how realistic you need things to be and how personal you want to be.

Machine Learning Models for Data Synthesis: ML models are very vital for placing together accurate units of facts. Deep getting-to-know and artificial neural networks are two techniques that may be used to make faux records that look plenty like actual-international tendencies and distributions.

Within the following few elements, we are going to cross into more element about every of these simple ideas, searching at what they mean for business research and the way to use faux information most correctly.

17.8 IDENTIFYING MARKETING DATA REQUIREMENTS

Before entering into the way to make faux facts and how it could be used in advertising, it is critical to recognize what kind of statistics is needed for marketing take a look at. To do that, you need to recognize the crucial factors, connections, and developments that are associated with the commercial enterprise dreams. When figuring out what marketing data you want, right here are a few matters to reflect on consideration on:

17.8.1 Define Marketing Objectives

Make sure all of us knows what the project's dreams and ambitions are. Having clear goals will assist you in accumulating data, whether you are trying to parent out what customers want, what market developments are occurring, or how well your advertising and marketing efforts are running.

17.8.2 Identify Key Variables

Figure out which factors are maximum essential and ought to be within the records set. This ought to include psychographic traits, buying records, interplay measures, and demographic facts.

17.8.3 Consider Data Sources

Look into viable information sources that could come up with statistics about your target market and the way they act as customers. This may want to consist of internet polls, social media websites, non-public databases, and data vendors that are not part of the enterprise.

17.8.4 Evaluate Data Quality

Check the first-class and dependability of the data assets, which can be handy. Make sure the data is correct, updated, and related to the look at dreams.

17.8.5 Understand Regulatory Requirements

When you collect and take care of patron information, you should consider records security rules like GDPR, CCPA, and HIPAA. Make certain that the regulations are followed to protect customers' privateness and stay out of trouble with the law.

17.8.6 Account for Sample Size and Diversity

Discern out the proper pattern length and make certain the records set is various to get a collection that is consultant of the target marketplace. This ought to include the usage of stratified selection to make certain that everyone categories and agencies are properly represented.

By cautiously defining the advertising and marketing facts desires, researchers can make sure that the mixed information correctly matches the tendencies and behavior of the goal marketplace. This permits them to gain deeper insights and make higher decisions.

Once the advertising information needs were figured out, the following step is to make fake information that looks plenty like real records while nevertheless shielding privateness and safety. The steps below are commonly a part of the procedure of creating faux facts (Figure 17.1):

1. **Data Collection:** Get the statistics you want from a variety of assets, along with actual patron statistics, polls, and outdoor databases. Make certain that the facts you acquire are accurate and include all the factors that are needed.
2. **Data Pre-processing:** Remove any mistakes, outliers, or statistics that are not in shape with the rest of the data by cleansing and pre-processing it. To enhance the great of the data, this can include normalizing the data, filling in lacking numbers, and function engineering.
3. **Model Selection:** Pick the proper modeling strategies for making faux records. Statistical modeling, information processing, or device mastering techniques like generative adverse networks (GANs) or variation autoencoders (VAEs) may be part of this.

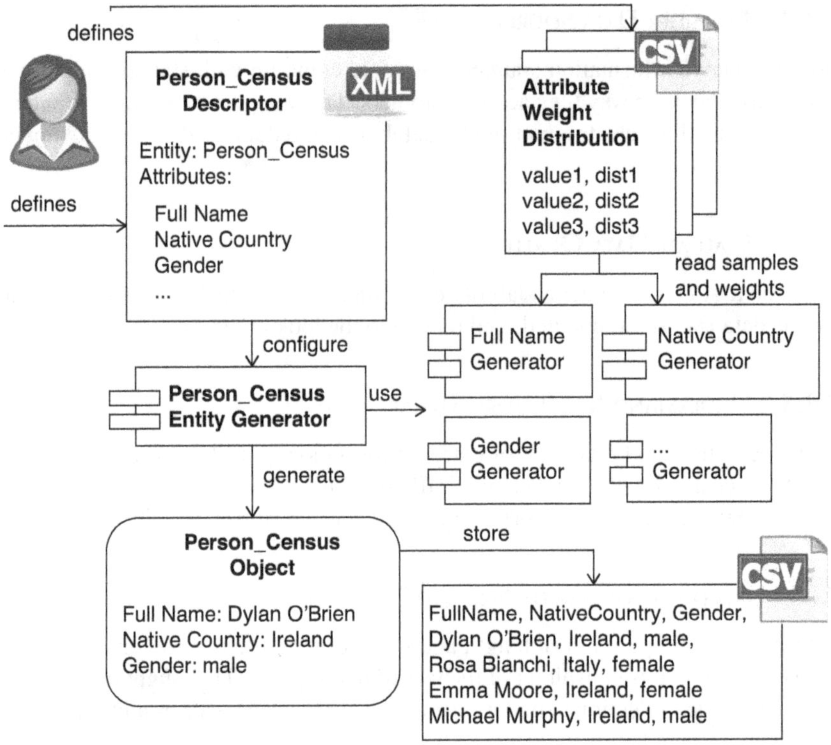

FIGURE 17.1 Synthetic data generation process.

4. **Model Training:** Use the pre-processed facts to educate the selected model the way to discover trends and stages within the facts. This is performed by means of making the version settings as appropriate as they may be in order that the artificial information and actual facts are as close as feasible.
5. **Evaluation and Validation:** Use validation techniques like cross-validation or holdout validation to check how nicely the found out model works. Check the created data's excellent through contrasting it to actual data and ensuring it keeps essential statistical features and hyperlinks.
6. **Privacy Preservation:** To make the artificial records anonymous and preserve private data secure, use techniques that protect privacy. To make sure that records security guidelines are accompanied, this could consist of different stages of privateness, ok-obscurity, or different approaches of anonymization.

By the use of a deliberate approach for growing synthetic information, researchers can make actual information units that exactly reflect the traits and behaviors of the goal market while nonetheless defending their privacy and protection.

17.9 TOOLS AND TECHNOLOGIES

Several tools and technologies may be used to create faux records for advertising studies. These gear can be used to model, train, and evaluate generated records in several unique approaches. These are some equipment and strategies that can be often used:

17.9.1 Synthetic Data Generation Platforms

Some platforms, like Synthon and Tonic, are made only for making artificial statistics. These platforms have smooth-to-use gear and models that can be already made for combining statistics from specific areas.

17.9.2 Machine Learning Libraries

Open-supply software program gadget mastering libraries including TensorFlow, PyTorch, and sci-package-learn make it clean to construct and use gadget getting-to-know fashions to create faux statistics. Many strategies and strategies in those applications may be utilized for modeling complex data distributions.

17.9.3 Privacy-Preserving Tools

ARX and the Privacy-Preserving Synthetic Data Generation (PSDG) modules are two examples of tools that guard privacy and cover personal data in artificial statistics units. Differential privateness and anonymization methods are the privateness-improving techniques that these gear use.

17.9.4 Data Visualization Tools

Tools for information visualization, consisting of Tableau and Power BI, may be used to peer and examine faux facts units. This enables specialists to discover indicators of traits within the records.

17.9.5 Custom Software Solutions

Businesses also can make their software program solutions which can be specially made to fulfill their records advent desires. To make fake records that suit their wishes, these solutions would possibly use secret algorithms, records processing procedures, and privacy-defensive features.

Researchers can accelerate the manner of creating faux facts and get excellent information units for research on marketing using those tools and technologies.

17.10 APPLICATIONS OF SYNTHETIC DATA IN MARKETING

There are a whole lot of ways that synthetic records might be utilized in marketing research. Here are a few important programs (Figure 17.2):

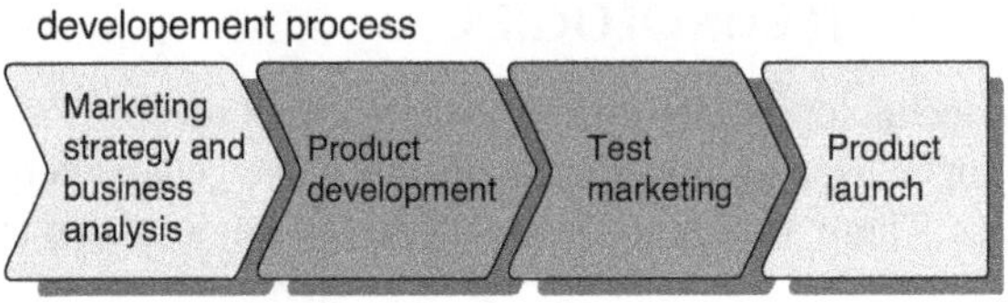

FIGURE 17.2 Applications of synthetic data in marketing.

17.10.1 Customer Segmentation

You can divide clients into groups primarily based on their demographic, psychographic, and behavioral tendencies using fake records. Marketers can analyze more approximately the specific needs and want of the target audience they are targeting using placing collectively faux information factors into clean groups.

17.10.2 Predictive Modeling

Synthetic data can be used to teach predictive models that may guess how customers will act, what they will purchase, and market trends. By searching out similarities in faux statistics, marketers could make models that could inform what is going to take place inside destiny and find boom opportunities.

17.10.3 Personalized Marketing

Marketers can make personalized marketing efforts which might be based on what each client needs by way of the usage of synthetic facts. Marketers can send messages and deals that are extra applicable to every group of clients by way of setting together facts about beyond contacts, purchases, and online conduct.

17.10.4 Product Testing and Innovation

Fake records may be used to look at how human beings react to new items, characteristics, and advertising plans. Marketers can check diverse kinds of merchandise and advertising techniques in a safe placing earlier than setting them available on the market by means of developing faux facts units that look like real-life conditions.

17.10.5 Market Simulation

Fake statistics can be applied to make fashions of the way markets work and how competitors might act. Marketers can examine how various factors affect customer conduct and market effects by way of making fake data that indicates exceptional market conditions.

Overall, fake records is a flexible and effective tool that marketers can use to examine greater approximately how clients behave, run focused marketing tasks, and make decisions based totally on facts to reach their agency's objectives.

17.11 CUSTOMER BEHAVIOR ANALYSIS

Businesses want to know how their clients act to make their goods, services, and advertising processes work better. The take a look at of how human beings use items, manufacturers, and advertising systems is called consumer behavior evaluation. Some critical components of customer behavior analysis are these:

17.11.1 Purchase Behavior

Looking at how regularly, these days, and how much people spend once they buy something. Businesses can enhance how they deal with their inventory, set expenses, and run promotions by understanding what objects human beings purchase as well as once they purchase them.

17.11.2 Engagement Metrics

Keeping track of ways engaged clients are at one-of-a-kind points of touch, like after they go to your website, connect with you on social media, or open your emails. Businesses can parent out how well their advertising and marketing is running and wherein they can make modifications by monitoring such things as fees of clicks, quotes of bounces, and the quantity of time spent on their website online.

17.11.3 Customer Preferences

Using polls, remarks paperwork, and market studies to find out what clients want, what they are interested in, and what they want. Businesses can make certain their merchandise and messages attain the right people using dividing customers into agencies based on the matters they like.

17.11.4 Churn Evaluation

predicting and reducing consumer turnover using finding early caution signs and putting in region techniques to keep customers. Businesses can forestall customers from leaving by using looking at things like client happiness, how regularly they purchase, and how often they address customer service.

17.11.5 Segmentation Analysis

Putting human beings into separate groups based on their demographic, psychographic, and behavioral trends. Businesses could make their marketing and product offers greater engaging and pleasurable for customers with the aid of mastering the specific wants and desires of various agencies of clients.

Overall, consumer conduct evaluation enables organizations to apprehend their customers' likes, dislikes, buying conduct, and why they purchase matters. This allows them to improve their advertising strategies and preserve clients coming returned.

17.12 MARKET SEGMENTATION AND TARGETING

Market segmentation is the procedure of splitting the market into separate businesses of humans who have similar wants, desires, and behaviors. Targeting means choosing positive organizations to concentrate on with specific advertising plans and merchandise. Some vital components of choosing and segmenting the marketplace are:

17.12.1 Segmentation Criteria

Figuring out what demographic, geographic, psychographic, and behavioral elements are most important for each organization. Age, gender, income, way of life, and buying habits are all not unusual department factors.

17.12.2 Segmentation Methods

Using statistical techniques like choice trees, cluster evaluation, and component evaluation to find beneficial marketplace businesses is known as categorization. Businesses can efficaciously divide their target organization using looking at customer facts and locating patterns.

17.12.3 Targeting Strategies

Coming up with approaches to attain particular groups of people with custom-designed advertising substances and deals. This may want to imply the usage of centered commercials, personalized email advertising, and product pointers which might be based on what the purchaser wishes.

17.12.4 Positioning

Putting manufacturers and items in a way that meets the wants and needs of particular businesses of people. Businesses can stand proud of rivals and connect to their intended clients by way of emphasizing their particular value offers and blessings.

17.12.5 Measuring and Comparing

Always keep an eye fixed on and judge how nicely focused and segmented strategies are operating. Businesses can figure out how nicely their marketing is operating with the aid of maintaining the tune of key overall performance signs like new customers, customers they preserve, and patron happiness. This way, they could make selections based on facts to make their plans even higher.

In the give up, marketplace segmentation as well as focus allows businesses to locate and awareness of the maximum valuable groups of customers. They can also make sure that their advertising campaigns and merchandise are tailor-made to fulfill the precise desires of every institution, which enables them to get a fine return on their funding.

17.13 PRODUCT DEVELOPMENT AND INNOVATION

Innovation and product improvement are the processes of making new goods, capabilities, and services that fulfill customers' converting wants and desires. Here are some essential parts of arising with new merchandise and thoughts:

17.13.1 Market Research

Looking into the market to find unmet needs, new trends, and probabilities to provide you with new thoughts. Businesses can discover holes in marketplaces and locate probabilities to make new products by getting comments from customers, competitors, and specialists within the subject.

17.13.2 Idea Generation

Coming up with new goods and enhancements through brainstorming meetings, feedback from customers, and running together with other people inside the company. Businesses can provide you with new merchandise with the aid of encouraging a mindset of creativity and innovation.

17.13.3 Prototype Development

Making mock-ups and prototypes to check and verify ideas for new products. Businesses can discover possible issues and make modifications to their designs before setting the product on the market with the aid of asking consumers and different important humans for feedback early on within the improvement method.

17.13.4 Testing and Iteration

Putting the product through beta assessments and pilot packages to get comments and make it better primarily based on how human beings use it. Businesses can find ways to improve the product revel and make it higher with the aid of tracking key overall performance measures like usefulness, happiness, and engagement.

17.13.5 Sell and Marketing

Making plans for the way to promote the brand new product and how to promote it to individuals who will purchase it. Targeted commercials, public relations efforts, and special deals can help organizations get humans enthusiastic about a new product, which could cause more income and adoption.

Overall, innovation and the creation of merchandise help corporations stay ahead of the opposition set themselves aside from rivals, and adapt to clients' changing needs and wants.

17.14 CHALLENGES AND LIMITATIONS

Customer conduct studies, marketplace segmentation, targeting, and product development are all useful tools for businesses, however, they also have a few problems and restrictions.

17.14.1 Data Quality

Making certain that the customer facts used for evaluation and categorization is correct, complete, and dependable. Bad facts could make it tough to get accurate insights and make focusing strategies that do not paintings.

17.14.2 Privacy Concerns

Dealing with privacy worries and following the guidelines when accumulating and studying customer information. To hold customers' consideration and observe information security legal guidelines, agencies need to ensure they get the right permissions and maintain non-public information safe.

17.14.3 Segmentation Accuracy

Make sure that the criteria and strategies used for segmentation are accurate and accurate. When segmentation is not carried out properly, advertising strategies can move off target, and chances to connect with goal organizations efficiently may be misplaced.

17.14.4 Competition and Saturation

How do we cope with greater opposition and complete markets in corporations that already have a number of them? To stand out and get a piece of the market, businesses ought to always provide you with new ideas and ways to do matters differently.

17.14.5 Rapid Changes in Technology

Getting used to rapid changes in technology and converting customer tastes. To keep up with new trends and changes within the market, companies want to be short and adaptable.

Overall, organizations want to recognize how to cope with these issues and restrictions to get the maximum out of client behavior research, market segmentation, targeting, and product creation, and to achieve long-term achievement and increase.

17.15 DATA QUALITY AND FIDELITY

While the use of generated information in advertising studies or any other facts-pushed assignment, the data have to be accurate and precise nice. Let's take a better take a look at these thoughts:

17.15.1 Data Pleasant

It approaches how correct, complete, steady, and reliable the records is. To ensure that synthesized statistics is of appropriate great, you need to do the following:

- **Accuracy**: artificial records need to accurately healthy the patterns and distributions of actual statistics. To make sure that the artificial facts kind of suits the houses of the original information, careful modeling and evaluation are wanted.
- **Completeness**: The synthetic data need to have all of the attributes and factors that are wished for studies. This should mean filling in lacking numbers or adding more features to the information set to make it fuller.
- **Consistency**: Different information factors and elements in artificial statistics should all be equal. Data that is not consistent or would not fit up can lead to fake thoughts and incorrect assumptions.
- **Reliability**: Synthetic data should be reliable and repeatable, this means that the procedure used to create it needs to continually supply the same effects. To make certain the fake data is reliable, this desires robust modeling techniques and evaluation steps.

17.15.2 Data Fidelity

The stage of information fidelity is how closely built data matches the actual-world activities it attempts to replicate. When it comes to advertising research, maintaining excessive data accuracy methods:

- **Preserving Relationships**: When making artificial facts, the relationships and connections that were gifted within the unique records should be saved. This way retaining the tune of how variables rely on each other and recording the complicated relationships that affect how humans act.
- **Capturing Variability**: The variety and variability seen in real records should be reflected in artificial facts. To do this, you need to make statistics factors with several one-of-a-kind numbers and distributions to show how one-of-a-kind the target group is.
- **Avoiding Bias:** Fake data should have no bias or skewness that might exchange the effects of the studies. To do this, you want to carefully choose the modeling techniques and assessment steps so that there's little bias and the underlying facts within reason are shown.

Making certain that the data is accurate and of high best is crucial for getting proper insights and making clever picks in marketing research. Researchers could make faux data for evaluation more useful and dependable by using the following great practices and validation strategies.

17.16 ETHICAL CONSIDERATIONS

When it comes to using fake facts in marketing studies, ethics are very essential. Here are a few critical moral matters to think about:

17.16.1 Privacy Protection

When creating and analyzing fake information, it miles very crucial to hold human beings' privacy secure. Researchers need to ensure that faux information sets have no PII (personally identifiable facts) that might be used to invade humans' privacy.

17.16.2 Informed Consent

Making sure that humans whose statistics are used to make faux records deliver their permission. This way, making it clear to customers why the statistics are being gathered, how it will be hired, and any risks or outcomes that might come with it.

17.16.3 Accountability and Transparency

Making sure that the system of accumulating records is open and responsible. Researchers must write down and proportion the steps they took to make fake data, alongside any flaws or biases that exist in the facts.

17.16.4 Fairness and Equity

Making sure that using fake facts for studies and making choices is truthful and identical for each person. When researchers make faux facts, they need to be privy to the biases or discrimination that could appear and take steps to reduce those risks.

17.16.5 Data Protection

Putting in area sturdy records safety method maintaining faux facts from moving into the wrong hands or being misused or shared without permission. To maintain non-public information safe, this includes encoding, admission to limits, and regular safety exams.

Researchers can ensure that using faux records in advertising studies does not violate human beings' rights and dignity at the same time nonetheless adding to our expertise and know-how of the concern via sticking to ethical standards and principles.

17.17 REGULATORY COMPLIANCE

Another important component to consider while using fake facts in market studies is the way to comply with the regulations, especially about information safety and privacy laws. Here are a few important guidelines you need to understand approximately:

17.17.1 General Data Protection Regulation (GDPR)

GDPR is a large records protection law that covers how the private records of humans in the European Union (EU) is processed. It has strict policies on how to accumulate, technique, and save statistics. These guidelines encompass ways to get permission, maintain data as small as possible, and supply humans with the right to be forgotten.

17.17.2 California Consumer Privacy Act (CCPA)

The CCPA is a California country privacy law that gives people certain rights over their records, such as the proper to see, delete, and refuse to have their statistics bought. Businesses that collect and use the personal facts of California citizens should observe positive regulations about privacy and consumer rights.

17.17.3 Health Insurance Portability and Accountability Act (HIPAA)

This is an American government law that protects the privacy and protection of protected fitness records (PHI). It applies to healthcare people, fitness plans, and commercial enterprise companions who address protected fitness statistics (PHI). It has strict regulations for maintaining facts safe and personal.

17.17.4 Other Regulatory Frameworks

The use of faux records in advertising studies may be ruled through one-of-a-kind regulatory frameworks relying on the commercial enterprise and place. Researchers need to understand and observe the regulations so that they do not get into problems with the regulations and need to pay fines.

When collecting, processing, and reading synthetic statistics, it is essential to pay near interest to statistics management, privacy rules, and legal duties to make sure that rules are observed. Researchers can decrease their ethical threats and build faith with each client and regulatory officials by following the policies set by using regulators.

17.18 CASE STUDIES

In marketing studies, case research displays how faux information is used within the actual global to clear up commercial enterprise issues and gain new insights. Below are a few examples to show what I imply:

17.18.1 Market Segmentation and Targeting

A Save uses faux statistics to divide its customers into corporations and find the most valuable businesses for centered advertising and marketing. The company divides clients into agencies based totally on their shopping behavior, private tastes, and where they stay by looking at fake statistics units crafted from client transaction facts and demographic information. This shall we the commercial enterprise to make its classified ads and offers greater relevant to every institution, which results in higher involvement and income charges.

17.18.2 Product Development and Innovation

A commercial enterprise that makes customer goods uses fake facts to see what feedback and preferences humans have for brand-spanking new product thoughts. The organization attempts extraordinary product capabilities, package designs, and pricing techniques in a digital world by making faux record sets that replicate exceptional styles of customers and their choices. This allows the agency parent out which product ideas are the maximum likely to paintings and then placed them on the top of the list for similarly testing and development. This leads to successful product income and more market share ultimately.

17.18.3 Customer Behavioral Analysis

A virtual advertising and marketing company makes use of faux facts to look at how customers interact with and purchase matters on different online structures. The business enterprise learns about consumer tastes, material picks, and income pathways by making fake statistics sets that look like real-life exchanges between customers and websites, social media websites, and e mail campaigns [1]. In turn, this helps the corporation improve its virtual marketing plans, content creation, and campaigns to get new customers so that its customers can get greater involvement and income.

These case research display how faux data can be used in many unique regions of marketing research, together with market segmentation and focused on, product improvement, and reading how customers behave. In a market that is getting an increasing number of aggressive, companies can benefit useful insights, make better decisions, and grow via the usage of fake statistics.

17.19 SUCCESSFUL IMPLEMENTATION IN MARKETING STRATEGIES

To use manufactured facts successfully in advertising plans, they want to be carefully deliberate, carried out, and evaluated. Here are some of the most critical things that made it paintings:

17.19.1 Clear Objectives

Set clear dreams and targets for the way you will use synthetic data for your advertising plans. It is important to have a clear photograph of what you need to obtain while you are seeking to enhance purchaser segmentation, customize advertising messages, or make advertising and marketing efforts greater powerful.

17.19.2 Data Integration

Make it easy to apply fake information in marketing gear and techniques that might be already in location. To upload fake statistics to advertising structures, CRM systems, and analytics applications, should mean making custom facts flows, APIs, or connections.

17.19.3 Testing and Validation

Use strict checking out and validation processes to ensure that the faux data is accurate and dependable. To make sure that the insights you get from fake facts are steady and reliable, you must examine them with insights you get from real data.

17.19.4 Iterative Improvement

Use what you analyze from faux information analysis to preserve converting and improving your advertising strategies. Keep a watch on key performance signs (KPIs) and make changes to your advertising and marketing techniques as needed to get quality outcomes.

17.19.5 Cross-Functional Collaboration

Get the advertising, statistics technology, and IT teams to paint together across capabilities to make certain that their use of fake information for marketing initiatives is aligned and powerful. To get the most out of faux information across the company, inspire people to share their facts and paintings collectively.

17.19.6 Measurement and Evaluation

Set metrics and dreams to peer how well and what kind of impact faux information-pushed advertising techniques have. Track KPIs like new client increase, and purchaser retention, and go back on investment (ROI) to see how properly advertising campaigns are doing.

By following those recommendations and pleasant practices, corporations can use faux facts to improve and guide their advertising strategies, get customers extra worried, and attain their business desires.

17.20 COMPARATIVE ANALYSIS OF MARKETING INSIGHTS DERIVED FROM REAL VS. SYNTHETIC DATA

By taking a take a look at marketing ideas from the actual and pretend facts side with the aid of facets, you could learn a lot about the professionals and cons of the use of faux information for advertising studies. Here is a look at how the two methods compare:

17.20.1 Data Quality and Consistency

Real records normally have higher statistics and accuracy than faux records as they indicate how actual customers act and engage with manufacturers. Synthetic information, alternatively, can be made in huge quantities and tailored to precise use cases. This makes records evaluation extra bendy and green.

17.20.2 Privacy and Compliance

Because in my view identifiable facts is eliminated from synthetic facts, there are no privacy troubles that include actual data. This makes certain that information protection laws like GDPR and CCPA are accompanied, which makes artificial statistics a better choice for research and evaluation.

17.20.3 Bias and Generalization

Real information may additionally have biases or limits that come from the way it became amassed, like sample bias or choice bias. On the opposite hand, synthetic statistics can be made to lessen mistakes and ensure that the goal institution within reason is represented.

17.20.4 Cost and Accountability

The cost and ease of access to real information can be high, and it cannot usually be available or smooth to get. Because synthetic facts are made in a lab, it could be made for a whole lot much less money and can be modified to shape unique looks at wishes, which makes it less difficult to get admission to and greater useful.

17.20.5 Validity and Reliability

The price and dependability of insights drawn from synthetic information depend on how accurate and practical the system of making the synthetic facts is. Even though simulated statistics can very intently reproduce the degrees and styles of actual statistics, they may now not be capable of fully capturing complicated behaviors and interactions [2].

In general, real and fake data have their execs and cons on the subject of marketing look at. When marketers integrate data from both assets, they can get a fuller photograph of how customers act, what they like, and how the market works. This helps them make higher alternatives and grow their organizations.

17.21 FUTURE TRENDS AND DIRECTIONS

The future of manufactured data for advertising and marketing research could be shaped using several traits and guidelines, consisting of:

17.21.1 Improvements in Data Synthesis Methods

New statistics synthesis strategies, consisting of machine-studying algorithms and fashions that might be generative, are making it feasible to create fake fact sets that are more real-looking and sundry.

17.21.2 Combining with AI and Automation

Combining faux information with technology for artificial intelligence (AI) and automation is making the procedure of making records more efficient and making it less complicated to analyze and make selections in advertising research.

17.21.3 Pay Attention to Privacy and Protection

People are getting more involved approximately recording privacy and protection, so there's more recognition on developing privacy-protecting approaches to create and examine fake statistics while still following the regulations.

17.21.4 Personalization and Customization

Synthetic statistics make it viable for personalized and customized marketing techniques by giving businesses facts approximately the likes, dislikes, behaviors, and wishes of each purchaser. This permits them to supply their target audience with more relevant and interesting reports.

17.21.5 Standards and Collaboration Inside the Enterprise

Rules and recommendations for moral and responsible usage of fake statistics in studies on advertising are being made with the aid of running collectively with governing our bodies, academics, and those within the enterprise.

17.21.6 New Uses

Synthetic facts are being used for more than just marketing studies. It is getting used to finding fraud, comparing hazards, and planning for specific eventualities as organizations search for new methods to use records to make strategic selections.

In well known, the future of fake facts for marketing studies looks vibrant. As it continues to be stepped forward and used, corporations will find new approaches to gain insights, make the patron revel in higher, and gain an aggressive aspect in the age of technology.

17.22 ADVANCES IN DATA SYNTHESIS TECHNIQUES

Improvements in facts synthesis strategies have modified the sector of making synthetic data, making it possible to create greater accurate and varied statistics units that can be used in many contexts, together with marketing studies. Here are some crucial advances:

17.22.1 Generative Adversarial Networks (GANs)

GANs are a powerful manner to make fake statistics by coaching two neural networks, a producer and a discriminator, to compete with each other. For this purpose, GANs are extremely good for marketing research due to the fact they can make information samples that might be very near actual record styles [2].

17.22.2 Variation Autoencoders (VAEs)

VAEs are a one-of-a-kind kind of generating model that learns to keep and retrieve information samples in a hidden area. By figuring out how the statistics are based, VAEs could make fake statistics with plenty of different variations while keeping crucial statistical features like correlations and distributions.

17.22.3 Models That Exchange Things

Models that use transformers, like GPT (Generative Pre-skilled Transformer) and BERT (Bidirectional Encoder Representations from Transformers), have shown promise in creating fake textual content and language data. Self-interest procedures are used by those models to find lengthy-range dependencies and make text that makes experience and is important to the state of affairs.

17.22.4 Domain-Specific Synthesis

Improvements in techniques for area-unique synthesis make it possible to create new records this is specific to certain fields or make use of. For example, in healthcare advertising studies, strategies for developing synthetic facts would possibly awareness of accumulating medical data, demographics of sufferers, and remedy outcomes to make it easier to analyze and make selections about healthcare advertising techniques.

17.22.5 Synthesis That Protects Privacy

Some methods, like differential privacy, shared mastering, and homomorphic encryption, make it feasible to create fake facts while protecting human beings' privacy and protection. With those privacy-protecting strategies, marketers can use private records for research without placing customers' privacy at hazard or breaking statistics protection legal guidelines [3].

Overall, those enhancements in information synthesis techniques are spurring new thoughts and letting entrepreneurs make extremely good synthesized information sets that can be used for greater correction take a look at evaluation and selection-making.

17.23 THE ROLE OF ARTIFICIAL INTELLIGENCE AND MACHINE LEARNING

It may be very important for advertising research to use artificial intelligence (AI) and gadget-gaining knowledge (ML) to create, examine, and use faux data. In this way, AI and ML help the manner:

17.23.1 Data Generation

AI and systems gaining knowledge of algorithms, like GANs and VAEs, are used to make fake records that look plenty like actual statistics. These algorithms take samples of existing records and use them to make new facts and points with comparable statistical features. This lets marketers make fake record sets that appear to be fact sets for analysis.

17.23.2 Data Analysis

AI and system getting to know are used to examine fake statistics and find insights that can be used. Machine-gaining knowledge of fashions can be taught with faux statistics to bet how humans will act, spot market developments, and make advertising methods work higher, which facilitates humans making choices.

17.23.3 Personalization and Targeting

Recommendation systems that are driven through AI use fake information to tailor advertising messages and pointers to all people's likes and dislikes and how they act. Marketers can use device studying algorithms to ship tailor-made advertisements, product suggestions, and unique offers to particular companies of customers through searching at faux data units. This increases consumer interaction and conversion costs [3].

17.23.4 Predictive Analytics

AI and ML models taught on faux facts can are expecting destiny tendencies and consequences. This lets entrepreneurs bet on how clients will act and change their techniques to match. Some predictive analytics methods, like regression evaluation and time collection forecasts, use faux information to discover developments and make predictions based on the facts. This helps with advertising and marketing selections and allocating resources.

Overall, AI and ML technologies assist entrepreneurs use fake data extra efficaciously, which ends up in new thoughts and higher advertising and marketing method decisions.

17.24 IMPACT ON MARKETING STRATEGIES AND DECISION-MAKING

Whenever fake statistics are utilized in advertising and marketing procedures, it adjusts how choices are made and the way nicely businesses do. The following indicates how faux information impacts advertising plans:

17.24.1 Improved Insights

Marketers can use artificial information to get a much wider and greater varied set of information samples, which lets them do a greater thorough analysis and research more about customer behavior, tastes, and marketplace trends. Incorporating faux statistics into advertising and marketing efforts and product development can help groups research greater approximately their target audience and make better picks about price advertising and marketing.

17.24.2 Enhanced Personalization

entrepreneurs can tailor advertising and marketing messages and products to everybody's likes and dislikes using the usage of artificial records. Marketers can find specific agencies of customers utilizing reading faux information sets. They can then make certain that their ads and messages are more applicable to those organizations, which ends up in higher interplay and conversion charges.

17.24.3 Risk Mitigation

Marketers can try advertising plans and tasks in a digital international before placing them into motion within the real international. Marketers can locate risks and opportunities by simulating unique conditions and identifying how they may trade client conduct. They can then use records to make selections that reduce dangers and maximize returns on investment.

17.24.4 Cost Savings

Making fake information is an awful lot cheaper than accumulating and analyzing real statistics, so it can be used in preference to actual information for advertising take a look at and evaluate. By using faux facts, marketers can make first-class use of their assets and make their advertising and marketing plans as effective as feasible, which saves them money and facilitates them to make extra cash [4].

By using faux information in advertising and marketing strategies, organizations could make smarter choices, encourage new thoughts, and advantage of an aggressive aspect in a marketplace that is turning into an increasing number of data-pushed.

17.25 CONCLUSION

The use of fake information in research on advertising and marketing has become a game-changer, supporting marketers to get around problems with information protection, safety, and entry to even getting to know more approximately how customers act and the way the market works. The strength of AI and system studying, along with enhancements in facts fusion methods, have completely changed how entrepreneurs accumulate, examine, and use statistics to make selections.

When entrepreneurs use faux statistics, they can personalize, target, and improve their campaigns with new methods. This results in greater involvement, higher conversion rates, and a better return on investment. To make sure facts are fine, confidentiality, and compliance, social, criminal, and technical issues ought to be carefully thought through earlier than faux records may be used.

As the sphere of artificially generated statistics adjustments, entrepreneurs want to keep up with new traits, and standards of excellence, and look at areas to get the maximum out of it as a tool for riding innovation and meeting business dreams. In the digital age, marketers can get ahead of the competition and provide their customers with higher reports by using the usage of faux information to guide and enhance their approaches to advertising.

17.26 RECOMMENDATIONS FOR MARKETERS

Based on what we have mentioned so far, right here are some pointers for marketers who want to use faux information in their campaigns.

17.26.1 Understand the Potential

Teach yourself and your collaborators about the professionals and cons of the use of fraudulent statistics in marketing research. Stay up to date on new traits in methods for combining data and tendencies in AI and gadget studying.

17.26.2 Start Small and Scale Steadily

Before moving on to bigger projects, try out faux data in smaller initiatives or take a look at research first. Find specific take a look at questions or use instances in which fake information may be beneficial, and attempt out special ways to collect and examine the statistics.

17.26.3 Ensure Data Quality and Privacy

When creating and analyzing faux records, place facts accuracy, privateness, and compliance first. Strong confirmation and verification strategies have to be used to make certain that faux records units are accurate, reliable, and private.

17.26.4 Collaborate Across Teams

Encourage groups from advertising, statistics technology, and IT to paint together so that you can use the information and tools that are available to make synthetic facts-pushed advertising plans paintings properly. To get the maximum out of fake information, get move-practical groups to percentage thoughts, trade thoughts, and work collectively on tasks.

17.26.5 Stay Ethical and Transparent

When the use of fake records for advertising and marketing research, observe moral regulations and best practices. Be clear approximately how you propose to apply fake statistics and what its limits are.

REFERENCES

1. Emam, K., Mosquera, L. and Hoptroff, R., 2020. *Practical Synthetic Data Generation: Balancing Privacy and the Broad Availability of Data*. O'Reilly Media.
2. Gal, M. S., & Lynskey, O. (2023). Synthetic data: Legal implications of the data-generation revolution. Iowa L. Rev., 109, 1087.
3. Pathare, A., Mangrulkar, R., Suvarna, K., Parekh, A., Thakur, G. and Gawade, A., 2023. Comparison of tabular synthetic data generation techniques using propensity and cluster log metric. *International Journal of Information Management Data Insights*, *3*(2), p. 100177.
4. Soni, H.K. and Sharma, S., 2021. Big data analytics for market prediction via consumer insight. In S. Sharma, V. Rahaman, G. R. Sinha (eds) *Big Data Analytics in Cognitive Social Media and Literary Texts: Theory and Praxis*, pp. 23–46. Springer.

18 Measuring Marketing Effectiveness and Return on Investment

Nelapatla Swetha, Ponthala Harshavardhan, Tolem Kusuma, and M. Chithik Raja

18.1 INTRODUCTION

Effective marketing and Return on Investment (ROI) measurement are essential tools for companies navigating the ever-changing world of modern trade. In a world where making decisions based on data is crucial, assessing the success of marketing initiatives has become essential. It emphasizes the critical function of ROI assessment, highlighting the importance of knowing which marketing channels and strategies produce the best results and which ones need to be improved. Measuring the effect of marketing initiatives is not just a metric exercise; it is a strategic necessity that enables companies to optimize their marketing budgets, deploy resources wisely, and ultimately increase ROI [1]. The main objectives are based on giving readers a broad overview of tactics, indicators, and best practices that are crucial for negotiating the complexities of calculating marketing ROI and effectiveness. Through an exploration of diverse measurement methodologies and Key Performance Indicators [KPIs], the objective of this second paper is to equip enterprises with practical insights to evaluate the effectiveness of their marketing initiatives. It also addresses the difficulties that come with measurement, providing a sophisticated viewpoint that goes beyond simple numerical analytics. This paper serves as a thorough guide, navigating the constantly changing field of marketing analytics and revealing new trends that have the potential to fundamentally alter how companies assess and maximize their marketing expenditures in the future; it also aims to provide businesses with the knowledge and resources they need to measure and improve the effectiveness of their marketing initiatives in a market that is changing quickly through a thorough analysis of relevant literature.

18.2 LITERATURE REVIEW

Businesses must measure marketing effectiveness and ROI in order to assess the effects of their campaigns and make wise resource allocation decisions. The dynamic nature of the marketing environment, with its multitude of channels and intricate customer journeys, poses difficulties in precisely measuring the value produced. In the past, metrics such as website traffic or surveys measuring brand awareness

DOI: 10.1201/9781003472544-18

were frequently linked to marketing effectiveness. A greater variety of metrics, such as website conversion rates, Customer Acquisition Costs (CAC), and social media engagement, have become accessible with the growth of digital marketing [2]. Although these metrics offer insightful information about campaign performance and customer behavior, it is possible that they do not fully account for the long-term effects on brand value and Customer Lifetime Value (CLV). Scholars emphasize how crucial it is to establish precise goals and choose relevant metrics that support them. A more comprehensive understanding of the customer journey and a more precise ROI calculation are also made possible by the integration of data multiple sources, such as marketing automation platforms and Customer Relationship Management (CRM) system.

18.3 UNDERSTANDING MARKETING EFFECTIVENESS AND ROI

A basic grasp of marketing effectiveness and ROI is essential when it comes to marketing evaluation. The success of marketing initiatives in accomplishing their stated objectives and yielding measurable outcomes is measured comprehensively as marketing effectiveness this goes beyond simple measurements and includes a variety of aspects such as building brand recognition encouraging customer interaction generating quality leads converting leads into sales, and eventually generating revenue beyond superficial metrics effective marketing produces observable results that make a substantial contribution to a company's overall success and long-term growth.

Conversely, ROI is a measure of financial success that compares an investment's initial cost to its profitability and cost-effectiveness in the context of marketing. ROI offers a lens through which companies can access the amount of money made or revenue brought as a direct result of their marketing initiatives relative to the resources used in those initiatives. Stress that ROI is an important metric that provides information about the efficacy and efficiency of marketing initiatives as well as their capacity to produce quantifiable business results.

The relationship between marketing efficacy and ROI has a mutually beneficial relationship, with marketing efficacy serving as the foundation for measuring ROI. A higher ROI can only be achieved through positive outcomes which are largely driven by effective marketing strategies and tactics. According to [3], optimizing marketing effectiveness through tailored messaging targeted campaigns, and strategic resource allocation becomes the driving force behind businesses successful achievement of their overall marketing goals and maximum ROI for companies hoping to successfully navigate the complexities of today's marketing environments and achieve long-term success a sophisticated grasp of these ideas is therefore imperative.

18.4 APPROACHES TO MEASURING MARKETING EFFECTIVENESS AND ROI

Quantitative techniques like tracking KPIs and using analytical tools are used in conjunction with qualitative techniques like customer feedback and brand perception evaluations to measure marketing effectiveness, and ROI businesses can get through a grasp of how their marketing strategies affect important business goals by examining both objective and subjective data these facilities well-informed decision-making campaign optimization and efficient resource allocation to guarantee a profitable return on marketing expenditure

18.4.1 Traditional Approaches (e.g., Marketing Mix Modeling)

Conventional techniques for calculating ROI and marketing efficacy include Marketing Mix Modeling (MMM) to measure the effect of marketing efforts on sales performance. MMM analyzes past sales data and marketing spending across multiple channels, which assists companies in comprehending how various marketing strategies and channels affect overall sales and profitability.

18.4.2 Digital Analytics and Attribution Modeling

Digital analytics and attribution modeling are now indispensable tools for determining the ROI and efficacy of marketing campaigns; thanks to the growth of digital marketing, digital analytical tools like Google Analytics monitor user activity on various digital platforms and offer insights into campaign performance use behavior and convention paths businesses can better understand the relative influence of each a marketing channel on conversions and return on investment by using attribution modeling which allocates credit to various touchpoints along the customer journey.

18.4.3 Customer Lifetime Value (CLV) Analysis

The goal of customer lifetime value (CLV) analysis is to quantify the long-term value that a customer brings to a company during the course of their relationship. The net present value of future customer revenues is computed by factoring in things like average purchase value retention rates and customer acquisition costs in order to maximize long-term profitability, businesses can use CLV analysis to identify high-value customer segments, prioritize acquisition and retention efforts, and optimize marketing strategies.

18.4.4 Multi Touch Attribution

As numerous interactions with a brand frequently lead to a conversion multi touch attribution models give credit to various touchpoints throughout the customer journey. A more sophisticated understanding of the ways in which various marketing channels and touchpoints contribute to conversions and ROI is offered by these models, which include linear attribution, time decay attribution, and algorithmic attribution multi touch attribution helps companies better allocate resources and maximize budgets by capturing the entire customer journey.

18.4.5 Marketing ROI Software and Tools

Marketo, HubSpot, and Adobe Analytics are a few examples of marketing ROI software and tools that offer sophisticated analytics and reporting features to gauge marketing efficacy and return on investment. These tools facilitate the real-time tracking of important metrics and KPIs, automate reporting procedures, and integrate data from multiple sources in order to optimize marketing strategies and maximize ROI. They assist businesses in gaining actionable insights into campaign performance, pinpointing areas for improvement, and making data-driven decisions.

18.5 KEY PERFORMANCE INDICATORS (KPIS) FOR MEASURING MARKETING EFFECTIVENESS

Key performance indicators (KPIs), which offer businesses actionable insights across multiple dimensions, are essential for evaluating and optimizing marketing effectiveness awareness metrics provide insight into the visibility and reach of marketing campaigns by measuring how well messages connect with the intended audience such as brand awareness and social media mentions [4]. Click-through rates and social media interactions are examples of engagement metrics that go deeper and show how interested users are in marketing content.

Conversion metrics move the emphasis to observable results and assess how well marketing campaigns motivate desired behaviors campaign effectiveness can be quantitatively measured with the help of metrics like conversion rates and return on ad spend which help businesses determine how successful their campaigns are in reaching their goals. Metrics related to customer retention such as customer lifetime value and churn rates are used to assess how well marketing is doing at building enduring connections and retaining customers.

Finally, financial measures provide a comprehensive understanding of how marketing affects corporate performance. Businesses can optimize budget allocation and resource utilization by using marketing ROI cost per acquisition and marketing contribution to revenue, which establishes a clear connection between marketing investments and financial results. When combined, these KPIs provide a thorough framework that helps companies monitor, evaluate, and adjust their marketing tactics, which promotes ongoing development and long-term success in a changing market.

18.6 CHALLENGES IN MEASURING MARKETING EFFECTIVENESS AND ROI

Businesses face several obstacles when measuring marketing effectiveness and return on investment. One major challenge is data fragmentation and silos, whereby data from different sources such as marketing campaigns, sales activities, and customer interactions is frequently kept in separate repositories. This fragmentation impedes a comprehensive understanding of marketing impact by making it difficult to integrate and analyze data effectively.

Another level of difficulty is added by attribution complexity, particularly in the digital sphere. Before converting, consumers engage with a variety of touchpoints through a variety of channels, making it difficult to pinpoint the exact role played by each touchpoint. Accurate evaluation requires sophisticated attribution models and analytical methods.

The difficulty for companies with protracted sales cycles or complex purchasing procedures is determining how marketing efforts affect conversions and ROI. It may take a while for prospects to go through the sales funnel, making it difficult to attribute marketing touchpoints directly to them [5]. Cross-channel and cross-device tracking becomes more difficult. Marketing channels and devices proliferate because consumers interact with brands on a variety of platforms, so it is necessary to develop capabilities that precisely attribute conversions across channels and devices.

Finally, there is a challenge in attaining marketing accountability and alignment with overall business outcomes. Effective communication collaboration and alignment with other departments including sales finance and operations are imperative for marketing teams as they face pressure to demonstrate measurable results and ROI. Strategic planning, cutting-edge analytics, and cooperation across organizational functions are required to address these issues and guarantee a thorough and precise evaluation of marketing effectiveness and ROI.

18.7 BEST PRACTICES FOR EFFECTIVE MEASUREMENT

Businesses can use a variety of strategies to overcome the difficulties in gauging the ROI and efficacy of advertising, beginning with the establishment of specific goals and key performance indicators (KPIs) that are in line with overarching organization objectives maintaining SMART (specific, measurable, achievable, relevant, and time-bound) objectives offers an organized framework for monitoring advancement and assessing accomplishments. Setting up baselines and comparing performances to competitors and industry standards provides an essential contextual framework for performance assessment. Businesses can establish realistic goals, identify trends, and monitor their progress over time by monitoring past metrics and industry benchmarks, which promotes a strategic approach to optimization. Investing in a strong data infrastructure and integration skills becomes essential.

The challenges associated with data fragmentation and silos are lessened by implementing data management systems and integrating disparate data sources, such as marketing automation platforms and customer relationship management (CRM) systems, which centralize data and enable seamless exchange.

Businesses can implement robust attribution models such as linear attribution, time decay attribution, or algorithmic attribution to achieve accurate attribution, which is crucial. These models address attribution complexity issues by providing a thorough understanding of the customer journey and enabling businesses to attribute credit to each of the six touchpoints based on how they contribute to conversions.

Finally, encouraging a culture of experimentation and learning is essential for ongoing development. By incorporating these strategies, businesses can improve their capacity to measure marketing effectiveness and ROI, opening the door for informed decision-making and sustained growth in a dynamic business environment. As stated in reference [6], teams can foster innovation and drive better results by embracing testing experimentation and data-driven decision-making.

18.8 EMERGING TRENDS IN MARKETING ANALYTICS

The combination of machine learning (ML) and artificial intelligence (AI) is radically changing the field of marketing analytics with their ability to provide automated optimization personalized recommendations, as well as predictive analytics. These technologies are completely changing the way businesses analyze data scale data sets combed through by AI-powered algorithms, which then use the patterns they find to forecast future events and dynamically optimize marketing campaigns in real time.

Another aspect of this revolution is predictive analysis and forecasting, which uses historical data and statistical models to forecast future trends, behaviors, and results in order to improve marketing performance. This helps businesses to recognize opportunities, anticipate customer needs, and make proactive, well-informed decisions.

This is further enhanced by real-time marketing analytics, which enables companies to track, examine, and react instantly to shifts in customer behavior and market dynamics. Businesses can maximize ROI by personalizing marketing messages, adjusting campaigns dynamically, and seizing emerging opportunities by utilizing real-time data insights.

Voice of the customer (VoC) analytics is gathering and examining consumer opinions, stances, and preferences from a range of touchpoints. Businesses can learn a great deal about the needs, problems, and expectations of their customers by actively listening to them. This gives them the ability to modify their marketing plans and product offerings to better suit the needs of their target audience and build closer relationships.

But as marketing analytics become more sophisticated, companies must deal with ethical and privacy issues. Businesses must maintain compliance and openness in their data practices due to strict regulations like the CCPA and GDPR, which place restrictions on consent and data privacy at a time when consumers are more conscious of data privacy. Addressing these issues is essential to establishing and preserving consumer trust [7]. Businesses that use these technologies not only improve their analytical skills but also have to navigate ethical issues in order to establish a foundation of trust with their clients.

18.9 CASE STUDIES AND EXAMPLES

These case studies and illustrations show how businesses in a variety of sectors use ROI tracking Attribution modeling and advanced analytics to access marketing efficacy and improve their marketing plans. Businesses can improve the effectiveness of their marketing campaigns, make well-informed decisions, and allocate resources more efficiently by embracing a data-driven approach and utilizing insights from analytical tools.

18.9.1 Procter and Gamble's Marketing Mix Modeling

Marketing mix modeling is a tool that Procter & Gamble (P&G) uses to assess the performance of its advertising campaigns in various product categories and geographical areas. P&G can optimize its marketing mix by reallocating resources to high-performing channels and tactics, leading to improved ROI and profitability by analyzing historical sales data and marketing spending [8].

18.9.2 Google Analytics Attribution Modeling

Google Analytics provides attribution modeling tools that let companies monitor and examine the customer journey through various channels and touchpoints. Businesses can optimize their marketing strategies for maximum effectiveness by using attribution modeling to gain insights into the relative impact of various marketing channels on conversions and ROI [9].

18.9.3 Amazon's Customer Lifetime Value Analysis

To identify high-value customer segments and customize marketing strategies to their unique requirements and preferences, amazon uses CLV analysis. Understanding it is customer long-term worth allows Amazon to make acquisition and retention investments that will pay off in the long run, resulting in steady growth and profitability [8,9].

18.9.4 Coco Cola Multi Touch Attribution

Coco cola evaluates the effectiveness of its marketing campaigns across a range of channels and touch points by using multi touch attribution models coco cola can maximize return on investment and accomplish its business goals by optimizing its marketing mix and allocating resources more wisely by knowing how various meeting initiatives affect customer behavior and lead to conversions [8,9].

18.9.5 Salesforce's Marketing Cloud ROI Tracking

With the help of salesforces' marketing cloud, companies can track ROI and evaluate the immediate financial effects of their marketing initiatives. Businesses can track the ROI of their marketing campaigns, find areas for improvement, and make data-driven decisions to optimize their marketing strategies and investments by integrating data from multiple sources and applying advanced analytics [8,9].

18.10 IMPLICATIONS FOR BUSINESSES

Robust measurement of marketing effectiveness and ROI yields significant advantages that enhance decision-making resource allocation, accountability, and competitiveness. A thorough grasp of the actual effects of marketing initiatives can help companies find optimization opportunities, reduce risks, and promote profitable and sustainable growth.

The measurement of marketing effectiveness and ROI has a substantial impact on budget allocation and strategic choices. Businesses can identify underperforming channels and tactics by using the measurement's insights to reallocate resources to high-impact projects and optimize the marketing mix for optimal return on investment. This improves the strategic alignment of organizational efforts by guaranteeing more effective resource utilization and creating a clear connection between marketing initiatives and overarching business goals.

Furthermore, by offering a standard framework and vocabulary for performance evaluation, efficient measurement promotes organizational alignment and accountability. Marketing teams can synchronize their endeavors with more expansive business objectives, monitor advancements in relation to KPIs, and effectively illustrate the significance of their input to stakeholders across the entire enterprise. Insights from measurement actively contribute to the improvement of strategies and tactics, fostering a culture of continuous improvement and encouraging transparency and collaboration [10]. All things considered, efficient measurement is essential to fostering both strategic and operational excellence in companies, providing a route to long-term prosperity and competitiveness in ever-changing market conditions.

18.11 CONCLUSION

In conclusion, for businesses hoping to succeed in the cutthroat business environment of today, measuring marketing effectiveness and ROI is not only a need but a strategic imperative. This essay has offered a thorough examination of the complexities involved in measuring marketing performance, covering everything from comprehending the core ideas of ROI and marketing effectiveness to going over different strategies, obstacles, and new developments in the field of marketing analytics.

It has been clear from the conversation that measuring marketing effectiveness and ROI accurately is important for several reasons. First, it helps companies evaluate the results of their marketing campaigns, pinpoint their strong and weak points, and make data-driven choices to maximize efficiency. Secondly, it offers a foundation for resource allocation and strategic planning, assisting companies in setting priorities and concentrating on projects that yield the highest run-on investment. Thirdly, it encourages transparency, accountability, and alignment within businesses, making sure that marketing efforts are in line with overarching business goals and that stakeholders are aware of the value that marketing campaigns bring.

The study has emphasized several measurement strategies including more recent approaches like multi-touch attribution modeling and customer lifetime value analysis, as well as more established ones like digital analytics and marketing mix modeling. Additionally, it has covered KPIs at various customer journey stages such as awareness and engagement conversion retention highlighting the significance of a comprehensive app to measurement. The conversion did, however, also address the difficulties in determining marketing ROI and effectiveness including data fragmentation, difficult attribution, and protracted sales cycles.

In addition to a dedication to promoting an environment of experimentation, learning, and continuous improvement within the organization, addressing these challenges calls for investments in data infrastructure integration capabilities and nine sophisticated analytical tools.

The study has identified future directors in marketing analytics such as the expanding use of machine learning and AI real-time analytics and VOC analytics. These developments give companies new chances to understand consumer behavior better tailor their marketing strategies and maintain a competitive edge in the digital era.

In conclusion businesses need to measure marketing effectiveness and ROI well in order to succeed in the fast paced cutthroat business world of today businesses can attain their goals promote sustainable growth and maximize the potential of their marketing initiatives by adopting best practices taking advantage of new trends and overcoming obstacles.

18.11.1 Recap of Key Findings

In summary businesses must measure marketing effectiveness and ROI to access the effects of their marketing initiatives and make wise decisions businesses can obtain actionable insights into their marketing performance and maximize the impact of their strategies by utilizing emerging trends in marketing analytics defining clear objectives and KPIs and adopting appropriate measurement approaches.

18.11.2 Recommendations for Future Research

Future studies on ROI measurement and marketing efficacy may examine sophisticated analytics methods for forecasting and predictive modeling such as AI & machine learning to increase consumer trust and confidence research may also concentrate on addressing issues with data privacy ethics & regulatory compliance in marketing analytics.

18.11.3 Closing Remarks

Effective measurement of marketing effectiveness and ROI is essential for promoting business success in a highly competitive and complex business environment. businesses can optimize marketing strategies maximize ROI and accomplish growth objectives in the digital age by investing in strong measurement capabilities utilizing data driven insights and cultivating a culture of experimentation and learning.

REFERENCES

1. Ranjan KR, Sugathan P, Rossmann A. A narrative review and meta-analysis of service interaction quality: new research directions and implications. *Journal of Services Marketing.* 2015;29(1):3–14.
2. Hoffman DL, Fodor M. Can you measure the ROI of your social media marketing? *MIT Sloan Management Review.* 2010;52:41–49.
3. Webster C. A note on cultural consistency within the service firm: the effects of employee position on attitudes toward marketing culture. *Journal of the Academy of Marketing Science.* 1991;19:341–346.
4. Homburg C, Vollmayr J, Hahn A. Firm value creation through major channel expansions: evidence from an event study in the United States, Germany, and China. *Journal of Marketing.* 2014;78(3):38–61.
5. Dybvig A. Truly maximize the ROI of sales' and marketing's expenditures with demand-driven planning. *Journal of Corporate Accounting & Finance.* 2015;27(1):45–53.
6. Armstrong S, Esber D, Heller J, Timelin B. *Modern marketing: what it is, what it isn't, and how to do it.* McKinsey & Company; 2020.
7. Taylor CR. Artificial intelligence, customized communications, privacy, and the General Data Protection Regulation (GDPR). *International Journal of Advertising.* 2019;38(5):649–650.
8. Leeflang PS, Wittink DR. Building models for marketing decisions: past, present and future. *International Journal of Research in Marketing.* 2000;17(2–3):105–126.
9. Shmueli G, Bruce PC, Patel NR. *Data mining for business analytics: concepts, techniques, and applications with XLMiner.* John Wiley & Sons; 2016.
10. Ambler T, Roberts JH. Assessing marketing performance: don't settle for a silver metric. *Journal of Marketing Management.* 2008;24(7–8):733–750.

19 Emerging Technologies Shaping the Future of Marketing

Adarsh Reddy Pannala, Prudviraj Reddy Singireddy, Adith Raj, and Chinna Swamy Dudekula

19.1 INTRODUCTION

Generative artificial intelligence (simply "Generative AI or GAI") has been the key factor responsible for large-scale acceptance of AI in enterprises (Kshetri et al., 2023; Dwivedi et al., 2023, 2024). GAI is the part of AI that can generate completely new content like images, text, or video (Susarla et al., 2023). Though organizations are enjoying benefits of all functional areas from this breakthrough technology (Dwivedi et al., 2024), marketing has been the domain which has been positively influenced by recent innovations in generative AI. Usefulness of generative AI is clear in industries like advertising and marketing where quality materials are needed to interact and communicate with consumers and stakeholders (Fintechnews Switzerland, 2023).

It goes without saying that the use of generative AI is rising significantly in marketing. As of March 2023, generative AI tools have been used by 73% of organizations in the United States, such as chatbots in activities and marketing (Dencheva, 2023a). Around 32% of companies give preference to sales and marketing applications of Generative AI, and 44% of organizations prefer use cases of customer operations like chatbots (Davenport, 2023). AI market was estimated to reach $15.84 billion in the year 2021, while it is estimated to cross $107.5 billion by the year 2028 (Dencheva, 2023b).

Generally, using digital technologies can be helpful to companies to deliver timely, personalize, and relevant information through the selected platform, that is, improving overall consumer satisfaction (Buttle & Stan, 2015). Better experience leads to more attention toward brands and products (Grewal et al., 2017), which ultimately increases firm performance and customer loyalty. Initial findings suggest that generative AI has a significant and stronger impact than previous technologies on marketing outcomes and processes (Kshetri et al., 2023). It is majorly because of the ability of GAI to generate easy-to-customize and human-like text, videos, and images to provide a huge range of robust tools to marketers to optimize the processes of content creation.

Generative AI is perceived by marketers is a significant booster of productivity. For example, over 82% of participants in a survey expected improvement in productivity to adopt GAI in comparison to only 4% of participants who expected a decline

DOI: 10.1201/9781003472544-19

in productivity. This survey was conducted by a non-profit research and membership group, "The Conference Board (2023)." However, the benefits of generative AI in promotion is exceeding their roles as merely time-saving or cost-cutting tools. Generative AI can do things that may not be possible for humans. For example, generative AI enables companies to boost marketing and sales and provide personalized experiences in a way that humans cannot do. GAI provides benefits like the capabilities of dynamic messaging with the use of a personal touch to send the ideal marketing message at the best time to consumers as per valuable and informed data. For example, customized text, relevant imagery, and predictive suggestions can scale personalized in various important moments in a cost-effective manner (Bernard, 2023).

This book chapter will cover the following sections. First of all, this chapter will explore some of the recent studies related to generative AI and AI tools. In the next sections, it will provide an overview of some of the real-life applications of AI in marketing and its current status. Next, it will discuss the factors contributing to the use of generative AI. Finally, it will conclude findings with implications for researchers and marketers and future research directions.

19.2 LITERATURE REVIEW

Generative AI can generate life-like images and augment creativity and disrupt the economics of producing marketing content. Though there is anecdotal evidence available on quality visuals created by GAI, there is a lack of knowledge of the effectiveness of these models in context of marketing. Hartmann et al. (2023) explored the disruptive potential of "text-to-image diffusion models" for generating visual marketing content while evaluating the performance of human-made and AI-generated images systematically across those dimensions of marketing like "social media engagement (comments and likes), human perception (realism and quality), and click-through rates (CTRs) of banner ads." Over 17,000 evaluations for 1,500 artificial images have been collected with 13 "text-to-image diffusion models." They found that AI-generated pictures can easily look better than images made by humans regarding realism and perceived quality, get comparable engagement in social media, and have more than 22% CTR in field experiments with over 86,000 impressions.

Explored the factors affecting the adoption of generative AI in digital marketing. The researcher conducted a questionnaire survey among 411 participants who are "Content Managers/Strategists, Digital Marketing Managers, and Social Media Managers." The study focused on challenges and opportunities in adopting generative AI. Machine learning (ML) models showed different accuracy levels for forecasting adoption. The highest accuracy was obtained by Support Vector Machine (SVM), i.e., 83%. Decision Tree and Random Forest showed the value of variables like scalability, efficiency, cost-effectiveness, personalization, and content generation.

Social media services like Instagram and Facebook have allowed customers to know about the products before buying. It has also diversified consumer needs and preferences. As online channels expand and preferences are diversified, it is important for organizations to offer personalized marketing. Personalized marketing approaches are vital to improving consumer engagement. There is a cost involved in writing marketing messages to provide personalized communication. There are also issues related to the complex development of models and the generation of quality messages automatically. Lee et al. (2024) proposed a Persuasive Message Intelligence (PMI)" service using the prominent "Large Language Model" to automate personalized messages.

Generative AI has also impacted the growth of conversational marketing conducted inclusive review on integrating anthropometric design and generative AI in conversational marketing. First, they explored psychological factors of anthropomorphism focusing on its role to improve user experience by building the feeling of familiarity. In this paradigm, generative AI can create conversational agents that can generate accurate, human-like responses. Then, research examined the implications of Gai on marketing and consumer engagement. It focuses on the potential benefits and challenges which improve satisfaction and user interaction. This study focused on the balanced approach to conversational marketing.

19.3 RESEARCH GAP

Several studies have been conducted on the use of generative AI in the field of marketing (Kunz & Wirtz, 2024; Huh et al., 2023; Peres et al., 2023; Paul et al., 2023; Polonsky & Rotman, 2023). There is a vast research gap on real-life applications of these AI tools and their impact on marketing and financial performance of firms. GAI plays a vital role in different aspects of marketing. This book chapter fills this gap by focusing on key applications of generative AI.

19.3.1 Objectives of the Study

- To discuss real-world applications of generative AI in marketing.
- To discuss the factors contributing to the applications of GAI in marketing.

19.4 RESEARCH METHODOLOGY

Digital marketing has recently faced a paradigm change driven by changing behaviors and technological innovation. With latent capabilities to redefine campaign strategies and content creation, the advancement of GAI presents a new front for businesses. However, adopting those disruptive approaches is usually combined with a blend of skepticism and enthusiasm. Knowing the challenges and opportunities for the adoption of Generative AI in marketing is important for both scholars and marketers. This chapter gives valuable insights into harnessing these technologies to improve marketing, while defining challenges that should be met to promote large-scale implementation and acceptance. This chapter fills most important knowledge gap by defining those factors that contribute to the implementation of generative AI.

Generative AI especially provides significant advancements in terms of scalability, efficiency, and personalization in generating content. It is important for successful campaigns. This advancement also has some challenges like complexity of AI tools, the need for human intervention, reduced creativity, and problems in combining these techniques in marketing models. This understanding is vital to make data-driven decisions for businesses on adoption of such tools and to tailor AI programs aligning with the needs for marketing. This chapter adopts descriptive research design, which employs secondary data collected from various sources like research papers, publications, media sources, etc.

19.5 REAL-WORLD APPLICATIONS OF GAI IN MARKETING

A lot of AI tools have been developed for marketing (Figure 19.1 and Table 19.1). One of the best examples of generative AI is "ChatGPT, developed by OpenAI." It is a well-known "GAI tool among the common public and marketers. Bank of America conducted a survey in June 2023 among 1,100 internet users aged 18–55 years and found that ChatGPT is one of the most preferred AI chatbots among participants, and it is used by 59% of participants. It is also reported that "51% of participants were also using Microsoft Bing and 31% of participants were using Google's Bard (Quarles, 2023)." Similarly, as per a survey by a provider of AI-based solutions for marketing chat, Botco.ai, ChatGPT was the best choice as one of the marketing experts for their tools based on generative AI (Butler, 2023).

Some of those tools are foundational models like "DALL-E2, Midjourney, and GPT4 and others are the models tuned for marketing only like Copy.ai and Jasper.ai." Though ChatGPT responds to text-based commands, GPT-4 is the most modern GAI tool of Open AI, which can be used by paid users as it also accepts images.

The advanced capabilities of GPT4 for language generation would enable marketers to generate better-quality content with ChatGPT. Content created by GPT-4 is supposed to be more relevant and engaging to the audience. The fine-tuning capabilities of GPT-4 can help digital marketers to tailor content and messaging for users, while fostering more personalized experience. Though a lot of generative AI tools used by marketers are helpful to generate text-based content like Jasper. ai, Copy.ai, and Peppertype.ai, other tools like DALL-E2 can generate life-like visuals and artworks as per text-to-image prompts. Additionally, digital marketing

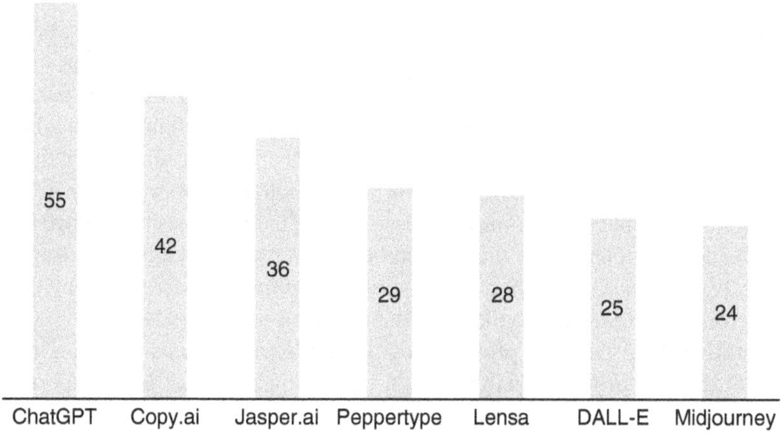

FIGURE 19.1 Marketing professionals using various generative AI tools. Source: Butler (2023).

TABLE 19.1
Some of the Generative AI Tools for Marketing

GAI Tools	Uses in Marketing	Applications	Resource
ChatGPT and GPT-4[a]	Stimulating and brainstorming the process of creativity, creating personalized solutions, and creating marketing content	Tome, which provides AI-based storytelling tool, enables consumers to generate presentations with online videos, documents, and digital content. In addition, Khanmigo is a GPT4-based tool by Khan Academy which provides interactive and personalized learning experiences for teachers and students.	Kshetri (2023)
AI Sandbox by Meta[b]	Generating background with image cropping and text prompts	This solution is used by "Jones Road Beauty" to generate more ads quickly. It can create quicker cycle by reducing the time needed to refine, develop, and revise ideas, concepts and designs to achieve the needed results.	
DALL-E2 by OpenAI	Generating art and custom images based on prompt	Mattel, a toy company, generated new model car of Hot Wheels. Omneky, a generative AI ad platform, created graphics for ads in social media.	
Midjourney[c]	Generating pictures as per text prompts	PrimeCare, an elderly care management firm, uses art generated by this platform for blog posts.	
Peppertype.ai[d]	Generating context-based, short-form copies and generating descriptions of products	Used by over 800 businesses like Adobe, Meta, and Amazon, as of October 2021.	Kshetri et al. (2023)
Jasper.ai[e]	Generating marketing content like product descriptions, blog posts, ad copy, and company bios	An insurance firm Goosehead Insurance generates marketing content like blog posts for online learning center of the company as well as email campaigns for existing and potential clients. Social media content is repurposed to enhance engagement and reach.	Kshetri et al. (2023)
Copy.ai[f]	Designing marketing content and ad copy	Used by Airtable, cloud-based database service and collaborative platform.	Kshetri et al. (2023)

[a] https://chatgpt.com/
[b] https://theaigrid.com/
[c] https://www.midjourney.com/
[d] https://www.peppercontent.io/peppertype-ai/
[e] https://www.jasper.ai
[f] https://www.copy.ai/

giants like Meta have made their own generative AI tools for clients. For example, a GAI Sandbox generated by Meta provided access to marketers to three tools in May 2023. The first tool enables marketers to use different versions of an ad copy in Insta or Facebook profile of a company. When a marketer enters ad copy, several versions of the copy are suggested by the generative AI to test. The second tool generates background using text prompts. Text prompts can be used by a marketer to describe style or background. The generative AI tool provides marketers with images to text their impact. The third tool consists of the feature of image cropping to generate visuals in various "aspect ratios" for different media like stories, social media posts, or short content.

It was found that there is a rise in the use of generative AI among marketers and also in demand (Table 19.2). Junior and mid-level marketers are known to have higher adoption for GAI in comparison to senior marketers (The Conference Board, 2023). The traits of marketing experts using generative AI are consistent with a huge population. A huge population of youth have used ChatGPT in comparison to older adults, according to a new survey in July 2023 by Pew Research Center.

TABLE 19.2
Applications of Generative AI among Marketers

Survey	Participants	Findings	Source
Salesforce and YouGov	Conducted among 1,029 marketers from May 18 to 25, 2023	Generative AI is used by 51% participants. Other 22% of participants planned to use those tools soon. Over 5 hours of working hours are saved per week.	
Botco.ai, an AI-based marketing chat provider	Conducted on 1,000 marketers in March 2023	Generative AI tools used by 73% of participants to generate marketing content. Some of the applications are cost-efficiency, improved creativity, performance, and augmenting human creativity.	
Boston Consulting Group	Conducted among over 200 CMOs from various industries in eight nations across Asia, Europe and North America	70% of participants are using generative AI and 19% of them were testing. Some of the top applications are simulating creative thinking, generating content rapidly, personalizing user content, and improving customer service.	Ratajczak et al. (2023)
The Conference Board	Among 287 communicators and marketers in August 2023	Over 87% of participants experimented with or used AI tools. Some of the major applications are personalizing user content or customers, generating content rapidly, and improving customer service.	The Conference Board (2023)

19.6 FACTORS CONTRIBUTING TO THE APPLICATIONS OF GAI IN MARKETING

There have been a lot of factors contributing to the applications of generative AI in marketing. Proper knowledge of such tools may show why those tools are widely used in some environments and by some firms. First of all, a lot of well-known generative AI tools like ChatGPT which show best performance in terms of "perceived ease of use," which is a significant contribution in deciding technology adoption. ChatGPT is one of the most popular generative AI tools among marketing professionals in marketing as it has a very friendly interface performing a lot of tasks related to marketing (Figure 19.1). A lot of marketing experts are also known to consider GAI tools for generating images like Stable Diffusion, Midjourney, and DALL-E2, and sophisticated graphics can be developed and used by almost everyone.

Additionally, generative AI shows the best performance when it comes to trialability, describing the ability of potential adopters to try or experiment with a product before formal adoption on a limited basis. Trialability has been increased as generative AI tools like ChatGPT are free and they have increased rapid growth in user base.

Third, though all of the generative AI tools for marketing are not available for free, cost of using majority of them are not huge. Most of those tools do not need expensive software (Chen, 2023). Similarly, OpenAI provided DALL-E to new users with 50 free credits during the first few months of use. After that period, they would have got 15 free credits for the next few months. Even though OpenAI decided to discontinue the feature of free trial, the cost of using that tool is very reasonable.

Fourth most important factor is the availability of a lot of Generative AI tools for marketing. Though ChatGPT is used most widely for marketing, a lot of similar tools have been generated (Figure 19.1). For example, Jasper.ai provides tool for AI writing for creating marketing copy like product descriptions, blog posts, ad copy, and company bios. It provides different generative AI models tailored to customers' needs. It works with other generative AI tools providers like Google, OpenAI, Meta, and Anthropic to meet different clients' needs (O'brien, 2023).

The last most important factor is ability to finetune or tailor generative AI models for different types of content like marketing content. There are around three approaches of models on official content of organization. Generative AI tools are trained by a lot of organizations with prompts but using huge volumes on content require special techniques like vector databases, embeddings, and similarity models. Those fine-tuning can train GAI models on specific services or products of the company.

19.6 CONCLUSION

This study has provided an insight to the transformation of important activities and areas by generative AI in the field of marketing. This study focuses on some of the modern applications like insight generation, personalization, and content creation. It is worth noting that such uses are interconnected. It is possible to use insights with generative AI as a foundation to develop better content and improve user engagement.

Similarly, personalization is vital to create content. This study discussed the roles of generative AI in personalizing content. All in all, generative AI is a very effective tool for personalized content for marketers to build a strong customer engagement and experience. Generative AI can also be used as a tool to improve productivity and efficiency of marketers and reduce costs. It can also improve lead generation for marketers.

Though generative AI tools cannot replace experiences and skills of human teams completely, they can perform several marketing tasks at higher speed, lower cost, and more efficiently as compared to human workforce. For example, previous models were not much effective for personalization. Similarly, traditional AI models showed poor performance in scalability. Generative AI can develop automation to generate highly personalized content as per customer journeys and interactions to achieve personalization. There are different capabilities of Generative AI observed in this study which are diverse for individual and organizational learning.

19.7 FUTURE RESEARCH DIRECTIONS

Future studies can explore different applications of AI. For example, improved customer service is one of the best applications of generative AI. This way, large language models (LLMs) can be compared with chatbots when it comes to improve customer service in future studies. Future studies can also focus on using generative AI for various marketing roles. Scholars can compare performance of chatbots and LLMs in terms of various measures like scalability, customer experience, usage, etc.

19.8 IMPLICATIONS FOR RESEARCHERS AND MARKETERS

Generative AI tools like ChatGPT can enhance the value proposition of a company by developing personalized solutions that can be helpful to consumers to solve new challenges. This way, researchers can examine different ways for LLMs to develop value propositions. Earlier studies have observed that there is a positive impact of personalization on cognitive and emotional well-being of customers. This way, researchers can compare the impacts of generative AI-based personalization on cognitive and emotional consumer behavior.

On the other hand, generative AI tools can be used by marketers to generate smart responses at personal level to automate and develop the best tailored marketing strategy. They can use these tools to generate and distribute highly personalized content, recommendations, offers, and experience at the right time.

REFERENCES

Bernard, H. U. (2004). Established and potential strategies against papillomavirus infections. *Journal of antimicrobial Chemotherapy*, 53(2), 137–139.

Butler, R. (2023). Where Are Marketers on the Generative AI Adoption Curve? Available at https://www.cmswire.com/digital-experience/where-are-marketers-on-the-generative-aiadoption-curve/.

Buttle, F., & Stan, M. (2015). Customer Relationship Management: Concepts and Technologies (3rd ed.). Routledge.

Davenport, T. H. (2023). Hyper-Personalization for Customer Engagement with Artificial Intelligence. *Management and Business Review*, *3*(1), 18–55.

Dencheva, V. (2023a). Share of Marketers Using Generative Artificial Intelligence (AI) in Their Companies in the United States as of March 2023. Available at https://www.statista.com/statistics/1388390/generative-ai-usage-marketing/.

Dencheva, V. (2023b). AI in Marketing Revenue Worldwide 2020–2028. Available at https://www.statista.com/statistics/1293758/ai-marketing-revenueworldwide/#:~:text=In%202021%2C%20the%20market%20for,than%20107.5%20billion%20by%202028.

Dwivedi, Y. K., Kshetri, N., Hughes, L., Slade, E. L., Jeyaraj, A., Kar, A. K., ... & Wright, R. (2023). "So What If ChatGPT Wrote It?" Multidisciplinary Perspectives on Opportunities, Challenges and Implications of Generative Conversational AI for Research, Practice and Policy. *International Journal of Information Management*, *71*, 102642.

Dwivedi, Y. K., Pandey, N., Currie, W., & Micu, A. (2024). Leveraging ChatGPT and Other Generative Artificial Intelligence (AI)-Based Applications in the Hospitality and Tourism Industry: Practices, Challenges and Research Agenda. *International Journal of Contemporary Hospitality Management*, *36*(1), 1–12.

Fintechnews Switzerland. (2023). The Implications of ChatGPT and AI Models on Fintech and Banking. Available at https://fintechnews.ch/aifintech/the-implications-of-chatgpt-and-aimodels-on-fintech-and-banking/57552/.

Grewal, D., Roggeveen, A. L., Sisodia, R., & Nordfält, J. (2017). Enhancing Customer Engagement through Consciousness. *Journal of Retailing*, *93*(1), 55–64.

Hartmann, J., Exner, Y., & Domdey, S. (2023). The power of generative marketing: Can generative AI reach human-level visual marketing content?. *Available at SSRN*.

Huh, J., Nelson, M. R., & Russell, C. A. (2023). ChatGPT, AI advertising, and advertising research and education. Journal of Advertising, 52(4), 477–482.

Kunz, W. H., & Wirtz, J. (2024). Corporate digital responsibility (CDR) in the age of AI: implications for interactive marketing. Journal of Research in Interactive Marketing, 18(1), 31–37.

Kshetri, N., Dwivedi, Y. K., Davenport, T. H., & Panteli, N. (2023). Generative artificial intelligence in marketing: Applications, opportunities, challenges, and research agenda. *International Journal of Information Management*, 102716.

Lee, E., Bristow, J., Faircloth, C., & Macvarish, J. (2024). *Parenting culture studies*. Hampshire: Palgrave macmillan.

O'Brien, M. W., Tremblay, P. E., Gentile Fusillo, N. P., Hollands, M. A., Gänsicke, B. T., Koester, D., ... & Zuckerman, B. (2023). Gaia white dwarfs within 40 pc–III. Spectroscopic observations of new candidates in the Southern hemisphere. *Monthly Notices of the Royal Astronomical Society*, 518(2), 3055–3073.

Paul, A., Tretheway, P., & Liu, L. (2024, March). Using Generative AI in Visual Media: New Technologies, Teaching Tools, and Trends. In Society for Information Technology & Teacher Education International Conference (pp. 847–850). Association for the Advancement of Computing in Education (AACE).

Pérez-Núñez, A. (2023). Exploring the potential of generative AI (ChatGPT) for foreign language instruction: applications and challenges. Hispania, 106(3), 355–362.

Polonsky, M. J., & Rotman, J. D. (2023). Should artificial intelligent agents be your co-author? Arguments in favour, informed by ChatGPT. Australasian Marketing Journal, 31(2), 91-96.

Quarles, C. (2023). *Systemic Inequality, Technological Innovation, and the Limits of Human Understanding* (Doctoral dissertation).

Ratajczak, R., Guziewicz, E., Prucnal, S., Mieszczynski, C., Jozwik, P., Barlak, M., ... & Facsko, S. (2023). Enhanced Luminescence of Yb3+ Ions Implanted to ZnO through the Selection of Optimal Implantation and Annealing Conditions. *Materials*, 16(5), 1756.

Susarla, A., Gopal, R., Thatcher, J. B., & Sarker, S. (2023). The Janus Effect of Generative AI: Charting the Path for Responsible Conduct of Scholarly Activities in Information Systems. *Information Systems Research*.

20 Customer Segmentation Techniques in Predictive Analytics and Generative AI for Data-Driven Marketing Strategies

Shalom Mariam Aeby, V. Vedhik Mohan Rao, and Nikhil Gupta

20.1 INTRODUCTION

In recent years we have seen a dramatic shift towards data-driven marketing strategies due to the rapid development of generative artificial intelligence (AI) including analytics and prediction, because their segmentation by consumers is essential to win the battle in modern marketing techniques.

Heterogeneous markets can be divided into homogeneous sub-segments through consumer segmentation, based on shared characteristics, behaviours, or preferences. The format consists of marketing that focuses on specific consumer segments, all of which are likely to increase in value as performance improves. The expansion had a significant impact on its growth.

Consumer segmentation has historically been based on major demographic criteria such as age, gender, income, and location. These demographic indicators remain relevant, but they offer limited insight into consumer behaviour and preferences. Marketers must use sophisticated segmentation tactics as customer expectations evolve and grow more complicated.

Companies are actually leveraging the promise of generative AI and predictive analytics to improve their customer segmentation strategies. Predictive analytics makes predictions about destiny tendencies and behaviours based on historic facts and statistical algorithms. This facilitates marketers to better understand the desires and possibilities of their target market. In contrast, generative AI generates new data and generates insights that are superior to those obtained from traditional analytics by using machine learning algorithms. A new era of precision, scalability, and adaptability in customer segmentation has begun with the merging of generative AI and predictive analytics.

Marketers may better segment their consumer base and spot subtle patterns and trends that were previously unavailable by utilising the power of these technologies.

DOI: 10.1201/9781003472544-20

This chapter will explore the development of client segmentation strategies, from conventional methods to state-of-the-art systems driven by artificial intelligence and machine learning. We will examine the advantages and difficulties of each method and offer helpful advice for putting sophisticated segmentation techniques into practice within the framework of data-driven marketing. This section provides a thorough overview of how to navigate the ever-changing field of consumer segmentation in the age of generative AI and predictive analytics.

Marketers can seize new chances of accelerating growth, improving customer satisfaction, and maintaining an advantage in a more cutthroat industry by comprehending the advancements and nuances of segmentation tactics.

20.2 TRADITIONAL SEGMENTATION TECHNIQUES

Throughout the past, marketers have classified their consumer base using a range of segmentation methodologies and then customised their approaches to marketing based on those categories. These methods generally involve segmentation based on demographics, geography, and psychography, each of which provides a different perspective on the behaviour as well as preferences of the consumer.

Segmentation based on demographics pertains to the division of a market according to distinguishable attributes including age, gender, income, occupation, education level, and size of family. Because of its accessibility and ease of usage, this strategy is among the most traditional and commonly used segmentation techniques. Through comprehension of the demographic makeup of their clientele, marketers may craft focused advertising strategies that appeal to particular customer segments.

Whereas geographic segmentation splits the marketplace according to geographic factors like nation, area, city, or neighbourhood. This method acknowledges how a variety of factors, including infrastructure, language, culture, and climate, can have a substantial impact on the interests and spending behaviour of consumers. Through customisation of marketing campaigns according to the distinct attributes of various geographical areas, advertisers can maximise their outreach and pertinence.

The psychology of consumers and behavioural characteristics, including values, beliefs, passions, occupations, mindsets, and personality characteristics, are further explored through the segmentation of psychographic data. By attempting to comprehend the fundamental desires and motives that shape consumer behaviour, this strategy enables marketing to develop more deeply personal and individualised advertising. For sectors like fashion, cosmetics, and expensive goods in which sentimentality and devotion to a brand are important, psychographic segmentation has proven particularly useful.

Although conventional segmentation methods have demonstrated efficacy in furnishing significant perspectives into consumer conduct, they frequently encounter constraints concerning precision and prognostic potency. Although useful, socioeconomic and geography-related variables may fail to capture the subtleties and complexity of personal preferences and behaviours. Psychographic segmentation, on the other hand, is more complex but might be difficult to apply at volume and can lack the precision for forecasting needed for efficient focusing.

Companies recognise the necessity for deeper methods of segmentation as the demands of customers increase and get more complex.

20.3 EVOLUTION OF SEGMENTATION METHODS

The rise of digital platforms and the exponential expansion of data have completely changed how marketers handle client segmentation. In the digital age, traditional segmentation strategies that only take into account psychographic, regional, and demographic criteria are insufficient to reflect the complexity of customer behaviour. Because of this, marketers are using more complex segmentation strategies that make use of rich data sources and cutting-edge analytical tools.

The emergence of behavioural segmentation represents one of the major developments throughout segmentation methodology. Behavioural segmentation is a substitute for conventional methodologies, which depend on static variables such as age or location. Instead, it involves recording real-time customer interactions across merchandise and brands. In order to identify significant patterns and trends, it entails evaluating transactional data, browsing habits, clickstream data, and metrics pertaining to engagement. Marketers can develop highly targeted ads that are based on individual behaviour rather than large demographic groups by knowing the habits and interests of their clients.

An increasingly potent kind of information for behavioural segmentation is transactional data. Through an examination of a customer's buying history, frequency, recency, and monetary value, marketers are able to discern different client categories according to their purchasing patterns. In contrast to infrequent or first-time shoppers, devoted clients seeking to generate regular purchases could need distinct messaging and incentives. By using behavioural segmentation, marketers may tailor their content as well as communications to clients according to where they are during the buying process.

Attitudinal segmentation grows increasingly popular as a useful tactic for comprehending consumer attitudes as well as preferences, in addition to behavioural segmentation. This method entails examining consumer mood as well as opinions from sources like social media exchanges, internet reviews, questionnaires, and direct consumer input. Algorithms for sentiment analysis can automatically categorise and examine text data to reveal information about the attitudes, feelings, and perceptions of consumers.

Marketers can obtain a deeper comprehension of the demographic they are targeting by combining behavioural data and attitudinal segmentation. For instance, pinpointing client segments that exhibit high levels of engagement but are unsatisfied with specific features of the good or service might help design focused campaigns for enhancement or retention. Additionally, developing content and message strategies that appeal to particular audience segments can be guided by an awareness of the preferences and interests of various client categories.

The necessity to adjust to the changing dynamics of consumer behaviour in the digital age has propelled the creation of segmentation techniques. Marketers may develop more relevant and impactful advertisements that are more tailored to their target audience by utilising sentiment analysis and behavioural data. We will look at how generative AI and predictive analytics are improving segmentation skills in the following section of this chapter, which will help marketers leverage data-driven marketing tactics to new heights of accuracy and efficacy.

20.4 INTEGRATION OF AI AND ML

The integration of artificial intelligence (AI) and machine studying (ML) era has spurred a paradigm shift in purchaser segmentation by means of providing marketers with computerised, statistics-driven techniques with formerly unheard-of scale and precision. In specific, system machine algorithms have advanced into notably effective tools for sorting through large datasets and extracting useful facts that would be challenging for human analysts to discover manually.

Customer segmentation based on shared traits or behaviours has gotten easier because of clustering methods like K-means and hierarchical clustering. These algorithms enable marketers to find discrete groups within their client base by automatically clustering customers based on predetermined criteria or attributes. Clustering algorithms uncover hidden linkages and associations by examining patterns in consumer data. These insights can be used to inform campaign personalisation and targeted marketing strategies.

Another method of segmentation is using classification algorithms, such as support vector machines, random forests, and decision trees, which determine which segment a new consumer will fall into depending on their characteristics or behaviour. By using past data, these algorithms create prediction models that group clients into pre-established groups or forecast the probability that they will fall into a particular group. Classification algorithms allow marketers to quickly discover and target high-value customer segments with customised offers and messages by automating the segmentation process.

Models based on deep learning have made segmentation easier by enabling them to evaluate unstructured data sources, including text, images, and videos. Machine learning methods such as recurrent neural networks (RNNs) and convolutional neural networks (CNNs) have been particularly adept at extracting valuable data from complex, diverse input sources. This makes it possible to further improve segmentation efforts through an in-depth knowledge of client attitudes and preferences.

For instance, deep learning models can extract important themes, feelings, and subjects pertinent to various client segments from the analysis of text data, including social media posts, reviews, and other textual data. Through the integration of textual insights into segmentation analyses, marketers can detect subtle patterns and trends that conventional segmentation techniques would miss, enabling more individualised and detailed targeting approaches.

Customer segmentation has been completely transformed by the merging of AI and ML technologies, which have improved and automated the analysis of enormous and varied datasets. Marketers can find significant client categories by using clustering and classification algorithms, and deep learning models enhance segmentation insights by examining unstructured data sources.

20.4.1 Automated Pattern Recognition

By using automated techniques for pattern identification, machine learning algorithms have completely changed the segmentation process. Clustering approaches have become essential tools for client segmentation based on traits, behaviours, or preferences among various algorithms. Notably, hierarchical clustering and K-means clustering techniques have been extensively used in this context.

A well-liked unsupervised learning technique called K-means clustering divides data points into a fixed number of clusters according to how similar their attributes are. K-means efficiently clusters data points that are near one another in the feature space by repeatedly optimising cluster centroids to minimise the within-cluster variance. When it comes to consumer segmentation, K-means clustering helps marketers find specific groups of customers that share similar behaviours or preferences.

Example: Based on client demographics, past purchases, and online interactions, a retail corporation segments its consumer base using K-means clustering. They divide the market into three categories: browsers, occasional shoppers, and frequent shoppers. The next step is to make recommendation and marketing campaigns especially for each cluster that allows you to increase income and engagement.

Similar to this, hierarchical clustering arranges facts factors consistent with how similar or assorted they may be into a dendrogram, or tree-like structure. With the help of this hierarchical technique, marketers can investigate the connections between various segments at several granularities. Through visual inspection of the dendrogram or algorithmic cutting at predetermined thresholds, marketers can discern significant subsets within their clientele, with each subset signifying a separate cohort with distinctive attributes.

Example: Hierarchical clustering is used by the telecom operator to group client data according to service choices and consumption trends. They find niches such as budget-conscious consumers, families, entertainment enthusiasts, and business professionals. The development of customised service offerings and customer support methods is aimed at meeting the distinct requirements of every segment and augmenting client happiness and loyalty.

20.4.2 Predictive Analytics for Segmentation

Marketers may automate the segmentation process and find trends in their data that would have gone unnoticed when utilising manual approaches by utilising these clustering algorithms. Thanks to the algorithms, marketers can now achieve previously unachievable levels of segmentation accuracy and granularity by analysing massive databases containing vast amounts of client data. In addition to streamlining the segmentation process, this computerised pattern identification creates the groundwork for more focused and successful marketing campaigns.

Marketers are able to make real-time adjustments to their segmentation strategies in response to the availability of fresh information due to the scalability and efficiency of device-learning algorithms. Marketing experts may additionally stay adaptable to transferring market conditions and converting consumer preferences via employing clustering algorithms to continuously examine consumer interactions, purchase patterns, and different pertinent records. This flexibility is especially beneficial in brief-paced fields where quick decisions can imply the difference between successful outcome and failure.

Marketing segmentation has modified as a result of automated pattern popularity strategies made feasible by means of gadget study algorithms. To be precise, clustering strategies like K-manner and hierarchical clustering have revolutionised this procedure. These algorithms enable entrepreneurs to obtain better granularity and accuracy in segmentation, resulting in extra-centred and successful advertising strategies.

These algorithms examine large datasets to locate applicable styles and segments. As an essential issue of purchaser segmentation, predictive analytics gives entrepreneurs essential insights into future behaviour based on historical statistics. With the resources of sophisticated statistical strategies and machine learning algorithms, predictive analytics allows marketers to project critical metrics like product choices, buy probability, and customer lifetime cost.

In customer segmentation, regression analysis—a basic predictive analytics technique—is frequently employed to find correlations between independent factors (such as demographic characteristics and historical purchasing patterns) and dependent variables (like future purchase intent and customer involvement). Marketers may accurately forecast future outcomes and quantify the influence of different factors on customer behaviour by fitting regression models to past data.

Regression analysis, for instance, can be used to forecast customer lifetime value (CLV), which measures the anticipated revenue a client will bring in over the course of their relationship with a business. Marketers can prioritise high-value segments for focused marketing campaigns and retention strategies by developing regression models that forecast each customer's lifetime value (CLV) based on historical purchase habits, customer demographics, and other pertinent characteristics.

Another effective predictive analytics method for consumer segmentation is time series forecasting, which makes predictions about future trends and behaviours based on existing time series data. By analysing historical data sets to find trends and seasonality, time series forecasting models—like ARIMA (Autoregressive Integrated Moving Average) and exponential smoothing techniques—allow marketers to project future demand and modify their segmentation strategies appropriately.

Retail businesses, as an example, may use time series forecasting to forecast seasonal variations in product demand and modify stock levels and promotional plans accordingly. Through client segmentation based totally on expected purchasing styles all through high-call for durations, marketers can also decorate their efforts to take advantage of beneficial instances and optimise return on investment.

Marketing professionals can optimise the return on funding (ROI) in their campaigns by segmenting their customer base based on anticipated behaviour. This allows for more effective strategy customisation. With the use of predictive analytics models, marketers may pinpoint high-potential customer groupings for focused acquisition campaigns, individualised chances for upselling and cross-selling, and proactive retention initiatives.

Customer segmentation now relies heavily on predictive analytics, which gives marketers the ability to predict consumer behaviour and adjust their tactics accordingly. Marketers may forecast important indicators like customer lifetime value and purchase likelihood by using techniques like regression analysis and time series forecasting. This facilitates the development of segmentation strategies and the creation of extra successful advertising campaigns. In a marketplace that is getting more and more competitive, entrepreneurs can capture new opportunities for boom and profitability by using predictive analytics.

20.4.3 Personalisation at Scale

The capacity to accomplish personalisation at scale in customer segmentation is one of the most amazing developments made possible by AI and ML. Marketers may deliver highly personalised marketing messages and product suggestions by using sophisticated algorithms to analyse individual customer interactions across many touchpoints and dynamically modify segmentation criteria in real-time.

The intricacy and variety of consumer tastes were often an excessive amount for conventional segmentation strategies to deal with, leading to conventional advertising campaigns that failed to connect with particular customers. But with the development of AI and ML technologies, entrepreneurs can now use huge volumes of data to develop precisely calibrated segmentation models that take into consideration the wonderful requirements and choices of every consumer.

Real-time evaluation of customer interactions and behaviours is crucial to personalisation at scale. Artificial intelligence (AI)-powered systems constantly stream and analyse facts from numerous resources, including internet site visits, email opens, social media interactions, and former purchase histories. Marketers may additionally personalise their communications and offers by gaining insights into the preferences, pastimes, and purposes of each customer with the aid of combining these records in real-time.

To create individualised product suggestion in real-time, an e-commerce business can, for instance, utilise AI-powered recommendation engines to have a look at a consumer's surfing history, previous purchases, and demographic information. A smooth and customised shopping experience that promotes repeat enterprise and strengthens purchaser loyalty can be created by the shop via dynamically editing the pointers primarily based on the client's interactions and remarks.

Furthermore, by using AI and ML algorithms, businesses may combine predictive analytics into their personalisation initiatives, moving beyond fundamental rule-based total segmentation. Marketers may additionally assume the demands of particular customers and proactively modify their messaging and services to match those wishes with the aid of ancient statistics to forecast future behaviour and possibilities.

Example: depending on a client's recent engagement patterns, a subscription-based service may use predictive analytics to estimate when a customer is likely to churn. The service provider can prevent customer churn and retain important consumers by implementing targeted retention initiatives, such as personalised discounts or loyalty awards, by proactively identifying at-risk customers.

Marketers can send highly relevant and timely messages to individual customers across numerous channels with personalisation at scale, enabled by AI and ML. Through the utilisation of predictive analytics and real-time analysis of large data sets, marketers can develop customised customer experiences that stimulate consumer engagement, loyalty, and eventually, business expansion.

20.4.4 Text and Sentiment Analysis

As AI and ML technologies boost, the opportunity for mass personalisation will grow, bringing in a brand-new technology for consumer-focused marketing processes. Textual data has come to be an essential supply of customer insights in the age of social media and online evaluations. It gives advertisers a plethora of statistics about the sentiment, opinions, and possibilities of their customers. Marketers have turned Neural language processing (NLP) strategies, a subset of artificial intelligence (AI), to examine text facts and extract actionable insights as a way to leverage the value of this unstructured data.

Marketers can systematise and realise human language in a way that intently resembles human comprehension through natural language processing algorithms. Large amounts of textual data from a variety of sources, including social networking sites, online forums, customer reviews, and survey results, can be parsed by these algorithms to find trends, moods, and interesting subjects.

One important usage of natural language processing (NLP) is sentiment analysis, which is the process of identifying the sentiment or opinions—whether positive, negative, or neutral—expressed in text data. Marketers can learn about consumer sentiment towards their brand, goods, or services by examining the tone of customer reviews, social media posts, and other textual sources.

Sentiment analysis, for instance, can show whether, during online interactions with a brand, consumers are expressing good sentiments like enthusiasm and contentment or negative sentiments like frustration and disappointment. Marketers can spot trends and patterns in consumer sentiment by compiling and evaluating sentiment data from various client segments, then adjusting their approach to target those customers

Customer profiles can be enhanced with sentiment-related attributes by including sentiment analysis in segmentation algorithms. Marketers can develop segments based on customer sentiment towards a brand or certain products by combining sentiment scores or sentiment-based attributes into segmentation criteria. This enables marketers to target distinct sentiment segments with their content and offers, resolving issues or building on favourable sentiments to increase consumer engagement and loyalty.

Additionally, text analysis methods like topic modelling can reveal hidden themes and subjects in textual data, giving marketers insight into new trends, client preferences, and interest areas. Through the examination of the subjects discussed in social media conversations, customer reviews, and other written materials, marketers can obtain important understandings of the elements influencing consumer attitude and behaviour.

With the use of AI and NLP-powered text and sentiment analysis tools, marketers may extract insightful information from textual data sources and apply it to segmentation models. Marketers can more successfully adjust their marketing efforts by gaining a deeper understanding of client preferences and opinions through the analysis of customer sentiment, discussion themes, and other textual qualities. Text and sentiment analysis will become more crucial to customer segmentation and customised marketing strategies as the amount and complexity of textual data increase.

20.4.5 Image and Video Analysis

The development of AI and ML has made it less complicated to analyse visual content, including snap shots and films, for segmentation functions in addition to textual facts. With the usage of computer vision algorithms, marketers can now benefit from a deeper understanding of purchaser choices and behaviour with the aid of extracting insightful facts from visible data. Machines can now perceive and comprehend visual stuff similarly to how humans see it, thanks to computer vision algorithms. With the help of these algorithms, marketers can access a multitude of data by using photographs and videos to recognise items, scenes, patterns, and even emotional indications. Example: computer vision algorithms can be used in the field of e-commerce to extract attributes like colour, shape, and design from product photos.

Marketers can learn about consumer preferences and spot popular products or trends by examining how customers engage with product imagery. Product recommendations, merchandising plans, and focused marketing efforts catered to specific consumer tastes can all be informed by this data.

Furthermore, video content may be used to analyse demographic data and behavioural patterns using computer vision algorithms, giving marketers important insights into their target market. For instance, using video content analysis, facial recognition algorithms may infer viewers' age, gender, and emotional state. This gives advertisers useful demographic information for audience segmentation. Marketers may also accumulate a deeper information of purchaser possibilities and behaviour by using incorporating picture and video evaluation into segmentation fashions.

For instance, a streaming carrier may appoint video evaluation to section visitors primarily based on their viewing conduct or favoured genres, at the same time as a style employer would possibly use photograph analysis to section customers based on their fashion options. Marketing professionals can improve personalisation efforts by means of using image and video analysis to provide clients with greater relevant and exciting content. For instance, an e-commerce platform may also appoint photograph evaluation to indicate visually similar merchandise to customers according with their surfing options or beyond buying pastime. In a similar vein, video analysis can be utilised by a streaming carrier to signify material based on viewer interests and possibilities. Marketers can advantage vital insights into the tastes and behaviour in their customers through the evaluation of snapshots and films using AI and ML algorithms. Marketers can attain a extra profound comprehension of consumer options by way of incorporating visible analysis into segmentation fashions. This allows them to provide their audience with more personalised and captivating experiences. The potential for image and video analysis in customer segmentation will only increase as computer vision technology develops further, giving marketers access to new growth and engagement options.

20.5 BEST PRACTICES AND CURRENT TRENDS

These models use past data to find patterns and trends, which helps marketers predict results and choose wisely when it comes to segmenting and targeting. Predictive analytics algorithms can identify which customers are most likely to respond to particular offers or campaigns by examining historical interactions, purchases, and engagement indicators. This information helps marketers craft messages and promotions that will have the greatest possible impact.

Marketers can dynamically segment their consumer base according to changing preferences and behaviours by using predictive analytics models. Through the continuous analysis of incoming data streams and real-time updates to segmentation models, marketers are able to adjust their plans and provide customers with personalised experiences that are memorable at every touchpoint. By using a dynamic approach to segmentation, marketing campaigns are guaranteed to be relevant and successful even when consumer demands and market conditions change.

By enabling marketers to react quickly to new possibilities and threats, real-time segmentation techniques—powered by streaming analytics and AI-driven decision-making—take this dynamic strategy to the next level. Streaming analytics tools allow marketers to monitor customer interactions, identify patterns, and make choices in milliseconds by ingesting and processing data in real time. Marketers can also automate segmentation and focus on decisions by using incorporating AI-driven selection-making algorithms into those structures. This ensures that the appropriate message reaches the right customer at the right time.

To become aware of clients who have abandoned their online shopping carts, for example, a retailer might also employ real-time segmentation strategies. The business may additionally then automatically send out customised email reminders with exclusive gives to these clients, encouraging them to complete their purchases. In a similar vein, a telecom issuer might also appoint real-time streaming analytics to perceive community congestion and dynamically modify fees and promotional offers to incentivize off-peak usage.

Predictive analytics models and real-time segmentation techniques powered by using streaming analytics and AI-driven selection-making are broadly used in trendy consumer segmentation practices. In modern-day statistics-pushed, speedy-paced industry, entrepreneurs can continue to be beforehand of the opposition, assume purchaser wishes, and create personalised experiences by way of using these modern-day techniques and generation.

20.6 FUTURE DIRECTIONS

Looking ahead to customer segmentation, it is becoming more and more clear that the combination of big data, generative AI, and predictive analytics will significantly change how companies see and interact with their customer. In addition to segmenting consumers based on past behaviour, sophisticated AI systems will also be able to predict future trends and preferences, giving marketers the opportunity to proactively adjust their plans for optimal effect.

Future customer segmentation will continue to be greatly influenced by predictive analytics as more advanced models that use enormous datasets to predict consumer behaviour with never-before-seen accuracy are developed. These models will foresee new trends and preferences before they appear in the market, in addition to identifying which consumers are most likely to convert or churn. Predictive analytics models will give marketers instantaneous actionable insights by integrating real-time data streams from several sources, such as social media, Internet of Things devices, and online interactions. This will facilitate quick and data-driven decision-making.

By combining fresh data and producing insights that surpass those of conventional analytics, generative AI—powered by deep learning algorithms—will significantly improve segmentation skills. With the assistance of these AI systems, entrepreneurs might be able to discover previously undiscovered markets and growth potential by revealing hidden patterns and correlations in records. Marketers can experiment with numerous segmentation strategies and expect feasible consequences prior to deployment by simulating and exploring "what-if" situations with the assistance of generative AI.

Hyper-personalisation—where every customer interaction is tailored in real-time based on dynamic aspects like context, sentiment, and intent—will also be a hallmark of the future of customer segmentation. In order to provide highly customised experiences across numerous channels and touchpoints, AI-driven personalisation engines will examine a wide range of data points, including past interactions, browser history, geography, and social media activity. Hyper-personalisation, from dynamically created content to personalised product tips, will permit marketers to construct significant relationships with purchasers at each factor inside the client adventure.

Technological trends in massive facts, consisting of edge computing and dispensed computing, will permit marketers to address and examine large volumes of facts at previously unheard-of speeds and efficiency. This will permit agencies to quickly regulate their segmentation strategies in response to moving consumer options and marketplace dynamics by permitting them to extract actionable insights from a number of complicated and diverse pieces of information in real-time.

Predictive analytics, generative AI, and big data technologies are expected to come together in the future of consumer segmentation, bringing with them an unparalleled level of personalisation and marketing agility. Businesses will be able to expect purchaser desires, offer customised experiences, and spur an increase in a marketplace that is becoming more competitive and dynamic by utilising the strengths of this modern-day generation.

20.7 CONCLUSION

The way that consumer segmentation tactics have developed over time is evidence of the revolutionary impact that generative AI and predictive analytics have had on the development of contemporary marketing strategies. Marketers have adopted progressively complex techniques to acquire a deeper understanding of consumer behaviour and preferences, ranging from conventional demographic and geographic segmentation to sophisticated behavioural and attitudinal segmentation.

Marketers can now phase records with remarkable accuracy, scalability, and efficacy through the integration of AI and ML technology, giving them the capacity to offer clients individualised experiences in more cutthroat surroundings. Marketers are able to make proactive, data-driven choices via the use of predictive analytics to anticipate future tendencies and preferences.

By revealing hidden patterns and connections in records, generative AI improves segmentation competencies and, in addition, facilitates entrepreneurs finding formerly undiscovered niches and boom prospects. Marketers can now create customised reviews that connect with customers at every touchpoint and dynamically modify their segmentation strategies thanks to this synthesis of generative AI and predictive analytics.

Looking in advance, the mixture of massive facts, generative AI, and predictive analytics guarantees to bring in a brand-new generation of advertising as a way to be marked by unheard-of personalisation and agility. Businesses will be able to anticipate consumer needs, provide customised reviews, and spur an increase in a marketplace that is becoming more competitive and dynamic by using the energy of the current era.

The improvement of customer segmentation strategies emphasises how important it is to include innovation and employ modern technology as a good way to stay ahead of the curve in the records-driven, in the fast-paced world of today. Marketers may additionally gain deeper insights into customer behaviour and possibilities by constantly changing and updating their segmentation tactics. This opens the door to the development of more hit and individualised advertising campaigns inside the destiny.

FURTHER READING

1. Othayoth, S. P., & Muthalagu, R. (2022). Customer Segmentation Using Various Machine Learning Techniques. *International Journal of Business Intelligence and Data Mining*, 20(4), 480–496.
2. Li, X., & Lee, Y. S. (2024). Customer Segmentation Marketing Strategy Based on Big Data Analysis and Clustering Algorithm. *Journal of Cases on Information Technology (JCIT)*, 26(1), 1–16.
3. Samidi, S., Suladi, R. Y., & Kusumaningsih, D. (2023). Comparison of the RFM Model's Actual Value and Score Value for Clustering. *Jurnal RESTI (Rekayasa Sistem dan Teknologi Informasi)*, 7(6), 1430–1438.
4. Istamova, M., & Diyor, X. (2023). Doing Business Based on Customer Segmentation. *Ethiopian International Journal of Multidisciplinary Research*, 10(12), 766–768.
5. Sharma, M. K., Vijai, C., Durga, C. V., Singh, N., Almusawi, M., & Janagi, R. (2023, December). Machine Learning Algorithms for Customer Segmentation in Data-Driven Marketing Strategies. In *2023 10th IEEE Uttar Pradesh Section International Conference on Electrical, Electronics and Computer Engineering (UPCON)* (Vol. 10, pp. 349–353). IEEE.
6. Wang, C. (2022). Efficient Customer Segmentation in Digital Marketing Using Deep Learning with Swarm Intelligence Approach. *Information Processing & Management*, 59(6), 103085.
7. Soni, V. (2023). Adopting Generative AI in Digital Marketing Campaigns: An Empirical Study of Drivers and Barriers. *Sage Science Review of Applied Machine Learning*, 6(8), 1–15.

8. Kasem, M. S., Hamada, M., & Taj-Eddin, I. (2024). Customer Profiling, Segmentation, and Sales Prediction Using AI in Direct Marketing. *Neural Computing and Applications*, 36(9), 4995–5005.
9. Verma, R. K., & Kumari, N. (2023). Generative AI as a Tool for Enhancing Customer Relationship Management Automation and Personalization Techniques. *International Journal of Responsible Artificial Intelligence*, 13(9), 1–8.
10. Ajiga, D. I., Ndubuisi, N. L., Asuzu, O. F., Owolabi, O. R., Tubokirifuruar, T. S., & Adeleye, R. A. (2024). AI-Driven Predictive Analytics in Retail: A Review of Emerging Trends and Customer Engagement Strategies. *International Journal of Management & Entrepreneurship Research*, 6(2), 307–321.
11. Nalini, R. (2024). Transformative Power of Artificial Intelligence in Decision-Making, Automation, and Customer Engagement. Ana Diogo, (eds.) *Complex AI Dynamics and Interactions in Management* (pp. 189–208). IGI Global.
12. Khan, A. R., & Aziz, M. T. (2023). Harnessing Big Data for Precision Marketing: A Deep Dive into Customer Segmentation and Predictive Analytics in the Digital Era. *AI, IoT and the Fourth Industrial Revolution Review*, 13(7), 91–102.
13. Tinkler, A. (2023). AI, Marketing Technology and Personalisation at Scale. *Journal of AI, Robotics & Workplace Automation*, 2(2), 138–144.
14. Taherdoost, H., & Madanchian, M. (2023). Artificial Intelligence and Sentiment Analysis: A Review in Competitive Research. *Computers*, 12(2), 37.
15. Dhabliya, D., Ugli, I. S. M., Murali, M. J., Abbas, A. H., & Gulbahor, U. (2023). Computer Vision: Advances in Image and Video Analysis. In *E3S Web of Conferences* (Vol. 399, p. 04045). EDP Sciences.
16. Hakimi, M., Katebzadah, S., & Fazil, A. W. (2024). Comprehensive Insights into E-Learning in Contemporary Education: Analyzing Trends, Challenges, and Best Practices. *Journal of Education and Teaching Learning (JETL)*, 6(1), 86–105.

21 Case Studies in Data-Driven Marketing

P. Santosh Sreeram Naidu, Shaik Iqbal Pasha, and P. Mohan Sai Manikanta

21.1 INTRODUCTION: BACKGROUND AND DRIVING FORCES

Over the last seven years, the Indian telecom market has seen the most intense business competition in its history after Jio was launched and the two giant players getting merged to become Vodafone Idea. BSNL is trying hard to withstand the market competition while players like Telenor and Aircel have just vanished from the market. But as we saw, while all these players were struggling to survive, the only player who fought back and still fighting back was Airtel. Bharti Airtel is one of the big telecom firms today with a healthy balance sheet and is stronger and sharper in terms of customer-focused business approach.

In the financial year 2021, Airtel was dealing with losses of 12,000 crores but in short span of 1 year they came back into profits of 8,305 crores as shown in Figure 21.1, and now in FY 23 while Jio made 1.19 trillion Rs in revenue, Airtel made 1.39 trillion Rs in revenue as shown in Figure 21.2, and in the past

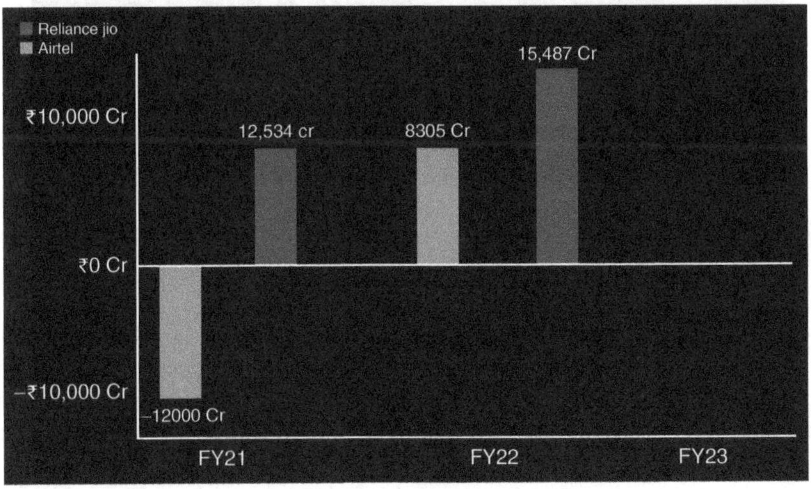

FIGURE 21.1 Net Profits of Jio and Airtel between FY 2022 and 2023. (Courtesy: Money Control.)

DOI: 10.1201/9781003472544-21

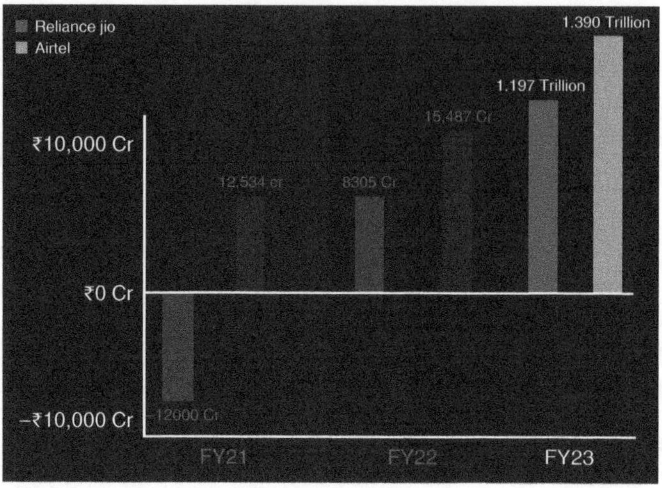

FIGURE 21.2 Revenue of Jio and Airtel as of FY 2023. (Courtesy: Money Control.)

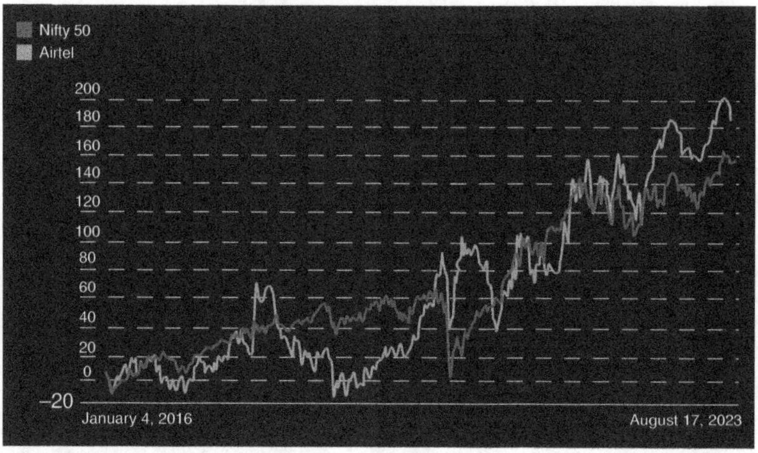

FIGURE 21.3 Airtel's stock performance vs Nifty 50 between 2016 and 2017. (Courtesy: Money Control.)

six-quarters Airtel stock prices also started outperforming the Nifty. If you see the graph as shown in Figure 21.3, after Jio's launch in September 2016, the stock underperformed compared to Nifty but over the past six-quarters Airtel's stock price has been consistently outperforming the Nifty by a healthy margin, so the question is what exactly did Airtel do to bounce back after the telecom shock of 2016?, what are the business strategies that helped Airtel beat Jio in this fierce competition?, what are the most important factors that will determine the result of this telecom war?

21.2 LITERATURE REVIEW

Lately, the crossroads of technology and business adopted data-driven marketing approaches gaining wider acceptance. For example, the authors [1] showed that business development's effectiveness through industry-driven API composition in market IT innovation is emphasized. These authors [2] add value through their work on the creation of user behavior-based personas from data, which is a new aspect of analyzing users' behavior. Next, the author [3] suggests that empathy and rationality be put together in data-based personas to make feel the user better. The author [4] analyzes the data pricing complexity and two-sided market models in his specific case study on Airtel Zero that contributes into the net neutrality debates. In his book, the author [5] examines the impact that business intelligence had on the activities of Bharti Airtel Ltd. and demonstrates a broad spectrum in the use of analytics, collaboration, and decision support for the transformation of society. The authors [6] study the transformational effect Jio Fiber has on India's digital market, thus generating an up-to-date picture of contemporary market dynamics. Also, the authors [7] participate in the discussion by investigating the rise of big data with digitization, which makes them realize that big data plays an important role in private consumer information and predictive analytics in digital marketing. This collection of literature is very comprehensive and helpful in developing a universal understanding of the diverse field of data-driven marketing, embracing new technological advancements, engaging customers on a personal level, and real-life practical examples.

21.3 DATA-DRIVEN MARKETING BY JIO

To understand the complex business work, we first must understand the complex division of the Indian market, and one of the best ways to study them would be to look at the video consumption segments in India. We have five types of customers. Firstly, there are 150 million dark TV homes where consumers have no access to TV or OTT but might have a feature phone or sometimes even a smartphone. Then we have free consumers who watch free TV as in they watch ads in exchange for content. This is very similar to us watching YouTube for free in exchange for watching the ads. As of 2022, in this sample of about 300 million customers, there were 45 million free TV users who watch these ads. Then we have the third type of customers who are on TV first customers, who form a base of 77 million customers. These customers pay for TV but do not pay for OTT platforms. This is because they usually get it bundled with their SIM card recharge. For example, if Sandeep was a TV first subscriber, he would pay for Tata Sky but would watch Hotstar for free because he got a subscription with a Jio recharge. Then we have the digital-first customers, who form 43 billion valuable users who pay for both TV and at least one OTT service, and lastly, we have the most valuable customers of all, who are only 2 million digital-only customers who consume only on digital platforms and rarely access conventional TV. Figure 21.4 shows the categorization of the video consumption segment of India with a data set of about 300 million customers. Considering the above segmentation of video consumption consumers, let's understand Airtel's business philosophy

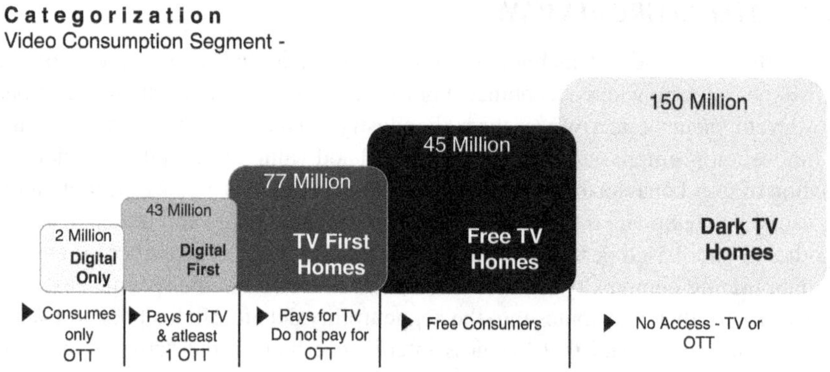

FIGURE 21.4 Segmentation of consumers based on video consumption as of the year 2022. (Courtesy: Think School.)

with a slogan that says if you call between speed and perfection, choose speed as perfection will follow as the course of things is moved. Now, we do say quality first. Speed always comprises principles of doing business that are really determined first. Initially At this scale and stage, they are bound to create societal value.

The business philosophy of Jio can be tagged as fortune at the bottom of the pyramid because Jio is not obsessed with just capturing the existing market, but with also creating a new market that did not even exist before, and they are doing that with four methods.

The first method lies in creating a market for phones at the bottom of the pyramid and here is where we have the Jio phone strategy. Reliance Jio has come true today to introduce India with intelligent smartphone by presenting the Jio phone. Jio phone is aimed at gaining customers who are using 2G feature phones that look like your old Nokia phones. Recently Jio released their Jio Bharat phone for as little as Rs 1,000, and along with it, they are also offering 500MP of daily data and unlimited calling for Rs 123 a month. Now, for instance, a daily wage owner who owns as little as Rs 5,000 a month is a game changer because right now, these customers are using 2G phones of Airtel, Vodafone, Idea, and BSNL, and now Jio aims to turn these customers into 4G customers, and this is such a huge customer base that them alone are targeting to reach 100 million users out of the 250 million feature phone users in India. To sum it up, if they take up Rs 103 subscription, that is Rs 100 billion in revenue, and the cherry on the cake is that these phones do not allow non-Jio SIM cards and have preinstalled Jio Pay, Jio Cinema, and Jio Saavn in their phones and considering the average lifespan of these phones to be 4 years, Jio will generate Rs 5,000 per phone over 4 years which is Rs 500 billion. So Jio will not just make 500 billion Rs but will also get 100 million more viewers to the Jio Cinema app, who will then watch IPL to increase its viewership, and then Jio can charge more sell ad slots on the Jio Cinema app. This is the first way Jio creates a market for itself by monetizing the bottom of the pyramids. The Indian Premier League was exceptional in terms of the number that the Jio Cinema app reported just during the opening weekend, and its stats look phenomenal. Jio Cinema for Tata IPL viewership record for the opening weekend of the tournament had got 147 Crore video views.

The second way in which they are tapping into the customers is by launching the cheapest mobile tariff plans, so coming back to Figure 21.4, these 45 million free TV consumers are more likely to have an entry-level smartphone like Vivo or Poco and just like dark TV customers, even though these users cannot pay for TV they can be monetized through ads on Jio Cinema and through the Jio sim card recharge and this is where their third method comes in, which is both streaming. Jio is majorly targeting these 77 million customers with Jio Cinema to make money from ads and these 2 million customers to pay for the Jio Cinema subscription. Lastly, Jio is also introducing low-cost products like laptops at a cost price of around Rs 16,500. This is all about the bottom-of-the-pyramid approach of Jio. Now, this does not mean that they are not interested in the top of the pyramid. For the top of the pyramid, they have Jio fiber, Jio 5G, and Jio postpaid plans.

So, to summarize this, Jio is targeting dark TV homes with 2G feature phones with their Jio phone strategy. They are targeting the dark TV homes with smartphones plus the free TV homes with their sports streaming ads. Jio is also starting to pay-TV homes, digital pay-TV homes with Jio Cinema subscription and Jio fiber. The digital first and digital TV homes are being targeted with Jio postpaid, Jio Cinema subscription, Jio fiber, and finally, Jio 5G. Jio wants to go deep into the bottom of the pyramid of India and wants to create a market for itself in the telecom market.

21.4 DATA-DRIVEN MARKETING BY AIRTEL

Airtel's approach is the opposite of that of Jio. The most important metric is something called ARPU or Average Revenue Per User. Now, as we saw in the Jio phone example, Jio would love to have a customer who generates a remedy of Rs 103 per month, which is at the bottom of the pyramid, whereas if you look at Airtel, they want to reach out to the low-value customers. In November 2018, Airtel implemented a subscriber cleanup initiative. In this process, Airtel deliberately lost over 49 million subscribers. In this way, Airtel was able to de-clock the network and clean up the inactive work for non-paying customers. Although this meant losing around 15% of its customers, Airtel could decrease its expenses and provide better service to well-paying customers.

Secondly, Airtel has no plans to launch a future phone, and thirdly, even for the customers who are using smartphones, Airtel has completely dropped the Rs 99 basic plan from 17 countries and has launched a Rs 150 package for all the customers, which means that if a customer wants to activate his SIM card number, he must pay Rs 155 minimum amount. When Jio has its minimum barrier at Rs 103, Airtel wants the minimum barrier to be Rs 155. Do you see that there is a 50% difference in cost? Fourthly, Airtel understands the telecom market and its own target audience very clearly. To put that into perspective, there are around 200 million feature phone users, with another 600 million smartphone users, 35 million postpaid users, and about 30 million homes in India that use broadband plus TV, and as customers move up this value chain, the average revenue per user increases. For example, from feature phones to smartphones, the average revenue nearly doubles from prepaid to postpaid. The average revenue again doubles from postpaid to broadband again and from broadband to converged homes, the revenue shoots up again. So, if you understand Airtel's approach, they are not interested in the future phone segment at all but instead they are interested in the postpaid customers. This is because postpaid customers are one of the most valuable customers in the ecosystem, and even though postpaid customers only form 6% of the adult customer base, they can generate around 25%–30% of Airtel's revenue which is because the average revenue per user in the postpaid segment is almost three times the revenue of the prepaid segment. This is the reason why Airtel and Jio both are obsessed with postpaid customers and when it comes to Airtel, they are prioritizing the postpaid customers in every possible manner. Firstly, they have identified 700 plus districts that have the highest number of high-quality customers and Airtel is expanding its tools in these high-value neighborhoods.

Secondly, Airtel is also leveraging its lending business service called Airtel Finance to turn prepaid customers into postpaid customers, and for this, Airtel is using a mechanism to build a credit score of customers using a combination of civil data and over 2,000 telecom attributes with which Airtel identified over 60 million credit worthy customers and the majority of these are currently prepaid customers. So, in the spending proposition, the company is nudging those users to move to postpaid. Hence, it is very similar to Ola, whereby using Ola postpaid, Ola started giving credits to people to turn them into valuable postpaid customers.

Thirdly, what I found to be fascinating is that Airtel literally tracks the customer experience of each device and it is chasing something called zero unfulfilled query stream because in FY2022, Airtel is receiving the greatest number of complaints and they got 10 times more complaints from its customers compared to Jio customer complaints. This means either Jio customers are getting the best service or the Jio customers are too lazy to register a complaint in the first place. In both cases, Airtel sees this as both a risk and an opportunity to serve the customers better. To improve this, Airtel has built an AI-based solution in collaboration with Nvidia to enhance the overall customer experience through its customer contact center, and lastly, the family plan has been such a massive hit that nearly 70%–80% of Airtel's postpaid customers are on family plans. This is how Airtel wants to catch hold of the valuable postpaid customers in the Country. If we see the graph as shown in Figure 21.5, that spike from March 2018 to

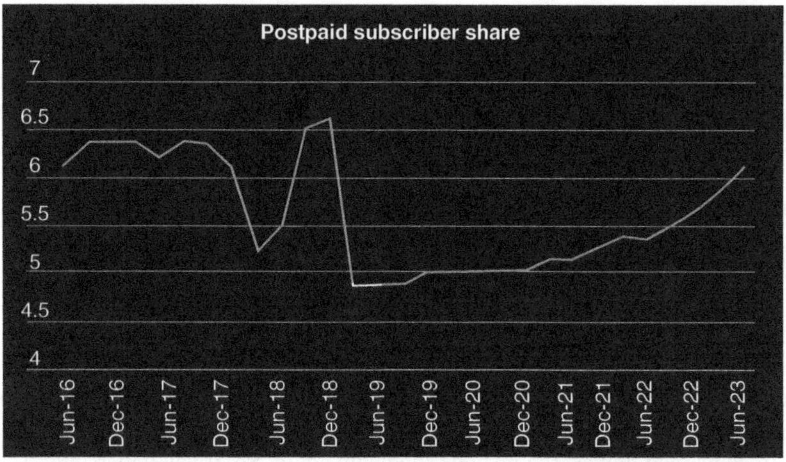

FIGURE 21.5 Graph depicting postpaid subscriber share of Airtel in the year 2018. (Courtesy: Economic Times.)

June 2018 is because of the merger of Telenor subscribers with Airtel and no reporting of subscribers by Aircel due to the closure of the business, but after that, if you see the postpaid customer base has grown steadily from 2019 to 2023 and the fun fact here is that Airtel is very careful with its prices, while Jio gives out two sims at Rs 499 and four sims for Rs 699, Airtel gives out two sims for Rs 599 and four at Rs 999. So, even in the postpaid segment, Airtel only wants premium customers and lastly Airtel and Jio both are very aggressively targeting home broadband as these home subscribers offer a potential average revenue per user of over Rs 1,000, which is almost five times the ARPU of Airtel right now but still Jio is far ahead because they have already laid out 1.1 billion km of optical fiber whereas Airtel is just at 400,000 km. While Jio already had 25 million homes connected in 2021, Airtel has just reached 25 million homes in 2023. To summarize this, Airtel is not interested in dark home customers who do not have feature phones and is also not interested in dark home customers who cannot afford the Rs 150 recharge and free TV homes. While Jio makes money with content via Jio Cinema subscriptions and ads, Airtel makes money via DTA subscriptions therefore digital first and digital only homes. Airtel has Airtel fiber, Airtel postpaid, and family-planned bundles, just like Jio. It is just that Airtel's plans are Rs 100 more expensive than Jio's because Airtel only wants quality customers with very high purchase power. Airtel went one step ahead to tap into the apex of the pyramid with something called a B2B service wing, which provides Internet connectivity to common people, and also provides Internet connectivity to giant businesses like SBI and HDFC banks. As of March 2023, Airtel's business reported 18,600 crores which is $2.2 billion in revenue, which was one-fifth of Airtel's total revenue. Airtel business is a market leader in enterprise connectivity business with a 33.67% revenue market share as of March 2023, according to Ken. Airtel business serves over 1,200 global enterprises, 2,000 large and 1 million small and medium businesses across India, and until then, Jio only held 3% of the enterprise creativity market share and now we can say that Airtel's competitor is not Jio but Tata Communications. Airtel's revenue and EBITDA both are far better than that of the Tatas in between the FY21 and FY23. So, to summarize, Airtel and Jio both are operating with a very different philosophy, while Jio wants to capture the bottom of the pyramid, Airtel wants to ease the top of the pyramid now. The fundamental reason as to why Airtel is not interested in the bottom of the pyramid whereas Jio was going so aggressive because Jio has a method to monetize these uses by adding them to the Jio Cinema viewership and then making money by ads. When it comes to Airtel, except for SIM card recharge, Airtel has no way to make money out of these customers, and eventually, the theory that the telecom companies have is that customers who will not buy a SIM card recharge will not buy a DTH and broadband separately. They will only buy all these services together in a bundled format, and if a person cannot afford to buy anything other than just the SIM card recharge, that customer will not be a valuable customer, so at the bottom of the pyramid, even if Airtel manages to get them as customers for their SIM card recharge they will not have the affordability to buy a DTH service or to buy a broadband connection so the customer lifetime value at the bottom of the pyramid for Airtel is far lower as compared to that of Jio which could simply sell a Jio phone add them to the viewership of Jio Cinema and make money by ads. This is the root cause of the fundamental difference in the philosophy of both these companies, and now there are three unanswered questions that will decide the fate of this battle in the next three years.

1. Will Jio's theory of making a fortune at the bottom of the pyramid with feature phones and laptops be successful? If so, then how viable is it in terms of profit margin that they can make by selling laptops for Rs 16,500?
2. Why does Reliance have two times more cables laid than Airtel? How will Airtel win the home broadband game?
3. Lastly with Reliance entering the B2B segment, how Airtel and Tata Communications will play the game differently in the B2B segment?

REFERENCES

1. Srivastava, B., Chetlur, M., Gupta, S., Vasa, M., & Visweswariah, K. (2018). Effective business development for in-market it innovations with industry-driven api composition. Usha Mujoo Munshi, Neeta Verma (eds.) *Data Science Landscape: Towards Research Standards and Protocols*, Springer, pp. 165–181.
2. Jung, S. G., Salminen, J., & Jansen, B. J. (2020, March). Giving faces to data: Creating data-driven personas from personified Big Data. In *Proceedings of the 25th International Conference on Intelligent User Interfaces Companion*, Cagliari, Italy, (pp. 132–133).
3. Jansen, B. J., Salminen, J. O., & Jung, S. G. (2020). Data-driven personas for enhanced user understanding: Combining empathy with rationality for better insights to analytics. *Data and Information Management*, 4(1), 1–17.
4. Sahay, A. (2016). *Airtel Zero: Data Pricing, Two Sided Markets Led Business Models and Net Neutrality.* Indian Institute of Management Ahmedabad, pp. 1–12.
5. Panigrahi, P. K. (2015). Business intelligence at Bharti Airtel Ltd. In R. P. S. Reddy, H. R. Rao, & V. Bharadwaj (Eds.) *Reshaping Society through Analytics, Collaboration, and Decision Support: Role of Business Intelligence and Social Media*, Cham, Switzerland: Springer, pp. 249–266.
6. Khurana, R. (2021). Jio Fiber: Disrupting the digital market in India. *Journal of Information Technology Case and Application Research*, 23(2), 115–138.
7. Okorie, G. N., Udeh, C. A., Adaga, E. M., DaraOjimba, O. D., & Oriekhoe, O. I. (2024). Digital marketing in the age of iot: a review of trends and impacts. *International Journal of Management & Entrepreneurship Research*, 6(1), 104–131.

22 Case Studies in Churn Prediction and Customer Retention

Vaishnavi Tadepally, Surya Shivannagari, and Dasoju Nikhileswar

22.1 INTRODUCTION

Customer retention and churn prediction are not only useful but also an integral part of any successful business. To summarize churn prediction involves stepping into the shoes of customers who may part company with a business, whereas retention is using strategies to keep customers loyal to the business. In this regard, product and branding strategies are very important because they usually support gains in revenue and the long-term stability of the company. The ability to predict churn and customer retention is a key ingredient for the success recipe of any business. Customer churn management is a crucial part of profitability stabilization which ensures sales revenues are not lost (Gattermann-Itschert & Thonemann, 2022). Unlike successful customer retention strategies that foster lasting relationships leading to increased customer lifetime value, those that fail result in a decrease in customer lifetime value and profitability of the company. As far as predicting customer churn and retaining customers is concerned, the use of different methods along techniques is the basis of success. Companies most likely apply data-driven techniques, delivering machine learning to customers' data for analysis purposes. Employing these techniques of identifying signals that suggest client attrition, gives a company, amongst other things, an unprecedented level of strategic edge. The processing of customer behaviour data is an extensive information harvesting and data refining process.

This allows us to consider that relevant data are extracted with which the foundation for the right result is built. Machine learning processes, including but not limited to decision trees, logistic regression, and neural networks, are used to understand the patterns and the presence of outliers in customer data. Predictive analytics, one important pillar of behavioural analysis of customers, is of great significance in both churn prediction and customer retention. Making use of past data, companies can model probability distributions and devise measures designed to prevent customer churn. This will, in turn, allow to use of managerial flexibility and be quick with the adoption of a retention strategy that pinpoints the unique interests of the customer and hypothetical steps. Consequently, it needs to transition from the forecast of the chances of customers churning to their retention, which depends on their review of the service quality past the initial stages of their experience (Abou el Kassem et al., 2020).

DOI: 10.1201/9781003472544-22

Certainly, with the depth of study of applied methodologies and techniques for understanding customers, software based on data and evidence becomes the heart of profitable programmes. Therefore, entrepreneurs and companies that take time to understand these notions of marketing communication structure will be in a better position to deal with the complexities of their interactions with their clients, hence building long-term success.

22.2 CASE STUDY 1: TELECOM INDUSTRY

22.2.1 Challenges in Customer Retention

In the Telecom market area, the security of customers' fulfilment is the most key and difficult work that needs deep study to understand it fully. Acknowledgement of these hindrances stands out as the chief element of the crafting of deliberations which improve the customer loyalty movement. This sector is struggling with aggressive competitiveness for clients as well as high-tech innovations, which make contract loyalty more difficult. The service provider has the persistent nuisance of churn to deal with as subscribers have been accompanied by the sensational deals flung at them by their competitors (Jain et al., 2020). This force nature aside may make companies receive pressure to be strategic in order to counter the effects of aggressive competition.

On the other hand, besides customer demands and expectations that are highly dynamic, customer retention has an additional challenge of keeping. Such an evolution of preferences becomes a key driver of change for telecom companies, which is the underlying need for them to adapt rapidly so that whatever they are offering matches the rapidly changing customer expectations. Personalization is extremely relevant to lasting customer engagement and customer satisfaction and therefore it can be said that personalization is instrumental in maintaining customer engagement and satisfaction.

The telecom sector operates in the context of cutting-edge technology and a thrilled customer audience. The overlap of these determinants provides the reasons why the comprehensive conceptualization of customer retention issues is significant. The acknowledgement of competitive forces, technological observations, as well as the gradual changes in customer dynamics can help telecom companies formulate effective strategies and be ready to face up against the risks posed by customer churn (Lalwani et al., 2022). By pursuing this mission, operators ensure the maintenance of their current customers and promote long-standing relationships between them and their customers based on science in the complex working environment of telecom operations.

22.2.2 Data Collection and Processing Methods

Overcoming these issues, data collection and preprocessing become the first step. Upward trends and jam-packed processes are critical for the business. Data cleansing which results in accurate and relevant data by managing and cleaning up very detailed data. Finally, we bring to the fore the most vital part: reliable data is the main bedrock upon which the prediction of churn would come out to be highly accurate.

Telecom operators manage to get access to this information by painstakingly creating databases on their clients' habits and likings that determine churn rates. Usage patterns bring to life the way people use the service offering, while Customer satisfaction feedback holds information on what people think of the service. This process includes well-thought-out structures of data, which makes the data flow easily and dissolves any mistakes that might exist there. The role of pertinent data should not be overlooked since it provides the base of the churn prediction that delivers impressive outcomes. Desired articles should have encouraging proof emphasizing the role of the dataset in being one of the key factors for ML algorithms to detect past patterns, make forecasts and predict them. This sort of data could improve the possibility of telecom companies to create and use Predictive models which are characterized by a high level of accuracy and that adapt to the constantly evolving way customers use the services provided. To be accurate, the most responsible component includes the data collecting and processing stages by the telecom companies when talking about their customer retention. It provides businesses with the ability to make competitive decisions based on an advanced understanding of the customer and related scenarios. In such a way, they can create a plan that triggers shifts in the delivered services or telecoms sector.

22.2.3 Application of Machine Learning Algorithms

In the customer churn industry, machine learning has a central role in assigning analytical skills. A multiplicity of approaches are in the arsenal of tools, such as decision trees, support vector machines, and ensemble methods, which are leveraged to exercise a thorough examination of a meticulously crafted dataset. Such algorithms arduously peel off intricate relations and correlations buried within the data, which then determine the predictive indicators of customer churn. Through the use of such models, where predictive models come into play, telecom organizations acquire the power to preemptively manage the issues, which is a further step in customer care service (Wu et al., 2021). Decision trees do this through their hierarchical structure that makes the data digested into discernible decision nodes and paths. Support vector machine is good at classifying the scattered data points, and it can identify key factors that influence churn. Ensemble methods combining different algorithms balance each model's strength, which leads to greater model accuracy. Utilizing the potential of machine learning, telecom companies get a competitive advantage in the identification of complex customer behaviours. The judgement of churn indicators provides the basis for foresight, which in turn allows these enterprises to develop personalized interventions, thus reducing the possibility of customer attrition (Fujo et al., 2022). Here, the complex designing of machine learning algorithms evolves to be a trigger for strategic expansion and customer retention in the dynamic telecom market.

22.2.4 Results and Insights

The adoption of machine learning to detect churn cases creates advantages and insights as well. Customers at high risk can be identified by business thus, retention strategies can be customized and tailored to meet individual needs. This proactive approach not only reduces churn but also increases the quality of service by targeting interventions to individuals. The study case findings revealed the particulars of the factors that are motivating customer choices. This understanding enables telecom firms to tailor their services better and give the users what they want and need more than just some hand-me-down products. By uncovering patterns and correlations from the data, companies can tailor and optimize their approaches, thus improving their retention strategy and technique (De Caigny et al., 2021). Generally, the use of machine learning not only prevents customer churn, which is part of a sensitive issue, but also offers an opportunity to develop a more educated perception of customer behaviour. It further enables telecom companies to get insights into this complex array of customer behaviours. Through this network, they try to develop a platform that would become responsive to the evolving needs of their consumers.

22.3 CASE STUDY 2: E-COMMERCE SECTOR

E-commerce is a big world, and knowing the factors that affect customer retention is mandatory. High competition and dynamic behaviours of consumers confront the industry with difficulties. These facets assist businesses where they can create an array of effective strategies for customer retention and ensure success for a business in the dynamic e-commerce marketplace.

22.3.1 Factors Influencing Customer Churn

In the e-commerce industry, amid the fierce competition in the market and the constantly changing consumer behaviours, customer churn emerges as a major problem. The competitive situation forces companies to compete for the consumer's attention. They may try to win them over with their diverse product lines. Furthermore, a quick shift in consumers' tastes complicates the challenge because businesses need to adjust frequently to meet new requirements of an increasing variety of preferences. Due to such a dynamic environment, customers might look for alternatives provided by other platforms, making them attractive due to competitive offers or a better match with their changing preferences (Devriendt et al., 2021). Therefore, businesses are challenged to keep the customers while still dealing with fluctuations that bring with them challenging intricacies, which demand that businesses have a strategic understanding of the relationship between competition and consumer choices. Overcoming these obstacles, the businesses have the knowledge that is vital to the development of inventive retention strategies designed to specifically meet the needs of the e-commerce industry, which in turn promotes continued patronage.

22.3.2 Predictive Analytics in E-Commerce

Concerning e-commerce, predictive analytics can be seen to be a major tool, making use of a data-based approach, especially machine learning algorithms, to determine and speculate customers' reactions with a particularly high probability of potential churn. Data-driven approaches employ large-scale databases comprising customer interactions, buying histories, and engagement patterns (Pondel et al., 2021).

Machine learning algorithms such as decision trees, neural networks, and ensemble methods are among the tools used in these analytical processes. As an example, the interactive decision trees can spot moments of customer interactions deciding about the possible way leading to a drop. The application of predictive analysis is not just in minimizing bare churn risks but in activating intervention strategies as well. By using big data to describe past behaviour, these algorithms affect the future behaviour of e-commerce platforms, enabling successful strategies among them. This may cover the idea of personalized marketing campaigns, customized offers, and increased service and support for clients who are looking like they are likely to drop off (Wagh et al., 2019).

To sum up, using predictive analytics analysis in e-commerce gives the platform a strategic edge as far as customer churn is concerned. Through the utilization of machine learning, companies can now not only predict challenges but also develop precise, data-based replies, allowing them to follow a more flexible and customer-focused plan against the competitiveness of retail over the web.

22.3.3 Enhancing Customer Retention Strategies

In the e-commerce sector, customer retention can be improved by implementing personalized strategies, for example, personalized marketing, loyalty programmes, and customer feedback analysis. Personalized marketing is tailor-made for individual needs, helping to develop a relationship with customers (Baghla & Gupta, 2022). Loyalty programmes represent a form of incentive programme aiming to attract customers to come back repeatedly with the promise of a reward after a mass of sales are made. Evaluating customer feedback helps businesses gain valuable responses that can be used when making changes. There is a heavy emphasis on tailoring approaches according to the characteristics of different types of customers, taking into consideration the various requirements and standards of the customer base (Li & Zhou, 2020). In this way, e-commerce platforms provide a more personalized and entertaining experience, consequently creating relationships that will be long-term and ultimately eliminating the danger of customer churn.

22.4 CASE STUDY 3: SUBSCRIPTION-BASED SERVICES

In subscription-based business models, comprehending customer churn is not just critical. This approach implies that customers pay for services on a routine basis, and one of the keys to its success is understanding all the reasons that the customer might go away. These elements often encompass customer dissatisfaction with services, pricing matters or changing customer needs. Such understanding gives businesses the chance to adjust their strategies and adapt to the customer's preferences while creating the opportunity for lasting relationships (Saleh & Saha, 2023). Subscription service will be the focal point of this case study outlining core reasons why consumers may become subscription cancellation prone and how to suggest solutions which will suit business in such a transaction.

22.4.1 Common Reasons for Customer Churn

The very reason that can help subscription services grow is to understand the types of customers who quit the services. Price matters, and buyers will likely go after alternative services which offer them better value. The category of service discontent, which commonly results from customers' frustration toward not-so-good customer support or poor features, is also one of the leading impediments mentioned. That said, the movement of customer tastes, for instance, a preference shift and a demand change, will push a subscription cancellation (Pondel et al., 2021). Sign-up costs may not go as well as expected if users feel that they are overpaying for the service without regretting the benefits they get out of it. The diversity of customer service dissatisfaction can be composed of such features as technical bugs, non-conformity of personal expectations or unanswered feedback from the side of the service provider. Consumer needs change dynamically with the diversity in consumer demands creating a need for businesses to follow standard rules of trends which the consumers at the margin can follow easily. The violation of such guidelines might have the consequences of weakening the business competitiveness and reducing its ability to keep up with the changing trends (De Caigny et al., 2020). The picture analysis will reveal this organization's reasons for the subscribers' churn in subscription services. And then the devised plan for churn will be created from these insights. Moreover, their strong awareness helps them to target specific pain points, better quality service, and change pricing strategy or make it in line with customer taste. This can be viewed as a chance that the companies will be able to take a preventive manner to these usual cases of fall off and will make the market for subscriptions more a-consumer-satisfaction and loyalty-oriented in nature.

22.4.2 Predictive Modelling Techniques

Subscription-based providers, among others, should apply forecasting techniques for measuring off-take rates and retention factors. The majority of businesses strengthen their algorithms, for example, logistic regression in predictive analytics or enhanced time-series analysis, to boost their forecasting skills. Like other approaches, logistic regression is applied by subscription companies in order to foresee the possible customer attrition rate (Fujo et al., 2022). Logistic regression may provide the right data needed from sources such as usage patterns, customer interactions and satisfaction ratings, which are then processed to get a probability score that assumes the possible chance of a customer unsubscribing. This population dynamics approach, therefore helps businesses to become proactive in setting aside high-risk customers and they can also adopt more targeted retention strategies. Besides, one of the most reliable resources, which is time-series analysis, is used to reveal the patterns and relations that repeat in time. For example, the data from the history of subscription allows one to find the long-term consumption behaviour, which may be the same with cancelled cases or a high probability the consumer will cancel (Tariq et al., 2022). Now, business can prepare their operational plan on the internet ground where they provide service subscriptions, and the analysis result will be the basis to determine their future customer behaviour. On the other hand, the use of these predictive modelling techniques will help the business subscriptions to be ahead of their competitors in keeping their most loyal customers, who are the main ones that matter. With a deeper understanding of churn causes and the use of state-of-the-art algorithms, companies can build the obtained knowledge into the core of their business practices to serve customers' needs fully by providing high service and optimizing pricing models. As a result, they not only reduce the risk of customer flight but also create a more responsive and customer-oriented atmosphere within a subscription-based services landscape (Gold, 2020).

In subscription-based services, customized retention strategies have to be put in place to address the individual needs of customers and produce loyalty through it. Companies adopt specific strategies such as personalized communication, exclusive benefits, or personalized service to create a better overall customer experience.

22.4.3 Implementation of Personalized Retention Strategies

Customer preferences, when understood, will help businesses to communicate with these people with related information. Such may be customized messaging through personalized emails, notifications, and any others that are tailored to match the interests of an individual and their usage pattern. Companies can build up their customers' ties by customizing their communication showing they know very well the specific needs customers have. The availability of exclusive offers significantly affects the retention of subscribers (Labhsetwar, 2020). By developing such mechanisms as individual discounts, special promotions, or access to limited content, the feeling of value for the customer is created. Along with that, these incentives ensure a steadfast subscription and instil the idea that the subscription aligns with the customer's pre-defined preferences. Customized services involve designing individualized services that address the unique needs of each subscriber and understanding the diversity that exists within the subscriber base. The attainment of this objective may be reached by possibly giving out personalized subscription plans for the customers, adding services based on their consumption, or possibly altering the user interface so that it suits the preferences of the customers (Mustafa et al., 2021). This personalization goes beyond the traditional fit-all model, yielding more unique and exciting services that will ultimately favour every subscriber. Subscription businesses have the ability to put forth personalized retention strategies for each customer that are developed by scrutinizing this data in detail. And by doing this, it reduces the cost of losing customers but it also takes the business to the next level of personalization and customer experience, enabling them to maintain a friendly relationship with their customers.

22.4.4 Analysis of Subscription Churn Patterns

In Churn analysis of subscription patterns, where customers churn out routine trends occurring ahead of what is evident is what we observe. The scope of the Data Trends Assessment consists of insights into the usage behaviour, clients' comments, and anger rates. First and foremost, we value the fact that this allows us to identify the reasons that contribute to the loss of clients. Discoveries of novel ideas that may be dissimilar to what could have happened due to data analysis will induce a deeper understanding (Zdravevski et al., 2020). Potential deviations in the subscription profile should be located at the ambiguous parts. For instance, the graphs that have a noticeable incline or decline worth inquiring into could be an indication of the operation of an external factor that affects the churn. For example, the kind of reaction during promotional times is predictable, people become customers as they enjoy the promos temporarily.

Moreover, grasping the period of triggers can cause tactical information. The company will be able to time the retention efforts better by monitoring when users are most likely to cancel their plans. For example, if a lot of customers cancel their subscription after a particular feature update, the reason could be the dissatisfaction of users and the need for some improvements. A thorough examination of churn patterns is an exposure of key data for businesses. Identifying recurring patterns, anomalies and the timing of churn provides organizations with useful data to act on. Therefore, the data-driven method is the right approach that helps to develop tailored retention strategies and use the subscription services in the best way to boost customers' expectations, not to make them churn.

22.5 CONCLUSION

In sum, client retention and churn prediction would play key parts in the capitalist growth of any business and significantly impact the telecom and e-commerce industries. To achieve the efficiency required for the success of the company in this scenario, identifying churn cases and applying personalized retention tactics for retaining customers over the long term is critical. As far as the communication sector is concerned, there are hurdles such as high market competition, technological advancements, and nature's customers (Pondel et al., 2021). Accurate forecasts, based on techniques driven by ML algorithms, take the leading position against these obstacles. With regards to data acquisition and processing, which involves both good data cleansing and usage pattern analysis along with customer satisfaction feedback to come up with the best churn prediction, data elevation will be the starting point. Using machine learning technologies such as decision trees, support vectors and some others enables telecom companies to special track personality traits which in the end contributes to less client churn.

Also, the e-commerce sector confronts consumer churns just like the others due to ferocious market competition and the transforming of customers' behaviour. With the help of predictive analytics driven by decision trees, neural networks and ensemble method types of machine learning algorithms, the chances of predicting the chance for customer churn are improved, and what can be done proactively to reduce this risk is realized (Wagh et al., 2024). Developing E-commerce customer retention strategies with personalized marketing programmes, customer loyalty programmes, and customer feedback analysis is the main purpose. Through offering personalized marketing based on the unique customer profile or smoking habits individual customers have, e-commerce sites build a strong brand image and hence, keep customers away from switching to competitors (Li & Zhou, 2020). These approaches not only bring methodologies and strategies together but also make them beneficial to businesses by providing information about customer's behaviour. That way, forward-leaning business strategies and plans are influenced by customers' needs and expectations. With the assistance of machine learning and predictive analytics, businesses can gain a competitive space in identifying predictors of customer churn and selecting appropriate measures to mitigate possible effects. If a shop's customer service is excellent in terms of retaining customers, this will also increase work efficiency and enhance customer satisfaction.

In a nutshell, the convergence of customer churn optimization and service retention attributable to intelligent data-driven tools and machine learning technologies is the foundation of the long-term growth of the global telecom and e-commerce markets. These methodologies help enterprises tackle the challenges connected with railing relationships, understanding consumer behaviour changes and shaping long-term prosperity.

REFERENCES

Abou el Kassem, E., Hussein, S.A., Abdelrahman, A.M. and Alsheref, F.K., 2020. Customer churn prediction model and identifying features to increase customer retention based on user generated content. *International Journal of Advanced Computer Science and Applications (IJACSA)*, *11*(5), 84–91.

Baghla, S. and Gupta, G., 2022. Performance evaluation of various classification techniques for customer churn prediction in E-commerce. *Microprocessors and Microsystems*, *94*, p. 104680.

De Caigny, A., Coussement, K., De Bock, K.W. and Lessmann, S., 2020. Incorporating textual information in customer churn prediction models based on a convolutional neural network. *International Journal of Forecasting*, *36*(4), pp. 1563–1578.

De Caigny, A., Coussement, K., Verbeke, W., Idbenjra, K. and Phan, M., 2021. Uplift modelling and its implications for B2B customer churn prediction: A segmentation-based modelling approach. *Industrial Marketing Management*, *99*, pp. 28–39.

Devriendt, F., Berrevoets, J. and Verbeke, W., 2021. Why you should stop predicting customer churn and start using uplift models. *Information Sciences*, *548*, pp. 497–515.

Fujo, S.W., Subramanian, S. and Khder, M.A., 2022. Customer churn prediction in the telecommunication industry using deep learning. *Information Sciences Letters*, *11*(1), p. 24.

Gattermann-Itschert, T. and Thonemann, U.W., 2022. Proactive customer retention management in a non-contractual B2B setting based on churn prediction with random forests. *Industrial Marketing Management*, *107*, pp. 134–147.

Gold, C., 2020. *Fighting Churn with Data: The Science and Strategy of Customer Retention*. Singapore: Simon and Schuster.

Jain, H., Yadav, G. and Manoov, R., 2020. Churn prediction and retention in banking, telecom and IT sectors using machine learning techniques. In S. Kumar, D. Bhattacharyya, & S. Biswas (Eds.), *Advances in Machine Learning and Computational Intelligence: Proceedings of ICMLCI 2019* (pp. 137–156). Singapore: Springer Singapore.

Labhsetwar, S.R., 2020. Predictive analysis of customer churn in the telecom industry using supervised learning. *ICTACT Journal on Soft Computing*, *10*(2), pp. 2054–2060.

Lalwani, P., Mishra, M.K., Chadha, J.S. and Sethi, P., 2022. Customer churn prediction system: a machine learning approach. *Computing*, 104, pp. 1–24.

Li, W. and Zhou, C., 2020, March. Customer churn prediction in telecom using big data analytics. In *IOP Conference Series: Materials Science and Engineering* (Vol. 768, No. 5, p. 052070). Bristol, UK: IOP Publishing.

Mustafa, N., Ling, L.S. and Razak, S.F.A., 2021. Customer churn prediction for telecommunication industry: A Malaysian Case Study. *F1000Research*, *10*, Article 117.

Pondel, M., Wuczyński, M., Gryncewicz, W., Łysik, Ł., Hernes, M., Rot, A. and Kozina, A., 2021, July. Deep learning for customer churn prediction in e-commerce decision support. In W. Abramowicz & A. Paschke (Eds.), *Business Information Systems* (pp. 3–12). Cham, Switzerland: Springer.

Saleh, S. and Saha, S., 2023. Customer retention and churn prediction in the telecommunication industry: A case study on a Danish university. *SN Applied Sciences*, *5*(7), p. 173.

Tariq, M.U., Babar, M., Poulin, M. and Khattak, A.S., 2022. Distributed model for customer churn prediction using convolutional neural network. *Journal of Modelling in Management*, *17*(3), pp. 853–863.

Wagh, S.K., Andhale, A.A., Wagh, K.S., Pansare, J.R., Ambedkar, S.P. and Gawande, S.H., 2024. Customer churn prediction in the telecom sector using machine learning techniques. *Results in Control and Optimization*, *14*, p. 100342.

Wagh, V. M., Panaskar, D. B., Jacobs, J. A., Mukate, S. V., Muley, A. A., & Kadam, A. K. (2019). Influence of hydro-geochemical processes on groundwater quality through geostatistical techniques in Kadava River basin, Western India. *Arabian Journal of Geosciences*, *12*, pp, 1–25.

Wu, S., Yau, W.C., Ong, T.S. and Chong, S.C., 2021. Integrated churn prediction and customer segmentation framework for telco business. *IEEE Access*, *9*, pp. 62118–62136.

Zdravevski, E., Lameski, P., Apanowicz, C. and Ślęzak, D., 2020. From Big Data to business analytics: The case study of churn prediction. *Applied Soft Computing*, *90*, p. 106164.

23 Leveraging Generative AI for Personal Branding

Jeevan D'Mello, Anisha Gupta, and Deepak Durga Prasad Timanani

23.1 INTRODUCTION

In the modern business world, where technology progresses at lightning speed, employing cutting-edge technologies is not only going to improve performance but also be a necessity to maintain a step ahead of the competition. The role played by AI has been tremendous, and the integration of Generative AI is the next level of this transformation, as there is an opportunity to revolutionize different sectors. Although its key features are currently tailored for businesses of all sizes and industries, it also has a strong presence within the realm of personal branding. This section will shed light on many sudden changes in personal branding strategies with the reliable aid of Generative AI.

Generative AI offers a huge opportunity to users to actively engage in shaping their online presence and narrative. Gone are the times when branding used to be crafted through communication of events and static content as a whole. Generative AI hands this power over to users, allowing them to craft content that can emotionally resonate with their audience. Through this technology, each individual is thus equipped with the means to create interesting stories that also remain responsive to shifting trends and the needs of an audience.

One of the most important effects of Generative AI on personal branding is that it gives the opportunity to develop better customer engagement. Such smart algorithms allow people to design visits that are tailored to their audience's specific needs, thus establishing stronger connections with them. What matters, either through thoughtful content recommendations or vivid interactive storytelling, is people making associations the brand, resulting in customer retention and brand loyalty. Moreover, Generative AI contributes to personal branding building, especially in the digital environment. Individuals can also streamline the content production process into one essential and uniform brand identity through online marketing channels. Generative AI can help streamline the content creation workflow, thus giving others the opportunity to focus more on the strategy.

Furthermore, Generative AI offers unique ways of being creative and using modern-day personal branding. People can find various and surprising subjects of content by using its capabilities while exploring exciting formats and new mediums to play around with. When it comes to Generative AI and its capabilities for visualization and storytelling, the door remains open for new discoveries and inventions, bringing a vast, vivid field for the development of individual branding.

DOI: 10.1201/9781003472544-23

FIGURE 23.1 The future of personal branding: crafted by AI.

Generative AI allows people to turn from mere tellers of a rather pre-designed brand story into its architects (Figure 23.1). It paves the way for liberating the shackles of static content and predetermined life stories, bringing out fresh dynamic emotional scenarios. Visualize a universe where your personal brands effortlessly morph according to your audience's evolution. Content changes to reflect their development, including their multi-faceted needs and desires. AI leverages the existence of low-skilled jobs to automate processes and free up humans for more critical thinking, which in turn increases their productivity within the working industry. The platform can be utilized for creative purposes like identifying unexpected themes of content, exploring new and innovative formats of content, and trying rising mediums. It is this continual evolution that ensures your brand storybook stays up to date and relevant and keeps your audience captivated.

23.2 UNDERSTANDING GENERATIVE AI IN THE CONTEXT OF PERSONAL BRANDING

AI that is generative with the aid of improvement algorithms and learning machines can produce texts by itself. It has now gone much beyond just stipulating instructions for simple repetitive tasks to creating artificial materials such as films, images, and videos with a human likeness to them. Recently, with the advent of technology, everybody has had the opportunity to be unique and build up their reputation or personal brand. Here are some of them:

23.2.1 Crafting Compelling Narratives

Nowadays, when information overload has become a common phenomenon, a convincing story is much more important than ever. It is through Generative AI that the partner will thus constantly have its back. While a personal brand may be a challenge, a different and believable story is one of the biggest hurdles. Incorporating Generative AI technologies which include Natural Language processing, is an important instrument that would make it possible for subjects to formulate their experiences, values, and dreams into attention-grabbing narratives [1]. By giving AI instruction based on crucial aspects of their own personal and career voyage, one can get inputs and styles that are the most prevalent in their target market. Therefore, there is no need to create separate content for different social media platforms, which saves time and reinforces uniformity in the message. The same applies when it comes to understanding consumer behavior and preferences with the end goal of creating messaging that can evoke the emotional responses necessary to ensure the success of personal brands.

23.2.2 Enhancing Customer Engagement

For personal branding, it may become a challenge to give content that is consistent and personalized at the same time. The customer experience aspect, however, is what must be fundamental for making the engagement activity a success [2]. AI becomes vital as it allows companies and people to reach and communicate in person with their audience on a larger scale with specific personalized storytelling. Whether it is through personalized email content, interactive social media updates, or engaging chatbots, demonstrating your marketing efforts to match their individual preferences definitely strengthens the brand-to-consumer relationship. AI algorithms can be trained to examine a target audience's needs and trending topics, coming up with customized content, from a post on social media to a blog article. Using the latest ad-driven tools, people may exercise the accessibility of the, keeping the carefulness criteria in display. This focused technique, in addition, connects with the customers in a way that makes them feel the experience and, at the same time it, boosts personal brand recognition.

23.2.3 Building Authenticity through AI

One concern often raised in the era of automation and AI is the potential loss of authenticity. However, when used judiciously, Generative AI can contribute to authenticity. Building authenticity using such technology involves a thoughtful and strategic approach to ensure that technology enhances, rather than replaces, the genuine aspects of an individual's personality.

Creation through AI needs to be strategic—it should be a companion of rather than instead of real-life personality traits. An example could be AI studying the preference for the way of communication and generating content in line with the person's voice. The analysis of data enables personalizing the content, as the right information must unite between the audience and the brand. Such an approach makes it possible to retain human nature together with digital abilities.

23.2.4 Optimizing Content Strategy

Apart from the fact that Generative AI produces content, with the knowledge of what drives audience behavior, preferences, and market trends, AI tools can therefore be used to improve the content strategy's effectiveness and maximize the impact and attitude on various platforms [3]. That is, discovering the optimal hours of the day for posting, the formats of content that are preferable, and the topics that interest the target audience most have to be included. Through the power of AI-driven analytics, individuals will be able to use the great potential of optimized content calendars and distribution strategies to add a greater range of hits, engagement, and conversion levels.

23.2.5 Scaling Personalized Communication

Generative AI is effective in that it enables the individual to achieve one-to-one level custom communication by automation of the message creation process for target user segments. By comparing data and occurring patterns through machine learning, AI tools identify personal preferences among audience members for the subsequent up-scaled content personalization. This ability develops meaningful conversations that keep the followers in line with various touchpoints. Such a gesture assures more involvement and loyalty. Through the personalization of email campaigns, social media interactions, or even chatbot correspondences, AI-based personalization boosts customer satisfaction and strengthens a connection between the brand and the audience.

23.2.6 Ensuring Brand Consistency

Consistency is the key to establishing trust and recognition through personal branding. Generative AI helps with making branding consistent by enabling content to be produced that follows set rules for style guidelines, voice, and visual interpretation to be used across all communication platforms. AI tools perform their job by taking into account the relational factors of existing brand resources and user-generated content. This way, they harmonize with a brand identity while meeting the needs of platform specifications and content format variation. Through that, all the content created by the brand reflects its values and builds up its image in the targeted audience's mind.

23.2.7 Enabling Data-Driven Decision Making

Generative AI facilitates data-behavioral trends-based analysis and offers aptness into audience inclinations, content fulfilments, and industry trends. With the power of AI technologies that provide deep-dive analyses, individuals get to integrate their knowledge about the higher demographics, engagement, and consumption patterns of their audiences. This gives them an opportunity to get all the information they need about personal branding so they can formulate a good strategy that will assist them to attain their goals into reality. Whether it is a fine-tuning of content strategies, distribution of limited resources, or catching new growth opportunities, AI-based advice allows people to remain flexible and true to the time characterized by a fast-changing digital environment.

23.2.8 Navigating Privacy and Security Concerns

The Generative AI tools used in building personal branding raise a lot of questions about people's privacy and security [1]. As we move toward personalizing content for our audience through collecting and analyzing data, there is a need for robust data protection measures and to comply with regulations. For instance, this could be via the de-identification of user data, explicit consent attainment about owning user data, and adoption of encryption protocols for the protection of confidential data. AI-powered personalization can only be achieved by giving high regard to audience members' privacy rights, which will result in trustworthiness and credibility, as well as in fulfilling the benefits of personalized serving.

23.2.9 Cultivating Community Engagement

Through the use of Generative AI, community engagement will be easier by allocating pertinent subjects, sparking discourses, and attaining collaboration from the community members. By means of sentiment analysis and topic modeling, AI tools make it possible to recognize what is happening in the communities or groups and thus allow for real-time engagement. Through AI content that not only begins conversations but also answers questions and weighs people's opinions, personal brands are strengthened through the creation of lively online communities. This brings about the creation of a desire of some sort among the listeners that leads to their constant engagement and support.

23.2.10 Evolving with Technological Advancements

With the progress of Generative AI technology, it becomes even more essential for people to follow the innovations in the field and to include them in their personal branding systems. Through the utilization of awakening AI tools and techniques, therefore, people themself are able to adjust to varying consumer behaviors and market dynamics and stay at the top of the competition in the digital arena. Such an exercise might involve trying out different content methods, utilizing AI-powered narrative tools, or discovering other options where audiences can be captured along various channels and platforms. Also, they will keep themselves abreast of new technologies in order to make their personal branding effective in a constantly emerging digital world.

23.3 CASE STUDY

23.3.1 Elon Musk

Elon Musk, the visionary entrepreneur behind companies like Tesla, SpaceX, and recently X (formerly Twitter), stands out as a compelling example of an individual who has effectively leveraged Generative AI for personal branding (Figure 23.2). This man, who is famous for his creative way of working on technology and space sciences, has successfully implemented AI technologies in his web presence and effectively

FIGURE 23.2 Amplifying brand with AI.

stabilized the brand in the market with his unique personal brand. Musk is able to automate the captioning of his tweets using algorithms so that they remain interestingly written and stylistic as well. Furthermore, AI assists Musk not only with the article restructuring but also with blog content upgrading, including the improvement of instruction in the writing style and the subject matter points for the relevant topics.

With AI-driven speech bots, Musk can create incredible voices that allow him to carry on conversations and connect with the audience in a way that they can view him as friendly.

Furthermore, Generative AI contributes to Musk's visual brand identity, ensuring consistency and innovation in designs for SpaceX missions, Tesla product launches, and campaigns at X. Musk's responsible use of AI underscores the importance of addressing ethical considerations, showcasing how the technology can be harnessed to amplify personal branding while maintaining authenticity and transparency.

23.3.2 Michelle Obama

Michelle Obama, the former First Lady of the U.S., smartly uses AI to reinforce her personal branding and social programs. By deploying AI algorithms geared to her target platforms – Instagram, X, and Facebook, she creates content that resonates with her audience, thus fostering meaningful connections and disrupting the status quo in education, health and social justice (Figure 23.3). AI integrated tools help documentary makers in creating multimedia content, which also tackles the most pressing societal challenges and is compelling thus driving positive changes. One of the prominent projects which Obama covers are through initiatives like Let's Move! Through the 6-year-old campaign and Reach Higher initiative, AI-powered chatbots enable to create personalized chat sessions, offering information and resources tailored to individuals' specific needs for their continued development and

FIGURE 23.3 Multimedia content creation with AI.

acts of goodwill. In addition to AI, her visual brand is also boosted by the fact that it helps her maintain a consistent and unique identity, in terms of images and content for platforms and across different campaigns. Obama's application of ethical issues and transparency in AI-driven social progress, places the weight of accountability on the individual to do what is right far and wide.

23.3.3 Javier Rodriguez

Javier Rodriguez, a health and wellness influencer, utilizes Generative AI as a means to boost his celebrity branding and popularity for personal holistic wellness. He uses social media, such as sites or online coaches, to assist AI algorithms in analyzing trends in the field of health, nutritional data, and lifestyle preferences (Figure 23.4). Then, Rodriguez produces content that informs and inspires his audiences to live a healthy lifestyle. Machine learning-directed chatbots have become the main tools of advice and relief for people trying to find out the answers to questions about correct fitness routines, nutrition, or any other mental wellness strategies, evoking a sense of belonging and improvement. Furthermore, Generative AI enables easy connection and differentiation of Rodriguez's personal brand with a unique touch in his images and marketing materials. He ensures that this paradigm is evident in his branding. These practices provide both holistic and end-to-end health repercussions and are employed in unison with technology to enrich people's lives worldwide.

23.3.4 Oprah Winfrey

Oprah Winfrey, the famous media magnate and philanthropist purposefully utilizes Generative AI to sustain her personal brand image and motivate her audience. By means of applying AI-powered tools, Winfrey creates engaging stories that really

FIGURE 23.4 AI personalizes wellness, builds community.

FIGURE 23.5 Harnessing AI for meaningful change.

matter to her audience, which she does by referring to her own life lessons and values (Figure 23.5). She works together with AI algorithms to make sure that her message-driven appeals are in line with the target demographics and emotional resonance and that there is also consistency on the different platforms. Tailoring of the content to individual preferences, Winfrey creates deep community bonds by issuing personalized social media posts and newsletters which help to strengthen an empowered feeling of belonging among her community. Concerns exist regarding authenticity in the digital age, but Winfrey displays how this tool would open the way for more genuine to be activated as it is used purposefully. Through AI, humanization of her brand becomes possible, as her persona is imbued with her voice and her brand values. She is able to bring technology and human connection in symbiosis, taking advantage of automation and brand relevance. AI assists in accomplishing this integrity-preserved personal development and the self-improvement goals of her audience which, in turn, contributes to her reputation as a trusted and relatable influencer. Applying AI helps her drive the change.

23.4 LOOKING AHEAD (FUTURE ASPECTS)

As technology continues to advance, the role of Generative AI in personal branding will undoubtedly evolve the digital culture between humanized creativity and artificial intelligence, which will probably reconstruct the next age of personal branding. The ones that will succeed in a business context are the ones that find the way to ride the ocean of the connection between robots and people. The implementation of AI powered by Generative Technology in personal branding approaches bolsters the transformative prospects for brands wanting to take the lead in the digital world. This can be achieved by drafting stories of personalizing content experienced by intelligently doing interactive engagements. Generative AI has applications that range from creating narratives to fun interactive activities where you can personalize your acts [3]. Such people, who equally put conscious thought into the utilization of these tools, are capable of unlocking fresh dimensions in their personal branding journey, standing the test of time in the business world, resulting in long-lasting and influential online presence.

Generative AI is an innovative force in personal branding that provides an array of advantages for nearly all aspects of content strategy, starting with audience engagement. Firstly, it makes content strategy more effective by interpreting data in order to customize content for the audience preferences and market trends, resulting in maximum efficiency and success. Secondly, it expands on personal communication by automating the customization of messages for the different individual audience segments, thus building deeper connections and more engagement at scale [4]. In addition, it assures brand consistency by making content that is in agreement with the defined style manual and visual style that is to be used, and this helps to establish the identity of the brand across different channels. Another advantage of generative AI is the exploring opportunities for a data-driven approach, which puts focus on the dissemination of audience demographics and content performance, thereby allowing the efficiency of the decision-making process. On that note, managing privacy and security issues is significant and therefore, safeguarding customers' private data by extensive use of data protection measures and adherence to regulations should be the key to sustaining trust and maintaining audience confidence. Moreover, generative AI promotes the audience's community involvement through a discussion around the trending subjects within the audience and thus builds the brand image around the online community. Lastly, we all have to be aware of technological advancements or we will be outdated and therefore not competitive, so individuals should strive to try fascinating forms of content and apply AI-powered storytelling techniques to ensure staying in the game. Specifically, with increasing utilization of generative AI in personal branding strategies, ways of growth for this field implement new forms of engagement, brand consistency, and audience connection that constantly change as the digital environment expands.

23.5 CONCLUSION

In conclusion, the introduction of Generative AI into personal branding signals a major shift in the way individuals create and deliver their online identities. Generative AI has the power to make users forge compelling stories and increase the number of clients and affect the way they promote their products and services. AI application can attain continuous flow of data insights that will improve their content strategy for cross-platforming. Privacy and security concerns should be addressed with each AI application based on ethical integrity [5]. In the future, as synthesis between personal branding and Generative AI keeps developing, the new tool for staying ahead and innovative in the dynamic digital world will be to be knowledgeable enough so as to not fear the new tools but to be ready to embrace them and let them help to create stories that are more involving, than ever before, to engage with the audience and to create everlasting impressions in their minds. As technology keeps getting sophisticated, those who handle the advantages of Generative AI well will not only survive but also reshape the future of personal branding with their online presence.

Now, the future of human identity in the virtual world is reshaped by Generative AI, and the same can be said about how people create and regulate their digital personas. It is no secret that social media is a powerful tool due to its ability to create personalized communications, intelligently analyze data via driven insights, and engage followers with the brand – all of these elements make for a deeper connection between audiences and the brand while retaining brand authenticity and relevance. On the accelerating discourse of the digital world comes the embracement of Generative AI in the personal brand strategy. There is no longer a choice but a necessity for those who desire an enduring and influential brand online. Through the adoption of innovation, ethics, and authenticity, individuals can exploit the whole capability of Generative AI to influence the future of personal branding, for which they may form new relationships and make a unique mark on the virtual world.

REFERENCES

1. Baskwill, A. (2023). Navigating Generative AI: Opportunities, Limitations, and Ethical Considerations in Massage Therapy and Beyond. *International Journal of Therapeutic Massage & Bodywork*, Vol. 16, pp. 1–4.
2. Kromalcas, S., Kraujalienė, L., & Ževžikovas, G. (2024). The Influence of Personal Brand Communication on Consumers. *Business: Theory and Practice.*
3. Tiautrakul, J., & Jindakul, J. (2019). The Artificial Intelligence (AI) with the Future of Digital Marketing. *SSRN Electronic Journal.*
4. Okonkwo, I., & Namkoisse, E. (2023). The Role of Influencer Marketing in Building Authentic Brand Relationships Online. *Journal of Digital Marketing and Communication.*
5. Nadeem, M. (2024). Generative Artificial Intelligence [GAI]: Enhancing Future Marketing Strategies with Emotional Intelligence [EI], and Social Skills? *British Journal of Marketing Studies.*

Index